Student Engagement Techniques

A Handbook for College Faculty

Elizabeth F. Barkley

JOSSEY-BASS
A Wiley Imprint
www.josseybass.com

The Jossey-Bass
Higher and Adult Education Series

Copyright © 2010 by John Wiley & Sons, Inc. All rights reserved.

Published by Jossey-Bass

A Wiley Imprint

One Montgomery Street, Suite 1200, San Francisco, CA 94104-4594—www.josseybass.com

Jossey-Bass books and products are available through most bookstores. To contact Jossey-Bass directly call our Customer Care Department within the U.S. at 800-956-7739, outside the U.S. at 317-572-3986, or fax 317-572-4002.

Jossey-Bass also publishes its books in a variety of electronic formats. Some content that appears in print may not be available in electronic books.

List from Provitera-McGlynn on pp. 121-122 used by permission.

Library of Congress Cataloging-in-Publication Data

Barkley, Elizabeth F.
    Student engagement techniques : a handbook for college faculty / Elizabeth F. Barkley.
        p. cm. -- (Higher and adult education series)
    Includes bibliographical references and index.
    ISBN 978-0-470-28191-8 (pbk.)
    1. Academic achievement—United States. 2. Classroom environment—United States. I. Title.
    LB2342.92.B34 2010
    378.1'25—dc22   2009029117

Printed in the United States of America
FIRST EDITION
PB Printing   10 9 8

HPB-Dallas
3860 La Reunion Pkwy.
Dallas, TX 75212
servicedfw@hpb.com

Items:

Qty	Title	Locator	Condition
1	Student Engagement Techniques: A Handbook for College Fa...	BSD-2-19-024-001-354	Good

Subtotal:
Shipping:
Total:

Marketplace: Alibris
Order Number: 4450879
Ship Method: Expedited
Customer Name: Marilyn Liebrenz-Himes
Order Date: 9/29/2019 12:00:00 AM
Marketplace Order #: 65618231-1
Email: liebrenz@gwu.edu

Thanks for your Order!

If you have any questions or concerns regarding this order, please contact us at servicedfw2@halfpricebooks.com

Contents

This book is dedicated to K. Patricia Cross—
my inspiration, teacher, and mentor for over thirty years.

Figures, Tables & Exhibits

Figures

Tables

Exhibits

Preface

IN MY EARLY YEARS as a teacher, "engaging students" wasn't even on my radar screen. I lectured, they listened; they studied, I tested—and that was that. Then I took a decade off to be an administrator, and when I returned to the classroom in the mid-1990s, things had changed. The handful of students sitting in front of me seemed mostly not to want to be there. Despite my enthusiastic efforts to engage them in a stimulating discussion, they stared at me with looks that ranged from utter apathy to outright hostility. It got worse. Three weeks into the term, the dean who had been hired as my replacement called me into his office. Stunned, I listened as he read from a legal-size pad a seemingly endless list of complaints from two particularly cranky students. This was my eagerly anticipated return to teaching. Although I had been a successful and popular teacher just ten years earlier, it was clear the old ways were no longer working. Because I was too young to retire, engaging students became my central concern.

I am not alone. Teachers in institutions across the country tell me that teaching today can be tough. The "twitchspeed" pace and multilayered delivery of modern media can make a lecture feel incredibly slow and boring; one student reported all the blood had left his head and he feared he'd pass out (El-Shamy, 2004, p. 24). Globalization and open door access have filled our classrooms with learners reflecting such a dizzying array of backgrounds and academic preparedness that teachers are often hard-pressed to find a collective starting point or the commonalities that create a sense of community. Abundant information at split-second access has redefined what students should be learning and created unprecedented opportunities for academic dishonesty. A panoply of pressures makes some classrooms a crucible of tensions that can erupt in incivility ranging from simple lack of consideration to overt aggression. For many of us teaching today, competing for the attention of our students and engaging them in meaningful learning is a profound and ongoing challenge.

But there is a flip side. Even if college teachers *did* have the performance skills and production support to put on a show that matches the level of sensory stimulation supplied by today's video and computer games, music videos, films, and television shows, it wouldn't matter—engaging students doesn't mean they're being entertained. It means they are thinking. Although the diversity of today's students can be a challenge, it also means students are bringing a rich array of experiences, insights, and ideas into the classroom. The information and communication revolution that places such demands on us can also transform our teaching role into something much more interesting than being a dispenser of information (and we even have tools that make it easier to catch plagiarism!). And finally, the stress we sense and the occasional outbursts in our classrooms also offer us opportunities to teach students how to resolve conflicts in ways that can contribute to a collectively safer, saner future.

This handbook was written for teachers like me who work in the trenches of academe. My primary purpose is to offer my teaching colleagues, current and aspiring, a wide variety of tips, strategies, and techniques that can help them transform what could be a daunting task into one that is stimulating and rewarding. To do that, I pulled from the literature on good teaching as well as the expertise of teachers in colleges and universities around the country. I have tried to create a compendium of useful, practical ideas that readers will find enhances the classroom experience for teachers and students alike. Very little in this handbook is new. My contribution is to pull it together into a single resource and cast it in a format accessible to busy, discipline-oriented faculty. I hope it will also be useful to faculty developers, instructional designers, department chairs, and other academic administrators interested in promoting teaching and improving learning.

Book Overview

This handbook is divided into three parts. In **Part One: A Conceptual Framework for Understanding Student Engagement,** I discuss a theoretical model for defining student engagement in the college classroom as the synergistic interaction between motivation and active learning. I also explore what student engagement looks like in practice, drawing from interviews with six college teachers with reputations among students for being effective, engaging teachers.

Part Two: Tips and Strategies offers practical advice on how to increase motivation, promote active learning, build community, help students learn holistically, and ensure students are appropriately challenged. This part contains fifty specific suggestions on topics such as how to learn student names, how to help students value what you are teaching, and how to use rubrics to grade effectively and efficiently.

Part Three: Student Engagement Techniques (SETs) includes step-by-step directions for fifty learning activities that can be used across many disciplines. The techniques are organized into categories based on learning goals ranging from acquiring basic knowledge, skills, and understanding to developing attitudes, values, and self-awareness. Each technique includes purpose and description, step-by-step directions, examples of the implementation of that technique in specific academic disciplines, online implementation, variations and extensions, observations and advice, and key resources. Rather than reading this book in a linear fashion, readers should thumb through it or start at the point that is most useful and appealing to them.

Sources

Student Engagement Techniques is really about effective teaching, and the literature on how to teach well is huge. I am not an educational psychologist, so especially in the conceptual framework that constitutes Part One, I relied heavily on Brophy's (2004), Svinicki's (2004b), and Wlodkowski's (2008) excellent syntheses of the research and literature on student motivation and on Sousa's (2006) informative and accessible work on how the brain learns. Readers who are interested in learning more about motivation or the brain are encouraged to go to these original sources.

For Parts Two and Three, I pulled from any source that had a good idea: books, journals, teaching and learning newsletters, corporate training manuals, Web sites, and even workshop handouts. Some ideas come from my own experience in the classroom; others from manuscript reviewers, colleagues, and students. I have tried to attribute accurately, preferably to published sources, but teaching ideas and techniques are often disseminated by word of mouth and become part of general lore and practice. If I failed to cite anything appropriately or misrepresented someone's ideas, please let me know at barkleyelizabeth@foothill.edu so that I can post a correction on my Web site and fix the error in a future edition.

Acknowledgments

I am deeply indebted to Thomas A. Angelo and K. Patricia Cross for their seminal work creating the prototype for this handbook with *Classroom Assessment Techniques: A Handbook for College Teachers* (1993). I worked with K. Patricia Cross and Claire Howell Major using the same structure for our book *Collaborative Learning Techniques: A Handbook for College Teachers* (2005). Pat Cross and I had continuing, lively conversations on student engagement as I worked on this book, and her writing and thinking have left an indelible imprint throughout its pages. My decision to dedicate the book to her is rooted in my immense gratitude for her inspirational guidance.

It was in a meeting with David Brightman and Jessica Egbert at Jossey-Bass that Jessica suggested writing a third handbook, this time focusing on student engagement. David, Jessica, and Aneesa Davenport have been incredibly supportive throughout the conceptualization, writing, and production of the book. I also want to express special thanks to James Rhem, who gave me encouragement at a critical point when the project had become overwhelming as well as substantive advice on the intellectual plot and structure of the book. For their support, insightful comments, and critical feedback, I want to express my tremendous appreciation to Jillian Kinzie, Kay McClenney, L. Dee Fink, Judith Ouimet, and Robert Smallwood, who read and commented on draft material at various stages. And for using her own excellent teaching skills both in providing constructive criticism as well as urging me to use my own voice in the writing, I am deeply grateful to Maryellen Weimer.

Thank you, too, to my faculty colleagues Judy Baker, Dolores Davison, Nicole Gray, Carolyn Holcroft, Scott Lankford, and Natalia Menendez, who shared their classroom-based experiences with me during interviews. I am also indebted to the members of my Instructional Team—Robert Hartwell, Milissa Carey, and Baomi Watson—for their collegiality and the ideas and insights on good teaching they offer on a daily basis. Additionally, I want to acknowledge my gratitude to Chris Garrett, Norman Vaughan, and the many educators who gathered at the first meeting of the Special Interest Group on Student Engagement at the International Society for the Scholarship of Teaching and Learning (ISSOTL) 2008 conference in Edmonton, Canada. They offered their ideas and, in several cases, went back to their campuses to gather feedback from students and colleagues on what "student engagement" meant to them. Finally, to my husband, I offer my deepest, heartfelt gratitude. Without his ongoing support and understanding, I would never have started this project, much less finished it.

The Author

ELIZABETH BARKLEY is a nationally known scholar, educator, and consultant. With over thirty years experience as an innovative and reflective teacher, her areas of interest include engaging students through active and collaborative learning; transforming face-to-face and online curriculum to meet the needs of diverse learners; and connecting learning goals with outcomes and assessment. She is author of *Collaborative Learning Techniques: A Handbook for College Faculty* (coauthored with K. Patricia Cross and Claire Howell Major, Jossey-Bass, 2004), *Crossroads: The Multicultural Roots of America's Popular Music* (Prentice Hall, 2006), and *Crossroads: Popular Music in America* (Prentice Hall, 2003).

Dr. Barkley has been the recipient of several honors, including the Carnegie Foundation for the Advancement of Teaching's California's Higher Education Professor of the Year, the Chair Academy's Outstanding Leadership Award for work with learning outcomes assessment, the Foothill-De Anza Community College District's Innovator of the Year in conjunction with the National League for Innovation in the Community Colleges, the Gerald Hayward Award for Educational Excellence, the Center for Diversity in Teaching and Learning in Higher Education's Faculty Award, and the California Community College League's Out-of-the-Box Thinker Award. She has also served as a leadership fellow through the American Council on Education and has been named a Carnegie scholar in the discipline of music by the Pew Charitable Trusts in conjunction with the Carnegie Foundation. Additionally, her course *Music of Multicultural America* was selected as the best online course by the California Virtual Campus.

Barkley holds a B.A. and M.A. from the University of California at Riverside and a Ph.D. from UC Berkeley. She has worked at Foothill College since 1977, including nine years as Dean of Fine Arts and Communications.

Part One

A Conceptual Framework for Understanding Student Engagement

Chapter 1

What Does *Student Engagement* Mean?

MOST OF US chose our field of scholarly endeavor because somewhere along the line we developed a passion for it. Part of the attraction of a career in academia is the opportunity to share our enthusiasm with others and possibly even recruit new disciples to the discipline. It is therefore very disheartening to look out into a classroom and see disengaged students who make little effort to hide their apathy. They stare at us vacantly or perhaps even hostilely when we attempt to pull them into class discussion, and then bolt for the door like freed prisoners the moment it seems safe to do so. Equally distressing are students who are obsessively focused on their grade but seem to care little about the learning the grades are supposed to represent. Why do some students bother to register for the course if they are not interested in learning what we are teaching? Why do some students go to such great efforts to cheat when they'd learn so much if they invested even half the effort in studying? Why is it sometimes so hard to get students to think . . . to care . . . to engage? These and similarly troubling questions are part of a national—even international—dialogue on student engagement.

The elements of the dialogue vary, largely because higher education today is astonishingly diverse. Although attention on student engagement at the moment seems to be focused on classes with hundreds of students, engagement can also be a challenge in courses with an average class size of twelve. While some teachers are looking for ways to challenge their students' higher-order thinking, others struggle to get students to show up—and then to take the earbuds out of their ears so that they can focus sufficiently to develop basic academic success skills. Today, teachers must find ways to engage students not only in traditional face-to-face courses but also in courses taught partially or wholly online.

The unifying thread is "engagement," but what *is* "student engagement"? Well, the answer is that it means different things to different people. Bowen, in an article appropriately titled "Engaged Learning: Are We All on the Same Page?"(2005), observes that—despite the number of recent vision statements, strategic plans, learning outcomes, and agendas of national reform movements that strive to create engaged learning and engaged learners—"an explicit consensus about what we actually mean by engagement or why it is important is lacking" (p. 3). My purpose in Part One is to construct a conceptual framework for understanding student engagement by first exploring the background of the phrase and then proposing a teaching-based model for what it means within the context of a college classroom.

Background

One of the earliest pairings of the term *engagement* with learning occurs in Pascarella and Terenzini's (1991) treatise on the impact of college on students: "Perhaps the strongest conclusion that can be made is the least surprising. Simply put, the greater the student's involvement or engagement in academic work or in the academic experience of college, the greater his or her level of knowledge acquisition and general cognitive development." A decade later, Russ Edgerton, in his influential *Higher Education White Paper* (1997, p. 32), pointed to the need for students to "engage in the tasks" that discipline specialists perform in order to really understand the concepts of the discipline. In this same paper, Edgerton coined the phrase *pedagogies of engagement*: "Learning 'about things' does not enable students to acquire the abilities and understanding they will need for the twenty-first century. We need new pedagogies of engagement that will turn out the kinds of resourceful, engaged workers and citizens that America now requires" (p. 38). Building on Edgerton's and others' work, Shulman (2002) placed engagement at the foundation of his learning taxonomy: "Learning begins with student engagement" (p. 37).

The National Survey on Student Engagement (NSSE) and associated efforts such as the Community College Survey on Student Engagement (CCSSE) aim to *measure* student engagement. They define *engagement* as the frequency with which students participate in activities that represent effective educational practices, and conceive of it as a pattern of involvement in a variety of activities and interactions both in and out of the classroom and throughout a student's college career. "Student engagement has two key components," explains NSSE's associate director, Jillian Kinzie (personal communication, 2008). "[T]he first is the amount of time and effort students put into their studies and other activities that lead to the experiences and outcomes that constitute student success. The second is the ways the institution allocates resources and organizes learning opportunities and services to induce students to participate in and benefit from such activities."

All of these usages of the term *engagement* work well when one is looking at general trends at the national and institutional level, but they aren't very helpful to college teachers who are trying to engage students on a daily basis "in the trenches." Many books and articles have been written on student engagement, and the discussions are rich and complex. Our understanding of student engagement continues to evolve and deepen as the dialogue continues. My purpose here is to contribute to this conversation by offering a closer look at what constitutes student engagement within the context of a single college class.

Toward a Classroom-Based Model for Understanding Student Engagement

College teachers tend to describe student engagement in one of two ways. The first is with statements like "Engaged students really care about what they're learning; they *want* to learn" or "When students are engaged, they exceed expectations and go beyond what is required" or "The words that describe student engagement to me are *passion* and *excitement*" (Barkley, 2009). These phrases reflect a view of engagement rooted in motivation. The etymological roots of the word *engagement* offer clues to this perspective. "Engage" comes from Middle English and its multiple meanings include pledging one's life and honor and charming or fascinating someone so that he or she becomes an ally. Both meanings resonate with teachers' motivation-based view of student engagement: we want students to share our enthusiasm for our academic discipline and find our courses so compelling that they willingly, in fact enthusiastically, devote their hearts and minds to the learning process.

The second way many college teachers describe student engagement is with statements like "Engaged students are trying to make meaning of what they are learning" or "Engaged students are involved in the academic task at hand and are using higher-order thinking skills such as analyzing information or solving problems" (Barkley, 2009). These teachers are relating engagement to active learning. They recognize that learning is a dynamic process that consists of making sense and meaning out of new information by connecting it to what is already known. Bonwell and Eison (1991) neatly define active learning as "doing what we think and thinking about what we are doing." Edgerton (1997) observes that "to really understand an idea . . . a student must be able to carry out a variety of performances involving the idea. . . . Students know about chemistry by reading and listening to lectures, but to really understand chemistry, students need to engage in the tasks that chemists perform." He adds that some teaching approaches (such as problem-based learning, collaborative learning, and undergraduate research) are "pedagogies of engagement" because they require students to be actively learning as they "do" the tasks of the discipline (p. 32). Bowen (2005) points out that the NSSE, "which assesses the extent to which these pedagogies are used, has become one de facto operational definition of engagement" (p. 4).

Whether teachers think primarily of the motivational or active learning elements of student engagement, they are quick to point out that both are required. A classroom filled with enthusiastic, motivated students is great, but it is educationally meaningless if the enthusiasm does not result in learning. Conversely, students who are actively learning but doing so reluctantly and resentfully are not engaged. Student engagement is the product of motivation *and* active learning. It is a product rather than a sum because it will not occur if either element is missing. It does not result from one or the other alone, but rather is generated in the space that resides in the overlap of motivation and active learning, as illustrated in Figure 1.1.

While combined motivation and active learning promote basic student engagement, some teachers are pushing for more: they want students to be truly transformed by their educational experiences. Although any learning, by definition, results in some level of change, transformative learning is deep

FIGURE 1.1.

Venn Diagram Model of Student Engagement

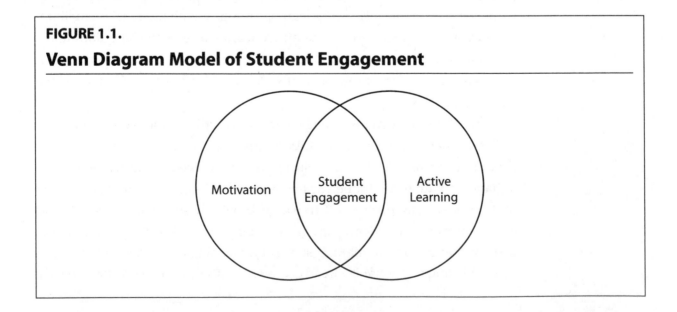

and thorough change. Cranton (2006) defines *transformative learning* as "a process by which previously uncritically assimilated assumptions, beliefs, values, and perspectives are questioned and thereby become more open, permeable, and better justified" (p. vi). It requires learners "to examine problematic frames of reference to make them more inclusive, discriminating, open, reflective, and able to change," and it can be "provoked by a single event . . . or it can take place gradually and cumulatively over time" (p. 36).

Transformative learning occurs when students are challenged intensely, creating the kind of growth described by Perry's upper levels of intellectual and ethical development ("Perry model," n.d.). In Perry's observations, most freshmen enter college as dualists, believing that there are clear, objective, right-or-wrong answers. One of the goals of a college education is to help students move beyond dualistic thinking to more complex stages as they learn to deal with uncertainty and relativism. As experiences challenge their thinking, students begin to see that truth is contextual and relative, and since there is not a single correct answer, everyone has a right to his or her own opinion. Eventually students recognize that there may be multiple answers to a question but not all answers are equal, and specific criteria such as empirical evidence and logical consistency can help them evaluate the usefulness and validity of knowledge claims.

In Perry's fourth and final stage, students come to recognize that they must make individual choices that require both objective analysis *and* personal values (Perry, 1998). As students' thinking matures to this level of sophistication, it is truly transformative. Interestingly, Bowen (2005) observes that students often resist teachers' attempts to promote transformative learning precisely because it "necessarily threatens the student's current identity and world view" and cites a study by Trosset at an elite liberal arts college that revealed that the majority of students did not want to participate in a discussion until they felt well prepared to defend their already firmly held views (Bowen, 2005). Some teachers consider transformative learning to be an element of engaged learning, but it may not be so much a required element as much as the result of sustained engagement or engagement that has achieved a higher level of personal intensity.

Motivation and active learning work together synergistically, and as they interact, they contribute incrementally to increase engagement. Rather than a Venn diagram where engagement is the overlap of active learning and motivation, thereby limiting the influence of each, engagement may be better described as a double helix in which active learning and motivation are spirals working together synergistically, building in intensity, and creating a fluid and dynamic phenomenon that is greater than the sum of their individual effects. (See Figure 1.2.)

FIGURE 1.2.

Double Helix Model of Student Engagement

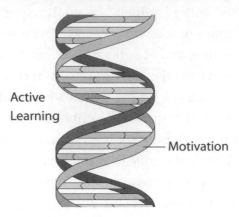

Active

Learning

— Motivation

Source: U.S. National Library of Medicine, DNA diagram (http://ghr.nlm.nih.gov/handbook/basics/dna)

Thus engagement occurs on a continuum: it starts at the intersection of motivation and active learning, but these two work synergistically and build in intensity. At the far end of the continuum are the transformative, peak experiences that constitute the treasured milestones of an education. As attractive and appealing as these experiences are, they are not sustainable on a constant basis—they'd be too exhausting. As college teachers, we can strive to increase experiences of deep engagement, reduce the incidence of indifference and apathy that characterize lack of engagement, and attend to the many ways we can adapt our teaching methods to enhance engaged learning throughout the range in between.

Within the context of a college classroom, I propose this definition: *Student engagement is a process and a product that is experienced on a continuum and results from the synergistic interaction between motivation and active learning.* Understanding basic principles drawn from the research and theory on motivation and active learning can offer insights into how to promote student engagement. Let us therefore begin by exploring the first element in our double helix model: student motivation.

Chapter 2
Engagement and Motivation

MOTIVATION IS a theoretical construct to explain the reason or reasons we engage in a particular behavior. It is the feeling of interest or enthusiasm that makes somebody want to do something. In the classroom, we want students to *want to learn*. So how do we accomplish that? Brophy (2004) proposes that motivation to learn is an acquired competence developed through an individual's cumulative experience with learning situations. It is a web of connected insights, skills, values, and dispositions that is developed over time. Some students come to our institutions and our classes with a high motivation to learn. Others are more motivated by the economic opportunities associated with the professions and careers they hope to have once they graduate. Regardless of a student's general disposition, motivation can be activated or suppressed in specific situations. Even a student who is generally motivated to learn may be less enthusiastic in a course that she feels coerced to take because it is a required element of the general education pattern. Conversely, a student who seems generally unmotivated to learn may become quite enthusiastic about the learning in a specific course.

Brophy defines motivation in the classroom as "the level of enthusiasm and the degree to which students invest attention and effort in learning" (2004, p. 4). This definition implies an internal state, a concept that differs considerably from the external manipulation of rewards and punishment that was emphasized in early, behaviorist studies of motivation. In the behaviorist approach, motivation was studied as a response to incentives and rewards, factors that are largely dictated from sources external to the learner. The behaviorist model suggests that teachers can develop motivated students by reinforcing the desired learning behavior that constitutes excellent work (attentiveness in class, careful and thorough work on assignments, thoughtful and frequent contributions to discussion), thereby encouraging students to continue these behaviors. If students are not able to engage in these behaviors immediately, they'll gradually improve if the correct behaviors are reinforced and incompatible behaviors are extinguished through nonreinforcement or, if necessary, suppressed through punishment.

Cognitive models of motivation started replacing behaviorist models in the 1960s, emphasizing learners' subjective experiences. Reinforcement was still important, but its effects were mediated through learners' cognitions. Among the cognitive models, needs models developed first. These models, such as Maslow's Hierarchy of Needs, propose that behavior is a response to felt needs, implying that basic physiological needs (such as sleep) must be met before higher-level needs (such as a sense of belonging) can be met. In terms of the classroom, this means that before students can focus on college-level learning, lower-level needs must first be met. In other words, students who are hungry because they're rushing between classes and haven't eaten or are tired because they worked late at their part-time job or studied all night for an exam will be distracted by their fundamental needs for food or sleep and not be able to concentrate on the coursework. Or as another example, the basic need for safety will discourage students from participating in a discussion and saying what they truly think or feel if they are anxious about rejection from their peers or criticism by their professor.

Both behaviorist and needs theories depict motivation as reactive to pressures, either from extrinsic rewards or internal needs. Theorists gradually began to acknowledge that humans are not always just pushed or pulled but are sometimes more proactive in their behavior; this led to "goals" models. Goal theories suggest students are motivated, for example, by performance goals (preserving self-perception or public reputation as capable individuals), learning goals (trying to learn whatever the instructor's task is designed to teach them), and even work-avoidant goals (refusing to accept the challenges inherent in the task and instead focusing on spending as little time and effort as possible in completing it). Studies by goal theorists and other motivational researchers contributed a great deal of information about the situational characteristics that predict students' tendencies to adopt different goals in achievement situations.

To apply goals theory to the college classroom, teachers try to (a) establish supportive relationships and cooperative/collaborative learning arrangements that encourage students to adopt learning goals instead of performance goals and (b) minimize the sorts of pressures that dispose students toward performance goals or work-avoidant goals. According to Brophy (2004), when these conditions are created in a classroom, "students are able to focus their energies on learning without becoming distracted by fear of embarrassment or failure, or by resentment of tasks that they view as pointless or inappropriate" (p. 9).

In the 1980s, intrinsic motivation theories combined elements of needs and goals models. Self-determination theory (Deci & Ryan, 1985, 2002), for example, suggests that at times we engage in behavior simply because we want to. Settings that promote intrinsic motivation satisfy three innate needs: autonomy (self-determination in deciding what to do and how to do it), competence (developing and exercising skills for manipulating and controlling the environment), and relatedness (affiliation with others through social relationships). Students are likely to be intrinsically motivated in courses that promote these three characteristics.

Today's theories about motivation combine elements of needs and goals models and emphasize the importance of factors within the individual. Brophy (2004) and Cross (2001) observe that much of what researchers have found can be organized within an *expectancy × value* model. This model holds that the effort that people are willing to expend on a task is the product of the degree to which they expect to be able to perform the task successfully (*expectancy*) and the degree to which they value the rewards as well as the opportunity to engage in performing the task itself (*value*). As with our model of engagement as a product rather than a sum (Figure 1.1), effort is also viewed as the product rather than the sum: it is assumed that people will expend no effort if either element (expectancy or value) is missing entirely. People will not willingly invest effort in tasks that they do not enjoy and that do not lead to something they value even if they know that they can perform the tasks successfully, nor do they willingly invest effort in even highly valued tasks if they believe that they cannot succeed no matter how hard they try. In short, students' motivations are strongly influenced by what they think is important and what they believe they can accomplish. Let us first explore the construct of expectancy.

Expectancy

Students' expectations are inextricably linked with their self-perceptions. Students must have confidence that, with appropriate effort, they can succeed. If there is no hope, there is no motivation. Cross and Steadman (1996) discuss three motivational theories that address student expectations: self-efficacy theories, attribution theory, and self-worth models. Self-efficacy theories (Bandura, 1977, 1982; Corno & Mandinach, 1983) suggest that students' *belief* about their ability to succeed at a learning task is more important than their actual skill level or the difficulty of the task. If a student is confident in her ability to perform a task successfully, she will be motivated to engage in it.

Attribution theory (Weiner, 1979, 1985, 1986) suggests that students attribute success or failure to a variety of factors such as ability, effort, luck, fatigue, ease or difficulty of the exam, and so forth, and that their belief is shaped by their perceptions of why they have succeeded or failed in the past. For example, if success depends on attributes over which they have control (effort), students are more likely to have confidence than when success depends on external conditions over which they have no control (difficulty of the exam). Three important dimensions of attributions are *locus* (whether failure or success is attributed to causes internal or external to the learner); *stability* (whether the attributed cause is permanent or temporary); and *controllability* (whether the learner has the power to influence success or failure).

Finally, self-worth models propose that people are strongly motivated to preserve their sense of self-worth. When students don't succeed, they would prefer to question—and have others question—their effort (they're lazy) rather than their ability (they're dumb) (Brown & Weiner, 1984; Cross, 2001). Based on this model, it is easier to understand why some students don't even try to accomplish a task if they believe there is low probability that they will be successful.

Covington (1993) found four typical student patterns that resonate with the experience of many college teachers interacting with students in the classroom. *Success-oriented* students are serious learners who want to perform well, and they usually do. They are predisposed toward engagement, as they enjoy learning for learning's sake. They find personal satisfaction in challenging assignments because they are accustomed to success and are able to preserve their perceptions of self-worth even in the event of an occasional failure. *Overstrivers* are also successful students and will take on challenging tasks, but they are not entirely confident in their ability and consequently worry constantly about their grades and performance. Anxious that each new learning task will be the one that exposes the lower level of ability that they have so far been able to conceal, they compensate by expending a great deal of effort to ensure that they do succeed. *Failure-avoiders* also suffer anxiety, but because they have not always been successful in school, they are afraid that if they fail at a specific learning activity, they will prove to themselves and others that they lack the ability to succeed. In order to preserve their sense of self-worth, they avoid tasks that are too challenging. Finally, *failure-accepting* students have become so accustomed and resigned to academic failure that they feel hopeless. They respond to learning tasks with indifference (school is irrelevant and unworthy of their efforts) or even antagonism, and they are neither satisfied with success nor dissatisfied with failure (Cross & Steadman, 1996, pp. 79–84). In short, they have disengaged from the learning process.

Although the role of expectancy has received considerable attention in the study of student motivation, value is also a critical variable. Most students are making the sacrifices necessary to get a college education because they believe in the value of the learning, the value of the degree, or both. Therefore, in our efforts to promote student engagement, we need to look at what the research says about how the concept of value influences student motivation.

Value

Some teachers find that the easiest and most direct way to spur students to invest time and effort in their coursework is reward strategies such as high grades, bonus points, praise, incentives such as release from work ("if you achieve x number of points, you do not need to take the final exam"), achievement recognition ("the three best projects were done by students X, Y, and Z"), and so forth. Kohn, in his influential *Punished by Rewards* (1993), is a leading critic of these approaches and sees such strategies as bribing students and shifting their focus away from valuing the task itself to valuing the consequences of task completion. He draws on research in the 1970s and 1980s showing that rewarding people for doing what they are already doing for their own reasons can decrease their intrinsic motivation and the quality of their performance because they develop a piecemeal mentality and do whatever will garner them the most rewards with the least effort. This is evident, for example, in the behavior of students who enroll in "easy A" courses rather than more challenging ones in order to preserve their GPA. In short, although strategies that provide extrinsic rewards may be quick fixes for increasing motivation, they may also be counterproductive to our efforts to help students develop the kind of intrinsic motivation to learn that we associate with truly engaged learning.

Csikszentmihalyi's (1993, 1997) concept of "flow" describes states of deep intrinsic motivation that sound a lot like deep engagement. He proposes that when we experience flow, action and awareness merge. We are so absorbed in the task at hand that irrelevant stimuli disappear from consciousness, and worries and concerns are temporarily suspended. We lose track of time; in fact, it seems to pass faster. The activity becomes autotelic, or worth doing for its own sake.

Wlodkowski (2008) notes that helping students achieve a sense of flow is more possible than many instructors realize, and he identifies the following characteristics as contributors: (1) goals are clear and compatible, allowing learners to concentrate even when the task is difficult; (2) feedback is immediate, continuous, and relevant as the activity unfolds so that students are clear about how well they are doing; and (3) the challenge balances skills or knowledge with stretching existing capacities (pp. 267-268). Brophy (2004) observes that while some people seem to possess a flow personality, seeking out challenges and taking great pleasure in stretching their limits, others rarely experience flow because they fear failure and avoid challenging situations (p. 11).

While the *expectancy* × *value* model offers a framework for identifying engagement strategies generally, it is also helpful in understanding and devising interventions for at-risk students whose low level of confidence and expectancy of failure have placed them in a state of almost chronic disengagement. For example, dissembling occurs when students recognize the value of the task but feel incapable of doing it either because they aren't certain of what to do or how to do it, or they doubt that they can do it. They then make excuses, deny their difficulties, pretend to understand, or participate in some other behavior designed to protect their ego rather than developing the task-related knowledge and skill. Evading is likely when success expectancies are high but task value perceptions are low, that is, students feel confident they can do the task but don't see any reason to do so and instead daydream, interact with classmates on topics unrelated to course content, think about their personal lives, and so forth. Finally, rejecting (active disengagement) is likely when both success expectations and perception of task value are low. Lacking either a reason to care about succeeding or the confidence that they could do the task if they tried, they become passive or smolder with anger or alienation, rejecting the task and don't even feel the need to dissemble or pretend to themselves or others that they are capable of doing it. Understanding the causes of lack of engagement can help identify strategies for re-engaging these students. Table 2.1 summarizes the anticipated student responses to engaging in a learning task when the expectancy or value aspects are influenced positively or negatively.

Expectancy and value are important constructs in our growing knowledge about student motivation, and the implications for classroom practice are fairly straightforward. Basically, teachers can increase student motivation by taking steps to increase the *value* of the learning to students and helping students hold optimistic and positive *expectations* about their ability to succeed.

TABLE 2.1.

Students' Responses to Tasks Related to Expectancy and Value Perceptions

	If a student expects to succeed and . . .	If a student does not expect to succeed and . . .
. . . VALUES THE TASK,	the student will probably engage in the task, eager and happy to focus on developing knowledge and skills by seeking to discover meanings, grasping new insights, and generating integrative interpretations.	the student might dissemble and make excuses, pretend to understand, or deny having difficulties, focusing more on protecting the ego than on developing task-related knowledge and skill.
. . . DOES NOT VALUE THE TASK,	the student might evade the task by doing the minimum that is required to get the task done, but his or her heart and mind won't be engaged in it; attention will be scattered, drifting to competing interests.	the student will probably resist or reject the task. If the task is required, the student will do it resentfully, angry at being coerced into a perceived unpleasant, pointless activity that may also prove to be embarrassing and reinforce negative self-perceptions of low ability.

Source: Based on J. E. Brophy, 2004, *Motivating students to learn* (Mahwah, NJ: Erlbaum), pp. 19–20.

Conclusion

Motivation is the portal to engagement. An unmotivated student has checked out emotionally and mentally from the learning process. Students who are motivated to learn, however, will actively seek the information and understandings that constitute engaged learning. Just as a classroom filled with students who are genuinely motivated to learn can be teaching nirvana, it can be teaching hell trying to work with students who are apathetic, bored, or even hostile; or who are so compulsively obsessed with grades that they badger us incessantly to improve theirs on every assignment; or who seem deliberately to take on strategies that are self-defeating. Understanding the complexities that underlie motivation can guide us in our efforts to set up conditions that enhance students' eagerness to learn. This is a first and critical step toward increasing student engagement.

Chapter 3

Engagement and Active Learning

ALTHOUGH THE TERMS *teaching* and *learning* are typically paired, those of us who teach know that students don't always learn. When I complained about this early in my teaching career, a colleague chided me: "Saying 'I taught students something, they just didn't learn it' is akin to saying 'I sold them the car, they just didn't buy it.'" As Angelo and Cross (1993) point out, learning can—and often does—occur without teaching, but teaching cannot occur without learning; teaching without learning is just talking (p. 3). Since helping students learn is our primary goal as teachers, how do we best accomplish that? The simplest answer may be to set up conditions that promote active learning. "Active learning" is an umbrella term that now refers to several models of instruction, including cooperative and collaborative learning, discovery learning, experiential learning, problem-based learning, and inquiry-based learning. Active learning puts into practice over a half-century of research that demonstrates that to truly learn, we need to make an idea, a concept, or a solution our own by working it into our personal knowledge and experience.

It is easy to confuse active learning with physical activity, thinking that, for example, simply breaking a class into small groups so that more students have a chance to participate will result in student engagement. This belief is reinforced by NSSE and CCSSE survey questions that ask students to report how often they've participated in group activities, with the assumption that the larger the number, the more engaged that institution's students are. Although pedagogies such as cooperative/collaborative learning are more likely to encourage engagement than others, it is not safe to conclude that if students are talking to each other, they are learning. It is equally risky to conclude that students are learning when they are listening to other students talking.

Active learning means that *the mind* is actively engaged. Its defining characteristics are that students are dynamic participants in their learning and that they are reflecting on and monitoring both the processes and the results of their learning. As Cross (1998b) notes, a chess player may sit for hours without talking or moving, but his or her mind is actively engaged in studying the layout of the pieces and strategizing the next move. Highly skilled listeners who are involved in a lecture by self-questioning, analyzing, and incorporating new information into their existing knowledge are learning more actively than students who are participating in a small group discussion that is off-task, redundant, or superfluous. This definition of active learning, where students make information or a concept their own by connecting it to their existing knowledge and experience, is critical to student engagement. An engaged student actively examines, questions, and relates new ideas to old, thereby achieving the kind of deep learning that lasts. Active learning is fundamental to and underlies all aspects of student engagement.

The Cognitive Basis of Active Learning

Neuroscientists are making remarkable discoveries that help us understand what happens within our brains when we are learning. To better understand how active learning occurs, it is useful to have at least a fundamental understanding of its neurological basis. Several books explain the brain's functioning to educators and general audiences, and the following paragraphs are a synthesis of information provided in some of these sources (Wlodkowski, 2008; Sousa, 2006; Ratey, 2002; Diamond & Hopson, 1998) as well as sources about learning techniques (Barkley, Cross, & Major, 2005; Cross, 1999).

What We Know from Neuroscience

The brain is composed of cells called *neurons*. Neurons start out as round cell bodies, each of which grows as many as 100,000 short branches called *dendrites* as well as a single long root known as an *axon*. Neurons act like tiny batteries, receiving information through the dendrites, sending it as a signal down the axon where chemicals called *neurotransmitters* are fired across a gap called the *synapse* to be received by the dendrites of another neuron. As the neurotransmitter enters the dendrites of a neighboring neuron, it sparks a series of electrochemical reactions that cause the receiving neuron also to fire through its axon. The process and reactions continue in a sequence until there is a pattern of neuronal connections firing together.

Bombarded with thousands of stimuli that create these events every moment of our lives, neurons stay in a state of readiness for hours or even days. If the pattern is not stimulated again, the neuronal network will decay and the perception will be lost. This keeps our brain from getting cluttered with useless information. If, on the other hand, the pattern is repeated during the standby period and the associated network of neurons fires together again, the web of connections becomes more permanent. Each neuron and its thousands of neighbors intertwine to form an extraordinarily complex, interconnected tangle consisting of about 100 trillion constantly changing connections. Through repetition, some connections are strengthened and we "learn," while connections that are seldom or never used are eliminated and we "forget."

Thus, dendrites are the main way by which neurons get information (learn), the axon is the main way the neuron sends the information (teaches), and everything we know and understand has been preserved as a network of neurons in our brain. When adults learn, they build on or modify networks that have been created through previous learning and experience. If the new information fits easily with the old information, it is said to be assimilated. If the new information challenges the existing information to the extent that the existing structure needs to be revised, it is said to be accommodated (Svinicki, 2004b, p. 11). The more dendrites we have on which to hang or attach new information, the easier it is to learn and retain new information. The greater number of basic neuronal networks we have, the easier it is to form more complex networks. From a neuroscientific viewpoint, therefore, learning is long-lasting change in neurons and existing neuronal networks. When teachers promote active learning, we are helping students grow dendrites and activate and build on existing neuronal networks.

What We Know from Cognitive Psychology

Findings from neuroscience parallel models of the working mind envisioned by cognitive psychologists, who postulate a structure of the mind known as the *schema* (in plural form, *schemata*). Cross (1999) provides a useful definition:

> *A schema is a cognitive structure that consists of facts, ideas, and associations organized into a meaningful system of relationships. People have schemata for events, places, procedures, and people, for instance. A person's schema for a place, such as a college, might include concepts such as location, reputation, the characteristics of the student population, the*

*style of campus architecture, even the location of campus parking lots.
Thus, the schema is an organized collection of bits of information that
together build the concept of the college for each individual. When someone mentions the college, we "know" what that means, but the image
brought to mind may be somewhat different for each individual. (p. 8)*

We can readily imagine the rich schema that would be in the mind of
someone who had taught at or attended the college (including memories of
courses, classrooms, and professors) and contrast it with the relatively
sparse schema of someone who had simply heard of the college. We can
also readily see the potential for errors and misunderstanding if the person
confuses the college with another college with a similar name or a college
with the same name that is in a different state.

The value of a well-developed schema is revealed in research on the differences between the learning of novices and experts. The expert quickly
grasps new information in useable form because connections to existing
knowledge are numerous. The learning of a novice, in contrast, is labored
and slow, not because the novice is less intelligent than the expert, but
because connections between new information and existing schemata are
sparse—there are no hooks on which to hang the new information, no way
to organize it (Cross, 1999, p. 8; de Groot, 1966). Each schema changes and
grows throughout life as new events, filtered by perception into the schema,
are organized and connected to the existing structure to create meaning.
Thus new information results in meaningful learning only when it connects
with what already exists in the mind of the learner, resulting in change in
the networks that represent our understandings.

The Role of Transfer in Active Learning

When activating prior learning to make sense of something new, the brain
searches for any past learnings that are similar to, or associated with, the new
learning. If the experiences exist, the corresponding neuronal networks or
schema are activated, reinforcing the already-stored information as well as
assisting in interpreting and assigning meaning to the new information.
Svinicki (2004a, p. 99) notes that there are many types of transfer discussed
in the literature, but two types are the most important for purposes of
instruction. The first is positive-versus-negative transfer. If the connections
are accurate, the search results in positive transfer that can aid the learner in
understanding and integrating new learnings. If, on the other hand, the connections are incorrect, the result is negative transfer, which creates confusion

and errors. For example, when teaching Romance languages to English speakers, teachers frequently encounter positive transfer (for example, *mucho* in Spanish sounds similar to *much* in English) and negative transfer (*librairie* in French sounds like *library*, but it means "bookstore") (Sousa, 2006, pp. 138–139).

The second type of transfer is near-versus-far transfer. This distinction refers to the type of task: near-transfer tasks are those that look very much alike and follow the same rules, whereas far-transfer tasks are ones that follow the same rules, but they are transferred to a different setting. Far transfer requires more thinking on the part of the learner. Svinicki (2004b, pp. 100–101) offers driving a mid-level automatic sedan as an example: if you've driven one, you can easily drive any other because the steering wheel, gear shift, windshield wipers, and turn signals all look alike and are in the same position. If, on the other hand, you get into a car that is very different (such as a convertible, stick-shift sports car), your normal driving responses are not instantly triggered and you have to stop and figure out where everything is. The rules are the same, but the car looks different. Moving between different mid-level automatic sedans is a near-transfer task, moving from a mid-level automatic sedan to a stick-shift sports car is a far-transfer task.

Several factors affect the quality of transfer: similarity/difference, association, and context and degree of original learning.

Similarity and Differences

How similar a previously encountered situation is to a new situation affects transfer. Interestingly, it appears that the brain generally stores new information in networks that contain similar characteristics or associations, but retrieves information by identifying how it is different from the other items in that network. For example, the visual appearances of people we know seem to be stored in the network of what humans look like (such as torso, head, two arms, two legs) but if we are trying to find someone we know in a crowd, we will look for the characteristics that distinguish him or her from other people in the group (such as facial characteristics, height, voice). Obviously when there is high similarity with few differences, distinguishing between the two becomes more difficult (Sousa, 2006, p. 143). Thus the potential for negative transfer is higher when concepts, principles, and data, or the labels for this information, are similar. For example, in music, "whole tone" and "whole note" sound similar, but the terms represent very different concepts (*whole tone* is a specific distance between two pitches, and *whole note* is the rhythmic duration of a single pitch).

Association

Learning two items together so that the two are bonded or associated also affects transfer, and when one of the items is recalled, the other is spontaneously recalled as well. When we hear or read the word "Romeo," we unconsciously add "and Juliet," or when we think of a trademark symbol such as McDonald's golden arches or Apple's apple logo, we immediately think of the associated product (Sousa, 2006, p. 145). Since everything we know and understand is preserved as a network of associations, the more associations we make, the greater the number of potential places we have to attach new information and the easier it is for us to learn and retain that information. In short, the more we learn and retain, the more we *can* learn and retain.

Context and Degree of Original Learning

Emotional associations can have a particularly potent influence on transfer, as emotions usually have a higher priority than cognitive processing for commanding our attention. Math anxiety—the fear and tension that interferes with some students' ability to manipulate numbers or solve mathematical problems—is an example of the association of a negative feeling with a content area. Students with math anxiety will try to avoid situations involving math in order to spare themselves the negative feelings associated with it. In contrast, people will devote hours on hobbies because of the feelings of pleasure and satisfaction they associate with these activities (Sousa, 2006, p. 145).

Not surprisingly, the quality of the original learning also strongly influences the quality of transfer to new learning. If the original learning was thorough, deep, and accurate, its influence will be much more constructive than learning that was originally superficial. At the college level, we work with the students' cumulative "prior learning" during K–12, over which we have little control. Because we have greater control over what students learn when they are with us in college (especially at the department/degree level), we should take extra care to help students connect positive feelings to new learnings and ensure that foundational material is taught well, as everything that is learned in these courses becomes the basis for future transfer.

The Role of Memory in Active Learning

Once students learn something, we want them to remember it. There are currently several different models describing memory, but a basic and generally accepted classification divides memory into two main types: short-term and long-term.

Short- and Long-Term Memory

Short-term memory gives continuity from one moment to the next and allows us to carry out hundreds of tasks each day by holding the data we are dealing with at the moment, but then letting it go so that our brain can turn its attention to other things. Short-term memory occurs when the brain works with new information until it decides if and where to store it more permanently.

While short-term memory is supported by transient neuronal networks and functions as temporary storage, long-term memory is retained for greater lengths of time—days, decades, even an entire lifetime. It is structurally different from short-term memory in that it is maintained by permanent cellular changes that have been created by neuronal connections distributed throughout the brain.

We want students to remember important new learning long term, so how do short-term memories become long-term memories? Research suggests that there is a special window of time during which this transition occurs: the time needed for neurons to synthesize the necessary proteins for "long-term potentiation" (LTP). An initial stimulation triggers communication across the synapse between two neurons; further stimulation causes the cells to produce key proteins that bind to the synapse, cementing the memory in place. If the memory is to last for more than a few hours, these proteins must bind to specific synapses and actually change the cellular structure.

The Importance of Sense and Meaning to Long-Term Memory

The criteria by which short-term memory determines whether information should be stored for the long term is complex. Information tied to survival or information that has a strong emotional component has a high likelihood of being permanently stored. In classrooms, where these two kinds of information are generally minimal or absent, two other factors come into play.

One important factor is whether the information makes sense—does it fit with what the learner already knows about the way the world works? When students say that they don't understand, it means that they cannot make sense of what they are learning, and hence they probably won't remember it. The other important factor is whether the information has meaning—is it relevant, is there some reason for the learner to remember it?

We remember some information just because it made sense even though it wasn't particularly meaningful (this is the kind of data people recall when they are doing crossword puzzles or playing games such as Trivial Pursuit).

We also remember information just because it had meaning (we had to memorize it in order to pass a test) even though it didn't make sense.

Of the two criteria, meaning is more significant. For example, telling a student that she needs x number of units in her academic major for a degree at your institution but y number of units at an institution in another state makes sense, but the student will be more likely to remember the number of units at her own institution because it is more meaningful and relevant to her educational plans. Brain scans have shown that when new learning is readily comprehensible (it makes sense) and can be connected to past experiences (it has meaning), retention is dramatically improved (Sousa, 2006, pp. 49–51).

Retention

The process by which long-term memory preserves a learning so that it can be located, identified, and retrieved accurately in the future is called *retention*. Retention is influenced by many factors, but a critical one is adequate time to process and reprocess information so that it can be transferred from short-term to long-term memory. The encoding process from short-term memory to retention in long-term memory takes time and usually occurs during deep sleep. Research on retention shows that the greatest loss of newly acquired information or a skill occurs within the first 18–24 hours, so if a student can remember the information after 24 hours, there is a higher likelihood that it is now in long-term storage. If a student cannot remember the information after 24 hours, it is most likely not permanently stored and will not be retained.

Conclusion

Learning is a dynamic process in which the learner literally builds his or her own mind by constantly making and changing connections between what is new and what is already known. Deep, long-term learning occurs when changed connections result in reformatted structures—whether these structures are described as schemata or neuronal networks. As much as we (and often our students) would like to think that we as teachers can simply transfer knowledge into learners' brains, it is just not possible. Students need to do the work required to learn. We can help them by reversing our typical roles in the classroom. Instead of standing in front of the classroom working hard to present information as clearly as possible to students who are expected to sit quietly and absorb it, we can set up conditions where they are doing more of the work.

Chapter 4

Promoting Synergy between Motivation and Active Learning

IN OUR MODEL of student engagement, motivation and active learning are twin helices that work together synergistically. How can we promote this synergy? I propose that three classroom conditions function somewhat like steps or rungs between the two sides of the double helix spiral. These conditions integrate elements of both motivation and active learning and thus contribute to the synergy that promotes increased levels of engagement.

Condition 1: Teachers Can Promote Synergy by Creating a Sense of Classroom Community

If we had only our own observations of the ubiquitous use of cell phones on campus, we'd probably conclude that staying connected to other people is important to today's students. But this desire to be part of a social community is also reported in the research. In *Millennials Go to College*, generation analysts Howe and Strauss (2007) identify Team-Orientation—with its tight peer bonds and expectations to stay in constant contact with large circles of friends and acquaintances—as one of the seven core traits that define the current generation attending college. In the video *A Vision of Students Today*, student participants in the digital ethnography project at Kansas State University report that they average two hours a day on the cell phone and will read 1,281 Facebook profiles over the course of a year (Wesch, 2007). Exploiting this predilection for social connections, college marketing departments publish "viewbooks" filled with photos of students in groups talking amiably together. Used as recruitment tools, the books send a visual message to prospective freshmen that they will find a vibrant campus community at that institution.

Recognizing the importance of campus community is not new. Residence halls, student clubs, campus activities, and sororities and fraternities are all *extracurricular* ways that institutions foster a sense of social community. Across the curriculum, educators hope students will work diligently to become part of a community of scholars. In between the extracurricular social community and the earned membership into the scholarly community, which is typically signified by graduation, is the *curriculum*—the courses where students have traditionally been expected to do their work individually and independently. Students sit in rows facing the professor and are urged to refrain from talking to each other because that is disruptive and distracting. Fortunately, this model is now changing, with many educators proposing that optimal, engaged classroom environments are those in which the teacher and students perceive themselves as members of a learning community.

Although there is debate in the literature over the definition of *learning communities* (with "purposeful pairing of courses" a common definition), for our discussion of student engagement in a single classroom, we use Cross's definition: "groups of people engaged in intellectual interaction for the purpose of learning" (1998c). The term *learning community* seems appropriate for two reasons. First, it places the emphasis on learning. Second, the term suggests that this learning occurs within a community—a group of people working together with shared interests, common goals, and responsibilities toward one another and the group as a whole (Brophy, 2004). In a learning community, the overarching goal is learning, but this learning is best achieved in environments where students feel a sense of belonging and where they feel comfortable responding to questions even when they are unsure of the answer and seeking help from the teacher or from their peers when they don't understand. Building learning communities that help students feel connected to rather than isolated or alienated from the teacher and their classmates addresses a basic, motivational human need to be part of a social community.

Participating in the collaborative activities that are a fundamental component of a learning community also promotes active learning. Active learning means students are building their own minds through an active, involved process in which they make an idea, a concept, or a problem solution their own by assimilating it into their own understandings. In the traditional model, teachers stand at the front of the room and teach by "telling" students what they have learned with the expectation that they will transfer this knowledge into students' heads efficiently and accurately. In the active learning model, teachers create conditions in which students do the work, actively making connections and organizing learning into meaningful concepts. The advantages of cooperative and collaborative learning for actively engaging students are clear when compared with more traditional methods—such as lecture and large-group discussions—in which only a few students typically can, or do, participate.

The effectiveness of promoting the interaction that characterizes a learning community is well documented. Pascarella and Terenzini's (1991) first synthesis of the research on college's effect on students concluded that a large part of students' gains in factual knowledge and a range of general cognitive and intellectual skills is determined by the extent of students' interaction with faculty members and student peers in and out of the classroom (p. 620). In their follow-up work synthesizing research conducted in the 1990s, Pascarella and Terenzini (2005) state that the "broad spectrum" of research on group work as a pedagogical approach suggests that "collaborative learning approaches can significantly enhance learning" (p. 103). They describe a study that used data from over one thousand students in fifty-seven classes and found that the greater the emphasis on collaborative learning and the lower the emphasis on grades, the more likely students were to use the higher-order learning strategies of elaboration, comprehension monitoring, and critical thinking (Pascarella & Terenzini, 2005, p. 180).

In another study, Pascarella and Terenzini (2005) did their own meta-analysis using raw data from a meta-analysis of forty-three experimental and quasi-experimental studies that considered the effects of cooperative versus individualistic or competitive learning approaches on general problem-solving skills. Four types of problems were considered: linguistic (problems solved in written or oral language), nonlinguistic (problems represented in pictures, graphs, symbols, mazes, or formulas), well-defined problems with precise operational procedures and solutions (such as a chess problem), and ill-defined problems (problems without clear procedures or solutions, such as deciding which car to buy). Pascarella and Terenzini concluded that "college students learning in cooperative groups had a statistically significant advantage in overall problem solving of .47 of a standard deviation" and that the advantage in problem solving was essentially the same for both well-defined problems and ill-defined problems (p. 180).

Collaborative learning is also in alignment with the model that knowledge is socially constructed rather than discovered. Bruffee (1993), in his philosophy of nonfoundational social construction, proposes, "We construct and maintain knowledge not by examining the world but by negotiating with one another in communities of knowledgeable peers" (p. 9).

Finally, building classroom learning communities in which all students feel respected and valued may also address criticisms that current approaches to measuring student engagement are part of a dominant paradigm that fails to take into consideration theories about marginalized groups, focusing too much on the student and his or her lack of engagement and not enough on exposing the existing structures that disempower students. They emphasize the responsibility of institutional agents to create more empowering and engaging conditions for all students to succeed. College teachers can support institutional efforts toward this goal by helping all students feel that they are included, honored, important, contributing members of a learning community. In short, creating conditions in which students interact with each other as members of a learning community promotes student engagement and creates synergy between motivation and active learning: it fulfills the basic human need to be part of a social community and also encourages students to learn actively as they collaboratively construct, reconstruct, and build their understanding.

Condition 2: Teachers Can Create Synergy by Helping Students Work at Their Optimal Level of Challenge

One of the fundamental principles of learning is that tasks must be sufficiently difficult to pose a challenge, but not so difficult as to destroy the willingness to try (McKeachie, 1994, p. 353). Somewhere between "been there, done that" and "dazed and confused" lies the optimal level of challenge that engages students. Vygotsky (1978) invented the term "zone of proximal development" (ZPD) to suggest that learning is productive when learners are operating in a situation that exposes them to concepts and ideas just slightly above their current level of development. The theory, applied to student engagement, suggests that engaged learning occurs in the gap between a learner's current understanding and potential understanding. Working at the optimal challenge level creates synergy because it straddles both motivation and active learning.

In terms of motivation, Brophy (2004) suggests that anxiety and a mismatch of task to skill are the chief threats to the flow potential that characterizes deep engagement. When students face challenging tasks but do not think they possess the necessary skills, they experience anxiety; when skill is high but the task is not challenging, students become bored; when both challenge and skill level are low, students become apathetic. All three qualities—anxiousness, boredom, and apathy—characterize lack of engagement. From the perspective of active learning, an important aspect of schema theory is that the mind not only decodes what is said or written and makes the connections to existing knowledge, but it also supplies much that is not present.

Cross (1993c) describes work done by Crawford and Chaffin on how readers construct meaning. They offer the simple sentence, "The little girl heard the ice cream man and rushed upstairs to get her piggy bank," and explain that most of us reading that sentence *know* what it means, even though the sentence itself says nothing about ice cream vendors moving along the street or ringing a bell, about liking or buying ice cream, or about a piggy bank containing money. The reader supplies that information from past experience and makes the interpretation based on what he or she already knows. To someone raised on a ranch in Wyoming, all sorts of puzzling questions might arise. How did the little girl "hear" the ice cream man? Why did she rush upstairs instead of going into the ice cream store? Given the diversity in many college classrooms today, imagine the confusion of someone raised in a bustling high rise in Hong Kong: a man made of ice cream? What is this odd American association between pigs and banks?

Meaningful learning requires some combination of both the incoming message and prior knowledge. For new learning to take place, it has to be related to what the learner already knows. If students have nothing to connect new information to—no associational hooks on which to hang the data—they may feel bewildered and overwhelmed. Therefore it is essential for a teacher to understand how students are incorporating new information into what they already know in order to help students work in their optimal challenge zone and achieve the deep, meaningful learning essential to engagement.

The challenge for teachers is that classes generally have a minimum of 15–20 students who are often quite diverse. Because individual learners within a class most likely have different learning gaps and hence have different zones of optimal challenge, how can a teacher possibly individualize the curriculum to meet each student's unique needs? Is it inevitable that some students will be bored, and others confused and frustrated? Not necessarily. Assessment, teaching students metacognitive skills, and empowering students as partners in their own learning are three broad approaches to helping students work in their optimal challenge zones.

Assessment and Feedback

Learners need to know how well they are doing and how they can do better. Effective teaching is not simply providing information—a textbook, video, or podcast can do that as well and often better. Rather, a teacher's value comes in the careful observation, analysis, and feedback to a learner that enables improvement.

Summative, Formative, and Educative Assessment

Summative assessment is the summary evaluation at the end of a topic, unit, or program, usually to produce a grade. It is essentially product focused. Tests are the traditional vehicle for this type of assessment.

Formative assessment is more process-oriented and developmental in nature. Its primary purpose is to provide feedback that encourages adjustments and corrections. Both summative and formative types of assessment are valuable and necessary and, in practice, often blended.

A term used by Wiggins (1998, pp. 12–13) that seems to incorporate both summative and formative aspects is *educative assessment*. Educative assessment is deliberately designed to promote as well as measure learning. Critical elements include identifying and communicating learning goals to students; specifying the criteria or evidence that will be used to determine whether the students have met the goals; and providing students with rich, timely, individually relevant feedback that provides opportunities for intervention and adjustment before it is too late.

Authentic Assessment

Wiggins and others also stress *authentic assessment*, an approach that developed out of the concern that conventional assessment instruments tend to focus on the more superficial and easily tested aspects of knowledge and do not replicate the kinds of challenges that adults face in the workplace, civic affairs, or their personal lives. Authentic assessment aims to be realistic, which means the task reproduces the ways and the contexts in which a person's knowledge and abilities are "tested" in real-world situations. This typically involves the student "doing" the subject. Instead of reciting, restating, or replicating through demonstration what he or she was taught or what is already known, the student has to carry out the kind of exploration and work that constitutes "doing" in the discipline.

Second, authentic assessment requires judgment, innovation, and efficient and effective use of a repertoire of knowledge and skills to negotiate a complex task or solve complex problems. In other words, authentic assessment requires students to integrate multiple elements. Third, authentic assessment is formative, allowing appropriate opportunities to rehearse, practice, consult resources, and get feedback on and refine performances and products (Wiggins, 1998, pp. 23–24).

What constitutes an authentic assessment task is discipline- and course-specific. For example in a history course, rather than testing whether students can remember the facts of history, an authentic assessment task might ask students to research a controversial historical account to determine the facts. Because authentic assessment tasks seem more relevant and also tend to be more interesting, students are often more motivated to do them than they are to do conventional assessment activities. Additionally, because of their greater complexity, they allow for a range of responses that can encourage students to work within their optimal challenge zone.

There are many different ways to approach assessment, but to be effective in improving teaching and learning, assessment strategies involve the same basic steps: (1) identify a learning goal; (2) select an assessment technique that will measure to what extent the goal has been achieved; (3) apply the assessment technique; (4) analyze the results of the assessment and share the results with the student(s), ideally providing an opportunity for student feedback; and (5) respond to the results and implement any necessary change in teaching strategy or course content (Fenton & Watkins, 2008, pp. 6–7).

Teaching Metacognitive Skills

Students who reflect on their learning are better learners than those who do not. Being aware of oneself as a learner and constantly monitoring the effectiveness of one's learning involves *metacognition*, a term used by cognitive psychologists to describe the "executive function" of the mind. Many different strategies can help learners acquire new information and integrate it with existing knowledge as well as retrieve stored information. These strategies include previewing, summarizing, paraphrasing, imaging, creating analogies, note taking, and outlining. Most experienced learners use strategies such as these to keep their attention focused on the task and their minds actively engaged. Many novice learners do not know or use these strategies.

For new learning to take place, it has to be related to what the learner already knows. The challenge for some students—particularly underachieving students—is that existing knowledge is poorly organized and distressingly sparse. Cross (1993c) offers the analogy of a clothes closet. It is rather easy to hang clothes in a well-organized closet and retrieve them ready to wear. Shoes, whether running shoes or dress shoes, go on the floor; blouses and shirts are short and can be hung in tiers; some clothing, such as slacks, go on special hangers; and other items, such as sweaters and knits, are probably best folded and placed on shelves. The point is that storing and retrieving items is easy when you understand and implement the organizing principles of the closet. If, on the other hand, you just toss things into the closet every which way (and shut the door quickly in the hopes that nothing will spill out), then it will be a challenge to find the shirt you are looking for or both of a pair of socks.

Metacognitive strategies require activity on the part of learners, not for grading purposes, but for the pedagogical purpose of actively monitoring and controlling their own learning processes. Teachers can help students develop the metacognitive strategies that enable them to exert more control over the quality of their learning. After all, in the final analysis, the learners themselves are in the best position to determine whether they are learning at their optimal level of challenge.

Empowering Students as Partners in the Learning Process

Because optimal challenge zones are determined by each student's unique needs, it helps if the student is an empowered partner in the learning process. When students have the power to make decisions regarding their own learning, they can take steps to ensure they are working in their optimal challenge zone. Weimer (2002) identifies sharing power with students as the first of five key changes required to shift to learner-centered teaching. Her chapter on the balance of power opens with this paragraph:

> How would you characterize today's college students? Empowered, confident, self-motivated learners? That is not how I would describe mine. The ones in my classes are hopeful but generally anxious and tentative. They want all classes to be easy but expect that most will be hard. They wish their major (whatever it might be) did not require math, science, or English courses. A good number will not speak in class unless called on. Most like, want, indeed need teachers who tell them exactly what to do. Education is something done unto them. It frequently involves stress, anxiety, and other forms of discomfort. (p. 23)

Weimer's description evokes a wonderfully clear and instantly recognizable image of disengaged students. She discusses power sharing from many perspectives, including summarizing the major themes in the writings of radical, critical pedagogues such as Freire and hooks, noting the emphasis they give to the influence of power on the motivation to learn and on learning outcomes themselves. She also observes, "[T]eacher authority is so taken for granted that most of us are no longer aware of the extent to which we direct student learning" (2002, p. 23), and she provides ample evidence of the power differential between teacher and students in typical college classes.

In Weimer's own teaching, she has noticed that when students realize she is not going to tell them what to do, they begin to exercise their power tentatively and anxiously, wanting feedback and needing reinforcement in order to move forward with a bit more confidence. "It is difficult to say precisely when it happens," she reports, "but one day, quite unexpectedly, the students are engaged and involved with the course and its content. There is an energy about the class, a kind of enthusiasm. Instructional nirvana does not descend. Not everybody is involved and engaged, and some activities and assignments still bomb. But student response to my efforts to share power has been the most eloquent evidence to me that learner-centered teaching is a powerful pedagogy" (2002, pp. 30–31). Empowering students to be active partners in their learning requires a subtle but thorough shift in focus away from what the teacher is teaching to what and how the student is learning.

Providing students with high-quality assessment and feedback, helping students to develop metacognitive skills, and empowering students as partners in the learning process are three approaches to helping students work in their optimal challenge zone. These strategies also help create synergy by connecting active learning (a student stretches to learn something that is at the edge of his or her understanding) and motivation (this challenge is stimulating and positive because it is new and because it is within reach).

Condition 3: Teachers Can Create Synergy by Teaching so That Students Learn Holistically

As college professors, we flourish in the thinking world. When we consider college-level learning, we readily understand and value the acquisition, synthesis, and evaluation of knowledge that characterizes abstract thought. Bloom's taxonomy of the cognitive domain (Bloom, Engelhart, Furst, Hill, & Krathwohl, 1956), which classifies such behaviors into a series of hierarchical levels, has served as a guide to faculty in all kinds of institutions as they design and develop their courses. But learning involves more than rational thinking. Even the definition of cognition moves beyond pure intellectual reasoning to include processes such as intuition and perception. Furthermore, newer models of "intelligence"—such as Gardner's "multiple intelligences" (which includes a bodily-kinesthetic intelligence) and Goleman's "emotional intelligence" (which emphasizes the ability to monitor one's own and other's feelings)—challenge us to embrace a concept of learning that extends beyond logical thinking.

This broader, more inclusive perspective is also supported by neuroscience. Harvard clinical psychologist John Ratey (2002) observes that the new view is that brain and body systems are distributed throughout the whole person and we cannot separate emotion, cognition, and the physical body. In fact, he says, separating these functions "is rapidly coming to be seen as ridiculous" (p. 223). Thus, despite higher education's historical emphasis on the purely intellectual, many educators today recognize that the body, heart, and mind are all involved in learning, and that all three make contributions to engagement. Some educators, such as Wiggins & McTighe (1998), Shulman (2002), and Fink (2003), are suggesting new taxonomies that integrate multiple domains.

The Affective Domain

How students *feel*—about life, about themselves, about what teachers are trying to teach them—plays a critical role in how they learn. Many educators believe motivation, sometimes defined as the feeling of interest or enthusiasm that makes somebody want to do something, is at the heart of student engagement. As Wlodkowski (2008) points out, "[W]hen there is no motivation to learn, there is no learning. . . . [P]eople motivated to learn are more likely to do things they believe will help them learn" (pp. 5–6). Sharing Wlodkowski's emphasis on the importance of motivation, Shulman (2002) pairs motivation with engagement and identifies the two as the first stage in his table of learning (p. 2). Yet students' emotions have been the least studied and most overlooked aspect of classroom teaching.

Although Bloom's taxonomy of the cognitive domain has been one of the most influential constructs in education, far fewer teachers are aware of the taxonomy of the affective domain (see Tip and Strategy 48, "Incorporate multiple domains when identifying learning goals"). Most teachers put their efforts into designing goals and activities that help students achieve cognitive outcomes; few instructors identify or assess learning goals having to do with feelings.

Affect is the emotion associated with an idea or action; thus the affective domain includes our feelings, values, enthusiasms, and attitudes. In Chapter 3, we discussed the function of neurons and neuronal networks in active learning from primarily a cognitive perspective; let us take a moment here to explore their role in affect. From a neuroscientific perspective, affect is just as much a part of the brain's neuronal network as cognition. Although scientists used to think emotion was centered in the specific limbic area of the brain, Ratey observes that newer research demonstrates "emotion is not the conveniently isolated brain function that once we were taught. Emotion is messy, complicated, primitive, and undefined because it's all over the place, intertwined with cognition and physiology" (Ratey, 2002, pp. 223–224). Even though our emotional responses are distributed throughout the brain and body, scientists are starting to figure out how the different components interact.

Affect and Memory

At the center of the brain, sandwiched between the two temporal lobes, is the limbic region, an area that consists of a group of structures that regulate our emotions and our memory. Two of these—the hippocampus and the amygdala—perform essential roles in learning. The hippocampus plays a major role in consolidating learning and in controlling how memories are stored. Memories are not stored as a whole in one place; they are distributed throughout the brain in a dynamic, interactive system that the hippocampus helps retrieve and reassemble as necessary.

At the bottom of the hippocampus is a smaller structure called the amygdala. Since we are bombarded with perceptual stimuli every moment of our lives, our brain must determine what is most important so that we are not on overload. The amygdala is a vigilant monitor that reacts to experiences before we consciously understand them—especially to those that appear threatening or dangerous—by priming the brain to be alert for possible action. The amygdala performs this function by comparing incoming information to long-term memories of past experience and then deciding what the body should do. The "fight or flight" response is an emotional response that happens before one's thinking brain, the cortex, can get involved because stopping to think would take too long before a decision was made (Newquist, 2004; Wlodkowski, 2008; Ratey, 2002).

When we are not in life-threatening situations, the hippocampus and the amygdala work together to help us read nonverbal information and interpret social situations and understand and deal with our own and others' feelings. The upper cortex, which involves our thinking brain, and the lower limbic structures, which involve our emotions, are in continuous communication with each other. Interestingly, there are many more connections from the small emotional limbic center into the large logical and rational cortical centers than the reverse. When emotions overwhelm us (we become too scared or too excited), we can usually use the reasoning centers in our cortex to overrule and manage them so that we can stay in control of our behavior—but not always, causing us to react or speak before we think (Ratey, p. 228; Newquist, 2004; Wlodkowski, 2008).

Affect and Learning

Emotions impact learning in two distinct ways: the emotional climate in which learning occurs and the degree to which emotions are associated with the learning content. A positive learning climate, in which students feel comfortable, have a sense of rapport with their teacher and their peers, and believe they can be successful, leads to endorphins in the blood, which in turn give feelings of euphoria and stimulates the frontal lobes. A negative environment, in which students feel dumb, disrespected, or disconnected, leads to cortisol in the blood, which results in raised anxiety and refocuses frontal lobes to fight or flight (Sousa, p. 84). In terms of learning content, students are more likely to remember material in which they have made an emotional investment. This is why many teachers try to help students care about what they are learning by using simulations, role playing, journal writing, and relating what students are learning to real-world experiences.

Designing courses to address students' emotional states is valuable for several reasons. Tapping into students' emotions can inspire them to put forth their greatest effort, thus propelling them toward achieving their highest potential. Helping students care about what you are trying to teach them increases the likelihood that they will learn more deeply and remember longer. Recognizing and making adjustments when a student feels sad, stressed, or threatened can remove roadblocks not solvable by cognitive strategies alone. Collectively, students' feelings greatly impact the interactions and relationships that contribute to—or undermine—the sense of classroom community. In short, how students *feel* about what is happening in the classroom is critical to how they engage—or disengage—in the learning that teachers are trying to engender in the classroom.

The Psychomotor Domain

Physical learning has been around from the beginning, ever since people learned to use fire, water, and land for their own survival. Ratey (2002) discusses the degree to which humans, at least over the last few centuries, have tended to undervalue the importance of physicality to our human identity. We have believed that "civilized man" is above the animals because he can "think," whereas animals just "act." Physical movement was thought to be a lower brain function, and cognition a higher brain function that only humans have evolved. Until very recently, most people didn't think any portion of the "motor brain" did anything but react to incoming stimuli and monitor or implement motor functions. But scientists are rapidly finding that regions associated with physical functioning also play a large role in activity related to planning, calculating, and forming intentions. As Ratey (2002) observes, "Clearly, catching a ball involves the brain's motor function. But making a mental calculation does too. . . . [M]ounting evidence shows that movement is crucial to every other brain function, including memory, emotion, language, and learning" (pp. 147–148).

When we are first learning to do something physically, such as riding a bike or driving a car, we are using the "thinking" part of the brain, the cortex. But as the activity becomes better learned and more automatic, the responsibility for it shifts to neurons in the lower parts of the brain, freeing up neurons in the cortex for new learning. The process is the same for cognitive acts. The cortex is directly involved when we first learn our multiplication tables or how to formulate a grammatically correct question, but once these tasks are mastered, they are moved to lower parts of the brain and become automatic (Ratey, 2002, p. 149). Thus, the older view that the brain is composed of specific regions that are each responsible for isolated, discrete functions is inaccurate: motor function is crucial to some forms of cognition and to behavior, just as behavior is the acting out of movements prescribed by cognition.

The Psychomotor Domain and Memory

The psychomotor component is also evident in procedural memory, the memory responsible for recalling skills that you've learned over a long time. These kinds of memories are almost impossible to forget because your body and brain have worked so hard to create them. This is the memory that helps you remember how to play a musical instrument or throw a football or button the buttons on your shirt. Novice learners start out imitating the teacher or more advanced peers as they develop skills in taking notes, participating in discussions, and performing laboratory procedures. As they move toward being experts, they become increasingly capable of doing these well on their own, ultimately attaining an unconscious mastery of the skills and often even adapting them in ways that best meet their individual needs.

Acknowledging the role of the psychomotor domain in engagement may be a stretch for many academics, but the doing of the visible, auditory, and kinesthetic activities of active learning involve psychomotor skills. Thinking and feeling are internal, but they are expressed and often worked out through talking, writing, reading, and performing actions. At all stages of learning, students with learning styles that respond best to kinesthetic experiences will be more engaged in learning tasks that incorporate aspects of the psychomotor domain. Finally, teachers know that even the most attentive and well-intentioned students cannot stay focused when they are sitting idly and physically inactive over long periods of time. Therefore, where possible and appropriate, effective holistic engagement strategies include psychomotor dimensions, even something as simple as getting students reenergized and refocused by having them stand up and move around the room to talk to each other or find partners for group work.

Integrating the Cognitive, Affective, and Psychomotor Domains

In some fields, experts must be skilled in all three domains. An accomplished classical pianist must be able to read abstract musical notation, memorize thousands of notes, create a unique interpretation synthesizing what he knows and understands about the piece's historical context with what he believes to be the composer's concept, blend this with his personal artistic vision, and perform physically in a nuanced manner at split-second speed within stressful situations. Similar domain spanning is evident in the work of actors, surgeons, archeologists, athletes, and others. From one perspective, student engagement may be the process and product of spanning domains and taking advantage, in an intentional way, of the contributions of each.

Many of the current thinkers on education recognize this. Fink (2003) proposed his taxonomy of significant learning because he believed that higher education was expressing a need for new kinds of learning: leadership and interpersonal skills, ethics, communication skills, character, tolerance, and the ability to adapt to change (p. 29). These kinds of learning go beyond the cognitive domain. Shulman's table of learning (2002) involves cognitive, affective, and psychomotor elements and is integrative and cyclical rather than hierarchical. The expanded concepts of Fink and Shulman are supported by other new approaches. In *College Learning for the New Global Century: A Report from the National Leadership Council for Liberal Education and America's Promise* (Association of American Colleges and Universities, 2007), for example, educators are urged to abandon narrow learning and to promote essential learning outcomes such as knowledge of human cultures and the physical and natural world, personal and social responsibility, and integrative learning.

Arguably the most effective—and engaging—learning environments integrate domains. The learning activities that teachers design to help students progress cognitively will be most successful if students are engaged on an affective level (enjoying the tasks and giving them their full attention) and, when appropriate, a kinesthetic level (applying the theoretical and abstract by doing a physical activity). In our double helix model of engagement, teaching for holistic learning can contribute to synergy because it supports active learning—learners are thinking and caring about what they are doing and doing what they are thinking and caring about—and enhances motivation—many students find domain-spanning activities intrinsically interesting and enjoyable; other students find domain-spanning activities necessary to be more successful learners.

Conclusion

Motivation and active learning are twin helices that work together synergistically. Teachers are more likely to promote student engagement when they implement strategies that increase this synergy. Helping students feel as though they are part of a learning community, ensuring as much as possible that students are appropriately challenged, and establishing classroom conditions where students can learn holistically create synergy because they integrate elements of both motivation and active learning.

Chapter 5

Additional Facets to Consider

STUDENT ENGAGEMENT is complex, and the model of student engagement as the synergistic interaction between motivation and active learning is simply one contribution to an ongoing discussion on both what student engagement means and how to promote it. Our understanding continues to evolve and deepen as the dialogue continues. Before turning to how this theoretical model plays out in the practice of the college classroom, I would like to touch on a few additional facets.

Engagement Is Individually Referenced

What is motivating to one student may not be motivating to another. A fundamental characteristic of active learning is that students must connect what is being learned to what is already known, and what one student knows is not the same as what another knows . Thus the blend of motivating factors and active learning that promotes student engagement is unique to each individual learner. Acknowledging that engagement is referenced individually, teachers who create engaging classes manage to find ways to challenge and support students at many different cognitive and developmental levels as well as create an affective environment that helps all students feel as though their presence and participation in the course matters.

Engagement Is a Multidirectional Partnership

While the teachers should do everything they can to create classroom conditions that promote engagement, it is ultimately the student's choice to engage in learning. Teachers and students share responsibility for engagement and will be more likely to achieve it if they consider themselves partners in the teaching/learning process. Interestingly, when students surveyed at different types of institutions and in four different countries were asked to define what *student engagement* meant to them, most of their descriptions echoed those of faculty: "The term *student engagement*, to me, means getting the students more involved in their own learning and becoming active learners" and "*student engagement* means feeling motivated, being challenged, excited about the new." One student responded at length:

> *Students are engaged when they are treated with respect. If low expectations are set, the students will not feel that they are being challenged, and will tend to not care about the class. I do not mean that by setting high expectations, the professor is being unrealistic. High expectations would simply result in creating an atmosphere where students feel comfortable to test their limits of knowledge. [Teachers can engage students] by creating class discussions where everyone feels they can participate, even if an incorrect answer is given. It is amazing to think that many college students are still afraid to raise their hand in class to give their opinion. I think that as soon as they feel comfortable doing this, they can feel that the classroom is a time for true growth, not just a time to get a passing grade, as they move on to the next mediocre class. I think this can be accomplished by giving assignments to students that force them to question their present reality, and the reality of those around them, as it relates to the subject of the class. (Barkley, 2008)*

Teachers who have empowered students as true partners in the learning process frequently report that many students are tentative at first, but they eventually accept and enjoy the responsibility and become much more engaged learners.

It is also much easier for teachers to create engaging classes if they are doing so within a supportive institutional environment. Recognizing how institutional and classroom influences interlace, the National Survey of Student Engagement (NSSE) and its sibling surveys define *student engagement* as a pattern of involvement in a variety of activities and interactions both in and out of the classroom and throughout a student's college career, emphasizing the institutional climates that promote engagement. As such, the five clusters of effective educational practices that create the NSSE benchmarks for measuring student engagement bridge both classroom and institution-level experiences.

Cluster 1, "Level of Academic Challenge," asks students questions that address the nature and amount of assigned academic work, the complexity of cognitive tasks, and the standards faculty members use to evaluate student performance. Although these aspects are clearly determined by the choices individual teachers make in the design and implementation of each course, it is much easier for teachers to create courses with a high level of academic challenge in institutions that emphasize challenging academic work—just as it is very difficult for a teacher to uphold high standards in an institution where such standards are an anomaly.

Cluster 2, "Active and Collaborative Learning," recognizes the importance of students working together to solve problems and master difficult material. Teachers know that it is much easier to incorporate active/collaborative learning tasks if students have already acquired appropriate skills from participation in effective group work in other classes—just as teachers know it is challenging to reorient students to be active, collaborative learners if in most of their classes they are encouraged to be passive and competitive.

The remaining three clusters make even more explicit the importance of a student's experience outside of the classroom. Cluster 3, "Student Interactions with Faculty Members," includes course-based questions on discussing grades or assignments with teachers or getting prompt feedback on academic performance. This cluster also addresses how students work with teachers on activities other than coursework, such as serving together on collegewide committees, participating in community organizations, talking together about career plans, and working with the professor on research.

Cluster 4, "Enriching Educational Experiences," addresses exposing students to diversity, helping them gain an appreciation for other cultures, and using technology—all of which can be designed into the goals and activities of a single course. The cluster also includes internships, field experiences, community service or volunteer work, study abroad, and co-curricular activities.

Finally, Cluster 5, "Supportive Campus Environment," explicitly shifts attention to experiences beyond the classroom and emphasizes the importance of positive working and social relations among different groups on campus, including student services and administrative staff (Kuh, Kinzie, Schuh, & Witt, 2005, pp. 11–13).

Thus NSSE and CCSSE's definitions of student engagement encompass beyond-the-classroom student experiences, including those typically in the realm of student services (or in the case of some four-year institutions, residential life), and integrating student services and support into classroom settings (K. McKlenney, personal communication, December 16, 2008).

This book aims to help college teachers promote engagement within the context of a single classroom. Clearly teachers have the greatest control over what happens to students in the specific courses they teach, but their efforts to foster engagement will be both easier and more effective if their institutional environment is supportive. Additionally, engagement will be deepened if what students are learning in the classroom connects to the broader institutional, community, and global context. Robert Smallwood (personal communication, December 15, 2008) suggests, "In many respects, [student engagement is] a three-way partnership between students, faculty, and administration that results in a classroom environment conducive to maximizing student learning."

Engagement Results from a Systemic, Integrated Approach to Teaching

Although students may find one (or even several) course activities engaging, the kind of intense and sustained student engagement that most teachers strive for is a byproduct of a larger, integrated effort. This includes implementing the principles of good teaching, such as establishing clear and significant learning goals, holding students to high expectations, and giving them prompt feedback. But it also requires something both deeper and less tangible: approaching teaching with the aim to honor students by "genuinely engaging their spirit, their experience, and their perspective. A mere strategy does not create such a milieu. [It is] the result of a determined living harmony, a constancy of practices blended with ideals from the beginning to the end of every lesson of every session of every course" (Wlodkowski, 2008, p. 169).

Efforts to Increase Engagement Can Be Supported through Assessment

Most college teachers recognize that collecting feedback on students' learning can help them adjust their teaching approaches to make learning more efficient and effective. Similarly, if our goal is to promote engaged learning, we are likely to be more successful if we gather feedback on how well our efforts actually *do* foster engagement, and then adjust our teaching accordingly. The core purpose of assessment from this perspective is to educate and improve student engagement, not to audit it.

The National Survey on Student Engagement (NSSE) was designed to assess engagement at the institutional level to help institutions identify the quality of the undergraduate learning experience on their campus. The main purpose was "to identify aspects of the undergraduate experience inside and outside the classroom that can be improved through changes in policies and practices more consistent with good practices in undergraduate education" (NSSE, 2009). Unfortunately, the institutional-level data gathered from these surveys is not generally very helpful to individual faculty members trying to increase engagement in their classes. To address this issue, Judith Ouimet and Robert Smallwood (2005; Smallwood, 2009) created a classroom-based instrument called CLASSE (Classroom Survey of Student Engagement).

CLASSE is a pair of survey instruments that parallel the NSSE survey but focus on engagement in a single course. One of the survey instruments asks faculty to rate how important various teaching practices are to student success in that course, and the other instrument asks students to report on how often these practices actually occurred in the course. The survey can be customized to include items a teacher believes are important to a specific course. Together, the two surveys open "a dialogue between faculty's own sense of 'good practices' and the subtext of 'good practices' informing the design of NSSE" (Rhem, 2007, p. 1). This helps ameliorate a fundamental problem many teachers have with the NSSE instrument: it uses frequency of behaviors as an engagement indicator, but these behaviors may not reflect what teachers consider to be truly engaged learning. For example, the first question on NSSE asks students to report how often they ask questions in class. Many teachers believe that frequency of asking questions (like many of the other behaviors in the NSSE survey) is not an indicator that students are experiencing higher levels of learning. Most teachers would probably say that if students are asking good, substantive questions (instead of questions like "Will that be on the test?"), it shows that students are paying attention, thinking about what is going on, and feeling sufficiently comfortable in class to ask questions without fear of being criticized by their teacher or peers. These qualities all relate to engaged learning. Thus there is a general positive relationship between asking questions and student learning, and there is a correlation between engagement overall and student learning, but it is not as simple a relationship as some interpreters of NSSE data may think (Rhem, 2007).

CLASSE also addresses another problem. Smallwood and Ouimet found that when unfavorable NSSE data on student engagement came back, faculty often responded, "These less-engaged students are not *my* students," and that this reaction occurred at every sublevel or disaggregation of the survey data: "if the university got low marks, it was the school of X that had the disengaged students; if it was the English department, it had to be the nineteenth century area that had them" (Rhem, 2007, p. 1).

Whether individual teachers are correct or incorrect in their perception that *their* students are engaged, gathering data at the single course level provides the evidence needed for a more constructive conversation. Additionally, the data can help individual teachers more readily identify what is happening in their own classes so that they can more efficiently and effectively target improvement efforts. Finally, CLASSE puts control of assessing for student engagement clearly in faculty hands, ensuring teachers can use the feedback for improvement rather than auditing purposes. In fact, at this writing, faculty can administer CLASSE without administrative initiative or simply add key CLASSE questions to their usual course evaluation process (http://assessment.ua.edu/CLASSE/Documents/CLASSE_Student.pdf).

Although CLASSE is the best-known instrument for assessing student engagement at the classroom level and has the advantages of paralleling the NSSE instrument, teachers may find it is simplest and most effective to develop their own engagement assessment strategies. Classroom assessment techniques, for example, provide college teachers with a variety of ways to determine how well their students are engaged in learning. Whatever means teachers use to assess engagement in their classes, gathering appropriate feedback can help close the gap between what teachers think is happening in their classes and what students are actually experiencing.

Chapter 6

From Theory to Practice
Teachers Talk about Student Engagement

THERE IS NO single tip, technique, or strategy that offers a magic formula or blueprint for student engagement. What works for one student doesn't work for another; a technique that is a guaranteed winner for one teacher falls miserably flat when tried by a colleague; a carefully planned course that was a giddy success in the fall doesn't get off the ground in the spring. Yet some approaches and activities do engage students better than others. We have explored a conceptual framework for understanding student engagement as the synergistic interplay between motivation and active learning. However I am a teacher, and I know that the gap between theory and practice can sometimes be wide. Therefore, I want to move from theory to practice and share with you the perspectives of college teachers who work hard in the classroom to engage students in learning.

The teachers come from an array of disciplines, are at different stages in their careers, and have taught at institutions ranging from highly selective private universities to open-admission community colleges. I interviewed the teachers and consolidated their comments into individual "stories" (Barkley, 2009). Each of these teachers describes student engagement differently. Some promote engagement by dint of their forceful, charismatic personalities; others by their commitment to a clearly articulated pedagogical framework; and still others by clever and creative activities. My intent is not to test the theory nor to offer a comprehensive sampler of perspectives, but simply to enrich the model with glimpses into the engagement efforts of a few real teachers in real college classrooms.

Excerpts from the stories are shared here, organized under a dominant theme, but each story contains unique insights and perspectives regarding student engagement as well as elements that appear to be universal. Because each story comes from an actual teacher grappling with challenges in his or her own course, you will find a complex, messy mix of the theory discussed in Part One. I invite you to read actively, looking for the connections between theory and practice yourself. As you read, you might consider questions such as the following:

- What do the teachers do to help students see the value in what they are learning?

- How do the teachers set up classroom conditions that help students expect that, with reasonable effort, they will succeed?

- What kinds of activities and strategies do the teachers use to encourage students to learn "actively"?

- Is creating a sense of classroom community important to the teachers, and if so, how do they achieve it?

- How do the teachers ensure students are challenged appropriately— that the work is neither too hard nor too easy?

- In what ways do they promote holistic learning—helping students move beyond the cognitive realm to include affective or psychomotor elements?

Approached in this way, the stories not only make the theory less abstract, but they also form a bridge into the tips, strategies, and techniques that constitute Parts Two and Three of this handbook.

Engaging Students through Creative Learning Activities

Judy Baker is a senior faculty member with extensive experience teaching courses in the health fields in a variety of institutions. She has taught face-to-face courses (including courses designed for adult health professionals) and is also a leader in creating innovative courses for delivery online. When many of us think of exceptionally engaging professors, we think of somebody who is sociable, self-confident, and extroverted. Baker is passionate about teaching, but she is introverted, reflective, and shy. Since an assumption underlying this book is that there is such a thing as student engagement techniques, I'll begin this exploration of teacher perspectives on engagement by sharing her story, as her success is due primarily to her creative learning activities.

JUDY BAKER'S APPROACH TO TEACHING COURSES IN THE HEALTH PROFESSION   I hated lectures—hated, hated, hated, hated, hated them—and I swore when I became a teacher, I'd never inflict them on anyone. Being forced to sit quietly and passively while teachers talked at me was just something I could not tolerate.

I need to do things. If you give me a piece of equipment to assemble, I'll just start putting it together and refer to the manual only if I have a question. My need to be actively involved in my own learning was the first major influence on my teaching philosophy; the second was the radically changed environment that shapes the learning experience for today's students. When I was growing up, access to information was a privilege. We'd go to school to learn information and supplement what we learned in class with information from books in the library. It was a real treat to go from the small branch libraries to the main library and be surrounded by even *more* books filled with information. Students today have the reverse situation: they are already surrounded by information. They don't need to go to school or to a library to get it. They can get information in a second. It is at their fingertips, in multiple sources, and it doesn't have a nervous tic. What students need to learn today is how to sift through, evaluate, and apply information. In my courses it is important to me that students learn actively and that they do not just acquire information, but that they do something with that information. Here are some of the activities I do to engage students actively in their learning.

● ● ●

To Help Students Feel a Sense of Ownership of the Course

Instead of my creating the syllabus in advance, I use an activity that is essentially an adaptation of SET 49, "Student-Generated Rubrics." I provide students with a basic framework of topics typically addressed in a syllabus, and then ask them to generate the policies and procedures that will govern the course. I might start the conversation with a question like, "Where, as women, do you go for information on women's health issues?" Students typically respond, "To my mother" (or my sister, or a girlfriend). I point out that often to learn something, we go to someone we can trust, someone who is reliable. I explain that for this course, we need to set up a learning community of people we can trust. So for example, regarding group work, we air our pet peeves (e.g., "It is annoying when students don't contribute to discussions"; "I don't like it when students don't do their share of the work"; or "It bothers me when group members don't show up for class"). If we agree that a behavior is a major aggravation, we devise rules and consequences. If it is minor, we agree to live with it. Even for courses in which I don't work with students to generate the whole syllabus, I always give them an opportunity to offer significant input; for example, at a minimum, they establish test dates.

To further help students develop a sense of ownership of their learning, I provide them with a menu of learning activities from which they choose and contract for their final grade. Their choices include field trips, research, essays, reflective journals, interviewing professionals in the field, and so forth. One choice that is a real win-win situation is discussion-forum monitoring. I want students to participate in the online discussions, but it would take a huge amount of my time monitoring the forums to make sure nothing inappropriate is posted and that the discussion stays focused, to track who is participating, and to ask the kinds of questions that prompt deeper discussion. So one of the activities students can choose is to be "discussion moderator" for one week. Their responsibilities include facilitating the discussion and then providing me and other students with a synthesis at the end. Not only does this save me time, but it also gives students an important learning experience where, for example, they can see how challenging it is to facilitate good discussion as well as to practice (and demonstrate to me) higher-order thinking skills. As students make their choices, I try to encourage them to push themselves and take risks. Often they take on too much, so I provide them with an opportunity to renegotiate their contract at a later point in the academic term.

• • •

To Get a Better Sense of Student Starting Points

To ensure that students are appropriately challenged, it is important for me to know their starting points. I use SET 16, "Team Concept Maps," as one of the first class activities. I organize students into groups, provide them with newsprint and markers, and ask each group to create a cognitive map on the topic of the course, such as "women's health." The range in style and complexity of the maps is both surprising and illuminating. For example, in one course, a group drew an apple tree with women who were mothers, daughters, sisters, and cousins, reaching up to pick apples that symbolized various health issues. Another group was barely able to generate a few simple phrases. Yet a third group created a very extensive web of connected ideas and terms. As a reporting out activity, I ask a representative from each group to explain their map. This serves as a relatively non-threatening projective device in which students can safely articulate their personal "lived" experiences and level of knowledge about a particular topic. I make comments where appropriate to show how their maps connect with the themes of the course, or point out how the topic is much more extensive than one might think at first, or acknowledge the amount of expertise some of the students bring to the course. I then collect the maps. At the end of the course, I have students construct a map again so that they can show me, and themselves, how much they have learned.

• • •

To Motivate Students to Be Interested in What I Am Teaching

Students come to my Program Evaluation course not wanting to be there. They think the course is about crunching numbers, or they believe that they already know what I'm going to teach them, or they contend that it is not relevant to their lives or careers. I use SET 2, "Artifacts," to help students recognize the value of what they will be learning. I give each student a paper clip, a thumbtack, and a small clamp, and then I ask the students to identify what the three items have in common. After they've agreed on something like "the shared purpose is to fasten something," I ask a series of questions that lead them to judge the items along a variety of criteria such as value, quality, and function. My goal is to keep challenging students to deepen their thinking and refine their evaluation criteria. For example, I show them that a paper clip can be bent apart and used like a thumb tack to fasten something to the wall. Used in this way, it has advantages over a thumb tack because it doesn't poke me, but then I ask students to evaluate how securely and safely it fulfills this function. Throughout this process students are coming up with the principles of evaluation that provide the framework for the course. To do this in my online class, I ask students to gather the three items, reflect upon a series of prompts that I have provided, and write out their responses in an assignment that they submit to me. In my experience, although the online students do not have the benefit of the social interactions of the face-to-face classroom, their reports often consist of a deeper analysis.

• • •

To Help Students Recognize That They Contribute to Our Collective Knowledge

I want my students to understand that they have expertise that is important to contribute to the class. For example, in my women's health course, one of the topics is pregnancy. So I ask who among the students has given birth. Usually there are about 5–6 students in the class who have had babies, so I say, "You are the experts!" I recruit them as my experts for "Set 5: Stations." I set them up at different places around the room and have students move around to interview each mother using a few baseline questions I've provided. Probably the most important part of this activity is when the entire group compares the different responses to the same question. And here's another idea that helps them pool their shared knowledge. Instead of having students purchase an expensive textbook that often is full of obsolete information, I sometimes have them work together using a Wiki to generate their own textbook. [Note: This is a variation of SET 21, "Class Book," in Chapter 8.] The books that they have produced have been superb—in fact, I've suggested they sell them on e-Bay!

• • •

To Help Students Develop Empathy and Greater Cultural Understanding

One of my teaching goals is to help students develop empathy; this is an essential characteristic for effective health care professionals. Here's an example of an activity I use to help students develop this important quality. Many of the people who are drawn to health professions are conscientious about their fitness and therefore have a hard time relating to the struggles of "the fat kid in P.E." So as a learning activity, I ask them to make a list of things they are good at and things that they are not good at, and then I ask them to (a) choose one of the things they are not good at, (b) do it, and (c) observe their feelings. For example, a student might not be good at singing or public speaking, so as part of their contract for the course, they go up in front of the class and sing or give a speech. This helps them to understand how even though something may be easy for them, it may be extremely difficult for someone else.

As another example, many of the students are young and have difficulty being tolerant and empathetic with elderly patients who might not fill out forms completely or correctly. I ask students to submerge their dominant hand in a bowl of ice water while they use their other hand to fill out a form, and then I explain that this is why patients who are in pain or whose abilities may be compromised have trouble with what we perceive as simple tasks. Students discuss their experiences or reflect on them in a journal. Online students can do this activity just as well as face-to-face students.

It is also important for health care students to develop cultural competency because as practitioners, they may encounter families whose beliefs and assumptions differ from their training. For example, a Hmong mother may rub a coin against her baby's body until it is bruised, having been told by her mother that this is the way to treat fever or muscle aches. The bruising that can result from this practice may prompt a Western-trained practitioner to suspect child abuse. So I use SET 19, "Role Play," to help students learn to recognize and respond to folk remedies in appropriate, culturally sensitive ways.

● ● ●

To Promote Critical Thinking

Although I try to promote critical thinking throughout my course, I do have an activity that I have found to be particularly effective. It is a variation of SET 24, "Think Again." I ask a physician to come in and give a one-sided presentation on a course-related topic, such as Hormone Replacement Therapy. The specialist is very persuasive and so after she leaves, I ask students, "Now how many of you plan to use hormones, and why?" As they share their decisions, citing examples of things she said, I give the flip side until, one by one, I've provided a con argument for every pro argument in her presentation. Then I ask students to think again based on a fuller understanding of both sides of the issue. We close with a discussion on the importance of making informed decisions based on more than a single source of information, no matter how authoritative that source may be.

• • •

To Teach Metacognitive Skills

Sometimes when students are doing an exercise, they tell me that they think it is dumb or that they don't see its relationship to the class. But I try not to let students consider a learning activity finished until they have identified what they have learned from it. One mechanism I use to accomplish this is a reflective journal that is a variation of SET 41, "Learning Logs." Usually students can see why I assigned something after they have thought about it, but sometimes it takes until the end of the course. There have even been occasions where students contacted me many years later saying, "Aha, now I really understand why you had us do that."

To me, *student engagement* means that students are totally involved in the course—they "own it." To be truly involved in the course, it is important that students care about what they are learning, and to help them care, I use a variety of approaches such as those I just described.

Baker is not a "charismatic" teacher. In fact, in class, she is quite subdued. She doesn't expend lots of energy trying to captivate her students with compelling presentations. Instead, she creates engaging activities and then has students do the work.

Engaging Students through Personality

Natalia Menendez is a fiery, passionate English professor whose hand and arm movements dramatically underscore her commentary. She is particularly admired for a course in African American literature, but her comments here come from her experience teaching English Basic Skills, a remedial level course designed to prepare students for college level English. Her colleague, Scott Lankford, describes why he thinks she is such an engaging teacher:

Lankford: If you watch her working with students, she gets in their face—she looks them squarely in the eye and almost demands, "What do you *think*? I'm talking to *you*."

Menendez: *[laughing]* Well, I don't want to scare people. I try to be sensitive to body language, and if students are resistant to my tough-lady approach, then I "get in their face" when I write comments on their essays. I think it is important to interact with students directly. I insist on aisles between the rows of desks so I can walk to the middle rows and the back rows and talk directly to students.

Lankford: In her classes, there's no place to hide, no corners in which to escape. There is a physicality to her teaching; she reaches out to students. *She doesn't tolerate disengagement.* Sometimes teachers are afraid to do that, but when I watch Natalia, I recognize that quality from my own experience with great teachers, and then I try to be more like her when I return to my own classroom.

In her Basic Skills course, Menendez works with some of the toughest students to engage: students who have checked out emotionally from school and have little or no motivation; students who are trying to squeeze school in between crushing domestic, work, or athletic demands; and students whose prior experiences in school have fostered such negative beliefs in their own ability that they have developed chronically low expectations and a kind of numbed acceptance of failure. Coaches and counselors send their most challenging students to Menendez because they know she can handle them and help them succeed. Here are some of her comments:

NATALIA MENENDEZ'S APPROACH TO TEACHING BASIC/REMEDIAL ENGLISH

To me, *student engagement* is eye contact, careful listening, helping students learn to care about things that they didn't think they cared about. This can be anything from content to deadlines. Some students care about deadlines but not about content, or they care about content but not about deadlines. I want students to pay attention and care. It is not any secret alchemy; it is getting students to focus on the essential question, "What is this about, and what does it mean in my life?" Every activity we do in class is intended to give students a chance to see—even in difficult, obscure texts—how the issues of others are similar to the issues they face themselves.

One of the ways I try to help students is by making sure they know what I am trying to teach them. On the first day of the term, we have a discussion about the different kinds of writing. Then I say, "OK, check it out—I'm teaching *this* kind of writing." I contextualize it. "This kind of writing is not the best kind, it is not the smartest kind, it is just what we do here in college. Keep writing your poetry, your rap, your text messages, your e-mail, but if you are going to be here in college, you need to learn how to do *this* kind of writing." It is what I call my "coach talk": "We're learning to play baseball, and this is how we do it. If you do something different, there's no moral judgment involved, it's just that that's not how you play baseball—you're playing soccer, but you're here to learn to play baseball." I level the playing field and I name the game, and then we're ready.

What works best with my students is clear rules, clear boundaries. I encourage students to find their own voice, for example, by saying, "This is the topic. How could you play around with it?" But it has to be within the established structure. Some of my students have incredibly difficult lives. It is so humbling to hear what they go through to get here. My sense is that they need structure more than choices, so I don't change the rules for them, but I try to help them find their voice within those rules. And in response to all their reasons why they can't do something (and there are a thousand reasons), I find it helpful to acknowledge that they take three buses to get here; that they might not be able to afford the textbook; that if they are athletes, they practice hard and are exhausted. I comment, "Practice is hard, isn't it?" or "How's Coach? Have you had to run any hills lately?" Often it is personal drama that competes for their attention—someone in their family has been shot. When I sense it is something serious, I don't look them in the eyes but instead, I sit down in a desk beside them, facing the same direction, and I just ask softly, "So what's going on?" I try to "see" them better. For the men, especially, it makes a huge difference if you truly "see" them—even a little bit. They don't get any special dispensation from the rules, but it helps that I acknowledge they have lives outside of the classroom.

It all comes down to respect. I want students to know that I love spending my day with 20-year-olds, that I'm so glad that they take three buses or passed through fire and water to get here. I always have on what I call my "cold-sensitive radar." I sweep the room, looking for who's not engaged and then I ask, "Michael, what's up? You're in my class, you're here, you have thoughts, I want to know what you think."

Menendez does have interesting learning activities in her classes, but it is primarily her deep caring and dynamic personality that helps her engage students.

Engaging Students through Course Structure

Baker's creative learning activities and Menendez's charismatic personality are effective approaches to engaging students. Yet another approach is reflected in my own story of how I transformed my course. As I explained in the Preface, my return to teaching after a nine-year hiatus in administration was a catastrophe. My attempts to engage students involved a systematic overhaul of content, delivery, and grading. Although I didn't know it at the time, the transformation of my course structure has its philosophical roots in a pedagogical strategy called "differentiation" (see T/S 41). As a formal teaching approach, differentiation was developed by Carol Ann Tomlinson, a professor at the University of Virginia. She and her colleagues have written several books that provide both conceptual and practical background for how to organize a course around differentiation principles (Tomlinson, 1999; Tomlinson, 2001; Tomlinson & Eidson, 2003; Tomlinson & Strickland, 2005). Although I had not known Tomlinson's work when I made my course changes, I came to similar conclusions about individualizing options for my students. The following, drawn primarily from an article I wrote for *National Teaching and Learning Forum* (Barkley, 2006c), describes the four basic strategies that underlie the structural changes I made in the course to transform it from one that wasn't working, to one that is.

ELIZABETH BARKLEY'S APPROACH TO TEACHING MUSIC APPRECIATION

How do we find solutions to the challenges we face in the classroom? I suppose there must be examples where teachers read a book or participate in a staff development workshop or consult with a colleague, and then have an "aha" moment where they find the precise solution to the problem with which they are struggling . . . but this has never happened to me. Instead, solutions sneak up on me sideways. I probably read or hear something that lodges in my brain and lies dormant until a time when, on some deep, unconscious level, it morphs and moves with magnetic force to connect as a solution to a problem over which I'm puzzling. As I reflect now on the changes I made during the years I transformed my course, I realize I used four main strategies that changed the way my course was structured.

• • •

Strategy 1: Changing to Multicultural Content

As I struggled to engage students, I was struck by their diversity. For some reason (did I know this intuitively? or had I heard or read this? or seen it modeled in other areas of my life?), I believed that I needed to find the glue that could bind them into a community. After some reflection, I determined that the single unifying characteristic was "Americanness." Students were either American-born, immigrants hoping to become more "American," or international students intrigued by what it was to be American. The curriculum that I had been teaching was based on Western European "classical" music and I thought, "Hello, we're not a colony anymore." This traditional curriculum did not adequately address the interests, needs, or cultures of contemporary students who have come of age in an increasingly diverse, multicultural society.

Using ethnicity as a central organizing principle, I transformed the course into Musics of Multicultural America, which traces the development of genres such as the blues, jazz, folk, country, Tejano, Cajun, and salsa from their roots in the ethnic traditions of a specific immigrant group to their development into a uniquely American music. By changing from a European-based classical music survey course to an American-based multicultural music course, I was hoping to minimize the barriers to engagement that arose simply from lack of interest in course content. It is evident that treating these music styles seriously and exploring the historical and social context in which they developed also empowered students. Immigrant students found it fascinating to see how their home country's traditions had seeded and shaped new musical styles. Native students, especially students of color, were pleased to see their histories and contributions to the American musical mosaic validated. Soon after the content change, a young Latino student approached me and said, "This class is one of the few classes that tells the truth." An African American student commented, "I had no idea *my* people had such an influence on American music."

• • •

Strategy 2: Personalizing Course Delivery

As an administrator, I knew the importance of faculty "productivity"—the cost/benefit analysis that is determined at our institution by faculty/student ratio. Two factors create the productivity number: how many students enter the course and how many students complete the course. I was able to attract a large number of students into the course by revising the content to make it more appealing, but once students were enrolled, I needed to retain them. Common sense as well as institutional research indicated that students drop a course if they conclude they won't be successful in it. I found myself scrutinizing every conventionally accepted teaching technique, trying to find strategies that helped *all* students succeed. The various solutions I developed became a constantly expanding and continually evolving bag of teaching tricks I refer to as my "Safety Nets." For example, students couldn't be successful in my course if there were stringent attendance requirements (sick children, work demands, broken alarm clocks, late busses always get in the way). I decided to drop the attendance requirement and provide students with alternatives that would allow them to acquire information without having to do so solely through their presence in the face-to-face class. At first I simply placed lecture notes on reserve in the library; eventually I offered all materials completely online.

Making attendance optional enabled me to encourage students to attend the face-to-face class only if they *wanted* to be there (and to ask seemingly bored students with "'tude" to leave). It also allowed students who needed more opportunities to review the material (perhaps due to learning or language difficulties) or who could not be there due to unforeseen work or family obligations to still succeed. Over the years, I developed "Blended Delivery," a model in which students choose how they want to involve themselves in the class, selecting a point on a continuum that ranges from completely traditional, on-campus participation to completely online. Students are encouraged to select the point on the continuum that best meets their individual needs on a flexible and ongoing basis throughout the term. This helped students who couldn't make it to class still succeed; they didn't feel forced to drop just because a few absences early in the term destroyed their hopes for a good course grade. Strategy 4 also provided students with ways to save their grade should they have (for whatever reasons) a rocky start.

● ● ●

Strategy 3: Offering a Flexible Menu of Learning Activities

The baseline course used standard instructor-directed activities emphasizing lecture format and extensive textbook reading. Conventional lecture was boring and did not engage students. Reading was too challenging as many students had difficulty either because of poor skills or because English was not their native language. So I created a flexible new model with an array of alternative activities from which students could select to meet their individual learning preferences. Activities include field trips, interviews, film observations, concert and special event attendance, online quizzes, and research. I even offer a "wild-card" activity in which students develop their own project. Two interesting, recent examples of wild-card activities include a Native American student's video documentary on the traditional musical practices of her family's tribe and a hip-hop musician's re-imagining of a centuries-old English folk song.

Revisiting how students could learn course content, I avoided structuring learning activities in the sequential, passive, and pyramidal approach of traditional higher-ed curriculum and instead decided to give students the power to determine their own learning paths. To accomplish this, I reorganized the course into a series of topical modules. Within each module, I allow students to choose from a variety of learning activities. For example in the Native American module, a student might attend a powwow, visit a museum, compile an annotated CD of additional listening examples, or watch films such as *Dances with Wolves* or *Smoke Signals* instead of (or in addition to) attending lectures or reading from the textbook.

Students are encouraged to select which modules they wish to do, as well as determine the number of activities within each module they choose to complete. Some students do a few activities in all modules, hence obtaining a survey-level overview; other students choose fewer modules but do more activities, hence learning fewer topics but in more depth. Students also have some freedom to determine the order and time in which they complete the modules; the only thing that is fixed is a deadline framework which is nonnegotiable. (There are four major deadlines throughout the term; students can turn in as much work as they would like early—in fact some of the best students finish the course before the academic term is finished—but students are not allowed to turn in work late.) This format allows students to select activities based on their preferences, abilities, schedules, and learning style.

• • •

Strategy 4: Giving Students Greater Control over Their Grades

I use a variety of assessment strategies, connecting each assessment to the specific learning activity. For example, worksheets and quizzes assess acquisition of knowledge from reading. Students submit a portfolio [SET 45, "Face-to-Face In-class Portfolio"] containing in-class notes, discussion summaries, and personal reflections and insights to show what they learned from attending face-to-face classes. To demonstrate the quality and depth of their learning from activities such as watching a film or attending a cultural event, students write a critical essay for which I provide a detailed grading rubric. Although students cannot choose from different assessment methods for a single learning activity, they can choose learning activities that use assessment strategies they prefer.

Rather than a letter grade, each assessment generates a number of points. For example, a quiz earns up to 100 points; a film observation combined with a critical essay earns up to 200 points. Students earn their final grade by accumulating points, but the number of possible course points is significantly higher than the points required for a good grade (out of the 4,000+ points available, a student earns 2,000 for an A). This is a variation of contract grading. Contract grading individualizes the process and empowers students because students can be directly in control of whether they complete the work requirements for any given grade level.

Since standard contract grading can reward quantity rather than quality, I link each activity to appropriate standards through a rubric that uses a system known as Primary Trait Analysis. For example on a film essay, students understand that they will be allocated points in a range of 0–25 for each of the following four traits: (a) use of edited standard written English (ESWE), (b) accuracy and appropriateness of relating observations to course themes, (c) thoroughness and depth of discussion, and (d) thoughtfulness and creativity. If students do poorly in one trait area, they can compensate by working harder in other areas (thus an ESL student who loses points for incorrect grammar can still earn points for thoughtfulness). Or to get a better final grade, a student may need to do more activities. Clearly identifying how students earn points and providing more opportunities to earn points than are required for a good grade allows students to tailor their work to their own needs and goals and maximizes student choice and responsibility.

The above strategies had a critical impact on course enrollment. The "baseline" course (the class as I started teaching it) struggled to meet minimum enrollment, averaging about 45 students for the academic year. Each year the class attracted more students, and within five years enrollment stabilized at +/- 1,200 per year. As enrollment grew, I reached a point where I could no longer teach it on my own. I now coordinate a team of teachers. These colleagues work with me to solve problems and identify ways to improve the class. Any particular potency my own personality had on engaging students has long been diluted by the effect of working largely behind the scenes as the course's coordinator. And although we try to create interesting learning activities, there is nothing exceptional about any of them: students attend and take notes in classes that are primarily conducted as lecture-discussions; they take multiple-choice/true-false quizzes; and they write essays. So it appears to me that it is primarily the structure that engages students. (For more information on our efforts to identify and assess learning outcomes, see Barkley, 2006b.)

Engaging Students by Focusing on Motivation

In Part One, we discussed a model of motivation as the product of expectancy and value. This model proposes that two elements must be present for people to be motivated to do a task. First, they must expect that they will be able to perform the task successfully (*expectancy*). Second, they must find the task worth doing (*value*). The equation generates a product rather than a sum because it is assumed that people will expend no effort if either element is missing entirely.

Expectancy

It is difficult (theorists say impossible) for students to be motivated to learn if they do not believe they will be successful no matter how hard they try. The following story reflects a teacher's attempt to address students' expectations of success. Nicole Gray teaches both introductory and advanced level math classes. As a new teacher, she was frustrated with the traditional ways math in remedial and lower-level courses was taught. These courses enrolled a large number of students with math anxiety, students who were convinced they could not learn math. She was dismayed with the high attrition rate in these courses and concerned that students' needs were not being met. This excerpt from her story describes how and why she worked with her colleagues to address the problem by developing a mastery-learning program called "Math My Way." Her efforts to create a course that changes students' expectations of success addresses the expectancy component of motivation.

NICOLE GRAY'S APPROACH TO TEACHING BASIC/REMEDIAL MATH

Math anxiety is very real. I think that if you went into a social science class and asked a group of students, "Johnny is 5 years older than Suzie, and Suzie's 10, how old is Johnny?" they'd be able to answer you, no problem. You put those same students in a math class and ask them the same question and you hear and see "Aaaaaargh." All of a sudden they freeze up. They have been taught to be scared of math. There are so many people in the world who are scared of math, and because it is quite acceptable to be scared of math, they have no reason to get over it. Experience after experience tells them that they are bad at math, so every time they encounter math, they don't want to do it. As adults, they actually feel nauseous and crazy the first time they step into a math class. So half your battle is getting them to overcome that. I'm part psychologist and part math teacher— probably more psychologist.

I have a whole routine the first day of class, where I tell them why they're here, because they all know that this is college but it is high school or junior high math that they'll be doing in the class. I say:

> You are here because when you were growing up, you had adults in your life who were scared of math. One thing I've learned now that I have little kids is that if you're scared of something, they get scared of it, even if you try to hide that you're scared of it. Adults in your life taught you to be scared of math. Math in elementary and middle school is typically taught by people who don't have a degree in math. They don't like it, they don't know how to make it fun for you, and they ignore it, so you don't get the kind of time on task that you should be getting to build a strong foundation. And then you get to high school. What's the stereotype of a high school math teacher?

When I ask them that question, they're kind of shy at first, but I say, "Come on, tell me—I can take it." *[She laughs, putting her hands over her head as though to protect herself.]* And students describe the nerd with the pocket protector who doesn't know how to communicate, so then I say, "By the time you got to high school, maybe you had someone who really knew math, but they didn't know how to teach it to you. So now you have a different opportunity—you have someone who loves math and who can communicate and show you how it is good."

• • •

The Program "Math My Way"

"Math My Way" came about because we had more and more students needing math remediation coming in to the college level, and it seemed they weren't really getting what they needed. We had a researcher do some grade data analysis, and his data showed that a student who earned a C in one of the lower-level courses had only about a 15 percent chance of passing the next course. So some of us in the math department thought, "Why even bother giving Cs if you have students who pretty much aren't going to get through the next course?" I had felt for quite a while that the way my colleagues and I were teaching wasn't working: by the time students get to college, they've seen someone add fractions and multiply negative numbers probably twenty or more times. Seeing someone do it one more time isn't going to make a difference. I thought, "What students really need is more hands-on, guided practice."

The traditional teaching approach is to explain how to solve a problem on the board, then give students homework and have them practice problem-solving at home. Then students submit their homework and the teacher grades it and comments on it, but the comments are too late. Students need that information when they're making the mistakes, otherwise they start practicing things that are wrong, and fixing their wrong habits is really difficult to do. For a long time I'd been thinking we needed a program to help students work on these skills where we can give them immediate feedback and not let them practice those mistakes over and over again. So we divided the arithmetic and pre-algebra courses into ten modules, each focused on a specific area of skills building, and combined the modules into one course. Students work on one module until they master it.

Each module consists of computer drills and handwritten assignments, and students must do every assignment and every problem and get at least 87 percent correct before they move on to the next level. A typical class is "controlled chaos"; in one corner, the teacher is explaining a process to a small group of students, while in other areas students are working on computer drills or working on problems either alone or in small groups, with the TAs circulating among them to check and answer questions. I work hard to ensure students do the time on task that contributes to success, particularly leading up to the first exam, because if students can be successful on the first exam, they start building the confidence that can help them through the rest of the course.

If they can do well on the first exam, they say to themselves, "Oh my god, I _can_ do this!" In "Math My Way," knowing that they can repeat a test until they get it right does a lot to alleviate their anxiety. But in all the other courses, you still have to worry about student attitudes—I have to be a bit of a cheerleader ("Yea,

yea, you!") as well as a disciplinarian ("You have to do this work, and you have to do it now"). It's quite a balancing act, being mean and nice at the same time.

We try to make the math interesting and fun, although let's face it, it's hard to do that with these students—math just isn't fun for them. But I do try, for example, by just showing them how excited I can get about it—"Wow, look at this, isn't this thing cool?!" Or by keeping it lighthearted, like when they are learning repeating decimals, I might go "3333333333333 . . ." until a student finally yells, "Stop! OK, we get it!" It drives the point home in a light way, rather than just saying, "This 3 can go on forever." Or by showing its relevance, like when they were learning to do percent increase and percent decrease, I showed them how to calculate percentages in one step instead of the standard two. Then we talked about how they can now walk into a store and if something costs $30 and it is 40 percent off, they can quickly find out how much it is going to cost.

We also pair the content with study skills and games. For example, we tell them, "Map out how you spend every hour of your week to see how you're using your time so we can identify where you can put more study time in." We have them play "Math Bingo" or we bring in Sudoku puzzles and teach them how to play so that they can see the potential for math as recreation. We also talk about the history of math. For example, we explain that Pythagoras was a leader of a cult. When something is attributed to Pythagoras, you can't tell for sure whether or not he was responsible because he had so many people who worked with him but never took credit and attributed all their stuff to him. We explain to them that there were scandals when irrational numbers were discovered: one of the things mathematicians were trying to do was take a circle and find a square that had the exact same area. You can't do that without irrational numbers, and so people who suggested that there might be numbers that weren't ratios or integers were beaten and killed. So we bring in interesting information in the hopes that it will help students understand that they get math in a nice, neat little package, but it took hundreds of years to develop the systems that we have for doing things today. We hope that it helps them understand the enormous amount of knowledge they're trying to take in. It has all been canned now so it is easier to digest, but it took people a long time to develop.

"Math My Way" is not perfect, but it is much more effective than the traditional approach. The program is still new and we don't have enough students yet that have gone through the program to compare our students' success rates with the other populations, but the preliminary data looks good—although we aren't getting any more students through than in the traditional course, they're doing a lot better once they go on.

• • •

Linking with Campus Support

Neither "Math My Way" nor the other math classes are explicitly linked to campus-based student support programs, but we do encourage students to get involved with such programs. For example, Pass the Torch (PTT) is a program designed to help at-risk students by giving them a physical location to meet and by linking them with another student who functions as their mentor. I have been the trainer of the mentors for PTT, and I think that the secret to the program's success is that at-risk students have a "home" on campus that helps them to feel more connected to the campus. You get students in PTT who were doing really well before coming into PTT who continue to do well, and you get students who weren't doing well before coming into PTT and they continue not to do well, but then there are the students for whom PTT makes a big difference. You hear things like they feel that they have a place on campus to go to. It is hard in a commuter college where you don't have a dorm or a place that feels like home. Also, PTT assigns each student a mentor who works with them two hours a week, although the student can also come to the PTT office and study on their own there. (The office has a computer and resources for them.) I've had students in my class who fail the first exam and I tell them, "Go, get into Pass the Torch," and then later their mentor tells me that the student doesn't need help. I tell the mentor, "I don't know what's going on, but there's a big difference between how he was before he was in the program and now after he's been meeting with you. He now does all of his homework and it is perfectly done, so you're doing something." It's the accountability and personal connection of having an additional person looking over your shoulder asking, "How are you doing?" and "Did you do your homework?" as well having a physical location and a community on campus that gives them a sense of belonging.

The program "Math My Way" addresses the needs of students who doubt their ability to succeed in math. Most students in our classes do not have such low expectations nor need such concentrated intervention, but almost all "engaging" teachers have developed approaches that address in one way or another the expectancy aspect of motivation. Clarity of grading criteria, careful and thorough directions on assignments, expressing to students you are available to help them if they are struggling, are just some of the ways effective teachers foster motivation by helping students develop expectations that, with appropriate effort, they will succeed in the course.

Value

The other component in the motivation equation is value. Dolores Davison teaches history. Following are her thoughts on engagement focusing on her experience teaching the freshman, general-education, year-long core sequence on the history of Western civilization.

DOLORES DAVISON'S APPROACH TO TEACHING HISTORY

I am intrigued by alternative pedagogies and activities, but because I am constrained by large class size, huge content coverage requirements, and a fixed-seating classroom, I feel stuck with chalk-and-talk. My core teaching assignment is the year-long lower-division history of Western civilization sequence. The course fulfills a general education requirement, and because most students feel like they are forced to be there, they don't come in with a lot of motivation. Plus they have little background in studying history. I didn't realize how poorly prepared most students were until I started talking about the papacy and one student asked, "So what's the papacy?"

My challenge is getting students in a large class who are ill-prepared and don't really want to be there to become involved and then to push them to higher levels of thinking—all this within a course that includes learning a lot of information. To me, students are engaged in the class if they're interested, intrigued, want to do extra research, and ask for recommendations of additional sources or materials. They are engaged if they participate in discussions, bring forth personal examples, and are actively listening to the group instead of sitting in the back of the room with their head down listening to their iPod. Here are some of my strategies for achieving that.

•   •   •

Creating a Sense of Community

I want the course to feel welcoming and to build a sense of community, so one of the first things I try to do is to learn student names. That way, I can call on all students, maximizing participation by looking to the back row, for example, and asking, "Kevin, what do you think about this?"

I use a variety of strategies to learn names and set aside a few moments the first day of class for students to turn to someone they don't know and introduce themselves. Throughout the term, I encourage students to come to my office to talk. They talk with me over just about everything you can imagine, saying, "I can't talk to anyone else about this, but I can talk with you." I also attend student-sponsored cultural activities as well as sports events. Being approachable helps me to keep students engaged and persisting. As an example, here's an e-mail I received from a student who was struggling because his father was diagnosed with myeloma:

Hi Professor Davison:

Everything has been good. Thank you! His myeloma has lowered dramatically, the doctors are just in shock, because it was all over his body about

95% and it's down to like 10%. I thank you so much for being so sweet, when you don't have to. My father really appreciates this. If it weren't for your generosity, I probably would have dropped out again for the third time. Thanks for your support!!!!!

Making a difference in students' lives—like the one I apparently made in this student's—is what makes this work so rewarding for me.

• • •

Helping Students Connect to the Content on a Personal Level

It is also important to me that students make a personal connection to what we are studying, so I try to relate what they are learning in class as much as possible to their own lives. For example, when I talk about the spread of the Plague in the fourteenth century, I compare it to the AIDs crisis in the 1980s. I ask students, "Why would this be frightening? Why would people choose to become religious? or become atheists? How would this affect patterns in society?" That resonates with students, because so many students have been influenced by the AIDS epidemic in one way or another and are willing to offer examples that I can use to draw similarities between the AIDs crisis and the bubonic plague. Or when I talk about the bombing of Pearl Harbor, we discuss the similarities to the 9/11 attack on the World Trade Center.

In fact, I try to use these kinds of examples to help students get a better sense of what history is: I ask them to remember the specific things that they did on 9/11, and we discuss how that will be a defining moment in their lives, just as other generations will always remember when Kennedy was shot, or when the Challenger blew up. I say, "See, you are a part of history," and students go, "Oh, yeah," and it makes it all more interesting to them. I am also aware that several teachers in the history department are looking for ways to make their classes more meaningful to students by offering learning activities and projects that connect course work to community issues. For example, one of my colleagues has students working on a project with a local history museum.

• • •

To Promote Higher-Order Thinking

I try to move students beyond just memorizing the information, and to do that, I have them constantly writing. To help students learn to think and write at more sophisticated levels, I scaffold the assignments. For example, my first assignment is a historical biography, an analytical essay on a particular person of their choice—someone who interests them—from the historical period we are studying. It is a good first assignment because it is the easiest kind of history paper to write and students can be successful at it.

I give students a grading rubric ahead of time that carefully explicates their task. On one side of a matrix I list the criteria for the paper, such as "an effective biographical description to make your figure vivid and interesting"; "strong analysis based on historical documentation of the impact and actions of the individual"; and "clear opinion about how and why this figure is significant to his/her own era and beyond her/his lifetime (if relevant) with full explanations." Each criterion has a number of points possible and a column where I can specify whether a student is strong/good/fair/poor on that particular dimension. I include a column for comments on each criterion and additional space for general comments.

By specifying every component and then weighting things accordingly, I clarify what students need to do and think about. For example, when I first used rubrics, I weighted formatting, grammar, and spelling aspects higher; now I think that those are not so important and have shifted the weight of the points to the substantive, analytical elements. The rubrics give students the specificity they need to be able to critically look at what they're writing and say, "Yes, I've accomplished the analysis portion to this degree with this depth of understanding, and I am demonstrating that in this paper." And when I'm assessing their work, I can say, "Yes, you have demonstrated this skill, but you have not demonstrated this other skill." It helps students learn to self-assess their writing because it provides a checklist against which they can compare their work before they submit it, and it provides an efficient mechanism for me to give students clear and substantive feedback when I return their graded essay. [See T/S 25 in Chapter 8 for more information about rubrics.]

Finally, I've found that what really engages my students are my own pictures of the places and things we're talking about. Because I travel so much, I have a gazillion photos. It adds to my "authenticity." For example, when we talk about the Plague and the Dance of Death, I can show students photographs of the Judgment Day paintings on the ceiling of the Duomo and explain how you're sitting in Mass and looking up at these scenes of judgment with body parts hanging out. Students say, "Wow, that's so cool. You were there!" Rather than just talking out of a book, this gives them images that are often more powerful, plus it makes things more real and that engages them.

When the class is finished, I always take the time to celebrate and honor their hard work. I'm known for bringing cookies and doughnuts to the final exam. It's a small thing to do to recognize their effort.

Engaging Students through Focusing on Active Learning

In the theoretical framework we discussed in Part One, I suggested viewing student engagement as that vibrant space in the overlap of motivation and active learning. All of the teachers I interviewed expressed their commitment to active learning. For example, when Baker was asked to identify her main objective, she responded, "My core goal? Students need to be active participants in their own learning. That means they don't just memorize information; they use higher-order skills such as application, evaluation, and synthesis." When asked to define what *engagement* means to her, Gray answered, "To me, student engagement is when students are actively involved in the learning process rather than just sitting there staring at you, hoping you'll make it easier for them by simply opening their brain and pouring the information in. In math, engagement is *the* most important thing. If you can get students engaged and practicing math, they'll make it through; if you can't, they won't. It's that basic."

Carol Holcroft is relatively new to teaching. She teaches microbiology and nutrition classes both face-to-face and online. One of her nutrition classes meets a general education requirement, but primarily her courses are required as part of the core sequence in vocational/professional programs. In sharing her insights here, she focuses on her microbiology course.

CAROL HOLCROFT'S APPROACH TO TEACHING LABORATORY SCIENCE

The problem I hear over and over again from employers is that students get the job and they know all these facts, but they don't know what to do with them, how to apply their theoretical knowledge to a real situation. My biggest goal, therefore, is to help students develop the higher-order critical thinking skills that help them bridge theory and practice. This is a challenge, because microbiology as well as the other science courses I teach are fact, fact, fact. It becomes even more difficult because a lot of my students haven't been taught or given the opportunity to think critically, and they're so used to being tested on information. Here are some of the ways I try to challenge students' higher-order thinking skills.

First, I try to use a "Think-Pair-Share" every day that requires students to practice "thinking" in response to an application prompt. Although I have a set of prearranged questions, often the best questions spring from the students themselves. I'll be talking about something in class, and a student will ask a question, and I tell them, "You know the answer—think about it." So I give them a minute or so to think independently, then turn to their neighbor and talk through both their thought process and their answer. Then I ask some of the pairs to share with the whole class. Even if someone nails the correct answer right away, I say, "Did anyone think differently?" Then I walk them through my own thinking process to the "right" answer. I stress to students that when they're in their practice as nurses or radiation therapists, there is not going to be someone next to them with the answer—they have to feel confident that they can find the answer and solve the problem on their own.

Another way I help students develop thinking skills is by asking them to write exam questions that require application of information. Most traditional exam questions don't test for application; they test for information recall. For example, a traditional exam question might be "Which of the following characteristics are generally present in gram-positive bacteria?" followed by a list of items from which to choose. In contrast, a question that asks them to apply the information rather than just recall it might be "Do you think a gram-positive or gram-negative bacteria would be more dangerous, and why?" Or when students study endonuclease, a traditional exam question might be "Endonucleases are enzymes that cleave the _____ within a polynucleotide chain," while an application question might be "Why do you think the bacterium made the endonuclease enzyme in the first place?"

It's much harder to come up with these kinds of questions, but because teaching students how to apply the information within a clinical situation is so important to me, this is how I have to test. I involve students in this process by, for example, saying, "Here's what we talked about today, so what was most important? In five minutes (or at home and then post on the Web site), write an exam question that's going to require you to apply this information, not just regurgitate it. How could you test a student's ability to apply this knowledge? Think like a teacher." Most students have not been taught to think like this very much, so sometimes they don't like me [*laughs*], but I just tell them I'm trying to move them to higher-order thinking. By the end of the course, they get pretty good at it!

● ● ●

Creating a Sense of Community

There are several things I do to foster a sense that we are a learning community. We do this silly little exercise the first day of class where everyone gets out of their chair and goes outside. I lay out the boundaries for an imaginary map of the valley and identify a few key geographical markers and then ask students to go stand where they live. When everyone is in place, I say, "Look around you. See the other students who live in your area—look over here, this student lives on your same street! Perhaps you could form a study group." It's a fun icebreaking activity that also gets them out of their seats and moving physically. [See T/S 30 in Chapter 9 for other icebreaker ideas.] I give students the opportunity to meet others because some students really thrive on that, but I don't make it mandatory because other students feel uncomfortable with it. I also ask students in both the face-to-face class and the online class to post an introduction, explaining why they are taking the class, their hobbies and interests, and I invite each student to respond to two other students' postings.

In my online class, students are also required to participate in a certain number of discussions, and this contributes to their sense of community. A particularly effective online discussion thread is something I call "The Study Forum." Since I tell students that one of the best ways to learn is to explain something to others, I advise students that if they get stuck, they should post a question (not just a what-is-the-answer question but a more reflective question, like "I've been thinking about this and looking at the information in the book, but I still don't understand why, or how, or ..."). Other students in the class are encouraged to respond by explaining their own thinking about the issue. I give students extra-credit points for participating appropriately and constructively in this forum. I do monitor it closely to make sure they are reinforcing information correctly, but that particular forum is a great mechanism for helping students refine their thinking skills.

The forum also meets another need: in my classes, students have a wide range of abilities. Some students are older and already have a skill set in science. For example, this term I have a student who has a bachelor's in environmental science who is retooling for a career in nursing. She catches on to everything very quickly. I also almost always have one or two students who are immigrants who were doctors or dentists in another country. Their training doesn't really count here in the United States, so they are taking my course either to prepare for U.S. certification or just to learn the English vocabulary. These kinds of students are particularly fun because they challenge me. Then there are also students who have no science background but need a job and have decided to become a nurse because they hear that it is a dependable kind of career. The Study Forum discussion thread provides an opportunity for the less skilled students to ask questions and the more expert students to answer them.

• • •

On Using Technology in the Class

I teach some courses totally online, but I also use a course Web site to support my face-to-face course. I use it to communicate with students both privately and as a group, to track grades, give practice quizzes for review, and collect essay assignments. An important component of the classes is the discussion forums, such as the Study Forum I mentioned earlier. Although the focus of the course is the learning of scientific facts, concepts, and principles, when I can, I introduce ethical issues. This is easier in courses that have a social component, but wherever it's appropriate, I try to ask things like "Given the science that we learned in the class, what do you think about these issues?"

I want students to be self-reliant and independent in finding answers to questions themselves, and this often involves looking up information on the

Internet. To help them do this well, I use a variation of SET 22, "WebQuests." I form teams, have the teams identify a controversial topic that has a clear pro/con side (e.g., genetically modified/engineered food, or the healthful aspects of drinking milk), and then have the teams search for two Web sites with opposing perspectives. I provide students with a list of credible criteria and some red flags to look for in a Web site. The teams then analyze the sites and write a synthesis of the information that represents their best efforts at a balanced, accurate viewpoint. They post their analysis and synthesis along with the URLs of the Web sites they chose. Then all students are asked to critique two of the other students' analyses, taking into account the credibility of the Web sites they used.

Many of my colleagues currently think the concept of "online labs" for science courses is blasphemy, but I can imagine that online labs may play an increasingly important role in extending educational opportunities for students. The experience wouldn't be identical to one in a fully equipped college laboratory (laboratory equipment such as microscopes and many of the materials are just too expensive to replicate in a noninstitutional environment), but if the course is a general education course, is it really an absolute requirement that students learn to use a microscope? They'll never use one on the street or at home. It is an interesting activity—but is it crucial? Science educators are coming up with alternatives to formal laboratory experiments, such as kitchen labs where students either purchase the ingredients themselves at the grocery store or get pre-packaged lab kits that are mailed to them. The experiments are not as sophisticated as those done in the campus laboratory, but maybe that's not the point— maybe it is the thinking and learning the scientific method that is most important.

Holcroft is explicit that active learning is her primary goal, and she engages students by ensuring every activity in the course—from discussions to exams—moves students toward this goal.

Engaging Students through a Combination of Approaches

All the teachers' stories so far have reflected a mix of the theoretical aspects regarding student engagement we have explored in Part One, but this last story seems to do that to a particularly high degree. Scott Lankford is a senior faculty member in the English department. He teaches American literature and gay/lesbian literature, but focuses his comments here on the teaching approaches he uses in his basic freshman English course.

I hope what students would say was engaging about my teaching is that their experience in the course transformed their sense of themselves and that I am absolutely crystal clear about my expectations. Those are my two goals. First, I try to lay out the task and the tools as clearly as possible, because I think so often students (especially students who have struggled through school) don't understand what they are being asked to do and why they are being asked to do it; it is deeply frustrating for them. Second, I am trying to get them to retell or transform their own story, their life story as they tell it to themselves. I am looking for this deep transformation of how they see themselves. The combination of those two things is really powerful. Often there is a really evil English teacher in their past who has shaped their attitudes about writing. One evil teacher can place a curse on a student in the third grade that lasts throughout his or her education. Giving students the tools to tell their story clearly already transforms their story.

• • •

On Giving Students Choice

One of the ways I achieve clarity is by a collection of handouts that I believe empowers students with the tools they need to be effective writers. My handouts are also about choices—here are my top ten tips. I don't say there is only one way to do it, because that is what most students have heard all their lives. I say, "Great writers—whether they are professionals or students—have some combination of these characteristics. Look at this student's paper. She got an A. See how she did that? You can do it too. I don't want to make robots, I want to give you the skills to go with your own voice and style. Here's a grab bag, choose from it." I think it is important to give students choices. For example, I always give students the choice of doing alternative assignments. Most of my assignments require that the student engage directly with their own lives, responding in some way to the question, What does this text, reading, and so forth have to do with you? Most students can write best about themselves, but there is a 10–20 percent subset who can't or don't want to write about themselves. There may be cultural reasons, or it may not be their personal style or the way they think— whatever—but they are just not empowered by writing about themselves, so I give them an alternative.

• • •

On Building a Sense of Community in the Class

I'm of two minds about how to build community starting the first day of class. I used to do the syllabus kind of activity, but now I've moved to getting to the content as soon as possible. I go through the syllabus as fast as I can—ten minutes max—"Here are the essentials, boom, now let's start" and then I move on to content. Since all students won't have the books the first day, I take the first page from our first reading and put it up on an overhead. I try to make sure the book is engaging. Since I start with personal writing, I choose a memoir, and the first page usually opens with some sort of shocking confession from the person involved, and it has to do with fate and choices and how choices and fate change one's life. I try to find the questions that really engage students so that they want to raise their hands. I go into what I call my "Oprah mode." I don't worry about names, but I make sure everyone participates. We spend an hour discussing that page. I'm relying on the power of the author to build the community. Plus I'm saying, "Look how complicated this is—we've spent a whole hour on this and we still don't understand it. This is deep. We have to read it again. This isn't middle school or high school stuff. This is college level stuff, and I want you to think and I want to know what you think." My underlying message is this: "You want to be in my class? This is what it is going to be like."

Praise is really powerful. I look so hard for things to praise, because most of these students have never been praised ever by an English teacher. Once in a while, on a bad day, I still get into the blame game. "You're not here and you didn't turn in your paper," responding like a parent. I think that there's a better way to respond, and it doesn't mean I am going to extend the deadline or take back my late penalty, but it comes from a point of respecting the student. I ask them, "What happened?" I assume the best intentions. Responding to them in that way is very empowering for them. A teacher giving them respect is very unusual. Unlike privileged students at elite institutions who have grown up with a sense of entitlement and being respected, many of my students have never been treated with respect before. That message can be deeply empowering.

● ● ●

To Ensure All Students Participate in Discussions

After the first day, I have a trick I use to make sure that I call on every student in each class. It is very simple, but it keeps the few brainiacs from dominating the discussion and it requires the shyer students to speak up. I have a set of 3–5 cards, with a student name on each card, and I randomly shuffle the cards and draw from that. I tell students, "When your card comes up—and you never know when it's going to come up—you'd better be able to respond." If I have to repeat the question, I might say, "You're paying for this class, so why do I have to repeat the question?" If they don't have anything to contribute, I try to help them out but in a nonblaming kind of way. If necessary, I might eventually ask, "Did you do the reading?" A small amount of embarrassment is OK. I push even reticent speakers to speak up. I don't want to be culturally insensitive, but I have talked to non-native speakers sufficiently in my office to know their reasons for not wanting to speak up in class. I might say, "You need to speak up and practice your English. Isn't this why you came all the way across the ocean?" I try to help them out, but I keep the pressure on and don't let other students rescue them. I use this approach because if students don't think they are going to be called on, they start to sit back, they start to tune out, and as soon as they tune out, you've lost them.

• • •

Using the Psychomotor Dimension

Thinking through and writing out a good thesis is so important. So I've developed what might appear as a kind of goofy strategy for helping students understand the three components of a thesis, because if they don't do all three parts of the thesis for their essay, it is catastrophic for their essay. I justify its silliness because it works. It clarifies the components for students in a way that they never forget, and since clarity is my number-one teaching rule, I am OK with silly. I get the whole class to stand up and follow my lead for what I call "Thesis Calisthenics." I take the book that is the subject of their paper (for example, *Not a Genuine Black Man* by Brian Copeland) in my left hand and I raise my arm and ask them, "What is this book about? It is about Copeland's experience as an outsider." Then I raise my right arm and say, "Now you are going to talk about yourself, and your experience as an outsider, however you want to define that." And then I put my hands together and say, "Now you are going to bring these two together." Days afterwards, when we're still talking about the thesis, I can call on a student and as he struggles to respond, one of his peers might wave their left hand or their right hand or clap their hands together until the student remembers the framework. Students like it—especially the students who you might think would like it least. Goofiness can be really powerful. *[laughs]*

We teach students from all over the world with all kinds of backgrounds and levels of academic preparedness, and we're teaching them how to write academic essays. Another strategy I have found effective is to draw pictures of the paper on the board: five blank pieces of paper. Then I ask, "What goes on the first page?" and we write in the title, the intro, the thesis, and so forth, and I say, "This is the game, this is what makes a standard American essay." I had a French student who was so frustrated because she had been an extremely successful student in France but kept getting lower grades on her essays here in the United States. She just couldn't get it—and then one day, after I had drawn the picture for the tenth time, she exclaimed, "Oh, I get it, in the American essay, the conclusion is the beginning!" Our way is completely upside down from what she had learned in France, and it took those pictures to help it finally make sense to her.

And here's one more activity I learned from a colleague: "Cocktail Party." We all know how to put people into groups and what we should do to make group work effective, but I still find group work hard to do well, and this generation of students seems to resist it. Perhaps it is because they have had it done so badly and felt their time was wasted. But in this twist, I say something very specific like "Your paper is due in seven days. I want you to introduce yourself to one of your peers and explain your thesis. Don't just talk to your friends; meet someone new." Then everyone stands up and you handle it like a cocktail party. You present the prompt, and students mill around talking to each other usually in groups of 3–4. It is still "I'm going to tell you about my thesis paper and you are going to tell me about yours," but because students are standing up and moving around, they seem to accept the task and do it. As teacher, I am the power host—I make sure students are mingling, and if a student is standing by themselves, I'll help them mingle. What I love about this activity is that it breaks the "slouch"—you know the body language that says, "I'm not engaged"—where students look exhausted, like they just wish it would all be over, like they are close to being dead. *[laughs]*

• • •

On Using Technology

I believe technology can be truly transformative—so I've integrated the Internet, social networking, and even cell phones into my teaching in every way I know how. At the moment this involves using an Internet uplink and a computer projector to display everything from relevant YouTube video clips to discussing archived student work in class. I've found that blogs are an excellent way to display outstanding student work online; recently I've even tried interacting with other teachers and their classes around the globe (creating what Thomas Friedman calls a "flat earth classroom"). Outside class I'll use the comment features on blogs as a way to keep discussions going. Since this generation communicates so easily via short text messages, I let them e-mail questions to me anytime day or night. Don't get me wrong: it's not that I always respond! Instead I simply get a snapshot of what they've been thinking about, why they're stuck. Occasionally I'll use my BlackBerry to send back a very quick e-mail response, but usually I just lump all the most typical concerns together and address them in class the next day, explaining, "I've gotten a ton of e-mail messages about X lately, so let's talk."

I think the keyword for engagement is *outreach*. You have to reach out to students. You can't wait for them to reach out to you. The good students always have and always will reach out, but the struggling students don't know how to make the first move.

Keeping Oneself Engaged

Our focus up to this point has been on engaging students, but let's shift our attention momentarily to teachers. Just as it is essential to engage students, so is it important to get and keep ourselves engaged in our teaching, even after many years in the trenches. Much that I have talked about in Part One can be applied to teachers because I submit that teaching *is* learning, and what applies to students as learners applies equally well to teachers as learners. Teachers need to feel motivated to teach well. At a basic level, using the *expectancy* $\leftrightarrow$ *value* equation, teachers need to believe that with effort, they can create classroom conditions that are engaging to students. They also need to value good teaching—a disposition that can be reinforced by institutions that have structures in place that clearly expect and reward good teaching.

Teachers need to be actively learning from their teaching. Teaching is— or could be and should be—an exciting profession because there is always something new to learn. I don't know any teacher who takes teaching seriously who thinks they know everything there is to know about teaching and learning. In fact, the more experience one has as a teacher, the more one is likely to question one's own effectiveness. When teachers are engaged in their teaching, each day, each class, each student presents an opportunity to learn something new about our profession. Classroom research and the scholarship of teaching and learning are two avenues for keeping engaged in teaching by concentrating on how and what we can learn from our endeavors.

In addition, the three conditions that promote synergy between motivation and active learning and thus contribute to increased levels of engagement in students may also promote increased levels of engagement in teachers. Teachers who feel they are members of a community committed to excellent teaching (for example, they feel safe expressing concerns about classroom issues to their colleagues and asking for ideas on how to solve problems) are more likely to experience higher levels of engagement than teachers who feel isolated or even disrespected for their efforts to improve their teaching. Teachers who are teaching classes at their optimal level of challenge are likely to be more engaged than teachers who find their courses either overwhelmingly difficult to teach (such as mega-enrollment courses without sufficient support) or too easy (perhaps the teacher is bored and simply recycles in identical format the lectures and assignments he or she has used for years). Finally, teachers who are involved holistically in their teaching and, for example, truly *care* about their students' learning and development are likely to be more engaged than those who are emotionally detached because they see their role as primarily a dispenser of information. Based on this assumption that virtually everything we have learned about engaged learning is equally applicable to engaged teaching, here are comments from four of the teachers interviewed on the challenge of staying engaged in their teaching.

Holcroft: I am very involved in academic leadership and campus governance, and so I have a long to-do list beyond classroom teaching. I find toward the end of the term I'm just fried. A friend drew a graph for me that I think is just hysterical. The x-axis is time, and the y-axis is interest. Teachers start the course with lots of energy, really encouraging students to ask challenging questions. And they have lots of time to answer the questions. By the end of the course, teachers are so crunched for time they no longer have the interest or ability to deal with students' more difficult questions. The graph so well captures my sense that by the end of the term, when students have learned enough information and skills to start asking really interesting, deep questions, I'm exhausted. I'll check on the discussion forum and find this great question by a student and think, "I could spend an hour answering that—it's a wonderful question—but I've got this huge to-do list today!"

These comments capture one of the core challenges to teaching for engaged learning—it takes time, commitment, and hard work. Holcroft is an engaged and dedicated teacher, and she puts in the effort, but some teachers find trying to teach for engaged learning just one more pressure in a role already overburdened by research, publication, and committee meetings.

On the other hand, the rewards from teaching can be motivating and energizing, as is expressed by the following three teachers:

Gray: I stay engaged by teaching a variety of classes. If I taught only the lower-end courses and Math My Way, I'd burn out—but I also get to teach the advanced courses that keep me intellectually challenged. Also, the student successes are very rewarding. I had a student in pre-algebra when I first started teaching. She was retired from the military and was enrolled in the veterinary program. Every day, this is the conversation I had with her:

> *"Hi, V., so how are you doing?"*
> *She'd respond, "Well, I'm doing OK today, that homework last night wasn't so bad, but I looked ahead and I see that we're doing (bleah) and so today's the day I'm not going to be able to do it anymore and I'll have to give up on math."*
> *And I'd say, "OK, well, we'll see."*

And then she'd take her seat. Every day I had that exact same conversation with her. But she persevered, eventually changing her major to history with a minor in math, taking several courses in calculus as well as other advanced math courses. She earned a double credential and teaches history and math in a local high school today. But every day, she was convinced she wasn't going to be able to do it. We still stay in touch. *[laughs]*

Lankford: When I first came here from X (a prestigious private university), I looked at the senior faculty at this college and they had this youthfulness. There was a physical difference; they were not burned out. At X, the senior faculty were all hunched over and they looked exhausted, like they were on death's door. This was a way to look cool. It sent the message "I've spent my whole life in a library and I'm exhausted and my latest book was about this and I hate teaching." The joke was that a teaching award was the kiss of death. That's why I left and never looked back. I am not going to work in a place where a teaching award is a kiss of death. The best teachers have this inner light that comes from the fact that we love our work and deeply respect the students. I may have to deal with an occasional discipline problem or the frustration that a student just isn't getting it—but that is like 10 percent. Ninety percent of my day is just plain fun.

Menendez: I sometimes wonder how people who don't just really love teaching get through their day. It is spiritual to me. It is so inspiring to see these human beings in the room who are willing to let me be the person to teach them. I'm very grateful and joyful they're here. I don't say that to them—I play the tough guy—but my caring is radiating through as a subtext. When I was first here, the old guys always thought it was funny to make snide remarks about students. I walked away from that years ago. It feels so wrong on so many levels. These vulnerable people who don't have the privilege that we had—and I'm getting a salary for this? and health insurance? and I'm going to make fun of them? It just isn't right. Now it doesn't mean that I won't go to one of my colleagues and say, this student is driving me nuts! But that's for my own repair, so that I can get back in there and love them up the next day. You have to be humble. The persona has to be big, but we are serving, and inside we need humility. I am in a life of service, and a life of service is a life well lived, as everyone who does this kind of work knows.

These teachers are engaged in their teaching. I propose that it is because they find value in their profession, have developed expectations that they can teach well, find their work intellectually stimulating, are appropriately challenged, care deeply about their students' learning, and feel as though they are part of a community dedicated to high-quality teaching.

Conclusion

There is a popular saying "In theory, theory and practice are the same, while in practice, they're different." It's clever, but my sense is that these experiences of real teachers match up in many ways to the theoretical discussion we had earlier. I also think every one of the teachers I interviewed would have just laughed had I had the foresight to ask them if all students in their classes were engaged all the time. I know mine certainly aren't. Some years ago, in a mindless moment that might today land me a lawsuit, I threw a whiteboard marker at a student who was sleeping. With a degree of physical prowess I didn't know I possessed, I planted a big black spot on his forehead. "Stay awake," I said, "this is interesting." More recently, to make American roots music more appealing, I showed a video clip from Bruce Springsteen's *The Seeger Sessions*. After Springsteen talks about the need for every generation to both maintain and build upon folk music traditions, he breaks into a barn-bustin' version of "Mary Don't You Weep." I thought, "How exciting! How hip! How relevant!" After I turned on the lights and looked out on a room full of blank faces, one student asked, "So who's Bruce Springsteen?" And another rolled her eyes and added, "And why does he keep telling Mary not to eat?"

How do we find solutions to the problems we face engaging students in learning? Most likely from our own creative ideas or by talking to colleagues or by looking to the literature. But solutions to straightforward, clearly defined problems (what's an efficient way to learn student names?) are still easier to find than solutions to complex, ill-defined problems (how can I get my students to accept greater responsibility for their learning?). Still, the seeds of solutions to even the most complicated student engagement problems abound in the ideas we find in workshops, conversations with colleagues, and the good practice literature.

The purpose of Parts Two and Three is to provide the tips, strategies, and techniques others and I have found helpful in promoting engaged learning. Teaching can be tough, but by sharing, we help each other in the problem analysis and solution construction we struggle with consciously or unconsciously each time we enter the classroom and attempt to engage students in learning.

Part Two

Tips and Strategies (T/S)

THE FIFTY TIPS and strategies (T/S) that follow build upon Part One's conceptual framework of student engagement. This framework proposes that student engagement functions as a double helix in which active learning and motivation work together synergistically, building in intensity, and creating a fluid and dynamic phenomenon that is greater than the sum of their individual effects. Engagement does not occur if either of the two elements is missing: a student is not engaged if she is motivated but not learning, or if she is learning but doing so reluctantly. On a continuum from barely engaged to deeply engaged, students become more engaged as motivation and active learning build. Certain conditions promote synergy because they integrate elements of both. For example, students become more engaged when they feel that they are valued members of a learning community; when they are working at their optimal level of challenge, neither bored nor overwhelmed; and when they are learning holistically.

The tips and strategies come primarily from the good practice literature and are organized according to this conceptual framework: fostering motivation (Chapter 7), promoting active learning (Chapter 8), building community (Chapter 9), ensuring students are appropriately challenged (Chapter 10), and teaching for holistic learning (Chapter 11).

Tips and Strategies for Fostering Motivation

WHEN STUDENTS WANT to learn, they are more inclined to do what is necessary in order to learn. They pay attention in class, they take notes during a lecture, they study when they get home, and they monitor their own progress and ask questions when they don't understand. Many teachers find that if a student is highly motivated, most of the typical teaching and learning challenges disappear. This section includes tips and strategies for creating classroom conditions that enhance student motivation.

T/S 1 Expect engagement.

Expect students in your course to be engaged in learning, and resist settling for less.

If you have done everything you can to create classroom conditions that promote engagement and still see students who look bored or apathetic, talk to them privately. Tell them disengagement is not an option in your course, and invite them to suggest activities that will achieve course or unit learning goals that they'd find more engaging.

Even though a student who falls asleep in class may be truly exhausted from working all night or staying up late studying for an exam, sleeping students are not engaged students; a disengaged student undermines the morale of the entire class. Consider waking him up and suggesting he leave the room and walk around for a few minutes to get more oxygen into his system. Or move close to the sleeping student and talk to a student sitting nearby in a voice loud enough to wake up her neighbor.

Think about dropping the attendance requirement and giving students the choice of learning from materials on reserve in the library, the media center, or online so that if they don't find the classroom situation engaging, they have another option.

Just as overt displays of disengagement have a deleterious effect on classroom environment, so is enthusiasm contagious. It may not be reasonable to expect all students to be engaged all the time, but as the artist Niccolini observed, "By asking for the impossible, we obtain the best possible."

T/S 2 Develop and display the qualities of engaging teachers.

Teacher personality and behavior have a powerful impact on whether students feel motivated in a course. Building upon studies by industrial and organizational psychologists, educational researchers have found that even students who are not intrinsically motivated by their studies will put forth reasonable effort if they like and admire their teacher, just as they may become apathetic or resistant if they view their teacher negatively (Brophy, 2004, pp. 27–28).

Provitera-McGlynn (2001) summarizes research by Perlman and McCann, who asked seven hundred undergraduates to write complaints about teacher behavior in courses they had taken. Among the top ten complaints were "being unhelpful and unapproachable" and "intellectual arrogance—talking down to or showing lack of respect for students" (p. 63). Provitera-McGlynn (2001) observes, "Although they may use different language, students overwhelmingly report that classroom atmosphere is a critical variable in what motivates them to come to class and do well" (pp. 63–64).

This does not mean that you have to be false to your basic personality ("authenticity" appears in other lists of ideal teacher characteristics), but it does suggest that students will be more likely to engage in your class if you cultivate and display attributes of well-liked and respected teachers, such as energy, enthusiasm, passion, approachability, fairness, and optimism.

T/S 3 Use behaviorist-based strategies to reward learning rather than behavior.

The principles of behaviorism permeate education. To motivate students to do excellent work, teachers reward desirable behaviors through praise, bonus points, and exemptions from work, and they try to extinguish undesirable behaviors through nonreinforcement or negative reinforcement such as chiding, bad grades, and penalty points. Although these approaches may provide quick fixes, from the standpoint of most motivational theorists, they are control of behavior and not motivation of learning.

Brophy (2004, pp. 154–157) provides a thoughtful discussion of the issues, but the essential criticisms are that (1) these approaches focus on extrinsic rewards rather than encouraging students to develop their own sense of reward from the intrinsic pleasure of learning; (2) they can become "bribes" for what students should be doing anyway; and (3) they promote situational compliance rather than helping students develop the attitudes, values, beliefs, and self-regulated learning strategies we want them to use as lifetime learners both in and out of formal educational contexts.

Awareness of the issues can help you use incentives and rewards in ways that put the emphasis on learning rather than on manipulation of behavior. For example, make explicit that it is the learning and what the learning leads to that is of value rather than participation in or completion of an activity; recognize the degree of individual improvement rather than making peer comparisons; and in grading, emphasize the quality of accomplishment rather than quantity of work.

T/S 4 Use praise and criticism effectively.

Complimenting comes naturally to most teachers who care about students and who are striving to create a positive, supportive classroom environment. Unfortunately, praise does not always have the effect we intend. Kohn (1993) points out that some students do not attach much value to a teacher's praise and hence will not feel particularly rewarded when they receive it; others may feel insulted or demeaned if they feel they are being lauded for what they consider to be a minor accomplishment; and some students may find it embarrassing or irritating to be singled out in a way that draws their peers' attention to a behavior that might be considered conformity or obsequiousness. His central objection is that praise is manipulation of behavior. "We all want to be appreciated, encouraged, and loved," he comments. "The question is whether that need must take the form of what often looks like a patronizing pat on the head and saying 'Good boy,' to which I believe the most logical response is 'Woof'!" (in Brandt, 1995, p. 5).

Educators such as Kohn oppose praise on principle, viewing it as manipulative and contributing to a hierarchical relationship between learners and instructors. Following are suggestions for how to praise effectively in ways that are more empowering and respectful, drawing from Brophy (2004, pp. 167–169) and Wlodkowski (2008, pp. 368–369).

1. Praise in a timely manner with simplicity, sincerity, spontaneity, and other signs of authenticity. Don't dramatize, and use straightforward sentences ("I never thought of that before") instead of gushy exclamations ("Wow!") or rhetorical questions, which are essentially condescending ("Isn't that great!").

2. Praise the attainment of specific criteria that is related to learning, such as noteworthy effort, care, perseverance, or demonstration of progress, and specify the skills or evidence of progress that you are praising: "This essay does not have a single spelling, grammar, or syntax error. I appreciate the meticulous editing it so obviously reflects" rather than "Good work."

3. In general, praise privately. Wlodkowski (2008), for example, cites Plaud and Markus, who observe that in collectivist cultures such as many Asian societies, adults may prefer to receive praise indirectly as a member of a social group, rather than directly as an individual. He also cites a study by Jones, Rozelle, & Chang that noted Chinese adults did not want to be used as "good examples for others."

Just as praise is not always helpful, neither is criticism always harmful. Wlodkowski (2008) clarifies that constructive criticism is distinguished from general criticism in that it points out errors and deficiencies in learning but does not connote disapproval, disgust, or rejection. He suggests that it is particularly appropriate and may even be necessary in situations where the learning process is costly or involves a threat to human safety; when performance is so poor that to emphasize success or improvement would be ridiculous or patronizing; when performance has significant errors and there are few remaining chances for improvement in the course; or when a learner directly requests criticism. Constructive criticism is most helpful and motivating if it is informational, based on performance criteria, behavior specific, corrective, prompt, given privately, and offered when there are opportunities for improvement (Wlodkowski, 2008, p. 364).

T/S 5 Attend to students' basic needs so that they can focus on the higher-level needs required for learning.

Needs theories emerged as an alternative to behaviorist theories. Although they are now criticized for circular logic problems, Maslow's hierarchy of needs remains popular and influential. His model suggests that in the classroom, physiological needs (sleep, thirst), safety needs (freedom from danger, anxiety), and love needs (acceptance from teachers and peers) must be met before students can move on to the higher-level needs that we associate with engaged learning. This does not mean you need to be responsible for the care and feeding of your students, but it does suggest that if you teach classes in the early morning or right before lunch, you may be faced with students who are distracted and unable to focus simply because they are struggling with basic unmet needs. To adjust for this, consider incorporating activities that require social interaction and physical movement in early morning classes. Especially important to the college classroom is being aware of students' psychological needs and taking care to ensure students feel safe to say/write what they truly think or feel without fear of ridicule or criticism by either you or their peers.

T/S 6 Promote student autonomy.

Self-determination is the basic human need to have control over one's life. In the classroom, students are more motivated to engage in meaningful learning if they are acting of their own volition. The need for self-determination works hand in hand with helping students build self-efficacy: they are more likely to believe they are capable of achieving a particular goal if they feel they are in control of the actions required for success.. Student engagement is a partnership that requires students to accept responsibility for their learning, but accepting responsibility can be difficult when, as Wlodkowski (2008) observes, "instructors usually establish requirements, issue assignments, give tests, generally set the standards for achievement, often control the learning environment, and sometimes require learner participation" which can lead "students to the conclusion that instructors are more responsible for their achievement than they are" (pp. 189–190).

Following are some general strategies for promoting autonomy (Wlodkowski, 2008; Raffini,1996; Brophy, 2004):

1. Provide students with meaningful rationales that enable them to understand the purpose and personal importance of course activities.

2. Acknowledge students' feelings when it is necessary to require them to do something they don't want to do.

3. Give students choices among several learning activities that meet the same objective.

4. Allow students options in deciding how to implement classroom procedures.

5. Allow students to decide when, where, and in what order to complete assignments.

6. Encourage students to define, monitor, and achieve self-determined goals individually.

7. Help students to use self-assessment procedures that monitor progress as well as identify personal strengths and potential barriers.

8. Provide opportunities for students to assist in determining evaluation activities.

9. Avoid making students right, wrong, good, or bad based on their choices but instead emphasize accountability.

T/S 7 Teach things worth learning.

It's not surprising that students are more likely to feel motivated in a class if they believe they are learning things worth learning. Although a central goal for many of us is helping students understand and remember the basic facts, principles, and concepts of the discipline, the sheer abundance of information and the rapidity with which information is changing makes "mastery" of information an impossible and perhaps unwise learning focus. Wiggins and McTighe (1998) advise teachers to strive to help their students achieve *understanding*, as distinguished from simply *knowing*. "Enduring understanding" results from grappling with the big ideas and core processes at the heart of a discipline rather than memorizing and remembering lots of facts. In the handbook they developed to guide teachers implementing their model (McTighe and Wiggins, 1999), they suggest using a framework of three concentric circles to prioritize content. In the large, outermost circle, identify the content that is worth being familiar with. In the medium-sized circle inside it, identify the more important knowledge and skills. In the center circle, identify the essential understandings that anchor the course. Use this framework to guide decisions regarding learning activities and assessment.

Fink (2003) proposes a new learning taxonomy to help teachers focus on the kind of deep, permanent learning that goes beyond information gathering. It consists of the following categories: foundational knowledge, application, integration, human dimension (learning about oneself and others), caring (developing new feelings, interests, and values), and learning how to learn. He suggests teachers identify significant learning goals derived from the taxonomy. For example, in a microbiology course, a goal associated with the learning-how-to-learn category might be "A year after this course is over, I want and hope students will be able to identify important resources for their own subsequent learning" (p. 78).

Blumberg (2009) guides teachers through a process to implement Weimer's learner-centered model. She explains that in a teacher-centered approach, a core dimension is to help students build a knowledge base—which usually involves students memorizing the content. In a learner-centered approach, the teacher encourages students to transform and reflect on most of the content to make their own meaning of it (p. 19). As an example, she suggests an instructor might ask students make a chart or graph to summarize some material in the text or to develop associations between what they read or hear in class and their own lives or real-world phenomena (p. 22).

For those of us accustomed to teaching data-intensive courses, it is difficult to shift the emphasis from the learning of information to learning how to find and then use the information. Information recall is easier to teach, test, and maybe even to learn. Nevertheless, changing the focus of your course from content coverage (which is usually information-driven) to uncovering the content (which is usually process- and application-driven) is more relevant to the changed environment in which students must function both during and after college.

T/S 8 Integrate goals, activities, and assessment.

When learning goals, activities and assessment are carefully chosen and integrated to help students achieve significant learning goals that reflect a broader conceptual framework, it is easier for students to see the purpose in what they are being asked to do. This, in turn, can foster motivation. Following are three models for this integration. Teachers are encouraged to go to the original sources, as they are richly nuanced with both theoretical and practical information.

Wiggins and McTighe's Backward Design

At the core of this model is a three-stage sequence. In the first stage, teachers determine what students should know, understand, and be able to do. McTighe and Wiggins (1999) encourage teachers to use the three-circle approach described in T/S 7 to identify learning goals that will result in enduring understanding of core principles and concepts.

In the second stage, teachers determine what would constitute evidence that students have achieved the goals. To help teachers identify this, Wiggins and McTighe (1998) developed a six-facet taxonomy. If students have developed enduring understanding, they can (1) explain, (2) interpret, (3) apply, (4) demonstrate perspective, (5) empathize, and (6) demonstrate self-knowledge. They suggest using a continuum for evaluating evidence of each of the six facets. For example, the ability to explain can be evaluated on a continuum from "naive" to "sophisticated," and the ability to apply on a continuum from "novice" to "masterful."

The third stage, designing academic prompts, performance tasks, or projects occurs only after a teacher has determined the enduring-understanding goals and identified how one can assess the depth at which understanding has been achieved.

Fink's Significant Learning Experiences

The "significant learning" model was inspired by Fink's (2003) observations that many college teachers put together their courses by creating a list of eight to twelve topics (drawn either from the teacher's own understanding or from the table of contents of a good textbook) and then developing a series of lectures to go with it. He notes, "With the addition of a midterm exam or two plus a final, the course is ready to go" (p. 61). He explains that although this approach is fast and efficient, it focuses on organization of information and pays little or no attention to how that information will be learned. The result is usually learning that tends to be superficial and temporary.

Fink's (2003) more learner-centered alternative guides teachers through a twelve-step course design process that begins with determining what would constitute high-quality learning in a given situation, and then making careful choices regarding activities and assessment so that the combination contributes toward promoting a significant learning experience. The twelve steps are clustered into three phases. The initial phase involves building component parts such as identifying the learning goals, feedback and assessment, and teaching and learning activities. The intermediate phase guides teachers through processes to ensure the course is a coherent whole. And in the four remaining tasks of the final phase, teachers develop grading systems, identify possible problems, and conclude with evaluating the course and their teaching for further improvement.

Weimer's and Blumberg's Learner-Centered Teaching Weimer (2002) proposed five key changes teachers can make to promote learner-centered teaching. These changes involve the balance of power, function of content, role of the teacher, responsibility for learning, and purpose and processes of evaluation.

Blumberg (2009) uses Weimer's model to guide teachers on how to transform a course from the traditional, teacher-centered model to a more engaging learner-centered model. For each of the five dimensions, Blumberg suggests teachers pursue a five-step process: (1) understand each dimension and its components; (2) think about ways to transform a course in relation to each dimension; (3) identify the current status of your course for each component; (4) choose the components you want to transform; and (5) create a plan for the components you want to transform. She then suggests two additional steps to integrate all five dimensions: (6) review, group, and prioritize the changes you want to make; and (7) begin to change how you teach (pp. 68-69).

T/S 9 Craft engaging learning tasks.

Even if we have identified powerful learning goals, we still need to figure out what to have students actually *do*. The Student Engagement Techniques (SETs) in Part Three of this book offer a wide variety of ideas drawn from the good-practice literature that help teachers move beyond traditional lecture and discussion. Each technique includes step-by-step procedures as well as examples, variations, and observations and advice. Although the SETs provide the organizing framework, teachers must still do the creative work of designing interesting prompts. See Table 7.1 for examples of prompt stems to help you design engaging tasks.

T/S 10 Incorporate competition appropriately.

Today's students are accustomed to competition. They've competed in sports, video games, and science fairs and observed competition in contests and survivor-style television shows. Structuring competition or competitive elements in activities can add excitement, incentive, and just plain fun to classroom activities. Yet there is considerable debate about the value of competition in increasing motivation. Brophy (2004, pp. 171–172) summarizes the main reasons. First, competition is already built into grading systems, and because participation in classroom activities involves risking public failure, it may be counterproductive. Second, competition distracts students from using their own progress as the benchmark for learning. Third, competition can feel coercive when it is mandatory and the games and rules are imposed by authority figures with high stakes attached to the outcomes. Fourth, competition is only effective if everyone has a good (or at least an equal) chance of winning; however, the range of individual abilities in class makes this virtually impossible if competition is among individuals. Fifth, competition creates losers as well as winners (and usually many more losers than winners), which invariably causes at least temporary embarrassment and, for those who lose consistently, may result in permanent losses in confidence, self-esteem, and enjoyment of school.

Brophy (1987, 2004) and Wlodkowski (2008) offer research-based suggestions for how to structure appropriate competition to take advantage of the benefits while ameliorating the detriments:

1. Make participation in competition a choice;

2. Have the competition team-based rather than individual;

3. Establish conditions that ensure that everyone has a good (or at least an equal) chance to win (this is best achieved in teams that have been carefully balanced by individual ability); and

TABLE 7.1.

Sample Task Prompts

Question Type	Purpose	Example
Exploratory	Probe facts and basic knowledge	What research evidence supports _____?
Challenge	Examine assumptions, conclusions, and interpretations	How else might we account for _____?
Relational	Ask for comparison of themes, ideas, or issues	How does _____ compare to _____?
Diagnostic	Probe motives or causes	Why did _____?
Action question	Call for a conclusion or action	In response to _____, what should _____ do?
Cause and effect	Ask for causal relationships between ideas, actions, or events	If _____ occurred, what would happen?
Extension	Expand the discussion	What are additional ways that _____?
Hypothetical	Pose a change in the facts or issues	Suppose _____ had been the case, would the outcome have been the same?
Priority	Seek to identify the most important issue	From all that we have discussed, what is the most important _____?
Summary	Elicit syntheses	What themes or lessons have emerged from _____?
Problem	Challenge students to find solutions to real or hypothetical situations	What if? (To be motivating, the problem should be one on which students can make some progress on finding a solution, and there should be more than one solution.)
Interpretation	Help students to uncover the underlying meaning of things	From whose viewpoint or perspective are we seeing, hearing, reading? What does this mean? *or* What may have been intended by _____?
Application	Probe for relationships and ask students to connect theory to practice	How does this apply to that? *or* Knowing this, how would you _____?
Evaluative	Require students to assess and make judgments	Which of these are better? Why does it matter? *and* So what?
Critical	Require students to examine the validity of statements, arguments, and conclusions and to analyze their thinking and challenge their own assumptions	How do we know? *and* What's the evidence? *and* How reliable is the evidence?

Source: E. F. Barkley, K. P. Cross, and C. H. Major, *Collaborative Learning Techniques* (San Francisco: Jossey-Bass, 2005), p. 58.

4. Make conscious effort to ensure that the attention is focused on learning goals.

Brophy (1987, pp. 43–44) also notes that competition is more effective for stimulating intensity of effort than for inducing thoughtfulness or quality of performance. It is therefore best used with drills and practice tasks designed to produce mastery of specific skills or where speed of performance or quantity of output is more important than creativity, artistry, or craftsmanship. The bottom line is that competitions can be fun and effective for certain kinds of learning goals, but teachers should take care to minimize individual anxiety and risk of embarrassment.

T/S 11 Expect students to succeed.

Henry Ford, someone who knew a thing or two about success, stated his belief in the power of expectations when he said, "Whether you think you can or think you can't, you are right" (quoted in Cross, 2001, p. 14). Teachers can help support student motivation by expecting students to succeed. Teachers' faith in their students and commitment to actively supporting their efforts contributes strongly to the students' motivation and success. Teachers who believe in their students and expect success are more likely to get it than teachers who doubt their students' ability and are resigned to minimal or mediocre performance.

T/S 12 Help students expect to succeed.

One of the fundamental ways teachers can help students expect to be successful in their course is by ensuring that learning activities and assessment promote success through clear organization, appropriate level of difficulty, scaffolding of complex tasks, communication of standards, and fair grading. Beyond these baseline conditions, an important way to foster students' expectations of success is to help them attribute success to their own persistence and effort. You can help students recognize the link between effort and outcome in many ways (Wlodkowski, 2008, p. 195; Brophy, 2004, p. 386):

1. Model the effort/outcome linkage by talking out loud as you think through tasks. Show that learning takes time and may involve confusion or mistakes, but express confidence that you will eventually succeed if you persist working carefully and thoughtfully, searching for better strategies, or acquiring additional information.

2. Consider sharing with students that differences in success are due largely to differences in experience: students who have had more experience

with a particular task usually have more knowledge about how to do the task well.

3. Explain that even with some subjects such as math, writing, and the arts that are conventionally understood as ability-driven, students can learn strategies and gain the learning necessary to succeed. Reassure students and tell them that in order to gain the experience they need, they must be tolerant of mistakes.

4. Stress the effort-outcome linkage when you provide feedback, acknowledging progress and the accomplishments students have achieved that have resulted from their efforts.

5. Invite former students who started your course without much confidence but ended up being successful to share their tips for success with your current students. If having former students come to class is too difficult logistically, have students write out their tips at the end of the course and provide a collated, synthesized list of tips to students attached to the next term's syllabus.

In short, the best way to lead students to expect success is to structure the course so that they *can* succeed, and then show them throughout the course that if they try hard and persevere even when things are tough, they *will* succeed.

T/S 13 Try to rebuild the confidence of discouraged and disengaged students.

Despite your best efforts to help students expect to succeed, some students will remain convinced they will fail. These students are quick to attribute failure to a lack of ability and jump to the conclusion that they just can't do it. Brophy (2004) includes a whole chapter on rebuilding discouraged students' confidence and willingness to learn (pp. 119–150). He organizes these students into four types (pp. 119–121):

- students with limited ability who truly do have difficulty keeping up and have developed chronically low expectations and numbed acceptance of failure;

- students whose failure attributions or ability beliefs make them susceptible to learned helplessness in failure situations;

- students who are obsessed with self-worth protection and thus focus on performance goals but not learning goals; and

- students who underachieve due to a desire to avoid responsibility.

Strategies to support these different types vary, and teachers who consistently face discouraged students are encouraged to refer to the detailed, type-specific strategies Brophy (2004) provides. Following are some of his recommendations that are generally applicable to students who seem predisposed toward expecting failure.

1. Provide clear directions and structure, including dividing assignments into manageable parts with checkpoints and deadliness (see T/S 42, "Use scaffolding to provide assistance for complex learning," in Chapter 10 for other scaffolding ideas).

2. Emphasize personal causation by allowing students to plan and set goals, make choices, and use self-evaluation procedures to check their progress.

3. Help students establish realistic goals and provide them with encouragement that concentrates on their efforts and calls attention to their successes, guiding them to focus on trying to surpass their own prior achievements rather than competing with classmates.

4. Organize material into modules that allow for students to move at their own pace based on mastery learning principles, but monitor these students frequently and provide supplementary tutoring.

5. Set up "study buddy" systems so that low achievers can collaborate with higher-achieving students.

6. Guide students to tutorial programs or other kinds of campus support programs that can help them develop general college academic and study skills.

7. Help these students better understand themselves as learners—to explore which classroom situations they find comfortable and which provoke anxiety, and why; and to understand when they do or do not need help and become willing to get help when they need it.

8. Emphasize your role as a resource person who assists them in their learning efforts.

9. Finally, combine empathy for these students with determination and confidence that they will meet established learning goals.

Chapter 8

Tips and Strategies for Promoting Active Learning

LEARNING IS A DYNAMIC process that consists of making sense and meaning out of new information and connecting it to what is already known. To learn well and deeply, students need to be active participants in that process. This typically involves doing something—for example, thinking, reading, discussing, problem-solving, or reflecting. Following are tips and strategies culled from the literature that address various elements involved in promoting active learning.

T/S 14 Be clear on your learning goals.

"If you don't know where you are going, how will you know when you get there?" This bumper sticker phrase contains elements of truth for teaching and learning just as it does for travel and life. Acknowledging that sometimes the most rewarding experiences are those that surprise us, in general, when we want to go somewhere, it helps to know what the "where" is. In our courses, we want students to learn, but if we are not clear about what we want them to learn, we can waste a lot of time and energy, or worse, find that students didn't learn what we wanted them to learn after all.

Much has been written about identifying learning goals, and a whole vocabulary has developed with subtle distinctions between terms such as goals, objectives, and student learning outcomes. Consulting the assessment literature will help you through the process. Suggested resources are *A Taxonomy for Learning, Teaching, and Assessing: A Revision of Bloom's Taxonomy of Educational Objectives* (Anderson, Krathwohl, & Bloom, 2001), *Learner-Centered Assessment on College Campuses* (Huba & Freed, 2000), and *Teaching First-Year College Students* (Erickson, Peters, & Strommer, 2006), all of which include whole chapters on writing learning objectives. But in short, effective statements of intended learning outcomes or goals

- are student focused rather than professor focused;

- focus on the learning resulting from an activity rather than on the activity itself;

- focus on important, nontrivial aspects of learning;

- focus on skills and abilities central to the discipline and based on professional standards of excellence;

- are general enough to capture important learning but clear and specific enough to be measurable; and

- focus on aspects of learning that will develop and endure but that can be assessed in some form now (Huba & Freed, 2000, p. 98).

An unknown author said, "In absence of clearly defined goals, we become strangely loyal to performing daily acts of trivia." In the classroom, both teachers and students can waste lots of time and energy doing things that don't result in much learning. Once you are clear on what you want students to learn, you can make better decisions and choices about the kinds of tasks that will best promote active learning.

T/S 15 Clarify your role.

If your goal is to promote active learning, your role in the classroom changes, yet what that role should be is debated in the literature. Some educators contend that instructors should play a minimal role in shaping and directing the work of students. Weimer (2002), for example, stresses, "We must move aside, often and regularly" (p. 74). Others, such as Miller and her colleagues (1996), warn that "a common mistake of teachers in adopting an active learning strategy is to relinquish structure along with control, and the common result is for students to feel frustrated and disoriented" (Miller, Trimbur & Wilkes, p. 17).

How instructors operate in the classroom is influenced by their personal vision and philosophy about teaching and learning as well as the discipline, course objectives, class size, student experience, and unique characteristics of a particular class. Thus, some instructors see themselves as coaches— observing, correcting, and working with students to improve their performance; some prefer the role of facilitator, which implies arranging the learning environment to encourage self-directed learning; some use the term *manager*, emphasizing a sequential process of setting the conditions and managing the process to produce the desired outcomes; still others favor the role of co-learner, emphasizing the social function of constructing knowledge (Cross, 2003, p. 6). Although opinions differ, the literature seems to agree that today's college teacher must be more than a dispenser of information. Regardless of the role you decide to take, clarifying it for yourself helps you to be clear and consistent in your interactions with students.

T/S 16 Orient students to their new roles.

Students have different responsibilities in active learning than they do in traditional education. The primary method for orienting students to these new responsibilities and teaching students active learning skills lies in the learning tasks themselves: students will develop active learning skills if they are given tasks that ask them to apply concepts, solve problems, discuss issues, or reflect upon the factors that influence their thinking. Some students may not know how to make this shift; others may actively resist. Teachers may want to consider taking the time early in the academic term to explain why they have organized the course around active learning principles.

Rather than just explaining this to students, Silberman (2004) recommends starting the very first session with an activity that orients students to active learning. For example, in one of Silberman's suggested activities, the teacher writes the question "What makes teaching active?" on the whiteboard or an overhead and gives students time to think about what an instructor could do to make learning an active experience. As students offer their suggestions, the teacher writes them down. To close the activity, the teacher responds to the list, commenting on how well it does (or does not) correspond to the teacher's concept of active learning. Another activity, titled "Obstacles to Active Learning," is done in groups of 5–6. The teacher distributes an index card to each student and asks them to write one obstacle they foresee or have already experienced about getting other students in a class to be active and to work hard. Then students pass the index cards around their group and each person places a check on any card that expresses an obstacle he or she finds significant. The teacher then identifies the obstacles that received the most votes and responds to them. As an alternative, the teacher can ask students to suggest solutions to obstacles. Following is Silberman's (2004, p. 17) suggestion for a hands-on activity that demonstrates the importance of active learning:

Telling Is Not Teaching

1. Distribute blank sheets of paper to students, and then tell them some version of the following:

   a. "We are going to begin this class with an activity that shows us some important things about the teaching-learning process. Pick up your sheet of paper and hold it in front of you. Now close your eyes and follow the directions I will give you, but don't open your eyes to look."

b. Give the following directions while you do the same with your sheet of paper:

    i. "The first thing I want you to do is to fold your sheet of paper in half."

    ii. "Now tear off the upper right-hand corner."

    iii. "Fold it in half again and tear off the upper left-hand corner of the sheet."

    iv. "Fold it in half again and tear off the lower right-hand corner of the sheet."

c. "Now you can open your eyes, and let's see what you have done. If I did a good job of telling you what to do, and you did a good job of listening, all of our sheets should look the same."

Hold your sheet up for them to see; it is highly unlikely theirs will match yours or those of many of the other students.

2. Observe the differences. If any student's sheet doesn't match yours, ask them why not?

Students will probably respond, "You didn't let us ask questions" or "Your directions could be interpreted in different ways."

3. Tell students what a "poor job" you did as an instructor during this exercise. Not only did you not allow for questions, but you also failed to recognize an important fact about the teaching-learning process: Telling is not teaching. This means that what an instructor says (or does) is not the measure of success; what the learner says (or does) determines success.

4. Consider following up with an activity in which students respond to the following (adapted from Confucius):

When I just hear it, I forget.

When I hear and see it, I remember a little.

When I hear, see, and ask questions about it or discuss it with someone else, I begin to understand.

When I hear, see, discuss, and do it, it allows me to acquire knowledge and skill.

When I teach it to another, I start to master the topic.

T/S 17 Help students develop learning strategies.

Help learners become better able to direct and manage their learning by showing them how to use learning strategies. Learning strategies are devices or behaviors that help us retrieve stored information as well as acquire and integrate new information with existing knowledge. They include, for example, previewing, summarizing, paraphrasing, imaging, creating analogies, note taking, and outlining. Svinicki (2004b) provides a table of learning strategies that illustrates the kinds of strategies or tactics students can use for learning different types of information or skills. As she notes, "Many students have never been exposed to these different ways to approach studying or even to the idea that there are different ways to study." Table 8.1 is an excerpt from the table that Svinicki provides students in her classes.

Learning strategies are best incorporated into content-based learning activities, but an explanation (such as Table 8.1) might also be provided in handouts. For example, Weimer (2002) includes as appendices a collection of handouts about various learning strategies that could be attached to the syllabus; examples include "Notetaking Types and Characteristics to Help Students Succeed" and "Successful Students: Guidelines and Thoughts for Academic Success."

T/S 18 Activate prior learning.

Because active learning requires students to integrate new information or ideas into what they already know, it is helpful to have students participate in activities that activate prior knowledge. Some ideas for helping students discover what they already know about a given topic include:

- writing brief essays to describe what they remember and understand,
- interviewing each other,
- participating in a Think-Pair-Share that requires them to respond to prompts designed to elicit prior knowledge, and
- using graphic organizers (generating concept maps, filling in tables that include blank cells, and so forth) to stimulate recall of prior learning.

See also SET 1, "Background Knowledge Probe," in Chapter 12 for a structured activity to activate prior learning.

T/S 19 Teach in ways that promote effective transfer.

Active learners connect new ideas and information to already known concepts and principles as well as apply already known concepts and principles

TABLE 8.1.

Learning Strategies

To learn at this level:	The general strategy is based on:	Here is a sample strategy:	Comments
Basic definitions	Rehearsing	Use flash cards or anything that allows you to practice pairing a term with its definition.	These strategies help encode information into long-term memory.
	Organizing	Group similar words to make it easier to make connections among them. Identify examples and non-examples.	
Structural knowledge—how concepts go together	Recognizing key concepts	Pull out all the text headings and put them in outline format.	These strategies organize the concepts in terms of their relationships to other concepts.
	Recognizing relationships among key ideas.	Draw a concept map that shows what ideas are connected and how.	
Application of concepts to problems	Developing process steps	Write down the details of how the instructor or text uses examples to illustrate concepts. Then look for common steps or characteristics. Try your steps with a new example.	The strategies here create a repertoire of examples or mental models in which the concepts have been used. These can form the basis of case-based reasoning (using familiar cases to solve problems).
		For each example figure out why the procedure was used and what steps were taken.	This strategy has the learner figure out the steps for applying the concepts.
Analysis of problem situations	Looking for relationships	Use the transition words or other text markers to identify important components or relationships.	These strategies are designed to help the learner see the components of a situation more clearly and break the problem down into manageable chunks.
	Visually representing the problem	Use a comparative organizer to contrast assumptions, ideas, and evidence.	

Source: M. D. Svinicki, *Learning and Motivation in the Postsecondary Classroom* (Bolton, MA: Anker, 2004), excerpted from Table 6.1, pp. 125–127. Reprinted with permission of John Wiley and Sons, Inc.

to new situations. This involves a process known as *transfer*, which is the effect that past learning has on the processing and acquisition of new learning and the degree to which learners can apply what they have learned to new situations. Transfer is important both within a course or series of courses in an academic discipline (teachers strive for a cumulative effect as students keep building upon their skills or deepening their understanding) and between unrelated courses (for example, applying the writing skills learned in English classes to other courses). Research, unfortunately, has demonstrated that students are often not successful either in accurately connecting new material to existing understanding or in recognizing how what they learned can apply to new situations, suggesting that teachers need to be more intentional about helping students make connections between past learning and new learning. The following suggestions from Sousa (2006, p. 155) and Svinicki (2004b, p. 106) can help promote positive transfer:

1. When teaching similar concepts, highlight the differences up front by identifying and teaching them first or incorporating learning activities that require students to identify critical distinguishing attributes.

2. Use a variety of strategies to help students make associations. Metaphors, analogies, symbols, and images, for example, can help students understand and recall concepts or principles that you want them to transfer to a new learning situation.

3. Teach students how to recognize when to use a strategy at the same time you are teaching them that strategy. Additionally, teach a skill just before students will have the real opportunity to use it.

4. Make sure students have learned the task well enough to transfer it. Asking students to state the principles that have been learned and are being transferred can serve as a bridge between learning and practice.

5. In the early stages of the transfer process, make sure the learning situation is similar to the situation in which the material or skill will actually be used. Incorporate more variation later in the learning process to prepare students for variations in the real world.

T/S 20 Teach for retention.

Once students have learned material, teachers want them to be able to remember it. Because the ability to store, retain, and subsequently retrieve information is so fundamental to learning, "Remembering" is now the first level in the revision of Bloom's taxonomy of educational objectives (Anderson, Krathwohl, & Bloom, 2001). Three components help ensure that new learning is moved from short-term memory to long-term memory:

1. **Emotional connection**: If a student can make an emotional connection to the information, it is more likely to be stored permanently. Teachers can help students care about what they are learning by foregrounding the human dimension that underlies content. For example, rather than just having students read about an event, use images, films, and oral histories that convey the impact of the event on people's lives.

2. **Sense**: How well information makes sense and fits with what the student already knows also affects retention. Teachers can help students make sense of what they are learning by organizing learning into thematic units; crafting assignments that prompt students to identify the commonalities among diverse topics; asking students to brainstorm ways new learning can be applied in other situations; and asking students to create an analogy that illustrates similarities or differences between related topics.

3. **Meaning**: There needs to be a reason for the brain to remember information, and it is better if this reason extends beyond just being able to pass a test. Teachers can help students find meaning and personal relevance in a new topic by asking them to connect what they are learning to their past, to what is going on presently in the world around them, or to the professional or civic responsibilities they may have in the future.

Even if a student seems to have learned material, there is no guarantee it will be remembered in such a way that it can be located, identified, and retrieved accurately in the future. A critical factor in retention is adequate time to process and reprocess information so that it can be transferred from short- to long-term memory. This usually occurs during deep sleep. Research on retention shows that if a student can remember the information after twenty-four hours, there is a higher likelihood that it is in long-term storage; if a student cannot remember the information after that period, it will most likely not be retained. One way to help both yourself and your students assess for long-term retention is with pop quizzes for which students cannot prepare. If these quizzes are not graded but rather are administered only as part of a supportive, formative assessment process to show both students and teachers what is being stored in long-term memory, they can be effective ways to monitor retention.

T/S 21 Limit and chunk information.

Research has determined that the average adult's working memory can handle between five and nine items of information at once. Additionally, the average adult can process an item for ten to twenty minutes before mental fatigue or boredom occurs and attention drifts (Sousa, 2006, pp. 45–47). The implications for teachers who are presenting new material are (1) to limit topics or items to about seven; (2) where possible, to chunk smaller and similar components together; and (3) to break up presentations into sections interspersed with other kinds of activities such as discussion or writing.

T/S 22 Provide opportunities for guided practice and rehearsal.

Rehearsal reinforces learning and increases retention. Two major factors affect the quality of rehearsal: the amount of time and the type of rehearsal activity. In terms of time, there is an initial period in which the information first enters short-term memory. If the learner cannot attach sense or meaning to the new information, then it will most likely be lost. Providing sufficient time for a learner to review the information, make sense of it, and assign value and relevance increases the probability that the learning will be retained in long-term storage (Sousa, 2006, pp. 86–87). There are two types of rehearsal activity:

1. **Rote rehearsal** is used to remember and store information in the same form that it entered working memory, such as in memorizing a poem or the precise steps of a procedure. We can help students by teaching them strategies to remember lists, facts, and definitions such as mnemonic devices to associate abstract ideas with concrete objects, or number memory techniques or link systems (described, for example, in Bautista, 2000).

2. **Elaborative rehearsal** helps the learner process the information so that it is more meaningful. It takes more time but results in deeper learning. Elaboration strategies include forming associations, organizing information into categories, outlining, clustering concepts into taxonomic categories with shared characteristics, paraphrasing, summarizing, creating analogies, and self-quizzing.

It is important to make sure that practice and rehearsal are reinforcing information or skills correctly. As Sousa (2006, p. 97) points out, "practice does not make perfect, practice makes permanent." Therefore, monitor rehearsal carefully at first and give prompt, specific, corrective feedback to ensure the learning is correct.

T/S 23 Organize lectures in ways that promote active learning.

The *primacy-recency* (or serial position) *effect* is our tendency to remember best what comes first, second best what comes last, and least that which is in the middle. Although documentation of this effect dates to research as far back as the 1880s, more recent studies indicate why: The first items of new information command our attention because they are within the working memory's functional capacity. As time goes on and more information is added, the capacity of working memory is exceeded and the information is lost. Toward the end of the learning episode, the initial items in working memory have been processed to allow the brain to turn its attention to the arriving information. Sousa (2006, pp. 92–93) explains that retention during a learning episode is highest in a bi-modal distribution at the beginning (Prime-Time 1) and end (Prime-Time 2) and least during the middle (Down-Time; see Figure 8.1). Retention is also influenced by the length of the teaching episode.

Unfortunately, teachers often use Prime-Time 1 for relatively unimportant information processing such as monitoring attendance, distributing graded assignments, collecting homework, and so forth. By the time they get to presenting new, important information, students are already in their "down-time."

FIGURE 8.1.

Approximate Ratio of Prime-Time to Down-Time during Learning Episode

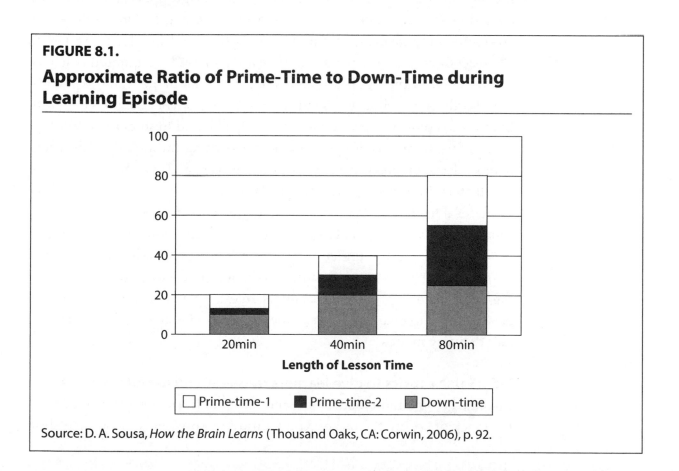

Source: D. A. Sousa, *How the Brain Learns* (Thousand Oaks, CA: Corwin, 2006), p. 92.

Limited attention spans combined with the primacy-recency effect suggest that it is generally most productive to divide class time into short segments of about twenty minutes, introducing new material at the beginning, then giving students opportunity to process the new learning, and moving on to closure activities toward the end. Organizing class time in this way significantly reduces the proportion of down-time. Although an obvious activity is to have students apply what they just heard in lecture, it is also useful to give students a brief break. Telling a story or a joke, playing some music, allowing students to talk off-task with their neighbors or even get up and stretch or walk around the room can reenergize students so that they can focus again during the next twenty-minute learning segment (Sousa, 2006, pp. 92–93). As a side note, Wilson and Korn (2007, p. 88) reviewed the research on student attention during lectures and conclude that it is clear that students' attention varies, but they recommend more controlled research if this assertion is going to be presented as empirically based.

T/S 24 Use reverse or inverted classroom organization.

Organizing curriculum according to the reversed or inverted classroom model (in which face-to-face class meetings are used to follow up on assignments done out of class either individually or as groups) can ensure that class time is used for effective active learning strategies. One of the early strategies emphasizing this approach is Just in Time Teaching (JiTT, 1999–2006). In JiTT, students complete a Web-based assignment (such as responding to a prompt based on reading a chapter in the textbook) that is due shortly before class. The instructor reads the students' submissions "just in time" to adjust the face-to-face session to respond to student needs. The face-to-face session is designed for active learning through mini-lectures, demos, classroom discussion, worksheet exercises, and even hands-on mini-labs that are informed by the instructor's analysis of student responses. This provides a feedback loop in which students' outside-of-class preparation fundamentally affects what happens during the subsequent in-class time.

This principle also underlies *blended delivery*, defined by Garrison and Vaughan (2008) as "the thoughtful fusion of face-to-face and online learning experiences" (p. 5). Table 8.2 offers an example of how a course might be structured to take advantage of the attributes of both online and face-to-face delivery modes.

T/S 25 Use rubrics to give learners frequent and useful feedback.

Imagine being blindfolded, alone, and trying to learn archery. Without the feedback of seeing the target, you would not know how close each shot

TABLE 8.2.

A Cycle of Tasks Blending Face-to-Face with Online Tools

Nature of Inquiry	Learning Activities	Use of Online Tools
Before a Face-to-Face Session		
Create a triggering event	Prereading assignment or activity on a specified topic or issue	Announcements tool
Determine learner's prior knowledge or experience with the topic or issue	Self-assessment quiz, survey, or discussion forum	Tests, surveys, discussion forums tools
During a Face-to-Face Session		
Respond to results	Instructor mini-lecture and/or tutorial to address results of quiz/survey	Display quiz or survey results
Explore the questions	Dialogue with teacher and fellow learners through whole-class or small-group discussion	Overheads or presentation software to project prompt or displays of support information
After a Face-to-Face Session		
Follow-up classroom assessment	Muddiest point (What are you still unclear about?) or one-minute paper (What did you learn from the class session?)	Survey tools or discussion forums
Further exploration and integration	Dialogue with fellow learners or additional reading/writing	Discussion forums or assignment tools
Tentative integration and initial phases of connecting theory to practice	Individual or group project work	Discussion forums, assignment tools
The Next Face-to-Face Session		
Resolution/application	Talking/listening/writing through review of online discussions, individual or group presentations	Display quiz or survey results
Introduction of next triggering event	Initiation of dialogue on the next topic or issue	Overheads or presentation software to project prompt or displays of support information

Source: Adapted from D. R. Garrison and N. D. Vaughn, *Blended Learning in Higher Education* (San Francisco: Jossey-Bass, 2008), pp. 113–127.

came to hitting the bull's eye. In fact, you'd probably have only a vague sense whether you hit the target at all. One of a teacher's most important responsibilities is giving learners feedback. Learners need to know what they are doing right and what they are doing wrong so that they can adjust their efforts and improve. Most teachers know this, but the time and effort it takes to provide timely, effective feedback can be a major obstacle, especially in courses with large numbers of students.

Rubrics are an effective solution. They are used today to explicate and grade a wide range of learning tasks, from standard written assignments such as essays and research papers to discussion participation, group work, oral presentations, laboratory reports, Web-page design, projects, and portfolios.

It takes time and effort to create an effective rubric, but once done, it saves time and effort (Stevens & Levi [2005, p. 18] say by 50 percent). Here are some of the benefits of rubrics for teachers:

1. Teachers are able to offer more complex, challenging assignments because they can present multiple components in a clear, organized manner, thus saving time and effort explaining assignments and clarifying expectations.

2. Grading can be more consistent and equitable (for example, between the first and last student's assignments the instructor is grading, or when work is graded by team teachers or teaching assistants).

3. The anguish of grading is reduced, because performance standards are clearly spelled out, and either the student's work meets the explicit criteria, or it doesn't.

4. Less time is needed to grade assignments and to justify or explain the grade to students who contest their grade.

5. Core learning goals and performance expectations can be reinforced when rubrics are used for multiple assignments.

6. Rubrics help teachers of the same course, sequenced courses, or similar assignments within a department or program communicate with each other about departmental or institutional standards, criteria, and assessment.

Rubrics have become such a popular assessment tool that Stevens and Levi (2005) introduce their book on rubrics in higher education with the comment that "professors like us who use rubrics often consider them the most effective grading devices since the invention of red ink" (p. 3). Students need feedback and instructors need to grade. Rubrics can meet both needs in an effective and efficient manner, providing the substantive, meaningful "educative" feedback that can help ensure students are on track and working in their optimal challenge zone.

Rubrics range in complexity, but Stevens and Levi (2005) identify four basic elements:

1. task description,

2. components of the task,

3. descriptions of the range of performance for each component, and

4. a scale (such as excellent/competent/needs work) to rate how well or poorly any given task has been performed.

Exhibit 8.1 is an adaptation of an excerpt from a comprehensive rubric for a presentation assignment in Stevens and Levi (2005, p. 91). It is provided as an example of how a rubric could clarify assignment expectations and provide extensive, personalized feedback to students while reducing the amount of time the instructor has to spend grading.

EXHIBIT 8.1.

Grading Rubric: Interculturalism in Contemporary Asian Performing Arts

Task Description: Each student will make a 5-minute presentation analyzing a contemporary artistic work from the field of theatre, dance, or music, identifying the various ethnic influences and addressing issues of interculturalism, such as cultural and political contexts, questions of identity, interethnic power relations, and notions of displacement. The presentation should include appropriate audio or film clips, photographs, maps, graphs, and other visual aids for the audience.

STUDENT'S NAME:_____

	Excellent	**Competent**	**Needs Work**
Knowledge/ Understanding (20%)	☐ The presentation demonstrates a depth of understanding by using relevant and accurate detail to support the student's thesis.	☐ The presentation uses knowledge that is generally accurate with only minor inaccuracies and information is generally relevant to the student's thesis.	☐ The presentation uses little relevant or accurate information. ☐ Little or no research is apparent.

Continued

EXHIBIT 8.1.

Grading Rubric: Interculturalism in Contemporary Asian Performing Arts (Continued)

	Excellent	Competent	Needs Work
	☐ Research is thorough and goes beyond what was presented in class or in the assigned texts.	☐ Research is adequate but does not go much beyond what was presented in class or in the assigned text.	
Actual points _____	**15–20 points**	**6–14 points**	**0–5 points**
Thinking/Inquiry (30%)	☐ The presentation is centered around a thesis that shows a highly developed awareness of artistic, cultural, or social issues and a high level of conceptual ability.	☐ The presentation shows an analytical structure and a central thesis, but the analysis is not always fully developed or linked to the thesis.	☐ The presentation shows little or no analytical structure and under-developed or no central thesis.
Actual points _____	**25–30 points**	**11–24 points**	**0–10 points**
Communication (20%)	☐ The presentation is imaginative and effective in conveying ideas to the audience. ☐ The presenter responds effectively to audience reactions and questions.	☐ Presentation techniques used are effective in conveying main ideas, but they are a bit unimaginative. ☐ Some questions from the audience remain unanswered.	☐ The presentation fails to capture the interest of the audience. ☐ The presentation is confusing in what it attempts to communicate.
Actual points _____	**15–20 points**	**6–14 points**	**0–5 points**
Use of Audio/Visual Aids (20%)	☐ The presentation includes appropriate and easily understood audio/visual aids, which the presenter refers to and explains at appropriate	☐ The presentation includes appropriate audio/visual aids, but they are too few; they are in a format that makes them difficult to	☐ The presentation includes no audio/visual aids or includes aids that are inappropriate or too small/short or too messy/complex to be understood, or the presenter makes no

	moments in the presentation.	use or understand; or the presenter does not refer to or explain them in the presentation.	mention of them in the presentation.
Actual points _____	**15–20 points**	**6–14 points**	**0–5 points**
Presentation Skills (10%)	☐ The presenter speaks clearly and loudly enough to be heard, using eye contact, a lively tone, gestures, and body language to engage the audience.	☐ The presenter speaks clearly and loudly enough to be heard but tends to drone or fails to use eye contact, gestures, and body language consistently or effectively at times.	☐ The presenter cannot be heard or speaks so unclearly that she or he cannot be understood. There are insufficient attempts to engage the audience through eye contact, gestures, or body language.
TOTAL Points _____	**8–10 Points**	**4–7 Points**	**0–3 Points**

Comments:

There are many variations to this example, and readers are encouraged to go to one of the excellent sources available on creating and using rubrics for in-depth discussion, directions, and models (for example, Stevens & Levi, 2005; Walvoord & Anderson, 1998; Wiggins, 1998). In addition, Rubistar, a free online tool, guides teachers through the process of creating quality rubrics: http://rubistar.4teachers.org/index.php.

Chapter 9

Tips and Strategies for Building Community

HUMANS HAVE A basic need to be part of a social community. Students will engage more in classroom-based learning if they feel that they are welcomed, valuable, contributing members of a learning community. Following are tips and strategies for creating conditions that build a sense of community in the classroom.

T/S 26 Move away from an authoritarian role.

In a true learning community, teachers and students are partners in the learning process. This requires a fundamental shift in the traditional balance of power between teachers and students. To emphasize how thoroughly teachers hold most of the power in traditional classrooms, Weimer (2002, p. 24) suggests teachers try to answer honestly such questions as, Who controls the pace at which content is covered (the calendar)? and Who controls and regulates the flow of communication, deciding who gets the opportunity to speak, when, and for how long? Most of us would answer "I do" to every one of her questions. Weimer's book *Learner-Centered Teaching* (2002) offers a wealth of insight and advice on how to shift to the shared power that characterizes a community of learners. The steps needed to make this shift go far beyond a single strategy or even cluster of strategies, and if you have become quite accustomed to a teacher-centered approach, making the required changes is difficult. For a clearer sense of what "learner-centered teaching" means, read Weimer's (2002) book, or Blumberg's (2009) guide to implementing Weimer's model, or books by authors with similar views (for example, Cranton, 2006).

Even if you are not prepared to completely transform the way you interact in the classroom, even small changes can communicate to students that you want to promote a sense of community. For example, in your course syllabus you could include a statement that explains your teaching philosophy and conveys that you view yourself and your students as members of a learning community. Try to minimize harsh, directive language. Singham (2005) discusses the authoritarian tone of many of today's course syllabi—"You will submit three projects" and "Students bear sole responsibility for ensuring that papers submitted electronically are received in a timely manner." About his own institution's faculty handbook, he notes, "the sections that deal with course syllabi are formal and defensive, as if a committee had looked at all the possible things that could go wrong and all the possible laws that might apply, and then had devised rules to prevent disaster" (Singham, 2005). A shift in tone, as well as including information that explicitly communicates your attitude about students, can make a huge difference in how students engage in your course.

T/S 27 Promote class civility.

Many teachers are increasingly concerned about student incivility in the classroom. Behaviors ranging from lack of consideration and respect to overt hostility and aggression undermine the sense of community and seriously disrupt the learning environment. Following are some strategies that may help you prevent or manage incivility:

1. Prepare a statement to include in the syllabus that clarifies expectations for behavior and lists what you find acceptable or unacceptable. ("Respect for the opinions of others is an essential characteristic for a learning community. Although it is likely you may not agree with everything that is said or discussed in this course, you are expected to behave and to express your viewpoints in a manner that is courteous and respectful. Please adhere to the same rules and expectations when you communicate online.")

2. Early in the term, elicit student help in creating a classroom civility policy that includes both expectations and consequences for unacceptable behavior.

3. Reduce student anonymity so that students are accountable for their behavior.

4. Establish a method for students to air grievances, such as designating a student ombudsman or using SET 42, "Critical Incident Questionnaire," in Chapter 10.

5. Confront problems when they arise.

6. Document incidences, and if the behavior is particularly egregious, ask other students who witnessed the event to write down their observations of what happened.

7. Know your institution's policies and procedures for addressing disruptive student behavior.

An online search using keywords such as "classroom civility" will provide examples of many institutions' policies and recommendations for managing incivility. Sorcinelli (2002) is a useful source for discussion of civility issues in large classes. Drawing from her own experiences teaching a large, lower-division lecture class, she talks about the erosion of classroom decorum that she and others started noticing in the early 1990s, defines what constitutes uncivil behaviors in large classes, offers reasons for why they occur, and suggests strategies such as decreasing anonymity and encouraging active learning for creating a constructive large-class environment.

T/S 28 Create a physical or online course environment that supports community.

Although few college teachers are in complete control of the physical aspects of their classroom, most teach in rooms that are designated for a particular discipline or discipline cluster. Consider underscoring shared academic interests by posting discipline-related art or posters on the walls. Try to have your courses scheduled in rooms with moveable chairs, desks, or tables. Their flexibility allows for arrangement in a circle or U-shape for whole-class work as well as various configurations for group work. These seating arrangements are more conducive to promoting a sense of community than fixed seats in rows.

In online classes, create an area for students to communicate with each other in ways not necessarily limited to course content. This could be as simple as setting up a discussion forum titled "Student Lounge."

T/S 29 Reduce anonymity: Learn students' names and help students learn each other's names.

Few students will engage deeply in a course in which they feel like their presence is neither noticed nor needed. One of the first steps toward building a learning community is being able to address students by name. Here are some strategies for learning student names. Several have the added advantage of going beyond just learning names to learning more about each student's background, aspirations, and interests.

- **Photo roster/seating chart**: Work with your institution's Student ID Office to create a photo roster and seating chart. Robert Smallwood (personal communication, December 15, 2008) describes the basic steps:

  1. Send a list of student ID numbers to the Student ID Office and ask the office to send you a jpeg file of the pictures that were taken when the students had their IDs made.

  2. At the first class meeting, inform students that you will be making a photo roster/seating chart based on where students sit at the second class meeting. (Create the seating chart using the Table option in Microsoft Word with columns/rows corresponding to the desk layout in the classroom.)

  3. Cut and paste each student's picture into the appropriate cell in the table.

  Smallwood notes that the University of Texas at Austin's photo roster process can be viewed at http://www.utexas.edu/student/registrar/classroster/roster.about.html#PR.

- **Name tents**: Cut 8½ × 11 inch card stock paper in half. Distribute the paper and markers. Ask students to fold the paper lengthwise to form a tent, and then print their first name in block letters on one side and their last name on the other. Students place their name tent at the front of their desk. Either collect the tents and have them available for pickup each class session, or tell students they must be responsible for bringing their name tent to each class. (Since a few students invariably forget, have materials available at subsequent class sessions so they can construct another.)

- **Group photographs**: Ask students to gather in groups of 4–6 for a photograph, make prints, and circulate the photographs with a fine-tip marker so that students can write their first name underneath their picture on the front and their full name on the back. This is particularly effective if students have already been formed into teams.

- **Video introductions**: Have students fill out basic information on an index card, then line up, submit their card, and introduce themselves while being videotaped. This has the added value of being visually memorable and allowing you to hear the correct pronunciation of their name.

- **Student info cards**: Ask students to attach a passport size photo to an index card and add identification info (such as e-mail address, telephone number, academic major, other courses taken in the discipline, career goals, and hobbies). You might also ask students to write a short paragraph on the back that can serve as a writing fingerprint to help you assess their language ability. Cards can be kept in a small file and used as flash cards until you learn the names. You can refer to the cards before meeting with students in order to refresh your memory. Instead of index cards, you can use a word-processing or publishing program to create a template of six cards on 8½ × 11-inch card stock.

Just as it is important for you to learn students' names, it is also important for students to learn each other's names. Below are ideas to help accomplish this.

- **Name game:** Students and teacher form a circle and (1) introduce themselves and then (2) recall and repeat names of those who have already introduced themselves. Some instructors vary this by asking students to add an alliterative adjective or descriptive comment. If some students have auditory processing difficulties or if many of the names are foreign, it is helpful to have students write their name on a card and show it as they introduce themselves. To reduce stress, encourage the group to help struggling students. Consider closing with the entire group saying all names together. If the class contains more than thirty students, form two or more circles, then repeat the process over subsequent days until everyone feels comfortable knowing all names.

- **Online self-introductions**: Ask students to write a brief paragraph introducing themselves to the rest of the class and post this on a designated forum thread. If the software allows, consider asking students to post their photograph or to select an appropriate avatar. To ensure that students take the time to read all the introductions, create a quiz or point-generating assignment based on details you have gleaned from the students' intros (for example, Who in the class moved here last year from Indonesia?).

- **Interviews and introductions:** Generate (or ask students to generate) a list of questions for students to ask each other (for example, What is your academic major? Why are you taking this course?). Ask students to find a partner and interview each other. Consider asking pairs to introduce each other to one or more other pairs, building in a snowball fashion. Alternatively, ask pairs to introduce each other to the whole class. If the class is large, ask 3–5 students to each introduce a peer to the class at the beginning of each class session until you have gone through the whole roster.

- **Academic "speed dating"**: Students move at a brisk clip through several face-to-face conversations with their peers, each conversation anchored by a prompt provided by the teacher and posted on a presentation slide. A buzzer is set for 2–3 minutes, and when it goes off, students must quickly find another partner with whom to participate in a brief conversation responding to the prompt. To use this activity on the first day, create prompts that focus on the syllabus such as "What is the purpose of the assignment on page 8?" as well as lighthearted prompts such as "Describe the most unusual or fun job you have held" (Eifler, 2008).

T/S 30 Use icebreakers to warm up the class.

Most students come to the first class feeling some level of anxiety, and studies show that two of their greatest concerns are whether they will like the teacher and how well they will get along with their fellow students (Provitera-McGlynn, 2001). The first days of the academic term set the tone for the remaining weeks of the semester, so it is essential that teachers make efforts to foster a sense of community right from the start. To foster development of a learning community, consider allocating at least a portion of the time for students to interact with each other. While many of the SETs in Part Three are designed to structure purposeful, learning-based student interaction, it may still be helpful to provide icebreaker activities early in the term to break down social barriers and help students feel comfortable.

Social Icebreakers

Social icebreakers use general and personal information to help students get to know each other. Although many students find social icebreakers fun, some may feel uncomfortable about sharing personal information. Give students the choice to not respond to a particular question and substitute another, or consider using the course content or policy/procedure icebreakers that follow the list here.

- **"What's in a Name?"**: Ask students to interview each other about the importance of their name, asking questions such as, Who named you? How was the decision for your name made? Are you named after someone? Do you like your name? Are there cultural reasons for your first and middle name? (Provitera-McGlynn, 2001).

- **"The Company You Share"** (aka "Stand Up/Sit Down"): Create a list of different categories of people, such as people who love chocolate, have brown eyes, are fluent in a language other than English, have moved here from a different country, have a close friend who is (or you yourself are) Hispanic American (Asian American, Arab American . . .) and so forth. As you read through the categories, have students form groups in different parts of the classroom (groups form and reform), or simply ask students to stand up and look around to see others who share that characteristic (adapted from Provitera-McGlynn, 2001).

- **"Preference Lists"**: Give students fifteen minutes to write down all the things they most enjoy doing and then identify each one as A (activity done alone), OP (activity done with other people), N5 (new activity they weren't doing five years ago), and $ (activity that costs money). Form groups or dyads and have students discuss what they learned about themselves. Particular attention can be given to gender and cultural differences and how they match or counter stereotypes (Brookfield & Preskill, 2005).

- **"Standpoint Statements"**: Ask students to write down five demographic facts that define who they are (such as ethnic heritage, gender, age, place of birth, and academic major or stage of education). They then write how these factors have shaped their standpoint—their view of life and the identity they present to the world. Next, ask them to assess the importance of these demographic facts. Finally, have them discuss their findings with partners or in small groups and look for commonalities and differences (Brookfield & Preskill, 2005).

- **"Revolving Circles"**: Ask students to pair up and one choose A and the other choose B. Have the A students form a circle with their backs toward the center of the circle, and have the B students form an outer circle facing the inner circle. Then give each student a handout with numbered prompts (such as "I chose my academic major because . . ." "If I could travel anywhere in the world I would go to . . . " or "I like or hate technology because . . ."). Call out a number and ask facing students to share their responses to the prompt. After a few minutes, call "time," ask students to move one person to their right, and then call out the number for a new prompt. If the classroom does not have sufficient space to form the circles, have students form two rows of equal numbers and stand facing each other, or form various sets of rows throughout the room, with the student at the end going to the opposite end of the line or joining a new line when time is up (About.com: Continuing Education, n.d.).

Sample prompts for icebreakers:

I chose my academic major because . . .

I enrolled in this class because . . .

My favorite movie is . . .

My favorite musician (or type of music) is . . .

If I could travel anywhere in the world I would go to . . .

My favorite food is . . .

The thing that makes me happiest is . . .

My family . . .

The most important thing in my life is . . .

To have fun, I . . .

I like or hate technology because . . .

I have or would like to have a pet . . .

If I could do anything I wanted, I would . . .

My dream car is a . . .

If I could say whatever I wanted to past (or future) generations, I'd say . . .

My favorite actor or actress is . . .

My best piece of advice to fellow (or future) students is . . .

My dream job is . . .

In ten years, I plan to be . . .

If I were a millionaire, I would . . .

The craziest thing I ever did was . . .

- **"Over the Rainbow":** Create an overhead transparency explaining a color key such as the one in Table 9.1. Ask students to circulate around the room, finding new partners to quickly share responses as you announce different colors.

Course Content Icebreakers

Subject matter, rather than personal information, can be used to foster a sense of community. Prompts and activities that focus on course content can help students identify and share prior knowledge, clarify learning gaps, give reassurance that others are at a similar starting place, and pique interest in what they will be learning. The following techniques are useful for this purpose.

- **"Common Sense Inventory":** Create a list of 5–15 interesting true-or-false statements related to the discipline or course. Ask students to form

TABLE 9.1.

Rainbow Color Key

Color	Meaning	Question
Red	Stop	What is one behavior or thing you wish the teacher or other students would not do?
Orange	Motivation	What motivates you to do your best in a course?
Yellow	Commitment	Describe a learning experience (within or outside of an educational setting) to which you gave your all.
Green	Money	What do you plan to do for your career?
Blue	Possibilities	The sky's the limit—what are your dreams and hopes for your future?
Purple	Royalty	If you were ruler of the universe (or president of the college or teacher of this class), what is the first thing you would do?

Source: Adapted from About.com: Continuing Education, *Ice Breakers*, http://adulted.about.com/od/icebreakers

pairs or small groups, and then discuss, decide, and mark which statements are true or false. Follow up by projecting a blank matrix on an overhead and asking groups to report out and explain their decisions. Record responses by placing tally marks in the T/F columns. After discussion of each statement or at the end of the activity, either give the correct response(s) or generate suspense by telling students they will learn the answers as the course unfolds (Nilson, 2003).

- **"Problem Posting"**: Have students form pairs or small groups, and ask them to identify problems (or topics, questions, issues, or information) that they think the course should address. Then ask students to report out, using their responses to reinforce or clarify course goals and content. If students suggest topics that you had not planned on covering but you consider appropriate, augment planned course content to include modules or activities on student-generated ideas (McKeachie, Hofer et al., 2002).

"Course Concept Mapping": Select a key word from the course title or identify a concept that is central to the course, such as How do we learn about the past? (for history) or What is music? (for music appreciation). Organize students into groups of 4–6 and ask them to generate word associations or related ideas as they draw a concept map. In a follow-up whole class discussion, ask team spokespeople to show and explain their maps, and use these reports as the basis for explaining the purpose or organization of the course (Davis, 1993).

Course Policies and Procedures Icebreakers

Developing shared understandings of course policies and procedures is another important element for promoting a learning community. The following ideas for activities can help students feel part of a community as they learn important course information and establish group norms.

- **Syllabus review**: Form groups of 4–6, identify a recorder, and ask students to generate a list of questions about the course. Pass out the syllabus, and ask students to read it to find the answers to their questions. Ask them to note any course information about which they had not thought to ask as well as questions for which they could not find the answers. Close with a whole class discussion on the syllabus based on students' unanswered questions and their discoveries about the course.

  As a variation, create a quiz with common questions regarding the course (such as How do I get an A? What is the first deadline? What is the make-up policy?) and distribute these questions to small groups along with the syllabus. Have the student groups find the answers in the syllabus (Millis & Cottell, 1998).

- **Establishing group ground rules**: If you are planning to use group work throughout your course, establishing group ground rules early in the course can help prevent problems and improve group functioning. Involving students in determining policies encourages buy-in and can help them to accept basic responsibility for observing and enforcing the rules. Create a grid with two columns, labeled "Helpful" and "Not Helpful." Form groups of 4–6 students and ask one person to serve as recorder. Ask students to take turns identifying behaviors that will be helpful or not helpful to the group, with the recorder writing down responses in the appropriate column. Using the completed grid, either ask groups to develop a list of ground rules for group behavior or ask groups to report out in a whole class discussion, using their ideas to create a class list of ground rules. Consider developing a completed grid in advance to ensure all productive and nonproductive behaviors have been identified. As a variation, provide a list of ground rules and ask students to select from the list those they think are most important.

- **Group learning contract**: A Group Learning Contract that outlines policies, procedures, and penalties regarding group work may be useful. The contract can be drawn up by either the teacher or the student, and can serve as a formal record, adding emphasis and legitimacy to the ground rules. It may be helpful to provide students with a sample form to use as a model (Knowles, 1986; see Exhibit 9.1).

EXHIBIT 9.1.

Group Learning Contract

For the next several class periods, I will be participating in a group to learn:

I am committed to participating effectively in this group learning activity and will strive to do the following: [Students supply their agreed-upon ground rules, such as the following examples.]

____ Come to class regularly and on time

____ Come prepared and ready to share in my group

____ Listen actively to what others have to contribute

____ Be supportive of the efforts and initiatives of others

If I do not follow these rules, I will do the following to compensate: [Students supply their own ideas or penalties.]

____ **If I miss a class,** I agree to ask a group member ahead of time to take notes for me. If it is an unintended and unavoidable absence, I will get the notes from a group member and make up any group work I missed.

____ **If I am unable to prepare for a class/group assignment,** I will make up for and do an additional proportional share of the work on the next assignment.

____ **If I notice or if someone points out that I am not listening,** I will stop what I am doing and immediately give my full attention to whoever is speaking.

____ **If someone notices that I am too critical or am otherwise unsupportive,** I will make efforts to watch my words and interactions in the future.

Signed _____   Date_____

_____

Source: M. S. Knowles, *Using Learning Contracts* (San Francisco: Jossey-Bass, 1986). Reprinted with permission of John Wiley and Sons, Inc.

T/S 31 Use technology to extend or reinforce community.

Technology offers a powerful array of tools to help promote classroom community. Even before the academic term begins, teachers can start setting up conditions that will foster a sense of community. If you have access to student e-mails prior to the term, consider sending a welcome letter in which you introduce yourself, tell students your hopes for the class, and invite students to come by and talk to you during office hours. You might also include questions for students, such as why are they taking the course, what their academic and career goals are, and whether they anticipate any particular challenges in the course; ask them to write you a letter with their answers that they will submit the first day of the term. (Hopkins, 2000).

On the first day of class, students can be asked to share e-mail addresses or cell phone numbers to communicate with each other about course projects. Participating in online discussion forums can be encouraged or a required part of the course structure. Automated response systems ("clickers") can provide immediate feedback in face-to-face classrooms on how students think or feel, aggregating the information into subgroups to show students how their responses compare to those of their classmates. Several Internet-based applications are specifically designed to support social networking. Although some require institutional support, many are available for free or at minimal cost and can be set up independently by a teacher, taking advantage of student-owned computers and the accessibility of computers in public institutions.

T/S 32 Be consciously inclusive.

Hall and Sandler (1982) conducted the first comprehensive study on the differential treatment of male and female students in college classrooms. They coined the phrase "chilly classroom climate" to describe the way teachers, often unknowingly, make female students feel unwelcome. Related research has demonstrated that the small and subtle inequities experienced by female students are also felt by students because of race, ethnicity, sexual orientation, age, disability, level of ability, language use, and social class. Sandler, Silverberg, and Hall (1992) believe that teacher-student interaction affects not only the classroom atmosphere but also individual students' learning, self-esteem, satisfaction, motivation, career choices, and so forth. To help faculty develop awareness and sensitivity, many institutions offer diversity training and workshops as part of their staff development training. It may also be helpful to videotape class sessions and then watch closely, looking for instances in which you may be unintentionally treating students differently. Building upon the research on chilly classrooms as well as her own research and experience on how to create a safe, inclusive classroom environment, Provitera-McGlynn (2001) offers these tips (pp. 64–68):

1. When you walk into class the first day (and every day), greet the class as a whole or greet students individually.

2. In your first class, tell the students what you prefer to be called, and ask them what they prefer to be called, noting this on the roll sheet.

3. In general, it works best to be consistent, calling all students by either their first or last names.

4. Take roll in every class session to show students that you value their presence and as a way of helping you (as well as fellow students) learn and remember all students' names.

5. Use students' names in class in ways that will boost their self-esteem, such as quoting a comment a student made earlier or praising a student for a particularly good question, comment, or work on an assignment.

6. Since the frequency of faculty-student contact inside and outside of class seems to promote student motivation, perseverance, and success, talk to students before and after class.

7. In surveys of student satisfaction with the college experience, students ranked interaction with professors as a very high priority (Astin, 1993), so be approachable, treat students with respect, show an interest in their learning, and be a real person to them.

8. Use humor, where appropriate, to create a more informal atmosphere.

T/S 33 Subdivide large classes into smaller groupings.

Effective strategies to create an engaging classroom environment include increasing the frequency and quality of student-teacher and student-student contact. Consider using assessment or diagnostic testing to determine student background in the course topic, and then invite the more experienced students to be available to offer advice and support to less experienced students. Or organize the class into communities of 8–12 students that support each other throughout the academic term. Depending upon course goals, students can work together formally on course projects or informally, helping each other by taking and sharing notes if a student cannot attend a lecture and encouraging each other when things get tough.

T/S 34 Involve all students in discussion.

To be a true learning community, *all* members must exchange information, ideas, and opinions. If you do not take steps to ensure all students participate, only a few students will speak up while the majority remain quiet, perhaps listening attentively but just as probably off in their own worlds daydreaming. To encourage students to stay attentive, consider creating a stack of cards with students' names or using a "Socrates jar" filled with slips of paper with individual students' names on them and pulling names randomly. Try to call on every student within a reasonable time frame depending upon the size of the class.

It is also important to help students feel comfortable in speaking up and saying what they truly think, believe, and feel. This is challenging because many students are afraid to take this risk, fearing that their comments might be viewed as wrong or stupid. If English is not their primary language, students may fear that they will use the language incorrectly, say the wrong word, or speak with an accent. Consider the following tips for starting and maintaining a good discussion (Davis, 2009; Barkley, Cross, & Major, 2005):

1. Take the time to craft an effective prompt that is open-ended and leads to issues rather than facts. (Avoid questions that have simple answers and can be perceived as quizzes in disguise.)

2. Consider creating prompts that are progressively more challenging. Asking an initial question that *all* students can answer establishes that the discussion is inclusive and reduces the possibility that some students will immediately disengage because they don't feel they have anything to contribute.

3. Use warm-up activities such as "Think-Pair-Shares" (in which students share their thoughts with a partner before sharing with the whole class). These kinds of activities help students collect and organize their thoughts and rehearse their response first in a low-risk situation, thus increasing willingness and readiness to speak in a large group.

4. Teach students how to benefit from discussion, pointing out to them the importance of sharing ideas, being receptive to alternative viewpoints, and showing respect for difference.

5. Consider paraphrasing a student's comments so that the student feels—and is—understood.

6. Ask a question to check your understanding of what a student has said. If a student makes a point and other class members look puzzled by it, ask a question that can help the student restate the point and clarify it for the class.

7. Mediate between students. If students are disagreeing, try to let them work it out, but if the conflict escalates and the discussion becomes heated, intervene to prevent a permanent breach. Statements like "These are both good points" or "You can see why there is so much controversy about this issue" or "Both sides have good arguments" can help ease tensions.

8. Point out or ask students to comment on the connections between students' ideas or remind them how the topic they're discussing relates to something they studied previously or will be studying or to something current in the news.

9. Compliment individual students on an interesting or insightful comment.

10. Help the class delve deeper into a topic by elaborating on a student's statement or suggesting a new perspective.

11. Students need time to think and to see that the instructor, too, needs time to think through problems, so allow time for silence.

12. Emphasize the main points as you reach them, and summarize and synthesize the entire discussion at the end.

T/S 35 Use group work effectively.

An important way to promote community is to have students work together in groups, but ensuring that group work is effective requires careful planning by the teacher. Thoughtful decisions must be made regarding how to form groups (size, heterogeneous or homogenous membership, and membership determined randomly, by instructor assignment, or by student choice); how to facilitate group interaction and solve common problems such as inequitable participation, off-task behavior, groups that don't get along, and groups that work at different rates; how to have students report out; and how to grade and evaluate work.

Some students resist group work, usually because they have had bad experiences with group activities in other courses. The most common student complaint is unbalanced workload: some group members don't do their share of the work, other group members try to "take over" and do too much. The best strategy to address this is to structure the activity so that there is both individual and group accountability.

An example of a group activity that achieves both individual and group accountability is Test Taking Teams (Barkley, Cross, & Major, 2005, pp. 163–167). First, students work in teams to prepare for exams. Then on exam day, students complete the exam individually and submit it to the instructor for grading. Before the teacher returns the graded individual tests, students rejoin their groups and take the exam as a group, reaching consensus on the answers and submitting a group response to the test. Individual students receive a combination of the two grades for their final test score that can be either the average between the two scores, or weighted in favor of the individual or group depending upon the teacher's values. Teachers can choose to emphasize the importance of the group's work by rewarding bonus points to the highest scoring teams.

Cooperative Learning for Higher Education Faculty (Millis and Cottell, 1998) and *Collaborative Learning: A Handbook for College Faculty* (Barkley, Cross, & Major, 2005) offer compendiums of information to help you integrate group learning activities effectively in your course.

T/S 36 Revisit icebreaker kinds of activities later in the term.

Although icebreakers are generally used early in the term to help promote a sense of community, they can also be used later to reaffirm, strengthen, and deepen social connections. You might use one or more of the icebreakers described in T/S 30, but modify the prompts to relate to a specific assignment or topic covered later in the term (for example, use an interview icebreaker but have students ask their interviewee questions about what they found to be most challenging, provocative, helpful, and so forth in a specific assignment).

T/S 37 Celebrate community.

Just as it is important to take steps to promote a sense of community at the beginning of the academic term, so it is important to celebrate and honor community at the end. Although this can be achieved through something as simple as an end-of-term class party, there are other activities that can keep the focus on learning.

- **Gallery of achievement:** Asks students individually or in groups to list their accomplishments (or the most important things they learned) on flip-chart paper that is then posted on classroom walls or in an online discussion forum. Ask students to walk around (or read through the online postings) and note achievements of others that they had not thought of but that apply to themselves. Survey the results and note the most popular, unusual, or unexpected accomplishments.

- **Class or group photos:** Close to the end of the term, take a photo of the whole class or groups of students. Right before you snap the picture, consider expressing your appreciation to the students and sharing observations of specific contributions they made that helped strengthen the class's sense of being a learning community. Present the photos to the students as a farewell gift on the last day of class, and consider keeping copies to be posted on the wall or collected in an album or webpage as a portrait gallery for future classes (Silberman, 1999, pp. 289–300).

- **Alumni invites:** Consider asking some of your best students to return to the class in a subsequent academic term to serve as tutors or teaching assistants, or to share their tips for success with new students.

Becoming a true learning community is hard work. It requires students to move beyond comfortable passivity and take risks, assume new roles, and develop skills that are different from those they are accustomed to using in many college classrooms. It requires students to work together and resolve conflicts in ways that acknowledge divergence of opinion and respect individual differences. It requires finding the overarching connections that help build a shared story. Recognizing and celebrating that the class has become a learning community can reinforce learning by helping to further cement ideas, concepts, and processes as it honors students for being active participants in their own learning.

Chapter 10

Tips and Strategies for Ensuring Students Are Appropriately Challenged

IF A LEARNING TASK is too easy, it can become boring; if a learning task is too hard, it can become frustrating. Either extremes can lead to disengagement. As McKeachie (1994, p. 353) points out, a fundamental principle of learning is that tasks must be sufficiently difficult to pose a challenge, but not so difficult as to destroy the willingness to try. When students are working at their optimal challenge level, they are more likely to be engaged. The tips and strategies in this section offer ideas for how to ensure students are appropriately challenged.

T/S 38 Assess students' starting points.

To ensure students are working in their optimal zone, it is essential to know their "starting points." Some disciplines already have widely used diagnostic tests (for example, the Force Concept Inventory in Physics and the California Chemistry Diagnostic Test) that can help you identify what topics or skills students have already mastered (Davis, 2009). But if such a test is not available in your field, you can develop your own by creating a list of key concepts, facts and figures, or major ideas.

SET 1, "Background Knowledge Survey" (in Chapter 12), is one strategy for uncovering students' prior knowledge. Nuhfer and Knipp's knowledge surveys (2003) are a much more extensive approach to determining what students know. A knowledge survey consists of course or unit learning objectives framed as questions that test mastery of the objectives. For example, if a core course learning objective in a science course is "Students will be able to distinguish science from other endeavors or areas of knowledge such as art, philosophy, or religion," the survey question will be "What specifically distinguishes science from other endeavors or areas of knowledge such as art, philosophy, or religion?" Rather than actually answering the questions, students respond to a three-point rating indicating their confidence to respond with competence to each query. Here are the directions from a sample survey provided by Nuhfer and Knipp (2003):

1. *Mark an "A" as a response to the question if you feel confident that you can answer the question sufficiently for graded test purposes.*

2. *Mark a "B" response to the question if you can answer 50% of it or if you know precisely where you could quickly get the information needed and could return here in 20 minutes or less to provide a complete answer for graded test purposes.*

3. *Mark a "C" response to the question if you are not confident that you could adequately answer the question at this time.*

The surveys are used to compare prior knowledge with how much students have learned by the end of the course or unit of study. Nuhfer and Knipp (2003) explain that knowledge surveys differ from pre-test–post-test evaluations because "[t]ests, by their nature, can address only a limited sampling of a course. In contrast, knowledge surveys cover an entire course in depth. While no student could possibly allocate the time to answer all questions on a thorough knowledge survey in any single exam sitting, they can rate their confidence to provide answers to an extensive survey of items in a very short time span." For an extensive discussion of the merits of this approach along with examples, see Nuhfer and Knipp's article "The Knowledge Survey" (2003) at http://www.isu.edu/ctl/facultydev/KnowS_files/KnowS.htm.

T/S 39 Monitor class pacing.

If you do not have the time or interest to adjust for individual learning needs, take steps to ensure that the class on the whole is functioning in an effective aggregate challenge zone. A simple way to do this is a classroom assessment technique known as the "Minute Paper" (Angelo & Cross, 1993, pp. 148–153): at the end of class students write and submit anonymously a couple of paragraphs in response to questions such as "What was the most important thing you learned during this class?" and "What important question remains unanswered?" Huba and Freed (2000, pp. 132–133) offer a variation on this technique. They suggest that at a point late in a class session (10–15 minutes before the end), students are asked to reflect on the class and in two minutes, think of any questions they want to ask or comments they would have liked to make, and write them on a piece of paper. The teacher collects the anonymous papers and in the remaining minutes of class, reads the questions/comments and answers or addresses them out loud to all. Strategies such as these help clarify and correct misunderstandings before students fall behind.

"Classroom Assessment Quality Circles," (Angelo & Cross, 1993, pp. 339–342) based on the Japanese management technique of establishing teams of workers and managers to address industrial planning and problem solving, offers a more comprehensive approach. Applied to an educational setting, the Quality Circle technique involves establishing one or more groups of five to eight students and meeting with them on a regular basis to listen to them as they offer structured feedback on course materials, activities, and assignments. It provides a vehicle for regularly collecting thoughtful responses from students about class sessions, readings, activities, and so forth, and also engages students by involving them in decisions regarding classroom operations. Students in the Quality Circles can serve both as advocates for their fellow students and as liaisons between the instructor and students, which can enhance communication in large classes. This strategy also indicates to students that you are serious about student learning and using student feedback to improve the course.

T/S 40 Help students learn to self-assess.

Help students evaluate their learning and learning process. This allows them to take responsibility for determining whether they are in their optimal challenge zone and adjust accordingly by doing additional review, seeking help, or challenging themselves to pursue more advanced work. For example, "Diagnostic Learning Logs" (Angelo & Cross, 1993, pp. 311–315) are essentially limited, tightly focused versions of the academic journals that many teachers already use. When responding to a learning session, students write one list of the main points that they understood and a second list of points that were unclear along with possible remedies for problems. Diagnostic Learning Logs tell teachers something about students' skills in recognizing their own learning difficulties in specific lessons, but the main virtue of this assessment technique is to make students aware of themselves as learners and to take more responsibility for analyzing their learning problems and doing something about them. SET 41, "Learning Logs" in Chapter 10 of this book, based on a technique developed by Weimer (2002), is another strategy for helping students gain information and insight into their own learning.

T/S 41 Differentiate course elements to meet individual student needs.

Nunley (2006) observes that education's bottom line is "if students are learning, you are teaching" (p. 129). She suggests that in formal educational environments, learning involves three steps: (1) teaching, (2) studying, and (3) assessment/testing. Although this three-part system seems logical and simple, problems arise through the traditionally narrow range of options and avenues we use for Steps 1 and 3. Teaching is almost always achieved through linguistic channels (we listen to spoken language and read the printed word), and assessment is almost always visual, linguistic, and fine motor activity involving reading printed words and manually writing a representation of our thoughts. Nunley (2006, pp. 129–130) urges teachers to remember that Step 1 (teaching) and Step 3 (assessment) are solely in existence for the purpose and benefit of Step 2 (learning) and that because educational environments have traditionally been so rigid in the way teaching and assessment are offered, we are seriously limiting success at the most important step—the learning.

Creating an effectively differentiated course is one way teachers can support individual students working at their optimal challenge zone. Differentiation is a pedagogical strategy developed by Carol Ann Tomlinson, a professor at University of Virginia, in which the teacher (1) makes a special effort to understand, appreciate, and build upon student differences and (2) designs the course specifically to encourage all students to work at a level that is appropriately challenging to them for maximum growth and individual success. She and her colleagues have written several books that provide both conceptual and practical background for how to organize a course around differentiation principles. Following are some ideas for differentiating a variety of course elements culled from several of these sources (Tomlinson, 1999, 2001; Tomlinson & Eidson, 2003; Tomlinson & Strickland, 2005):

- **Level:** Challenge students who already know a portion of the material to move to new, more advanced material or more complicated, complex applications of the material, and focus the efforts of students for whom the material is new on building a solid foundation.

- **How students access material:** Make content available through a variety of delivery mechanisms such as teacher presentation, textbooks, online, media such as films and recordings, and computer-assisted instruction.

- **Process:** Offer activities in a range of modes (for example, writing, discussing, creating), at varied degrees of sophistication, over varying amounts of time, or with varied amounts of teacher or peer support.

- **Product:** Replace some or all tests with other kinds of products such as essays, Web pages, media-based materials, presentations, demonstrations, role plays, models, and exhibits.

- **Classroom space:** Differentiate space by organizing a physical classroom in ways that allow students to work in a variety of configurations (individual, small-group, or whole-class work) and to change configurations smoothly and efficiently. (See Table 10.1.) Extend options through online delivery systems.

- **Materials:** Use technology, media, and traditional materials in a creative way to offer a wide variety of tools to support learning. To prompt learning, consider using quotes, charts, images, film clips, assessment results, Web pages, and podcasts. To provide variety in terms of how students construct materials to communicate their learning, consider using journals, presentations, exhibits, videos, audio recordings, Web pages, portfolios (hard copy and electronic), images (2- and 3-dimensional and computer generated), analysis and reflections, Wikis, and blogs.

- **Time:** Think of ways to use time flexibly within the external constraints of the academic term and class hour(s) by asking yourself questions such as, When is it best to work as a whole class, independently, or in small groups? Are there times when these can occur simultaneously? What should students do when some finish early? In the online environment, which activities are best done asynchronously and which ones synchronously?

The amount of variables to consider when thinking about differentiation can make the concept so overwhelming that college teachers dismiss it out of hand. But even Tomlinson (2001, p. 11) observes that effective differentiated classrooms usually include whole-class, nondifferentiated fare as the standard. In fact, she recommends that instructors differentiate only when they see the need and when they are convinced that modification will increase the likelihood that students will understand important ideas and use important skills more thoroughly. Furthermore, differentiation can be phased in, gradually adding more levels of options.

Some types of classrooms are more flexible than others, but faculty can differentiate learning activities in any kind of classroom. All classrooms can be used for individual activities (such as writing essays, stopping to reflect quietly) as well as traditional whole-class presentation and discussion. Table 10.1 offers suggestions for adapting various kinds of classrooms for small-group work (adapted from Silberman, 1996, and excerpted from Barkley, Cross, & Major, 2005, p. 51).

TABLE 10.1.

Differentiating Learning Activities in Various Classroom Settings

Fixed-seat auditorium or lecture hall	Students seated next to each other on the same level can form pairs or trios to engage in short brainstorming or brief discussions. Since groups are unable to work together for long periods in uncomfortable conditions, more complex collaborative assignments can be done outside of scheduled class time.
Laboratories	Laboratories most often contain workstations where groups of students can work together. Depending upon the kind of laboratory, groups of different sizes can form and re-form throughout the class session. For example in a computer laboratory, pairs might work best for an assignment, but for brief periods pairs could form together to form a quad.
Moveable chairs and desks	Students can form pairs, small groups, or a circle for whole-class discussion. Because students do not have a single shared workspace, writing together or manipulating pieces of paper in a graphic organizer may be challenging.
Moveable tables	The flexibility of this type of setting makes it ideal for a variety of group activities. In addition to pairs and pair-cluster arrangements, larger student teams can work together at a table. The tables can be pulled together to create one large conference table. The tables and chairs may also be arranged in a U shape. Almost any kind of group activity can be accomplished in this type of classroom.
Seminar	Organize the class into 2–3 groups; one group can work at the middle of the table, and the other groups can take different corners or ends of the table.
Large classroom with breakout space or rooms	Students can come together for a large session and then spread out for teamwork. This classroom allows groups to work independently on projects without disturbing other groups and is ideal for medium- or long-term groups.
Online class	Factors such as the level of students (lower division or graduate seminar?) and the size of the class (12 or 120?) influence how to form groups in online classes. In small classes with stable enrollment, it may work best to assign partners or triads early in the semester to work together throughout the term. In large classes with unstable enrollment and participation, it may work best to form larger groups of 8–12. Regardless of group size, identify groups (e.g., Group A, Group B), assign membership, and provide groups with their own "space" to discuss their work (e.g., a threaded discussion forum). Depending on the nature of the assignment, consider creating these forums as adjuncts to a whole-class discussion and/or providing only group members access to their group's discussion area.

Source: Adapted from M. Silberman, *Active Learning* (Needham Heights, MA: Allyn & Bacon, 1996), pp. 10–16, and excerpted from E. F. Barkley, K. P. Cross, & C. H. Major, *Collaborative Learning Techniques* (San Francisco: Jossey-Bass, 2005), p. 51.

T/S 42 Use scaffolding to provide assistance for complex learning.

When students are working on challenging projects, they need assistance to support them as they move from not knowing or not being able to becoming independent and competent. *Scaffolding* is a term used to describe the general strategy of breaking down multipart processes into smaller steps or providing students with examples, clues, prompts, reminders, and so forth to help them succeed at complex learning tasks. Just as in construction, a scaffold provides a temporary framework where workers can stand safely and access areas otherwise out of reach, a scaffold for learning provides students with support until they can solve the problem, perform a skill, or complete a task on their own. Following is an adaptation of scaffolding steps described by Wlodkowski (2004, pp. 185–186), with examples at each step to support students in writing a research paper:

- **Model:** Carry out the skill while students observe, or provide examples that students can imitate, such as completed projects or solved problems.

  To introduce the complex task of writing a research paper, form students into small groups, provide them with two research papers written by students in a previous class, with one being excellent and one being satisfactory. Ask them to identify the characteristics that make the one paper more effective than the other.

- **Think out loud:** Talk through the thought processes you would engage in as you carry out the task.

  For a research paper example, talk about how you might identify a topic, or how you would go about gathering and evaluating sources, data, and references; ask learners to share their own perceptions and processes about conducting and writing up research.

- **Anticipate difficulties**: Discuss with students areas where support is needed and mistakes are likely to occur.

  Talk about the strengths and weaknesses of Web research and how to paraphrase and cite sources appropriately to avoid plagiarism.

- **Break down an activity into smaller parts or provide prompts and cues:** Break down a complex process into smaller procedural steps or highlight important aspects of a project.

  Provide an outline of the steps involved, a grading rubric specifying quality criteria, or a checklist of questions such as, Have you included an in-text citation for every source you paraphrased?

- **Use reciprocal teaching:** Before students have completed the task, ask them to discuss their work with peers in order to obtain guidance and suggestions. *Form small groups in which students share drafts of their research paper to get and provide supportive feedback.*

Although some college teachers resist providing this kind of assistance and criticize it for "coddling" students, scaffolding can provide the support students require to persist on a difficult task that might otherwise become overwhelming. It can also guide students to do their best work. As Wlodkowski (2008, pp. 186–187) notes, the kind of assistance scaffolding provides should be just enough to keep students from getting lost, trusting them to chart the rest of their journey to learning on their own. It conveys the message that learners are not rugged individualists or solitary explorers, but rather, it embraces a vision of remarkable possibility nurtured by a caring community.

Chapter 11

Tips and Strategies to Promote Holistic Learning

MANY OF THE current thinkers on education recognize that learning involves more than rational thinking. Student engagement is increased when learning is holistic. Learning activities will be most successful if students are engaged on a cognitive level (they are thinking about what they are doing), an affective level (they enjoy what they are doing and give it their full attention) and, when possible and appropriate, on a kinesthetic level (they apply the theoretical and abstract by actually doing a physical activity). In this chapter are ideas for how to promote this kind of holistic learning.

T/S 43 Pick up the pace to hold attention.

El-Shamy (2004) observes that the speed at which people prefer to move through material is a critical generational difference in educational contexts. She proposes that teachers of the baby boom generation tend to teach "at a leisurely pace, punctuated here and there with a burst of energy, an involving activity, a small-group discussion." Younger students, who have grown up with the faster, more driving, unrelenting "twitchspeed" beat of MTV and its equivalent find the slower, sequential, linear delivery of such teachers "frustratingly slow and unnecessary" (El-Shamy, 2004, pp. 21–22). Nunley (2006) urges teachers to realize that they "just can't lecture fast enough." Citing Christakis et al., 2004, and Tervaniemi and Hugdahl, 2003, she explains that the reticular activating system, an area at the base of the brain that is responsible for focusing attention, has changed in recent years. Through constant exposure to video and computer games, the brains of today's young people have been trained to pick up and process new information at much faster speeds. When these students come into traditional classrooms, they are easily bored and have difficulty maintaining attention

(Nunley, 2006, pp. 37–38). Most college teachers have neither the skills nor the desire to "put on a show"; more importantly, engaging students means making them think—not entertaining them. Nevertheless, teachers who want to hold the attention of younger students should consider picking up the pace. El-Shamy (2004, pp. 21–29) suggests the following:

- **Immediately do something dynamic**: Start classes on time and begin with an opening activity that involves students doing something (not just listening to you talk). If possible, start with an experiential learning activity that illustrates a key learning point in a physical way, such as having learners experience the problem, the issue, or the situation first-hand. Other ideas include starting with small-group problem-solving, team competition, or even a quiz.

- **Move conceptually from A/V to multimedia**: Reconsider your approach to using media, shifting to music samples and short film clips taken from video games, movies, or real life (think YouTube); limiting overheads to ten seconds; keeping electronic slides to a minimum, using only graphics and a few key points rather than slides full of text; and interrupting longer videos to ask students questions.

- **Make it snappy:** Keep "telling time" short—quickly present a concept and then have learners do something with it—discuss it, apply it, critique it, reword it, draw it, or chart it. Move about the room, not in a way that is excessive or exaggerated, but don't stay in one location for very long. Incorporate rhetorical questions. Consider creating your own movie trailer (complete with commercials for other courses), and play it on the screen the first day of class. Or have a "quiz" related to the topic that will be covered in class projected on electronic slides set for automatic play. Have it play before class starts and during breaks, and offer a small reward (points, candy, prizes such as coffee cards) to students who answer all questions correctly.

- **Tighten up group activity time:** Give less time than you normally do for each activity. Tell participants exactly how much time they have to do an activity and then stick to that time limit, using a clock, stopwatch, or timer that can be seen and/or heard (pre-explain and agree upon a one-minute warning sign). Also limit the amount of time groups have for reporting out, explaining that there just isn't time to hear everything a group would like to share, so they should share only the most important information.

Obviously not all students will flourish in a classroom that has a fast pace; many learners will need or prefer a slower, more measured pace. But being aware of the preference of younger learners for a faster pace and adjusting for this may help grab and sustain student attention.

T/S 44 Offer options for nonlinear learning.

"Have you ever watched a twenty-something work or study?" El-Shamy (2004) asks. "There is nothing linear about it. There may be a book or two open, papers here and there, but the computer has two or three screens going at the same time while instant messaging alerts flash in the corner. Online, twenty-somethings move from site to site, taking in information, saving this, eliminating that." In college courses, we tend to ask students to do things one at a time and in sequential order. This is "not only boring to younger learners, but it is downright difficult." El-Shamy (2004, pp. 49–53) suggests teachers rethink and redesign courses to include more options, a variety of parallel processes, random access to an assortment of learning alternatives, and letting learners choose or devise their own pathway to get to the endpoint identified by the teacher. In addition to giving students choices from a variety of options such as those described in T/S 41, "Differentiate course elements," she recommends organizing the course into "stand-alones," or modules that can be done in any order and that encourage students to choose from a range of delivery styles—for example, some tutor-led, some classroom-led, and some online.

T/S 45 Use principles of universal design.

"Universal design" is an approach to designing a product or environment that is "usable by all people, to the greatest extent possible, without the need for adaptation or specialized design" (Burgstahler, 2008). In college teaching, it means designing our courses to be inclusive and barrier-free, thereby meeting the needs of more students. As Burgstahler (2008) notes, today's students "come from a variety of ethnic and racial backgrounds. For some, English is not their first language. Also represented in most classes are students with a diversity of ages and learning styles, including visual and auditory. In addition, increasing numbers of students with disabilities are included in regular pre-college and postsecondary courses. Their disabilities include blindness, low vision, hearing impairments, mobility impairments, learning disabilities, and health impairments. . . . Universally designed curriculum provides students with a wide range of abilities, disabilities, ethnic backgrounds, language skills, and learning styles multiple means of representation, expression, and engagement." Her

Web site, *Universal Design of Instruction* (http://www.washington.edu/doit/Brochures/Academics/instruction.html), includes practical suggestions for how to ensure that lectures, discussions, visual aids, videos, printed materials, labs, and fieldwork are accessible to all students.

T/S 46 Incorporate games.

Computer, video, and online games are an important part of the lives of today's college students. Research released in 2003, based on 1,162 students on twenty-seven college campuses, indicated that 65 percent were regular or occasional gamers and 32 percent played games during class that were not part of the instructional activities (Jones, 2003). Consider taking advantage of students' predilection for gaming by using games or game characteristics to infuse energy into course activities.

Commercial games such as *Civilization* and *Rise of Nations* already have academic and intellectual content. Many more games are being developed that have the disciplinary depth appropriate to support college-level classes. At some disciplinary and general academic conferences, vendors and teachers demonstrate electronic games designed to educate.

Even without using full-scale electronic games, teachers can take advantage of game characteristics (goals, rules, challenge, interaction) and types (puzzles, role-playing, strategy, board games, and so forth). For example, turn a review session into a board game by using a word-processing table function to make a 5-row/5-column grid and mark the center cell "start." Instruct students that the goal is to move in a spiral from start to finish. Create a set of game cards with a question on the front and the answer on the back along with an indication of the number of squares to move if the question is answered correctly. Form students into small groups and have students take turns pulling a card and asking a group member the question. Sugar (1998) and Yaman and Covington (2006) offer ideas and instructions for creating games that teach.

T/S 47 Teach so that students use multiple processing modes.

Most of us have heard for years that lecture is not as effective as active learning pedagogies. Research generally shows that the amount of retention corresponds to the degree to which a student is dynamically participating in the learning activity. In lecture, for example, students are sitting passively and concentrating primarily on processing verbal information just enough to convert what they are hearing into written notes. If the lecturer supplements the presentation with visual information (such as PowerPoint slides) or a demonstration (thus using physical movement), the students are processing both verbal and visual information, and retention increases. When the students themselves are active, retention dramatically increases. Sousa's (2006) summary of his and others' research on the impact of various teaching methods on retention is shown in Figure 11.1, which shows the percentage of learning that students can recall after twenty-four hours, when it is presumed to be in long-term storage. (See T/S 20, "Teach for retention," in Chapter 8 for additional information on retention.)

This is not to say that lectures should never be given (they are a particularly effective means to present in a short period of time a lot of information that is not available in other sources) or that other methods—for example, teaching others—should be used all the time (after all, students do have to initially learn what they are teaching others). Rather, the research suggests that students will retain more if they are using multiple senses to process information and are given opportunities at regular intervals to par-

FIGURE 11.1.

Pie Chart Showing Average Retention Rate from Different Teaching Methods

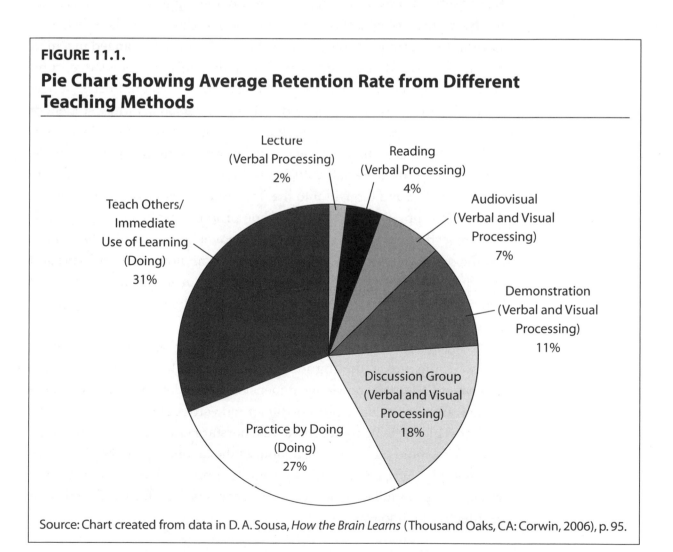

Source: Chart created from data in D. A. Sousa, *How the Brain Learns* (Thousand Oaks, CA: Corwin, 2006), p. 95.

ticipate in a variety of rehearsal activities that help them to make sense of the information.

T/S 48 Incorporate multiple domains when identifying learning goals.

As you identify learning goals, consider balancing goals that address the affective and psychomotor domains as well as the cognitive domain. Although there are several learning taxonomies that can be used as a framework for identifying learning goals (such as Fink, 2003, and Shulman, 2002), familiarity with Bloom's cognitive taxonomy (Bloom, Engelhart, Furst, Hill, & Krathwohl, 1956) and the contributions that he and his group made to understanding the affective and psychomotor domains make their taxonomies a useful starting point.

The Cognitive Domain Bloom's taxonomy of the cognitive domain was created by a group of educational psychologists to classify levels of behavior important in learning. It consists of six kinds of learning arranged in a hierarchical sequence. From basic to advanced, they include knowledge, comprehension, application, analysis, synthesis, and evaluation. In 2001, a new group of cognitive psychologists led by L. W. Anderson (a former student of Bloom's) and D. R. Krathwohl (one of the members of the original team) published a revision because they believed that many of the ideas in the original taxonomy were still valuable but they also wanted to incorporate new knowledge and thought into the framework (Anderson, Krathwohl, & Bloom, 2001, pp. xxi–xxii). Their revision proposes that learning occurs at the intersection of cognitive process and knowledge. Basically, they modified the original taxonomic levels (changing from noun to verb forms and replacing the terms *knowledge* and *synthesis* with *remember* and *create*) and then combined these with four knowledge dimensions: factual, conceptual, procedural, and metacognitive. (See Table 11.1.)

As teachers develop learning objectives, they place them at the intersection of the x-axis (the cognitive process) and the y-axis (knowledge dimension). Thus the knowledge dimension nouns determine what is being learned, and the cognitive process dimension verbs determine the cognitive level at which it is being learned. Teachers are encouraged to go to the source for a more thorough discussion, as the taxonomy can be very helpful when planning and organizing cognitive-oriented learning goals and activities. Less familiar to most college teachers is the affective domain and the affective taxonomy.

TABLE 11.1.

Bloom's Revised Taxonomy of the Cognitive Domain

	The Cognitive Process Dimension				
The Knowledge Dimension	Remember	Understand	Apply	Analyze	Create
Factual Knowledge					
Conceptual Knowledge					
Procedural Knowledge					
Metacognitive Knowledge					

From Krathwohl, David R., Benjamin S. Bloom & Bertram B. Masia. *Taxonomy of Educational Objectives, Book 2: Affective Domain.* Published by Allyn and Bacon/Merrill Education, Boston, MA. Copyright © 1984 by Pearson Education. Adapted by permission of the publisher.

The Taxonomy of the Affective Domain

The taxonomy of the affective domain, sometimes called Krathwohl's taxonomy, was produced by Bloom in conjunction with Krathwohl and published later (Krathwohl, Bloom, & Masia, 1964). This taxonomy addresses the manner in which we deal with things emotionally, such as feelings, values, appreciation, enthusiasms, motivation, and attitudes. The taxonomy begins with "receiving," followed by responding, valuing, organization, and characterization. Krathwohl's taxonomy suggests that all learning may begin with the affective domain: the very first step in learning is being willing to receive the information/knowledge that constitutes the foundational tier of the cognitive taxonomy. After simply being *willing* to do something comes *wanting* to do something—the essence of motivation—and this in turn leads to more complex levels, culminating eventually in the internalization of a system of values that directs all behavior. Affective learning is demonstrated by behaviors indicating attitudes of awareness, interest, attention, concern, and responsibility; ability to listen and respond in interactions with others; and ability to demonstrate those attitudinal characteristics or values that are appropriate to the test situation and the field of study. Table 11.2 shows the affective taxonomy with illustrative verbs and behavior descriptions that can guide teachers as they craft affective learning goals.

The Psychomotor Domain

Although Bloom and his colleagues proposed the psychomotor domain to describe physical ability, they never created subcategories. Others did, and perhaps the most relevant is one by R.H. Dave, a student of Bloom's. Table 11.3 shows Dave's taxonomy along with illustrative verbs and behavior descriptions that can be used as the basis for identifying learning goals in the psychomotor domain.

TABLE 11.2.

Learning Taxonomy: Krathwohl's Affective Domain

Level	Illustrative Verbs	Behavior Descriptions
Receiving refers to the student's willingness to attend to particular phenomena of stimuli.	Asks, chooses, describes, follows, gives, holds, identifies, locates, names, points to, selects, replies, use	Paying attention to a lecture, listening to others as they contribute in class discussion, staying open to exploration of controversial issues, respecting the rights of others
Responding refers to active participation on the part or the student.	Answers, assists, complies, discusses, helps, labels, performs, practices, presents, reads, reports, selects, tells, writes	Ranges from simple acquiescence (reads assigned material) to active response (pursuing and enjoying reading beyond the assignment), doing assignments, participating in discussion and small-group activities, questioning new concepts in order to understand them
Valuing is concerned with the worth or value a student attaches to a particular object, phenomenon, or behavior.	Completes, describes, differentiates, explains, follows, forms, initiates, invites, joins, justifies, proposes, shares, studies, works	Spans simple acceptance of value (desires to improve group skills) to the more complex level of commitment (assumes responsibility for the effective functioning of the group). Instructional objectives that are commonly classified under "attitudes" and "appreciation" would fall into this category.
Organization is concerned with bringing together different values, resolving conflicts between them, and beginning the building of an internally consistent value system.	Adheres, alters, arranges, combines, compares, completes, defends, explains, generalizes, identifies, integrates, modifies, orders, organizes, prepares, relates, synthesizes	Emphasis is on comparing, relating, and synthesizing values. Learning outcomes may be concerned with the conceptualization of a value (recognizes the responsibility of each individual for improving human relations) or with the organization of a value system (develops a vocational plan that satisfies his or her need for both economic security and social service).

| Characterization by a value or value set: The individual has a value system that has controlled his or her behavior for a sufficiently long time for him or her to develop a characteristic lifestyle. | Acts, discriminates, displays, influences, modifies, performs, practices, proposes, qualifies, questions, revises, serves, solves, uses, verifies | The student's behavior is pervasive, consistent, and predictable; thus the major emphasis is on the fact that the behavior is typical or characteristic of the student. Instructional objectives that are concerned with the student's general patterns of adjustment (shows self-reliance when working independently, revises judgments and changes behavior in light of new evidence, and so forth) would be appropriate here. |

Source: Adapted from "Learning Taxonomy: Krathwohl's Affective Domain," *University of Connecticut Assessment Web Site*, http://www.assessment.uconn.edu/docs/LearningTaxonomy_Affective.pdf

TABLE 11.3.

Taxonomy of the Psychomotor Domain by RH Dave

Level	Illustrative Verbs	Behavior Descriptions
Imitation	Copy, follow, replicate, repeat, adhere	Copying the action of another; observing and replicating a process or activity
Manipulation	Re-create, build, perform, execute, implement	Carrying out a task from written or verbal instruction; reproducing activity from memory
Precision	Demonstrate, complete, show, perfect, calibrate, control	Performing a task or activity reliably with expertise and to high quality without assistance or instruction; able to demonstrate to other learners
Articulation	Construct, solve, combine coordinate, integrate, adapt, develop, formulate, modify, master	Adapting and combining associated activities to develop methods to meet varying, novel requirements
Naturalization	Design, specify, manage, invent, project-manage	Automated, unconscious mastery of activity and related skills at strategic level

Adapted from A. Chapman, "Bloom's Taxonomy: Learning Domains" in R. J. Armstrong, *Developing and Writing Behavioral Objectives* (Tucson, AZ: Educational Innovators Press, 1975).

T/S 49 Include learning activities that involve physical movement.
It is difficult for students to sit for long periods of time. Some SETs in Part Three (such as SET 5, "Stations," and SET 12, "Split Room Debates") and some of the icebreakers in T/S 30, "Use icebreakers to warm up the class" (Chapter 9) provide ideas for activities in which students stand up and move around. Here are four additional examples in the literature of activities that involve physical movement:

- **Ball-toss:** This semi-review and wake-up exercise is particularly useful for re-energizing students when they have been working with material that requires heavy concentration. Craft an open-ended prompt (such as "In my lecture, what did you find particularly interesting? Important? Still unclear?"). Then have students stand up and form a circle facing each other. Toss a nerf ball or bean bag to a student and have him or her respond and then toss the ball to another student who also responds. Continue the exercise until everyone has caught the ball at least once and explained an important concept from the material just covered.

- **Snowballing (for discussion):** Give students a few moments to reflect upon and jot down answers to questions provided on a worksheet or projected on a transparency or presentation slide. Then ask students to pair up and share responses for about five minutes. After another five minutes, pairs join to form quads and exchange responses for about ten minutes, after which quads merge to create groups of eight. The process continues in increasing time intervals until the whole class is brought together at the end of the session. Although snowballing can sometimes have a frenetic, disjointed feel, the milling about and change in group configurations is sometimes "just the thing needed to shake students up a little" (Brookfield & Preskill, 2005, pp. 108–109).

- **Snowball:** Ask students to individually write brief responses on a blank piece of paper to a teacher-created prompt, then crush the paper into a ball and throw them around the room for a couple of minutes. When the teacher says "Stop," each student picks up a "snowball" and reads its contents at the instructor's request. This technique works well to get lots of ideas out on the floor (literally!) and is a fun and energizing way to break up long stretches of class time.

- **Cocktail party:** Invite students to move around, mingling with their peers as they participate in a discussion. The teacher acts as the host, introducing students and making sure everyone feels welcome and included. To contribute to the festive mood, the teacher might walk around serving non-alcoholic drinks and hors d'oeuvres from a tray (Brookfield & Preskill, 2005, p. 109).

T/S 50 Consider creating a graphic syllabus.

Course syllabi are typically text documents, but Nilson (2007) offers some compelling arguments for shifting to a graphic-based document—a one-page diagram, flowchart, or concept map of the topical organization of the course. After pointing out some of the reasons why text syllabi fail (with the main one being that students simply don't read them), she discusses how and why a graphic syllabus can enhance learning. For example, a graphic syllabus can use images, spatial relationships, and colors to show the global organization of a course as well as how component concepts, processes, and learning outcomes interrelate. This can be particularly helpful to learners who tend to think in pictorial, spatial, and sensate terms. A graphic syllabus may also help students retain material better and longer because students use both their verbal and visual-spatial memory systems (called "dual-coding material into memory"; Nilson, 2007, pp. 18–21).

To illustrate the difference between a text-based and a graphic syllabus, Nilson (2007) provides an excerpt from her course's original text-based syllabus (Table 11.4) followed by her graphic-based version (Figure 11.2).

TABLE 11.4.

Excerpt from Traditional, Text-Based Syllabus

Syllabus
Weekly Topics in SOC 123: Social Stratification
Dr. Linda B. Nilson

Weeks 1 and 2	What Social Stratification Is—Across Species, Through History, and According to Consensus Theory (Functionalism), Conflict Theory, and Lenski's Attempt at Synthesis
Week 3	Inequalities in Wealth and Income
Week 4	Inequalities in Power
Week 5	Review and Midterm
Week 6	Inequalities in Prestige; Measurements of Socioeconomic Status
Week 7	Inequality of Opportunity for Wealth, Income, Power, and Prestige. Social Mobility and Status Attainment.
Week 8 and 9	How Modern Stratification Persists: The Political System—Wealthfare, Welfare, and Pluralistic Representative Democracy
Week 10	How Modern Stratification Persists: Peoples Beliefs and Subjective Responses to Stratification
Week 11	Final Examination

Source: L. B. Nilson, *The Graphic Syllabus and the Outcomes Map* (Bolton, MA: Anker, 2007), p. 30.

FIGURE 11.2.

Excerpt from Graphic-Based Syllabus

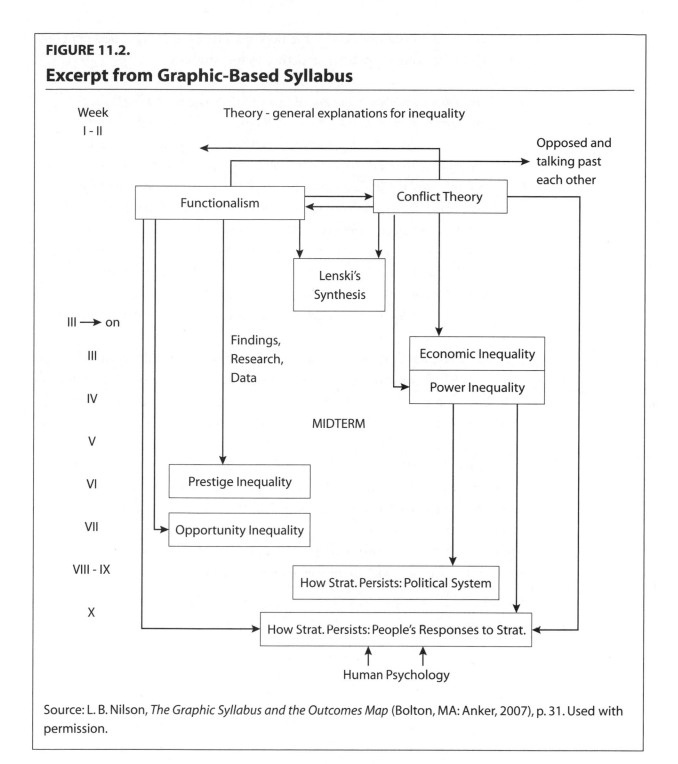

Source: L. B. Nilson, *The Graphic Syllabus and the Outcomes Map* (Bolton, MA: Anker, 2007), p. 31. Used with permission.

Nilson (2007) describes how the flowchart (Figure 11.2) helped her communicate the course's deeper structure to her students:

> *The graphic syllabus of my Social Stratification course shows that functionalism spawns research on inequalities in prestige and opportunity, which are measured in representative national surveys on a continuous quantitative (ordinal) scale. On the other hand, conflict theorists study economic and political inequalities, which the historical, documentary, and quantitative economic data that they use indicate are highly concentrated in a small elite class in most types of societies. Along with psychology, functionalism and conflict theory both contribute explanations for why social stratification persists, although conflict theory offers more and richer reasons. All in all, the two schools of thought complement each other, each filling in the knowledge the other fails to generate. (p. 32)*

She explains that the graphic helps her to show that the course is organized around competing schools of thought, which she hopes conveys to students a more complex, expert understanding of the subject. This helps them understand that "reality is more complex and messy than any human interpretation of it" (p. 32).

Nilson (2007) includes dozens of models from a variety of disciplines that show how graphics can be used to convey course information such as process, sequence/chronology, parallelism, and categorical hierarchy that are difficult to communicate in text alone. If we consider it important to teach for holistic learning, then finding new and additional ways to communicate course structure makes increasing sense.

Part Three

Student Engagement Techniques (SETs)

THE STUDENT ENGAGEMENT TECHNIQUES (SETs) are fifty field-tested learning activities that one or more college teachers have found effective in engaging students. Each SET promotes active learning by requiring students to participate in activities such as reading, writing, discussing, problem solving, or reflecting. Each SET can also foster motivation because most students find the activities interesting or valuable. The techniques are drawn primarily from the good practice literature. The format is modeled on the schema developed by K. Patricia Cross and Thomas A. Angelo in *Classroom Assessment Techniques* (CATs; Angelo & Cross, 1993) and continued in *Collaborative Learning Techniques* (CoLTs; Barkley, Cross, & Major, 2005).

Like the CATs and CoLTs, these SETs are similar to a collection of well-tested recipes. Each SET should be sufficiently clear for both new and experienced teachers to follow the step-by-step directions and be reasonably confident they will get good results. But my hope is that, rather than following the instructions precisely, teachers will use the SETs as accomplished chefs use recipes. Accomplished chefs use their knowledge and experience to experiment with recipes—substituting ingredients, adding new elements, tweaking the procedures, and basically using their creativity to adapt the recipe to their own needs and preferences. Please consider these techniques as guidelines and have fun modifying them to meet your unique instructional needs.

The SETs also resemble recipes in that they provide only the directions. Teachers, like cooks, must provide the actual ingredients. Just as flawed ingredients or a sloppy presentation can ruin the best recipe, so poorly conceived and framed learning prompts can undermine the effectiveness of a seemingly foolproof SET.

Finally, SETs are like recipes because some just won't appeal to you or your students. In this way, SETs differ from CATs and CoLTs. CATs are designed to help teachers gather data in order to assess and improve learning. If you follow the directions, you are pretty much guaranteed to collect useful data. CoLTs are designed to help teachers structure effective group learning activities. Again, if you follow the directions, you can be quite confident students will participate in an effective group learning activity. The correspondence between purpose and result for both CATs and CoLTs is strong; the correspondence is a bit more tenuous in SETs. This is because, as we saw in both the theory and practice in Part One, student engagement is a complex mix of motivation and active learning. Because motivation results from the interplay of many interrelated factors that are individually referenced, there is no guarantee that students in *your* class will be motivated by the technique.

Additionally, each SET is designed to promote active learning. But the truism underlying Dorothy Parker's wry pun on *horticulture* (you can lead a "horticulture," but you can't make her think) also applies to SETs: thinking is internal, usually invisible, and ultimately a student's choice. What you *can* be assured of is that each SET has a good track record for ensuring students will be actively learning and that they will find the activity sufficiently interesting or useful to be motivating.

Origin of the SETs

The SETs are drawn from a variety of sources: books, journals, corporate training manuals, Web sites, workshops, my own experience in the classroom, and ideas from manuscript reviewers, colleagues, and students. Some of the SETs are adaptations of CATs; a few are CoLTs. I have included Key Resources, but this section is not intended to provide the original source. In some instances, the techniques have been shared among practitioners for years, and it would be exceedingly difficult if not impossible to confidently identify an original source. In other cases, the original sources are not readily available should readers wish to examine them. Nor is the Key Resources section intended to provide the only sources available that describe the technique, since multiple sources exist for several of the SETs—many of which, it can be argued, are of equal importance. Rather, the section provides resources I found to be most useful either for the technique itself or for aspects within an example or variation.

How to Use the SETs

The SETs are organized into two main categories of broad learning goals, which are subdivided into more specific learning goals. Category I includes techniques to engage students in learning course-related knowledge and skills. It is subdivided into chapters on

- knowledge, skills, recall, and understanding (Chapter 12);
- analysis and critical thinking (Chapter 13);
- synthesis and creative thinking (Chapter 14);
- problem solving (Chapter 15); and
- application and performance (Chapter 16).

Category II includes techniques for developing attitudes, values, and self-awareness as learners. It is subdivided into chapters on

- attitudes and values (Chapter 17);
- self-awareness as learners (Chapter 18); and
- learning and study skills (Chapter 19).

Most of the SETs are presented as teacher-led (the teacher sets the parameters, crafts the prompts, presents the directions, and so forth), however almost all can be adapted so that they are student-led. Likewise, most are presented as group activities, but many can be easily assigned as individual work.

The best strategy is to thumb through the chapters and start experimenting with the SETs that seem like they would work for your teaching style, discipline, and class. You might start by looking at techniques in the chapter most closely corresponding to your teaching goals or challenges. Thus, if you are looking to develop your students' critical thinking skills, you might start by looking at the techniques in Chapter 13. If your course requires students to learn a lot of information, then you might first look at techniques in Chapter 12, "Knowledge, Skills, Recall, and Understanding." Using this approach, you may quickly find new ideas that you can incorporate easily into your existing teaching methods.

These categories represent my best attempt at sorting the techniques into clusters that share fundamental commonalities, but the dividing lines are not precise, and you are encouraged to scan through all the techniques. With some thought and creativity, most of the SETs can be adapted for a variety of teaching goals.

The SETs are organized according to the method originally developed for CATs (Angelo & Cross, 1993). My hope is that the parallel structure will provide teachers with an efficient way to correlate a SET learning activity to a potential assessment activity.

Format of the SETs

The fifty SETs are numbered sequentially and, within each category, appear essentially in order from least to most complex. Each SET is identified by a simple, descriptive name, usually the name as it appears in the literature. In some cases, I have changed or modified a name to something that seemed simpler or catchier. Sometimes a technique appears in the literature under multiple names and where possible, I have identified alternative names, usually in the Variations and Extensions section of that SET.

Essential Characteristics

At the top of each SET is a quick overview of important attributes.

> **Primary Mode**: This indicates whether the SET is basically designed for individual or group work. With slight modification, most group projects can be assigned individually, and most individual activities can be structured as collaborative projects.

> **Activity Focus**: Each SET typically involves students reading, writing, or discussing, but a few require other kinds of activities such as presenting, diagramming, performing, problem solving, or even visiting a site. If the kind of activity students do depends upon their specific role within a group or the way the teacher crafts the task, the activity focus is described as *Variable*.

> **Duration of Activity**: Most SETs can be done within a single class session. Those that take longer are identified with *Multiple Sessions*.

> **Online Transferability**: This is my assessment (low/moderate/high) of how well the SET can be adapted to the online environment given current technology.

Description and Purpose

This element provides a brief explanation of the SETs' key characteristics and distinguishing features. The assumption is that all SETs promote active learning and foster motivation—the twin helices of my model for classroom-based student engagement.

Step-by-Step Directions

Here I give instructions for what teachers or students need to do to prepare for or participate in the activity.

Examples

In this section, I include one or more examples that illustrate use of the SET in a wide range of disciplines and in both face-to-face and online classes. These examples have been pulled from the literature, shared with me by faculty colleagues, or drawn from my own experience as a teacher. I hope that readers will learn from examples in all fields and adapt the ideas for their own academic areas.

Online Implementation

This section describes how to adapt the SET for the online environment. Several factors made writing this component challenging. First, technology changes rapidly and this speed is in direct conflict with the enduring nature of print: information that is cutting edge at this moment will soon be out-of-date, and advances that may eventually become commonplace are not yet even imagined. Second, the sophistication of online courses and the level of assistance provided online instructors vary widely across institutions, making it difficult to provide concrete ideas for application. Third, readers will have different levels of students (lower division or graduate seminar?) and sizes of class (12 or 120?), which make it difficult to suggest specific online variations for the activities. But technology is growing in importance and I believe it is critical to offer some ideas for online implementation. I have therefore drawn from my own experience as an online instructor and the experience of my colleagues to offer general guidelines for adapting the SET to the online environment. Advice concentrates on two broad categories of tools: synchronous (such as Chat or Instant Messaging) and asynchronous (such as e-mail, Threaded Discussion, or Wikis).

Variations and Extensions

This section includes ideas and suggestions for ways in which the SET can be adapted, extended, or modified.

Observations and Advice

Here I include additional information I believe may help readers implement the SET successfully, such as caveats, benefits, and suggestions for grading and assessment.

Key Resources

As described above, this element contains one or more helpful sources for further information on the technique.

Chapter 12

Knowledge, Skills, Recall, and Understanding

THESE STUDENT engagement techniques (SETs) focus on engaging students as they learn the facts, principles, and ideas that constitute the foundational knowledge of the subject they are studying. Sometimes referred to as "declarative learning," this is the "what" of the course content and is generally represented by the lower tiers in learning taxonomies. The SETs in this chapter structure opportunities for students to organize, recall, understand, explain, and remember information and core concepts.

S T U D E N T
E N G A G E M E N T
T E C H N I Q U E

1

Background Knowledge Probe

Essential Characteristics

PRIMARY MODE	Individual
ACTIVITY FOCUS	Writing
DURATION OF ACTIVITY	Single Session
ONLINE TRANSFERABILITY	High

DESCRIPTION AND PURPOSE   One of the most important principles in both motivation and learning is working at a level that is appropriately challenging. Activities that are too easy are boring, activities that are too hard are discouraging, and either extreme leads to disengagement. The "Background Knowledge Probe" is a classroom assessment technique (Angelo & Cross, 1993, pp. 121–125) that helps teachers determine the most appropriate level at which to begin instruction.

Teachers develop short, simple, focused questionnaires that students fill out at the beginning of a course, at the start of a new unit, or prior to introducing a new topic. These probes help teachers identify the best starting point for the class as a whole. They also identify under-prepared students for whom remedial work may be needed and extremely well-prepared students who may benefit from tasks that are more challenging. The probes also help learners foreground their prior knowledge so that they can better interpret and assign meaning to new information.

STEP-BY-STEP DIRECTIONS   1. Before starting instruction on an important new concept, subject, or unit, consider what students may already know about it. Although their knowledge may be fragmentary, simplistic, or even incorrect, try to determine at least one point that most students are likely to know. Using this point as the starting place, make a list of less familiar points.

2. Based on your list of points, prepare two or three open-ended questions or a handful of short-answer questions that will probe the students' existing knowledge or understanding. Avoid specialized vocabulary that may be unfamiliar to students because that can interfere with their recall.

3. Write your questions on the board, an overhead transparency, or a presentation slide, or prepare a handout.

4. Explain to students that the purposes of the exercise are (1) to help them recall any relevant prior knowledge so that they can better connect it to what you will be teaching them, (2) to help them start the process of organizing their knowledge, and (3) to help you determine the most appropriate level at which to begin instruction. Assure students that their answers will not be graded.

5. After students have completed the probe, consider forming students in to pairs or small groups to share their responses.

EXAMPLES

Political Science

This professor knows that students start his class with a wide range of backgrounds in history and political science. To get a better sense of what students already know, he distributes a questionnaire that asks students to self-assess their current knowledge on a variety of names, terms, and concepts. An excerpt from the survey is provided in Exhibit 12.1.

The questionnaire continues with key terms and names such as *Republic, the Constitution of the United States,* and *James Madison.* Students submit their answers, which the professor quickly tallies and uses this profile of students' current knowledge to determine which topics he will spend more time on in class (Angelo, 2001).

• • •

Human Anatomy and Physiology

Professor Tish Oosells chose this SET to introduce a unit on the heart. She distributed a handout with an image of the exterior and interior structures of the heart and fill-in lines and arrows pointing to the different structures. She asked students to independently write in the names of as many of the structures they could recall. Then they worked in pairs to pool their knowledge to fill out a single handout, using three different colored pencils to represent individual and shared knowledge.

• • •

EXHIBIT 12.1.

Sample Questions from Political Science Survey

Political Science 100, Section 20

Background Knowledge Probe #1

Please circle the letter that best represents your current knowledge:

1. Federalism
   a. Have never heard of this
   b. Have heard of it, but don't really know what it means
   c. Have some idea what this means, but not too clear
   d. Have a clear idea what this means and can explain it

2. Separation of powers
   a. Have never heard of this
   b. Have heard of it, but don't really know what it means
   c. Have some idea what this means, but not too clear
   d. Have a clear idea what this means and can explain it

Music of Multicultural America

This professor uses a "Background Knowledge Probe" as both a pre- and post-assessment tool. She finds that the open-ended nature of the prompt helps capture a wide range of student knowledge and that the authentic nature of the task appeals to students. In addition to helping her assess students' starting points, the grid (Exhibit 12.2 is an example) helps her identify students with special expertise whom she can consider inviting to give an in-class presentation. At the end of the term, she has students fill out the grid again to assess how well they have achieved the course's learning goals. Students compare their responses on the pre- and post-grids, and they often report that it is gratifying to see how much they have learned. To ensure students are drawing from long-term rather than short-term memory (see T/S 20, "Teach for retention" in Chapter 8 for more information), she does not inform students of the assessment in advance, and she also assures students the results will not negatively affect their course grade. She quickly evaluates the grids by assigning one point for each substantive information item and gives the points to students as bonuses.

ONLINE IMPLEMENTATION This SET is easily implemented online as an assignment.

VARIATIONS AND EXTENSIONS
- Ask students to pair up and share insights or observations regarding their levels of background knowledge. Or have them pair up to create a composite assessment based on their combined knowledge.

EXHIBIT 12.2.

Music Background Knowledge Probe

Music of Multicultural America

Knowledge Grid

Name_____

Directions: You are hosting a visitor from another country who asks you about American music. At first you can't think of anything but the latest pop hits, but then you remember (1) how America is a nation of immigrants, (2) how immigrants brought the music traditions of their home countries with them to America, and (3) how the cross-fertilization of immigrant styles led to the creation of the new kinds of music that we call "American music." Use single words and short phrases to indicate the info and ideas you use to show your visitor you know what you are talking about.

	The Social/Historical Context	The Music (Representative Artists, Structural Characteristics, etc.)
Native American music		
Gospel		
Blues		
Jazz		
Country		
Urban folk revival		
Rock 'n' roll		
Tejano, Banda		
Salsa, Reggae		
Hip-hop, Rap		

- Consider using the information you glean to pair students into mentor relationships.

- "Knowledge Surveys" (Nuhfer and Knipp, 2003) are a more extensive approach to determining what students know. They can be used to assess information for an entire course, thus avoiding the piecemeal approach that can result from assessing background at the unit or task level. See T/S 38, "Assess students' starting points," in Chapter 10 for a more detailed description of this assessment method.

- In a variation called "Con-Venn-Tions" (Rogers, 1997), students are given index cards and asked to each write the 5–8 most significant points they know with respect to a given topic, one idea per card. In pairs, students share and organize their ideas, sorting the cards into three piles consisting of unique and shared ideas in order to develop a Venn diagram containing their pooled knowledge about the topic. They can use an actual Venn diagram or a simple table created in a word-processing program (see Table 12.1).

OBSERVATIONS AND ADVICE   If a student has little or no background knowledge, this activity may be demoralizing. If you suspect that some students in your class may fit this category, consider spending time up front building trust by assuring them that you want all students to be able to succeed and reinforcing that one of the ways you can help them succeed is by knowing all the students' starting places.

If what students already know is far more or far less than you expect, this SET can be overwhelming because it can challenge you to make major revisions in your instructional plans. Therefore, do not use this activity if you do not have the time, energy, and willingness to make adjustments if necessary.

KEY RESOURCES   Angelo, T. A., & Cross, K. P. (1993). Background knowledge probe. *Classroom assessment techniques*. San Francisco: Jossey-Bass, pp. 121–125.

Angelo, T. A. (2001). Speech at opening plenary session of the Central California Conference on Assessing Student Learning, California State University, Fresno, April 27.

Nuhfer, E., & Knipp, D. (2003). The knowledge survey: A tool for all reasons. *To Improve the Academy, 21*, pp. 59–78. Retrieved from http://www.isu.edu/ctl/facultydev/KnowS_files/KnowS.htm

Rogers, S. (1997). *Motivation and learning: A teacher's guide to building excitement of learning and igniting the drive for quality*. Golden, CO: Peak Learning Systems.

TABLE 12.1.

Sample Table for "Con-Venn-Tions"

Student 1's Ideas	Shared Ideas	Student 2's Ideas

S T U D E N T
E N G A G E M E N T
T E C H N I Q U E

2

Artifacts

Essential Characteristics

PRIMARY MODE	Collaborative
ACTIVITY FOCUS	Discussing
DURATION OF ACTIVITY	Single Session
ONLINE TRANSFERABILITY	Medium

DESCRIPTION AND PURPOSE
Based on the premise that images and objects can sometimes be more evocative than text, "Artifacts" uses visual representations and handheld items to arouse curiosity, stimulate ideas, and focus students when introducing a topic. Teachers provide groups of students with photos, specimens, charts, graphs, drawings, or objects that represent key ideas about a topic. Students then discuss the items in relation to instructor-designed prompts.

STEP-BY-STEP DIRECTIONS
1. Identify a concept you wish students to discuss that is rich, complex, important to understand, and lends itself to visual imagery or physical representation.

2. Collect or duplicate a sufficient number of objects or images to create a set for each group of 4–5 students.

3. Craft the prompts you will use to guide students as they examine the artifacts and write these on handouts, presentation slides, or overhead transparencies.

4. Decide how you will have students report out their findings.

5. Form groups of 4–6 students, explain the purpose and directions for the activity, and distribute items to each group of students.

Remedial Math

This professor gathered postcards with a variety of evocative images such as tightrope walkers, a cartoon of a man looking overwhelmed next to a stack of books, and a picture of Edvard Munch's painting *The Scream*. On the first day of class, she organized students into groups of five, gave each group a stack of postcards, and told students to pick out a card whose image best captured how they felt about learning math. She gave students a few minutes to discuss their choices in groups and then moved to a whole-class discussion about math anxiety. She found that the activity was a lighthearted, engaging way to start building trust and community by foregrounding students' fears and reassuring them that they were not alone in their nervousness.

• • •

Art History

Professor Al E. Gorical wanted students to understand how medieval Christian architecture used symbols and design elements to express a wide variety of spiritual concepts. Following a lecture in which he explained the meaning and significance underlying various numbers, colors, and objects, he distributed photos of different church facades as well as diagrams showing their structural layout. He formed students into groups of three and asked them to look closely at the images and identify and describe five or six uses of religious symbolism in the architecture of the churches.

• • •

American History

To start a discussion on European immigration and settlement in the United States during the nineteenth century, Professor Emma Grashon gathered a chart of statistics, excerpts from immigrant diaries, a photo of the Statue of Liberty along with a key to Bartholdi's use of symbols in the statue, and a collection of photos (a starving family on a farm in Ireland, a village in ruins following a pogrom in Russia and so forth), and asked groups to answer a series of questions on a worksheet related to why people came to America.

ONLINE IMPLEMENTATION For two-dimensional artifacts such as images, charts, graphs, and drawings, gather a collection and place it on a single Web page, craft the prompts, and ask students to discuss their responses and ideas in a threaded forum or submit them individually as an assignment. For three-dimensional objects, see the section titled "To Motivate Students to Be Interested in What I'm Teaching" in the first case study in Chapter 6. In the case study, J. Baker asks students in an online class to collect common household items and reflect on and respond to prompts in a written assignment.

VARIATIONS AND EXTENSIONS

- Although this activity was developed with graphic and physical objects in mind, written information (such as quotations, statistical data, and facts) can also be used by copying it onto index cards.
- Have students collect items (such as photos, drawings they've created illustrating a literature assignment, or specimens related to a biology or botany course) and create their own set of artifacts.

OBSERVATIONS AND ADVICE

Items that can be seen, touched, handled, and passed between students can engage students by helping to make abstract ideas or notions real.

Use this basic activity to stimulate discussion in response to a wide variety of prompts. For example, provide

- objects that represent different versions of an idea and ask students to compare and contrast the two;
- photographs of disease symptoms and ask students to offer diagnoses;
- different images of an event (for example, war photos, political cartoons, and military recruitment posters) and ask students to answer questions such as Whose viewpoint or perspective does this image reflect? What does it mean? Why was this image made?
- objects or images and ask students to evaluate their function or effectiveness in conveying a message with questions such as Which of these are better? Why?
- a series of pictures and ask students to put them into a sequence and construct a story.

KEY RESOURCE Dodge, J. (2005). *Differentiation in action*. New York: Scholastic, pp. 37–39.

**S T U D E N T
E N G A G E M E N T
T E C H N I Q U E**

3

Focused Reading Notes

Essential Characteristics

PRIMARY MODE	Individual
ACTIVITY FOCUS	Reading, Writing
DURATION OF ACTIVITY	Single Session
ONLINE TRANSFERABILITY	High

DESCRIPTION AND PURPOSE
This technique gives students a strategy for focusing their reading to help them become more efficient and effective learners. Prior to giving students a reading assignment, instructors identify 3–5 themes or concepts they want students to look for in the text and then choose corresponding keywords or phrases. Students use these keywords as headings for columns on a sheet of paper and enter reading notes in the appropriate column. The column headings direct students' attention to what is important and provide them with an organizational framework for writing notes about new knowledge and understandings.

STEP-BY-STEP DIRECTIONS
1. Decide what it is you want students to look for in a reading assignment and assign keywords or phrases. For example, if the assignment is Plato's dialogue *Crito*, the headings might be "Crito's values," "Socrates' values," "Use of analogies," "City or family versus the individual," and "My questions or responses" (Bean, 1996, p. 144).

2. Try out the keywords by creating columns and jotting down representative examples in the reading yourself, and then make any necessary adjustments.

3. Create a handout, or simply plan to give students the column headings and instruct them to create their own worksheet.

4. Explain the process to students, giving examples so that your expectations are clear.

5. As students read, they look for examples that correspond to the headings and write these down in the appropriate column.

6. Students submit their notes, or use them as study notes or as the basis for discussion with a partner.

EXAMPLES

English Literature

Professor Rita Booke decided to have students write an essay in class analyzing Joy Kogawa's *Obasan*, a novel about the relocation of Japanese Canadians to internment camps during WWII. To prepare them for an in-class essay analyzing how changes in perspective and style reflect the narrator's complex attitude toward the past, she created a handout with four columns with headings for different literary elements: point of view, structure, selection of detail, and figurative language. As students read, they looked for examples of these elements in Kogawa's writing and noted them in the appropriate column. Students were encouraged to bring their "Focused Reading Notes" to class for reference when they wrote their essays.

• • •

Music History

The textbook for this course was dense with data and information and many students found it overwhelming. To guide students, the instructor created a master template for each historical period; the column headings were (1) Genres and styles, (2) Representative composers and compositions, and (3) Characteristic treatment of structural elements. Students were asked to fill in the columns with information gleaned from their reading and use these worksheets as study guides for the data portion of the exams. She also asked students to submit completed worksheets on exam days prior to taking the test.

ONLINE IMPLEMENTATION

This is an easy technique to implement online. Prepare as you would for a face-to-face class, providing the explanation with columns, headings, and examples as an assignment that students submit either as an e-mail attachment or within your course's assignment tool.

VARIATIONS AND EXTENSIONS

• Use "Focused Reading Notes" as a preparatory activity for whole-class or small-group discussion, an essay, or an early step in a more comprehensive project.

• Instead of a worksheet with columns and headings, make an "Interactive Bookmark" to guide students as they read. Create a handout consisting of a vertical half-page bookmark listing prompts to guide students to take notes as they read independently. Prompts can focus on activities such as identifying cause-and-effect relationships, recognizing text structure, paraphrasing, inferring, and summarizing. This variation gives readers flexibility to choose the way they respond to the text (words, symbols, or other nonlinguistic elements). It can be used to engage students by activating prior knowledge, providing closure before moving from one subtopic to another, or to check for understanding and misconceptions. Here are some examples of prompts (Dodge, 2005, pp. 141–142):

Jot down a key idea expressed by the author.

Paraphrase what you have read.

Draw a symbol or picture to help you remember an important part.

Make note of something important (a quotation, a theme).

Make a connection between this text and your own experiences.

Make a connection between this text and another.

Make a connection between this text and something in the real world.

Write two questions that can be answered by the reading.

Predict what will happen next.

Note evidence of text structure.

Identify a confusing part.

Pose a question you want answered.

Give your opinion of what you read.

Create a metaphor or simile to help you remember an important word or idea.

OBSERVATIONS AND ADVICE Once students have become skilled at discovering key issues and themes in a reading, they can develop their own headings (Bean, 1996, p. 144).

If the entries in the columns will be uneven in terms of length (for example, sentences and terms), it may be more efficient to use a separate page for each heading.

KEY RESOURCES Bean, J. C. (1996). *Engaging ideas: The professor's guide to integrating writing, critical thinking, and active learning in the classroom.* San Francisco, Jossey-Bass, p. 144.

Dodge, J. (2005). *Differentiation in action.* New York: Scholastic, p. 141–142.

S T U D E N T
E N G A G E M E N T
T E C H N I Q U E

4

Quotes

Essential Characteristics

PRIMARY MODE	Collaborative
ACTIVITY FOCUS	Discussing
DURATION OF ACTIVITY	Single Session
ONLINE TRANSFERABILITY	Moderate

DESCRIPTION AND PURPOSE

Students select a slip of paper from a container filled with quotes from an assigned reading. They are given a few minutes to think about what they want to say in response to their quote, and then each student reads their quote and comments on it.

"Quotes" is an effective strategy for ensuring equitable participation because it provides all students a platform by which to join the discussion. It also underscores the instructor's commitment to the value of the assigned reading, addressing complaints that follow-up, in-class conversations do not draw explicitly enough on the text that students have been asked to spend time reading.

STEP-BY-STEP DIRECTIONS

1. Select 5–6 different sentences or passages from a text.
2. Type and copy these to create multiple slips of paper each containing one quote, and put them into a container.
3. Each student draws one slip of paper.
4. Students take a few minutes to think about what they want to say in response to their quote.
5. In an order controlled by students, the discussion continues with each student reading a quote and commenting on it, offering new insights or building upon or contradicting comments that have already been made.

Introduction to Shakespeare

Professor Rose N. Crantz uses a variation of "Quotes" as a means to stimulate whole-class discussion and detailed analysis of the dramatic works of Shakespeare. She selects a variety of quotes from one of the assigned plays. Students use the quote they've drawn as the basis for their contribution to the discussion. The first student to talk about a specific quote must provide, at a minimum, basic information about the quote (who said it and the dramatic context). Other students build upon these comments, adding insights regarding the quote's deeper meaning and relationship to the play's themes. She observes that the SET helps ensure students have done the reading and come to class prepared, that it gets discussion started quickly, and that the structure propels the discussion naturally as students must offer new and deeper insights as they build upon each other's contributions.

• • •

Principles of Advertising

In this course, the teacher selects slogans from a wide range of advertising campaigns spanning several decades and prints them on index cards. He then organizes students into groups, asks each group to draw 2–3 cards from the stack, and participate in a group discussion on the selected quote. To help focus the discussion, he provides students with a handout that includes a series of prompts asking students to determine the intended audience; to identify the idea, product, or service the slogan was designed to promote; and to analyze why, in their assessment, the slogan was or was not persuasive. He follows up with a whole-class discussion in which students identify the characteristics of effective advertising slogans, using the quotes their group analyzed to illustrate their points.

ONLINE IMPLEMENTATION

Although this technique is very effective when students are able to interact in the moment as they respond to their quote and to the comments of others, you can modify it for an online course by selecting 4–5 quotes and creating a forum for each quote, asking students to select a forum (or assigning them to a forum) to which they post comments on the quote.

VARIATIONS AND EXTENSIONS

- Ask students to find their own relevant quotes from a preparatory text. Quotes in the pre-reading can be statements that they especially liked or disliked, that best illustrated the major thesis, that they found most difficult to understand, and so forth. Students say where their quote is in the text (for example, "page 3, paragraph 5") and then read the quote while all class members follow along (Brookfield & Preskill, 2005, pp. 72–73).

- Instead of drawing quotes from an assigned reading, select a set of interesting quotes to use as a discussion stimulus.

- Organize students into groups, give groups a container with the quotes, and have students draw and comment on their quote in round-robin fashion.

OBSERVATIONS AND ADVICE   Give students sufficient time to think about their quote and formulate their ideas before starting the class discussion. The time required will depend on the nature, scope, and complexity of the quotes and the reading assignment from which they were taken.

KEY RESOURCE   Brookfield, S. D., & Preskill, S. (2005). *Discussion as a way of teaching: Tools and techniques for democratic classrooms.* San Francisco: Jossey-Bass, pp. 72–73.

STUDENT
ENGAGEMENT
TECHNIQUE

5

Stations

Essential Characteristics

PRIMARY MODE	Collaborative
ACTIVITY FOCUS	Multiple
DURATION OF ACTIVITY	Single Session
ONLINE TRANSFERABILITY	High

DESCRIPTION AND PURPOSE

This SET offers an alternative to traditional lecture. It engages students by requiring them to move around the room and interact with learning materials in an active way as they examine, question, exchange ideas with peers, respond to prompts, and formulate their own thoughts and commentary.

Exhibits can be simple (flip-chart paper with a question written on it) or elaborate (an interactive multi-sensory presentation). Displayed items depend on course content and instructional goals. Examples are written documents (such as letters, content summaries, quotes), visual documents (charts, photographs, art work reproductions), objects (cultural artifacts, biological specimens), and media (audio and film recordings). Learner interactions also vary and can include solving exhibit-posed problems, discussing responses to a prompt, using exhibit information to complete worksheets, or writing group or individual reflective essays.

STEP-BY-STEP DIRECTIONS

1. Select a topic that seems suitable for display and ask yourself what kinds of objects, images, documents, and other items could be included in an exhibit that would help students learn at a deeper, more engaged level than could be achieved from a more traditional method of accessing information such as reading.

2. Plan for exhibit logistics (number, type, and location of stations; items needed at each station; how students will move among stations; how

long they will have at each station; and so forth). Although it is possible to make a "progressive" exhibit (with each station building upon the learning acquired in the previous station), stand-alone stations are more practical because students can begin at different stations and start touring the exhibit at the same time.

3. Construct the exhibits and create and copy a group worksheet that gives directions and questions about each station in the exhibit.

4. Use class size, numbers of stations, exhibit layout, and complexity of interaction to decide on the size of the groups that will move through the exhibit together and whether multiple groups can be at the same station at the same time. Groups of 2–3 students are generally the most practical.

5. Divide the class into groups, explain the task, hand out the worksheet, and elicit questions.

EXAMPLES

African American Literature

This professor used "Stations" as a follow-up activity to reading Jamaica Kincaid's *Autobiography of My Mother*. She created six stations, each consisting of a taped piece of newsprint with a single question at the top. For example on Station 1, this was the prompt:

> This book starts with the following quote, "My mother died at the moment I was born, and so for my whole life there was nothing standing between myself and eternity; at my back was always a bleak, black wind." How does this set the tone for the book? What does this say about Xuela to you?

She organized students into groups of five, gave each group a different colored marker, and had groups start at different stations. Groups were asked to discuss the prompt and write their response onto the paper. At about ten-minute intervals, she announced, "Change stations" and groups moved to the next station. After students had visited all stations, she had groups go around a second time and put a check next to the response (other than their own) that they felt was most thoughtful and interesting. The activity closed with a whole-class discussion, and the group that had received the most checks next to their responses received bonus points.

•   •   •

Mathematics

To help motivate students in a remedial math course, Professor Al Gorithem wanted students to think about how understanding basic math principles could help them make better choices in their lives. He set aside one class session early in the term for students to walk around in small groups and tour an exhibit he titled "Math in Daily Life: How Do Numbers Affect Everyday Decisions?" He gave each group a worksheet to record their responses to problems posed at the five exhibit stations. Groups were allowed a specific amount of time at each exhibit, and when he announced, "Rotate," they moved on to the next exhibit.

The first station, "Playing to Win," consisted of a poster with a brief narrative describing the many ways people make decisions based on probability (such as sports bets, lottery tickets, poker, casino gambling, stock markets). Students were then asked to select a color-coded paper scrap out of a brown bag and compare their results against mathematical probabilities. The second station in the exhibit, "Savings and Credit," explained simple and compound interest. Using examples from savings accounts, loans, credit bills, and so forth, students were asked to solve problems that showed how paying attention to these percentages could make big payoffs in terms of their financial well-being. The remaining stations ("Population Growth," "Cooking by Numbers," and "Math: The Universal Language") contained similar displays and problems to solve. After the groups had visited all the stations, he held a brief whole-class discussion, then asked groups to submit their worksheets (adapted from Annenberg Media Learner.org, n.d.).

•   •   •

U.S. History

To help deepen students' understanding of the issues, historical significance, and human dimension of Watergate, (the political scandal stemming from the 1972 break-in by Republican operatives at the U.S. Democratic National Committee headquarters), Professor Vi O'Lashuns requires students to explore the Ford Library's online exhibit titled "The Watergate Files" (http://www.fordlibrary museum.gov/museum/exhibits/watergate_files/intro.php). The exhibit is organized into five display areas:

The Watergate Trial: May 1972–January 1973

Senate Hearings: February 1973–July 1973

Battle for the Tapes: July 1973–November 1973

Trials and Tribulations: February 1974–April 1974

The Aftermath: May 1974–September 1974

Each display area provides an overview, corresponding documents, a timeline, film clips and photographs, and brief bios of the people involved. To guide students through the exhibit, she created a worksheet containing questions requiring both objective and subjective answers and then had students write a reflective essay.

VARIATIONS AND EXTENSIONS

- Find online sites to create a virtual exhibit. A search for using "educational exhibits" as keywords will help you find a wide range of sites, including sites that are resources for finding other sites. For example, the Franklin Institute's *Resources for Science Learning* (http://www.fi.edu/learn/hotlists/jump.php) includes lists of educational and interactive exhibits such as "Linus Pauling: A Centenary Exhibit" and "The History of Computing."

OBSERVATIONS AND ADVICE

Posters containing relevant information can be hung on walls around the classroom. Most print shops can take a page created using standard word-processing software and expand it to poster size.

Because exhibits tend to be multisensory, this SET is more engaging than traditional lectures for visual and kinesthetic learners.

If the exhibits are complex, "Stations" can be time-consuming and labor-intensive. However, if you are able and willing to put in the investment, the payoff in terms of student engagement can be substantial. Well-designed exhibits can help students make connections between theory and practice, understand principles and concepts at a deeper level, and be an interesting and enjoyable change of pace. Furthermore, once developed, the exhibits can be used in subsequent classes, hence amortizing the effort over time.

If your classroom does not have the physical space to house an exhibit, there may be community space on campus for the exhibit.

Elicit the help of students.

Be sure to allow sufficient time at the end to disassemble and pack up the exhibits.

KEY RESOURCES

Brookfield, S., & Preskill, S. (2005). *Discussion as a way of teaching: Tools and techniques for democratic classrooms.* San Francisco: Jossey-Bass, pp. 107–108.

Tomlinson, C. A. (1999). *The differentiated classroom: Responding to the needs of all learners.* Alexandria, VA: Association for Supervision and Curriculum Development, pp. 62–65.

**STUDENT
ENGAGEMENT
TECHNIQUE**

6

Team Jeopardy

Essential Characteristics

PRIMARY MODE	Collaborative
ACTIVITY FOCUS	Discussing
DURATION OF ACTIVITY	Single Session
ONLINE TRANSFERABILITY	Low

***DESCRIPTION
AND PURPOSE***

The main focus of some courses is to help students understand and remember the basic facts, figures, and vocabulary that constitute a course or discipline's foundational knowledge. Often this material must be mastered before students can move on to tasks that require higher levels of thinking. Yet it is sometimes difficult to motivate students to put in the effort required to memorize such material. Modeled on the TV show *Jeopardy!*, this SET offers a fast-paced, energizing way for students to work together as they review this kind of nuts-and-bolts information.

Student teams take turns selecting the category and point value of cells on a grid that correspond to course content questions, and then compete to answer these questions correctly. As on *Jeopardy!* questions are presented in the form of an answer. For example, the correct response to the grid question "An Englishman considered to be the father of antiseptic surgery" is "Who was Joseph Lister?" Questions are organized in categories and vary in difficulty, with more challenging questions having the potential to earn more points. When the question is revealed, a team has an allotted time period to "ring in" with their response.

***STEP-BY-STEP
DIRECTIONS***

1. Choose the medium for your game board. For most teachers, the simplest medium is an overhead transparency, so the following preparation

steps will be based on this choice. See Variations and Extensions later in this SET for other mediums.

2. Decide on the number and type of categories (for example, People, Places, Events, Dates, Things), the number of questions for each category, and whether there will be more than one match. A match consists of one time through the entire grid.

3. On an overhead transparency (or other medium), create a simple table in which the columns correspond to categories and the row cells correspond to questions. In each cell, write in varying numbers of points. For an example, see Table 12.2.

4. Prepare questions and answers for each category, varying the level of difficulty and assigning each question one of the established point values.

5. Decide how teams will "ring in." The quietest and easiest method is for the team captain to raise a hand (or stand up) and say "Ready!"

6. Decide on and print out game rules and directions. "Team Jeopardy" can be played with many variations (see Variations and Extensions in this SET), but Exhibit 12.2 is an example of basic rules.

7. Divide the class into teams of 5–6 students and designate (or have teams choose) a team captain who will choose the cells and state the team's answer.

8. Post (or distribute) the rules, review them with the class, and answer any questions.

9. Decide which team goes first.

10. Proceed, following your established rules.

11. Cross off each cell as it is selected.

12. Keep score on the board using a simple score sheet such as Table 12.3.

TABLE 12.2.

Grid for "Team Jeopardy"

Category I	Category II	Category III	Category IV	Category V
5	5	5	5	5
10	10	10	10	10
15	15	15	15	15
20	20	20	20	20
25	25	25	25	25

EXHIBIT 12.2.

Rules for Team Jeopardy

1. Each team has a team captain who has 30 seconds to select a cell (for example, "Category I for 30 points").
2. Team A starts. Once the teacher reads the question, Team A has 1 minute to decide on its answer and "ring in."
3. Once the team rings in, the team captain has 30 seconds to state the team's answer to the whole class.
4. Correct answers earn the stated points, and the next turn moves to Team B.
5. Incorrect answers lose the stated points, and Team B gets an opportunity to answer. If that team answers correctly, it earns the stated points and has the opportunity to select a new category/point cell.
6. If a team cannot provide an answer, the team loses the points stated on the cell, and the opportunity to answer the question goes to the next team. If that team answers correctly, it earns the stated points and has the opportunity to select a new category/point cell.
7. At the end of the match, the team with the most points wins. In the event of a tie, the two teams will compete to answer a tie-breaker question.
8. Winning team members will be rewarded with the following number of points applied toward their final grade:

1st Place:	2nd Place:	3rd Place:
50 Points	30 Points	10 Points

TABLE 12.3

Score Sheet for "Team Jeopardy"

Team 1	Team 2	Team 3	Team 4

History of the United States

To motivate students to learn and remember the basic information that served as the knowledge foundation for the course, Professor James Town used "Team Jeopardy" as a review strategy to prepare students for both the midterm and the final exam. A week before the game, he provided students with a study guide that included names, dates, and core concepts. On the review day, he divided the class into teams of six students and led them through several fast-paced rounds of the game. Members of the three teams with the top scores were given bonus points that were applied to their exam scores. Students told him they enjoyed the change of pace from the usual lecture. He found that they also performed better on the objective portion of the exam.

ONLINE IMPLEMENTATION This SET does not transfer to the online environment.

VARIATIONS AND EXTENSIONS

- Eliminate the *Jeopardy!* twist and pose traditional questions as opposed to questions in the form of answers.

- To help visual learners and non-native speakers or to help all students if the questions are too complex to understand by listening to the teacher reading them, transfer each question to its own overhead transparency along with the category/point value in font large enough to be read by the students at their desks. Keep the transparencies organized by categories so that you can easily retrieve them during the game.

- Use this SET for problem-solving or more complex essay questions by extending the response time or having all teams work on a response simultaneously. For example, teams can compete to be the first to successfully solve a math or economics problem.

- Include one or more special "bonus questions" that are hidden behind regular questions and can be answered only by the team that selected that cell. The team can wager all or part of its accumulated points and have that amount either added to or subtracted from its total depending on whether the answer is correct.

- Reduce student anxiety over answering incorrectly by eliminating penalties.

- Instead of alternating teams, allow teams to compete simultaneously with individual team members ringing in to compete to answer the question.

- Vary the prizes. Instead of grade points, consider coupons for assignment exemption, candy, or gift coupons for coffee or fast food.

- If the class is large, consider having multiple games played simultaneously. Divide the class into an equal number of teams, subdivide into groups of two teams, and proceed with concurrent games of two teams competing against each other monitored by students who have been designated as game show hosts.

- To prevent a hot-shot team from collecting all the points from the higher-level cells early in the game, require that all columns in Row 1 be selected before moving to Row 2, then all in Row 2 before moving to Row 3, and so forth.

- Add variety to the game by selecting categories requiring different kinds of responses—for example, short answer, essay, image identification, role play, problem-solving. Increase point values as questions become more challenging.

- If you decide to use this SET on a regular basis, consider purchasing the materials to conduct a more official-looking game. Instead of using an overhead transparency, construct a game board out of cardboard or foam-core board (approximately 5×4 feet) and use 3×5 inch sticky notes for each cell. On the side of the note that faces the students, write the point value, and on the opposite side, write the corresponding question. For an even more professional appearance, invest in game show supplies. For example, Trainer's Warehouse (http://www.trainerswarehouse.com/) offers a wide array of supplies including different sizes of game boards and buzzers for ringing in.

- LearningWare (http://www.learningware.com/) offers software that helps you construct games and also incorporate them into online classes.

- Extend this SET by combining it with CoLT 12, "Test Taking Teams" in *Collaborative Learning Techniques* (Barkley, Cross, & Major, 2005). Form the teams prior to the game and have them study for the review game (which will prepare them for a subsequent exam) together. Use "Team Jeopardy" to review. On the day of the exam, have individuals take the exam and then, before you return the graded exam, have them take the exam again with their team. Individual grades can be a combination of that student's "Team Jeopardy" score, individual exam, and team exam.

OBSERVATIONS AND ADVICE   "Team Jeopardy" works best for review of a lot of fact-related information. It is not as effective for questions with subjective or highly involved answers.

The amount of time you wish to allot for this activity in combination with the extent of the material you wish to review will dictate the number of questions and matches. A typical "Team Jeopardy" game involving twenty-five questions for two matches takes 30–45 minutes. Shorten the game by using smaller grids (such as 3 × 3) or breaking the game into several segments, using only part of the grid at one time.

Provide students with a study guide to prepare for the game.

Game shows require clearly defined and established rules that are communicated up front. You are the rule maker, so you can customize the rules for the level of competition or collaboration you want, the type of questions you wish to ask, the ways in which you wish to reward or penalize, and so forth. Post or distribute the rules and go over them in advance. Most of the unproductive contentiousness that can arise due to the competition in this SET is due to unclear rules. For example, in the real *Jeopardy!* game show, contestants must answer in the form of a question. In an educational context, this rule is usually ignored and participants can say "Joseph Lister" without having to preface it with "Who is." It will save potential problems if you make this explicit as part of the game rules.

Timing is important in this SET. Establish times in advance, but know that the timing can be adjusted during the game if you find that the times are too long or too short. Depending on how you structure the game, you may need to set times for three elements:

Read time: How long teams have to read (or hear) and understand the question;

Ring-in time: How much time teams have before deciding they will try to answer; and

Answer time: How much time a team has to provide its answer.

Timers are crucial for effective game play because they keep things moving and fair. Kitchen timers work best because they free teachers from having to look at their watch.

If ring-in time is highly competitive, you can distinguish which team rings in first by using different kinds of noisemakers such as bells, whistles, and sound-effect makers.

Consider appointing a student as your assistant who can help you by keeping score, serving as a second set of eyes to see which team rings in first, crossing off cells, and so forth.

This SET can be particularly effective for test preparation as it helps ensure adequate preparation, thus alleviating test-taking anxiety. Furthermore, because it can be fun, students relax and are more open to learning and remembering.

"Team Jeopardy" promotes teamwork, encouraging students to use their classmates as a resource.

This SET gives immediate feedback to both the instructor and the students on how well material has been mastered. Students, particularly, can gauge what they are and are not understanding or remembering.

You can use this SET to clarify and expand on material. For example, if the question is "The type of soil conditioner that should be used when planting a new evergreen tree" and the response is "Peat moss," the teacher can elaborate by saying "Peat moss is essential to retain moisture, fertilize, and loosen hard soils."

Some students may get rowdy, or highly competitive students may resort to cheating or unsportsmanlike behavior. Professional sports offer ideas for penalties: consider giving a warning for the first infraction; deducting points as appropriate; giving non-offending teams free opportunities to answer and gain additional points; requiring offending teams or players to sit out one or more rounds or, in the worst cases, expelling them from the game.

This SET can be a single activity, but it can also be effective if used so that groups work together to review material on several occasions. This allows students to form strong bonds and to begin to feel responsible for each other's successes.

KEY RESOURCE   Yaman, D., & Covington, M. (2006). *I'll take learning for 500: Using game shows to engage, motivate, and train.* San Francisco: Pfeiffer, pp. 47–49.

S T U D E N T
E N G A G E M E N T
T E C H N I Q U E

7

Seminar

Essential Characteristics

PRIMARY MODE	Collaborative
ACTIVITY FOCUS	Multiple
DURATION OF ACTIVITY	Single Session
ONLINE TRANSFERABILITY	Medium

DESCRIPTION AND PURPOSE
"Seminar" helps students prepare for and participate in an in-depth, focused, and meaningful small-group discussion of a text. In preparation for class, students read a document, marking and prioritizing specific passages they want to discuss with the group, and writing a short essay about what they read in response to a prompt. Students bring their marked-up copies and essay to class, and they use these as their ticket to participate in a highly structured small-group discussion.

The steps students must take to prepare for the discussion encourage them to stay focused in their reading and to get more deeply into the source, even if they initially find it overwhelming or off-putting. The structure of the small-group discussion provides even shy and diffident students and non-native speakers with a platform to practice their voice. Additionally, the passages that each student reads are ones that they found to be most personally relevant and therefore require some degree of individual commitment.

STEP-BY-STEP DIRECTIONS
1. Select a text that is conceptually rich (a journal piece, a book chapter, a newspaper editorial) and duplicate it or provide a Portable Document File (PDF) online so that each student has his or her own copy to mark up.
2. Craft a prompt for a writing assignment that connects to the reading and will prepare students for participating in a discussion.

3. Create a handout that provides students with directions for both the reading and discussion. Consider incorporating Exhibit 12.3, "Identifying Good Seminar Behaviors."

4. Outside of class, students read the document, marking and then prioritizing the passages that they found to be most interesting, provocative, puzzling, and so forth and that they want to discuss with the group. They also write a brief essay in response to the instructor-developed prompt. This preparation is their ticket for assignment to a small group (although they do not submit the essay until the SET is finished).

5. The teacher forms prepared students into groups of 4–6. (Either dismiss unprepared students, or allow them to observe in fishbowl fashion, sitting in chairs outside a group, listening to the discussion but not participating.)

6. In round-robin fashion, each student selects one of his or her high-priority passages, identifies it (such as "page 3 paragraph 2") so that other group members can follow along, reads it aloud to the group, and then briefly explains why it was selected. The other group members listen and take notes but do not respond.

7. After every student has contributed, students respond to what they heard from one or two of the other participants.

8. Students enter into a free-flowing discussion, sharing what they learned or found most meaningful, and as much as possible connecting their comments to specific passages in the text.

9. After discussion, students add further comments, reflections, or insights as a postscript to their essays and submit them to the instructor.

EXAMPLES

Intro to American Literature

Professor Sal Inas uses "Seminar" regularly to provide a structure for both discussion and in-depth analysis of reading assignments. For example, as students read John Steinbeck's *East of Eden*, he organizes a "Seminar" around the theme of immigration and American literature, and asks students to mark up the text as well as write a brief essay in response to the prompt "When Sam and his wife Liza immigrate to America, what is it from the 'old country' that they bring with them, and why? How does living in America change them, and their children? What are the challenges and the opportunities America presents to the family?"

• • •

Cultural Anthropology

To help students explore anthropological perspectives on contemporary issues, this professor decided to use "Seminar" to have his students discuss a think piece on the challenges Bhutan, an isolated Himalayan Buddhist kingdom, faces as it opens to the Western world. She asked students to read through the article and mark it carefully, paying special attention to the topics of political organization, language, kinship, religions, and social inequality that they were studying in class. She also asked students to write responses to each of the following questions:

- Identify three examples the author provides on how tradition and change now coalesce in Bhutan.

- Discuss three concerns a cultural anthropologist might have regarding the impact of westernization on traditional Bhutanese culture.

Students used their marked-up articles and their written assignment as the basis for small-group discussions. The teacher believed that the activity helped deepen students' grasp of the concepts, theories, and methods used in the class, and by focusing on the challenges Bhutan was facing right now, that the activity helped give the course contemporary relevance.

ONLINE IMPLEMENTATION This technique is designed for a face-to-face environment. However, the basic steps can be adapted for an online class. For the reading stage of this SET, students can take notes on specific passages and write the essay and then submit these as an assignment. After submission, students can be assigned to a group to participate in an online discussion. To implement the SET without adaptation, students could scan and upload their marked-up documents and talk "in the moment" using synchronous tools such as teleconferencing or chat sessions—but these modifications are cumbersome and probably not worth the effort.

OBSERVATIONS AND ADVICE Most students will need guidance on how to read critically and how to contribute effectively to the discussion. Suggest to students that as they read, they keep in mind the following three questions and underline appropriate passages or make comments in the margins:

1. What does the text say? (Stick to straightforward facts.)
2. What does the text mean? (Look for the concepts or interpretations behind the exact words or inferences between the lines.)
3. Why is this important? (Share your personal analysis, reaction, or evaluation.)

To prepare students for good discussion, consider reviewing with them Exhibit 12.3, "Identifying Good Seminar Behaviors."

EXHIBIT 12.3.

Identifying Good Seminar Behaviors

When assessing seminar behaviors one can ask, How does a person contribute to the seminar? To what degree does he or she engage in the following three kinds of behaviors?

A. **Introduce substantive points:** A substantive point is one that is clearly a result of thoughtful reading and thinking about the assigned text and becomes the focus for group exploration lasting several minutes.

　Identify essential issues or questions the text is discussing.

　Point to the author's main hypotheses, claims, and supporting arguments and evidence.

　Point to important passages that need to be understood.

　Explain the complexities faced in exploring this text.

　Describe passages that are personally meaningful or connected to some shared experience.

B. **Deepen the discussion:** Help the seminar process with individual contributions that lead the group to discover new insights and understanding of assigned readings.

　Provide additional supportive quotes; explain relevance; ask clarifying questions.

　Share the thought process that was personally used in developing an idea.

　Paraphrase what the author means in a specific passage.

　Summarize the arguments being presented.

　Identify similarities and differences in positions being argued.

　Challenge an idea or present an alternative interpretation.

　Connect ideas from several participants or from other texts the group has read.

　Formulate insightful questions that spark group response.

　Introduce personal experiences that illuminate the text for others.

C. **Facilitate group exploration:** Focus on what the group is accomplishing more than on individual students' performance.

　Help to identify the goals and format for the group process.

　Keep the group on task.

　Focus group back to the text.

　Summarize for the group what has been discussed.

　Bring closure to one point and make a transition to a new one.

　Paraphrase someone's comments, identify what you don't understand, and/or formulate a specific question asking for clarification.

　Encourage nonparticipants by being alert to who wants to speak, or who hasn't spoken, and help them get the floor.

Indicate support by responding to a person's ideas, or complimenting them.

Show active listening by means of nonverbal cues like eye contact, nods, and smiles.

Become aware when dominating the discussion and then modify behavior.

Defuse a tense moment with use of humor.

Source: Used by permission of Jim Harnish.

KEY RESOURCE   Harnish, J. (2008). *What is a seminar? Seminar process to encourage participation and listening. Identifying good seminar behaviors.* Handouts distributed at Collaborative Learning Conference II: Working Together, Learning Together, Everett Community College, Everett, WA, February 22–23.

Chapter 13

Analysis and Critical Thinking

ONCE STUDENTS have acquired foundational knowledge, skills, and understanding, they must learn to *use* it in some way. As some educators have argued, information acquires value only when a student works with the knowledge to build something meaningful (concepts, principles, relationships).

The analysis and critical thinking student engagement techniques (SETs) in this chapter offer teachers ideas for structured activities that require students to break down complex structures into component parts, consider carefully the relationships, relevance, and validity of the parts to each other and to the whole, and to evaluate all of this as a guide to belief and action.

STUDENT
ENGAGEMENT
TECHNIQUE

8

Classify

Essential Characteristics

PRIMARY MODE	Collaborative
ACTIVITY FOCUS	Discussing
DURATION OF ACTIVITY	Single Session
ONLINE TRANSFERABILITY	Moderate

DESCRIPTION AND PURPOSE
"Classify" helps students achieve two common learning goals. First, it helps students understand how a discipline or subject's information is organized, but it does so in a way that requires students to infer the principles, thus learning the system at a deeper level than if they were simply "told" the system. Second, it helps students learn to identify component parts and to determine how the parts relate to the whole, which are essential steps in analysis.

Teachers gather a collection of items (such as specimens, images, or slips of paper with information written upon them) that represent subcategories in a classification system and provide a set to each group of students. Students examine, discuss, and sort the contents into categories based on shared features as they attempt to deduce the subject's classification system. A reporter from each group then explains the group's classification system and the rules used to guide their organization to the whole class. The instructor uses the students' ideas and principles as the basis for presenting and discussing the topic's established classification system.

STEP-BY-STEP DIRECTIONS
1. Identify a category of information that is important for students to understand, and write down the principles underlying that category's classification. Consider putting this on a presentation slide or overhead transparency to be used to guide whole-class discussion following the activity.

2. Determine how you will have students report out: Presentation? Reporting out as part of a whole-class discussion? Filling out a worksheet?

3. Gather representative objects or write down appropriate pieces of information on slips of paper or index cards. Collect or duplicate a sufficient number to create a set for each group of 4–5 students. If appropriate, put these into envelopes or containers. (If the classroom does not have desk or table space to allow sorting into piles, consider providing students with containers into which they can place items.)

4. Craft prompts to guide students as they examine the artifacts, and put these on handouts, presentation slides, or overhead transparencies. Here are some examples:

> "Look at these [plants, photos of paintings, excerpts from musical scores, index cards with information on them] and identify which ones are similar and which ones are different."

> "Discuss and write down the specific features you are using as evidence of each item's similarity or difference."

> "Review your features to determine a set of rules to guide you as you sort the items into separate piles."

5. Form groups, consider having them choose a group facilitator and recorder, and distribute a container of items to each group of students.

6. Have students participate in a discussion following the prepared prompts to come to consensus about how the items should be sorted.

7. Ask students to write out or present their classification system.

EXAMPLES

Art Appreciation

Professor Dee Sign had traditionally started the academic term with a lecture on the major historical epochs students would study throughout the course. Wanting to engage students more actively, she decided to try "Classify." She purchased postcards with images of paintings from museum shops, blackened out the identifying information on the back, and sorted them into piles so that each stack included 2–3 examples of different epochs. She formed groups of 4–6 students, gave each group a mixed-up collection of cards, and asked students to analyze the images in order to organize the cards into stacks with similar characteristics. After groups had discussed the images, Professor Sign moved to a whole-class discussion, asking each group to describe their system. As students reported out, she wrote their ideas on the board, expanding upon their observations and adding comments that introduced students to the different ways to look at and organize understandings about art (historical, topic, medium, and so forth).

• • •

Comparative Animal Physiology

At the end of two weeks of work on mammals, this zoology professor decided to use "Classify" to engage students as they practiced categorizing mammals visually. He formed students into pairs and distributed a handout that included a grid divided into boxes for the three mammalian subclasses: Prototheria, Metatheria, and Eutheria. He then projected numbered images of animals, with the examples more or less evenly divided among subclasses, and instructed students to write the number of the slide in the correct boxes on the grid. When the activity was complete, he projected a correctly filled-out grid so that student pairs could check their answers.

At the next class session he moved to a more challenging activity, asking students to individually categorize projected, numbered images of subclass Eutheria into seven of its major orders. Students were then asked to turn to a partner to compare results before he projected the correctly filled-out grid (adapted from Angelo & Cross, 1993, p. 161).

ONLINE IMPLEMENTATION Have students view images or text on a Web page and participate in the discussion component in team-specific discussion forums. Have teams share and compare their classification systems in a whole-class forum as a follow-up activity.

VARIATIONS AND EXTENSIONS

- Have students do their analysis individually outside of class and then use face-to-face time to share, compare, and contrast individual classification systems within their group.

- Rather than dividing the whole class into teams, use a "fishbowl" format in which some members sit in chairs outside a group, listening to group members discuss and identify shared and unique attributes, propose classification systems, and so forth, but not commenting. When they are finished, ask the observing students to review the proposed systems and make suggestions for any reorganization.

- Provide students with the classification system, and have students sort the items using the system. Although this variation foregoes the beneficial learning that can occur when the system is deduced, it provides a valuable assessment function by offering teachers information on how well students understand the system.

- As an out-of-class assignment, give students the classification system and ask them to find representative items. For example, given a taxonomy of plant types, ask students to search for and locate examples in their communities.

- Provide students with a container of items at the end of a unit to guide them on reflecting about what they have learned.

OBSERVATIONS AND ADVICE   If the classification system is not complex enough, this activity may feel like busywork. Conversely, some classification systems are too complex for this SET to be conducted effectively.

Suggest to students that they focus on broad, general categories at first, shifting to more specific subcategories as they develop more insights.

Encourage students to articulate the logic underlying their classification system.

If students create a system that is very different from the one used in the discipline, consider it a teaching moment to discuss their thinking.

KEY RESOURCES   Angelo, T. A., & Cross, K. P. (1993). *Classroom assessment techniques: A handbook for college teachers*, 2nd ed. San Francisco: Jossey-Bass.

Dodge, J. (2005). *Differentiation in action*. New York: Scholastic.

S T U D E N T
E N G A G E M E N T
T E C H N I Q U E

9

Frames

Essential Characteristics

PRIMARY MODE	Collaborative
ACTIVITY FOCUS	Reading, Writing
DURATION OF ACTIVITY	Single Session
ONLINE TRANSFERABILITY	High

DESCRIPTION AND PURPOSE   Instructors give individual students or student teams a template of sentence stems that provides the shape of a short essay but not the content. Students complete the sentences, expressing their ideas in their own words, but they do so within a clear and organized framework.

No teaching tool can guarantee that students will engage in hard, rigorous thought, but templates can stimulate and shape such thought, guiding them through the steps that constitute analysis and critical thinking and requiring them to make the key intellectual moves that they may not do on their own.

STEP-BY-STEP DIRECTIONS

1. Choose a course-related topic or reading assignment that you would like students to examine analytically and critically.

2. Decide on the specifics of the kind of thinking you want them to do: evaluate conflicting positions and decide which one is best, examine the validity of the arguments or conclusions, challenge their own assumptions, and so forth.

3. Write a brief essay that addresses your goals and has a clear rhetorical structure, then copy the essay and delete information from the copy so that you have a skeleton of the essay. The template could be very brief, such as this example:

Theory X proposes that _____ and is very useful because it offers insights into _____. On the other hand, Theory Y, which proposes _____, does a better job at explaining _____.

Or it can be more extensive, such as this example:

The author's main point in this essay is _____. The evidence she provides to support her view is _____. On the other hand, others argue that _____. To support their views, they point out that _____. The issue, then, seems to be whether _____ or _____. Our view is _____. Although we concede that _____, we maintain that _____ because _____.

4. Check to make sure that the frame clearly indicates the information students must add to make the essay complete, and make any adjustments.

5. Make copies of the frame along with directions to use as a handout for students, retaining the original as an assessment tool.

6. Distribute the "Frames" handout to each student or to groups of students, explain directions, and answer any process questions.

7. Students write essays using the frame as a guide.

8. Collect the essays, using your original essay to assess the students' essays.

EXAMPLES

Introduction to American Government and Politics

Professor Frank N. Privilege wanted his students to clarify their thinking on the issues related to the special benefits and advantages enjoyed by politicians. After presenting a lecture on the topic, he formed students into groups of three and distributed a handout with the following frame for them to complete and submit to him:

When it comes to the topic of the special privileges awarded politicians, most people agree that _____. Where this agreement usually ends, however, is on the question of _____. Whereas some are convinced that _____, others maintain that _____. Our view is that _____. Though we agree that _____,

we believe that _____. We think this issue is important because _____.

• • •

Workshop on the Scholarship of Teaching and Learning

To help workshop participants clarify, summarize, and communicate their individual research projects to others in their group, the facilitator, Lendol Calder,
crafted the following frame based on Graff and Birkenstein (2006):

In recent discussions of _____, a controversy has been whether _____. On the
one hand, some argue that _____. On the other hand, others say that _____.
The essential issue, then, is whether _____ or _____. My own thought is that
perhaps _____. To find out, I designed a research project to _____. My central question was _____. To help me draw conclusions, I relied on the following kinds of data: _____. My key methods for generating this data were
_____. Some of the problems I ran into were _____. But it was also quite
exciting when _____ happened. My findings are important because _____.

ONLINE
IMPLEMENTATION

"Frames" adapts easily to the online environment. Once groups are formed,
students can communicate through a Wiki, discussion forum, Web site
messaging, e-mail, instant messaging, or telephone. As they work together
to write the essay, they can send their contributions as e-mail attachments
and monitor individual contributions using the tracking features available
in standard word-processing programs or simply use different font styles.

VARIATIONS
AND EXTENSIONS

- Instead of a handout, use flip charts. For example, provide groups with
a frame that asks them to identify the main argument, the best line of
reasoning, the best evidence offered, the strongest counterargument,
the best evidence available to support the counterargument, and the
central issue between the two views. Give groups time to complete
their frame, write it on a flip chart, and then walk around and review
other groups' completed frames to identify the best frame (other than
their own). Follow with a discussion of the components, such as what
makes logic/evidence strong? Have students record these "standards"
of good thinking and apply them to new material. See if their standards need revising, and then ask students to apply the standards to
examples/material from everyday life (L. D. Fink, personal communication, 2008).

- "Frames" can be combined with other SETs to create a comprehensive
experience. For example, students can write a "Frames"-structured
essay as a closure activity to SET 10, "Believing and Doubting."

OBSERVATIONS AND ADVICE   In the preface to their book on the use of templates to guide students in academic writing, Graff and Birkenstein (2006) acknowledge that some instructors will fear that templates may encourage passive learning. The authors counter that templates can stimulate and shape thought, make explicit the deep structural thinking that underlies good academic argument, and help students by providing them with tools that guide them into thinking clearly and critically in a direct and immediate way.

Writing is not an easy task, and collaborative writing can be particularly challenging. Because of the structure "Frames" provides, it can help solve some of the essay organization problems typically encountered in collaborative writing.

"Frames" can help prevent the academic dishonesty sometimes associated with the conventional term paper assignment. The framework makes it impossible to do wholesale copying and discourages the copy-and-paste approach because of the difficulty of matching pre-existing writing to the information required to fill in the blanks. When this SET is used as a group assignment, it also discourages plagiarism because the group, rather than an individual, must do the writing.

The rigid structure of "Frames" can be both positive and negative. It is positive in that it requires students to fill in all the blanks, ensuring that they include all elements, and that these elements are combined in a finished product that has a clear organization and structure. This consistent and pre-established structure also makes students' essays easier to assess. But it can be frustrating to students if they don't think along the lines of the instructor-designed structure and want more flexibility to organize their thoughts and write their essays in their own way.

It is challenging to find the balance between providing sufficient information to make a supportive framework while still leaving enough information missing that students must think and use their own words to complete the frame.

KEY RESOURCE   Graff, G., & Birkenstein, C. (2006). *"They say/I say": The moves that matter in academic writing*. New York: Norton.

**S T U D E N T
E N G A G E M E N T
T E C H N I Q U E**

10

Believing and Doubting

Essential Characteristics

PRIMARY MODE	Collaborative
ACTIVITY FOCUS	Reading, Discussing
DURATION OF ACTIVITY	Single Session
ONLINE TRANSFERABILITY	High

DESCRIPTION AND PURPOSE

This activity helps students develop dialogical thinking, the active disposition to seek views different from their own and to construct arguments when informed proponents of opposing points of view are not available. It helps students see that scholarly articles and other assigned readings are voices in a conversation that they need to join. Complex and challenging texts will begin to make sense when students see their responsibility to participate actively as they read, imagining and considering alternative points of view as they evaluate an author's thesis, reasons, and evidence.

For the "believing" portion of "Believing and Doubting," students are asked to read a text empathetically, making a conscious effort to understand and appreciate the author's perspective and values. They make a list of reasons and arguments that support the author's viewpoint and use this list as the basis for a small-group discussion.

In the "doubting" portion of the activity, students reread the text and look for its weaknesses—making a new list as they raise objections and resist being taken in by the text's rhetorical force. The list they generate is used for an additional small-group discussion.

STEP-BY-STEP DIRECTIONS

1. Identify a controversy in your discipline that relates to your course goals, and find an article, newspaper story, or excerpt from a larger text that persuasively argues a single viewpoint.

2. Duplicate the article, post it online, or place it on reserve in the library.

3. Without revealing the "doubting" portion of the activity, explain to students that they are to read the text empathetically, making a sincere and conscious attempt to identify with and understand the author's feelings, beliefs, and values, and making a list of as many points as they can with which, from this empathetic viewpoint, they agree with the author.

4. Ask students to pair up or form small groups of 4–5 to discuss the ways in which they understood where the author was coming from.

5. As students report out in a whole-class discussion, create a cumulative list of their points on the board.

6. When you feel that most students genuinely understand the author's viewpoint, ask them to reread the text, but this time from a doubting perspective, making a new list of everything they can find that, when viewed from this critical perspective, they suspect may not be true, likely, or genuine.

7. Once again, ask students to pair up or rejoin their small groups to discuss the ways in which they now find the author's arguments flawed or reasons they may suspect what the author is saying is not trustworthy.

8. As students report out, create a second cumulative list of their points on the board, concluding the discussion with why it is important to resist being passive consumers of the written word and instead become critical readers and thinkers. Consider closing by asking students to generate a list of steps to critical reading, such as the following:

   • Try to determine who the author is—the purpose for writing the text, if there are any sponsors, and so forth.

   • Determine the target audience. This is helpful in deducing what the author is trying to get across, sell, or persuade the reader to believe.

   • Look for illogical arguments or fallacies, especially arguments that have no relevance to the subject and are used merely to persuade.

EXAMPLE

General Biology

To help students learn to read critically texts addressing ethical issues in the discipline, Professor Jenn Ettics selected an article that convincingly detailed how the creation, usage, and destruction of human embryonic stem cells is the first step toward reproductive cloning and how it fundamentally devalues the worth of a human being. She asked students to read the article to themselves in class, trying to understand the author's perspective as they created a list of the reasons why the article was persuasive. Students then discussed their lists with a partner. During the report-out, Professor Ettics created a composite list on the board. She then gave a presentation on the benefits of stem cell research. Since students now had a deeper understanding of the conflicting viewpoints, she asked them to reread the article, this time looking for potential flaws in the arguments. In the whole-class discussion that followed, she helped students create a guide for how to read critically that they could use in the future.

ONLINE IMPLEMENTATION

This technique is relatively easy to implement online. Form teams (or pairs), and have students communicate with each other through Web site messaging, e-mail, or telephone to develop a joint list of the reasons why they found the reading assignment persuasive, and then submit their list privately to you as an assignment. Create a cumulative list based on all students' submissions and post it for students to read. Then ask students to reread the text from the doubting perspective, communicate with each other to create a second joint list, and submit this list to you privately as an assignment. Once again, create a cumulative list and post it for all students to read. Create a discussion forum with prompts that ask students to reflect upon what they learned from the activity, focusing on the reasons why it is important to read critically and perhaps closing by generating a list of steps essential for critical reading.

VARIATIONS AND EXTENSIONS

- Instead of having students read an article, present pro and con sides of an issue in two mini-lectures. See the section titled "To Promote Critical Thinking" in the first case study in Chapter 6. In the case study, J. Baker uses this SET in a health class.

- Instead of using this activity as the basis for class discussion, have students submit their two lists individually along with a reflective essay on what they learned.

- Consider having students record which side they started on and whether they were persuaded to change their view, and then write a reflective essay on what it takes to change someone's mind.

OBSERVATIONS AND ADVICE

If you cannot find an article that is persuasive from a single viewpoint but that has sufficient logic or content flaws to allow for an effective analysis from a "doubting" perspective, consider finding two articles representing opposing perspectives. Have students read one article and make a list of persuasive points, and then read the other article and make another list of persuasive points.

Because this SET requires students to engage by viewing knowledge, information, and opinion critically, it is a useful tool for helping them learn to evaluate information on the Internet. The Internet is often the first (and sometimes only) source of information used by students in their research. While most educators agree that it can be a valuable resource if used correctly, many teachers are noticing a decline in the quality of student work because of reliance on Web sources for information. Browne, Freeman, and Williamson (2000) observe that many students are piecing together Internet-based information as if it were entirely factual, when in reality much information on the Web is unreliable, superficial, and can lead to misunderstanding because it is decontextualized. (Historical research, for example, involves recognition and appreciation of context, and the characteristics such as type, handwriting, layout, and paper quality that are important clues to a document's meaning may be missing in electronic text.) Although paper sources also have problems, some process of professional assessment has usually preceded their publication, suggesting that most print sources have at least some basis for belief. Relying upon the Internet for research also makes research seem easy and allows students to confuse bits of information with knowledge and to underestimate the need for careful evaluation. As students become increasingly dependent on the Internet for their information, participating in an activity such as "Believing and Doubting" can help them develop the critical reading skills that are essential to filtering through the enormous amount of information available on the Web.

KEY RESOURCE   Bean, J. C. (1996). *Engaging ideas: The professor's guide to integrating writing, critical thinking, and active learning in the classroom.* San Francisco: Jossey-Bass, pp. 142–143, 156–157.

**S T U D E N T
E N G A G E M E N T
T E C H N I Q U E**

11

Academic Controversy

Essential Characteristics

PRIMARY MODE	Collaborative
ACTIVITY FOCUS	Reading, Discussing
DURATION OF ACTIVITY	Single Session
ONLINE TRANSFERABILITY	High

DESCRIPTION AND PURPOSE

Student partners review material on a controversial topic in the field that has two opposing sides (A and B) and brainstorm arguments to support their assigned position. Pairs then split up and students move around the room, talking to other students on the same side (As talking to As) to come up with new arguments to strengthen their position. In quads, pairs present their arguments, then switch sides and argue the opposite side of the controversy, and finally work together to come to a consensus position.

This SET requires students to do in-depth analysis of an issue. Because students must discuss and argue both sides of a controversy, it can challenge students' existing assumptions and move them beyond simple dualistic thinking. Additionally, presenting their views and listening to the views of others can develop communication skills.

STEP-BY-STEP DIRECTIONS

1. Spend time finding and selecting an engaging topic that does not have a clear-cut answer and that would generate different views and opinions. Ideally, it is a topic that students can relate to and care about, but not one that is likely to make them too contentious or emotional.

2. Craft the controversy into a mini-case and create a handout that includes the case along with directions. Print the handout on two different colors of paper so that you can distribute one color to half the class and assign them Side A and use the other color to designate Side B.

3. Divide the class in half, distribute the handouts and ask students to read through the controversy and to privately come to an opinion about the dilemma.

4. Instruct students to use the two different colored handouts to guide them to form groups of four consisting of two pairs, one pair with each color.

5. Ask students within pairs to brainstorm arguments to make their case.

6. After a few minutes, ask student pairs to split up and walk around the room talking to others who have the same colored handout to gather new arguments to support their position.

7. Instruct students to re-form as quads and work with their partners for a couple of minutes to refine their arguments.

8. Tell Pair A to present their case while Pair B listens but does not comment.

9. Allow time for Pair B to ask clarifying questions. Then Pair B presents their case as Pair A listens and then asks questions.

10. After the questions, ask the two sides to switch and prepare to and then argue the opposite side of the controversy.

11. Once both sides have presented their arguments, ask the quad to come to a consensus on the controversy.

12. To begin the follow-up whole-class discussion, ask the quads who agreed with Side A to raise hands, and then do the same with Side B. Then ask how many students changed their opinion and invite them to explain why.

EXAMPLE

Art History

Professor Anne Cestral uses "Academic Controversy" to have students explore the question, Who owns the past? She presents a brief lecture on how museums around the world are being pressured to return artifacts that were bequeathed to them by private donors or bought in international auctions but which the source countries now say were originally taken from them illegally. The essential challenge is that nations like Greece, China, Egypt, Italy, Jordan, Iran, Turkey, and Pakistan—homes to the world's ancient civilizations—think of antiquities as national property that make an essential contribution to their modern national identity. Museum curators, historians, and others argue that products of ancient civilizations are also the heritage of all humanity, and as such, they should be widely available to the general public in order to educate, to encourage understanding and respect for the greatness of other cultures, and to help the world's people construct a human identity that transcends mere nationality. Professor Cestral believes participation in this SET challenges students to grapple with a fundamental dilemma in the discipline and deepens their understanding so that they are better prepared to address the issue either as future art historians or as citizens who care about the collections in their local, state, and national museums (Lacayo, 2008).

ONLINE IMPLEMENTATION

A technique similar to "Academic Controversy" but developed specifically for online teaching is called "Progressive Project." Students choose a topic for debate from an instructor-provided list and then are formed into pairs. Student A writes three pro arguments with supporting points and then sends this to Student B. Student B adds three con arguments with supporting points and submits the work to the instructor. The instructor gives the students' pro and con arguments to another peer pair who evaluate the strengths and weaknesses of both positions. The project along with peer evaluation is then submitted to the instructor (Conrad & Donaldson, 2004).

VARIATIONS AND EXTENSIONS

- Instead of forcing quads to arrive at a consensus that involves choosing one of the sides, ask quads to develop a compromise position or identify strategies that mediate between the two sides.

OBSERVATIONS AND ADVICE

Because "Academic Controversy" requires students to argue both sides of an issue, it is useful for helping students safely and candidly explore an issue without feeling pressure to express opinions only from the side that they perceive as popular or "politically correct."

KEY RESOURCES

Jacobson, D. (2002). Getting students in a technical class involved in the classroom. In C.A. Stanley (Ed.), *Engaging large classes: Strategies and techniques for college faculty*. Bolton, MA: Anker, pp. 214–216.

Millis, B. J., & Cottell, P. G. (1998). *Cooperative learning for higher education faculty*. Phoenix, AZ: Oryx Press.

STUDENT ENGAGEMENT TECHNIQUE

12

Split-Room Debate

Essential Characteristics

PRIMARY MODE	Collaborative
ACTIVITY FOCUS	Discussing
DURATION OF ACTIVITY	Single Session
ONLINE TRANSFERABILITY	High

DESCRIPTION AND PURPOSE

After a brief presentation on a topic or case study, students are invited to sit on one side of the room or the other corresponding to their position on a controversy related to a key course issue. Instead of the teacher selecting who is allowed to speak, students call on the next speaker after they have finished their own remarks. Students are encouraged to move to either side of the room as their attitudes change.

Debates provide a framework to help students develop more mature ways of thinking as they start to recognize the range of perspectives inherent in complex topics and internalize a view of knowledge that is dialogic, contingent, and ambiguous. This SET takes advantage of the teaching and learning opportunities inherent in debates, while providing a structure that allows students to move around in the room and to see how their own opinions and those of others can change as understanding deepens.

STEP-BY-STEP DIRECTIONS

1. Spend sufficient time selecting a controversial topic that is relevant to your course goals and that has two identifiable, arguable, and opposing sides that are appropriate to debate. Carefully craft the debate proposition into a one-sentence statement, such as "Scientists are justified in performing experiments on animals to develop products and medicines that benefit human beings." Proposition statements should avoid ambiguity yet be general enough to offer students flexibility in building arguments.

2. Determine whether students need any background information to address the proposition, and if they do, prepare them through lecture, assigned reading, discussion, or student research on the topic.

3. Identify the ground rules. For example, you may want to specify that a student can present only one argument at a time, or that each statement is limited to three minutes. Thinking about your ground rules ahead of time will also give you the opportunity to decide whether you want to assign any students a specific role, such as timekeeper.

4. Explain your ground rules and allow time for questions. Determine the dividing line in the classroom and identify which side represents pro and which side represents con.

5. Propose the motion, give students a few minutes to think about their beliefs, and then ask students to move to the section of the room that represents the side of the proposition they most support.

6. Ask a student on the pro side to start the debate, reminding him or her to finish by selecting the next speaker from the other side of the room.

7. When there are no longer new arguments being presented, announce that the debate is finished and ask students to return to their original seats. Hold a whole-class discussion to summarize the important issues and to give students the opportunity to discuss to what extent, if any, their opinions changed.

EXAMPLE

Educational Leadership

Professor Vi S. Principal wanted students to explore in depth a variety of topics throughout the term as well as clarify their personal opinions to prepare them for their roles as school administrators. She used "Split-Room Debate" to get lots of opinions out on the table. Her prompts included statements such as "Public schools should be allowed to teach creationism alongside evolution as part of their science curriculum" and "Voucher systems should be used to introduce choice and competition among schools." Following the closure discussion for each debate, she asked students to write an essay responding to the prompt by summarizing the issues from both perspectives and concluding with their personal viewpoints.

ONLINE IMPLEMENTATION Prepare as you would for a face-to-face debate. Write a paragraph that explains the rationale behind the debate, provides the discussion proposal, and gives assignment directions. Create a forum that poses the discussion prompt, and ask students to respond, alternating pro and con arguments. After the deadline, require students to read through the arguments, summarize and synthesize the debate, and conclude with their personal opinion. Although the online debate may lack the sense of immediacy achieved in an in-class debate, the essential characteristic of requiring students to alternate positions as they explore a topic from different perspectives is preserved. You may also consider posting a follow-up threaded discussion in which students can share whether participating in the debate changed their viewpoint.

VARIATIONS AND EXTENSIONS

- Instead of conducting this in a whole-class format, form teams or ask students to work in pairs to present opposing sides to each other.

- Identify a topic that has three clear sides, and set up a three-way debate.

- For a more comprehensive project, or if the topic is very complex, require students to do preparatory research.

- Ask students to write a follow-up paper describing issues that they clarified or confirmed, surprises they encountered, new information they gained, or whether their opinion changed.

OBSERVATIONS AND ADVICE

This technique works best if students have a reasonably deep knowledge or understanding of the topic so that they can make better arguments and rebuttals. "Split-Room Debate" is therefore best used after students have had time to investigate a topic through lecture, discussion, or reading assignments. Use this SET to introduce a new topic only if you are confident that the topic can be addressed through common knowledge.

Try to select a topic that you are fairly certain will generate opposing viewpoints. Consider using a preliminary assessment technique (such as CAT 28, "Classroom Opinion Polls," in Angelo and Cross, 1993, pp. 258–262) to identify attitudes ahead of time.

Choose a topic for which you can honestly see both sides. Part of the purpose of this SET is to help students carefully consider a side of an argument that is contrary to their own beliefs. It is therefore best if you do not have strong feelings for one or the other side yourself.

If, toward the end of the debate, most students have moved to one side of the room leaving just a few students defending a particular position, consider ending the debate and commenting on the students' courage in maintaining their positions despite peer pressure to do otherwise. You might also consider facilitating a discussion on what conditions must exist for one to change one's mind, and the difference between conviction and intransigence.

Explain to students that the purpose of this activity is to explore a topic in depth and that complex issues often have compelling arguments on both sides. Suggest that to aid their understanding, they share all the arguments they see even if they don't agree with them. In situations where a large percentage of students prefer one of the sides, this will help distribute arguments more evenly and allow some to say they don't know or to gravitate toward a middle position.

Preparing for, participating in, and listening to debates offers many benefits to students. Debates can increase motivation, promote logical thinking, and develop communication proficiency. "Split-Room Debate" is a quick technique to expose the class to a focused, in-depth, multiple-perspective analysis of issues. If students are also encouraged to contribute arguments that may be in opposition to their own views, it can encourage them to challenge their existing assumptions. This can move students beyond simple dualistic thinking, deepen their understanding of an issue, and help them to recognize the range of perspectives inherent in complex topics. In this way, this SET may also build appreciation for diversity and develop tolerance for other viewpoints.

The topic must be one that is engaging. It is especially effective when topics address issues that are contemporary and connected to students' lives.

In some contexts, students will tend to share similar opinions about issues or want to take the side that they perceive is popular or "politically correct." They may not feel safe arguing a side that is in opposition to their own or that they know is generally unpopular. If you are careful to set up a non-threatening environment and explain the purpose of "Split-Room Debate," however, students can enjoy arguing a variety of viewpoints.

Depending upon the importance of this SET to your overall teaching goals, you may want to choose an additional follow-up activity, such as asking students to fill out a "Pro and Con Grid" in which students list each argument in one column and balance it with a competing claim or rebuttal in a second column (CAT 10 in Angelo and Cross, 1993, pp. 168–171). This assessment technique provides you with a quick overview of each student's final analysis and understanding of both sides of the issue. A more complex assignment for use after the debate is "Analytic Memo" (CAT 12 in Angelo and Cross, 1993, pp. 177–180). For this activity, ask students to write a one- or two-page analysis of the issue, being careful to provide equitable coverage of both sides. You might suggest that they select a role such as policy analyst for a legislator or a consultant for a corporation's chief executive officer. Taking on such a role may make it easier for them to assume a position and it also establishes the writing audience.

KEY RESOURCE   Frederick, P. J. (2002). Engaging students actively in large lecture settings. In C. A. Stanley (Ed.), *Engaging large classes: Strategies and techniques for college faculty.* Bolton, MA: Anker, pp. 62–63.

S T U D E N T
E N G A G E M E N T
T E C H N I Q U E

13

Analytic Teams

Essential Characteristics

PRIMARY MODE	Collaborative
ACTIVITY FOCUS	Variable
DURATION OF ACTIVITY	Single or Multiple Session
ONLINE TRANSFERABILITY	High

***DESCRIPTION
AND PURPOSE***

"Analytic Teams" is a collaborative learning technique in which team members assume roles and specific tasks to perform when critically reading an assignment, listening to a lecture, or watching a video. Roles such as summarizer, connector (relating the assignment to previous knowledge or to the outside world), proponent, and critic focus on the analytic process rather than the group process (which entails roles such as facilitator, timekeeper, and recorder).

This technique is useful for helping students actively engage in the different activities that constitute a critical analysis. It can be particularly effective when it is used with roles that exist within the norms of the discipline. Giving students structured roles to play can increase participation among all members and equalize participation between active and less active contributors.

***STEP-BY-STEP
DIRECTIONS***

Select an assignment that requires use of a complex analytical process, and break the process down into component parts or roles. Although there are a variety of roles you can use depending upon the specific analytic process and your learning goals, the following examples can be applied to several kinds of assignments:

Proponent	List the points you agreed with and state why.
Critic	List the points you disagreed with or found unhelpful and state why.

Example-Giver	Give examples of key concepts presented.
Summarizer	Prepare a summary of the most important points.
Questioner	Prepare a list of substantive questions about the material.

To ensure that the assignment is appropriate for team analysis, take the time in advance to determine whether you could perform each of the assigned roles and that each role has a sufficiently challenging task.

1. Form student groups of 4–5, assigning each individual in the team a specific role and "job assignment."
2. Present the lecture, show the video, or assign the reading.
3. Give teams class time for members to share their findings and to work together to prepare oral or written presentations of their analyses.
4. Consider a closure strategy that emphasizes roles and component tasks. "Stand Up and Share" would be particularly appropriate for a fairly short activity, whereas a panel or poster session would be appropriate for more complex assignments.

EXAMPLES

Management Seminar

A professor in business management returned from a professional conference where he heard a stimulating, controversial keynote address in which the speaker proposed that business majors should be required to take more liberal arts courses. He obtained a tape of the speech to play for his class session on leadership. He used "Analytic Teams" in which individual students were given specific tasks that, combined, guided students as they identified and critiqued the speaker's arguments. Following their analysis, he asked each team to develop a list of recommended requirements for the business major.

• • •

History of the Americas

In this online class, Professor A. Joe Vexploration wanted students to understand different stakeholders' perspectives in the European conquest of the Americas. He did not feel that he could achieve this effectively through narrative text alone, so he decided to assign students to watch the film *The Mission*. Professor Vexploration knew that because the film was readily available at most local libraries and at video retail and rental stores, all of his online students would have access to it, regardless of their geographical location. The film, based on historical events that occurred in the borderlands of present-day Argentina, Paraguay, and Brazil around 1750, depicts the conflicts between the Spanish and Portuguese governments, the Roman Catholic Church, and the indigenous Guarani Indians. Based on his experience showing the film to students in his on-campus classes, Professor Vexploration knew that the film engaged students on the dramatic level. But he wanted to deepen the learning by helping his students to view the film more critically. He decided to structure the experience with "Analytic Teams." He organized students into groups of five, and asked all students to complete a worksheet in which they answered basic questions such as "When did Rodrigo decide to stop being a slave trade mercenary and become a Jesuit acolyte?" and "What did the Guarani Indians hang from a tree to warn Europeans to stay away?" He also created specific critical roles with assigned tasks:

- **Visual analysts** focused on how the film's director used camera angles, European and Indian clothing, physical settings, and props to underscore the contrast in cultural views and social status.

- **Music analysts** paid special attention to how Ennio Morricone's film score heightened viewers' perception of the culture clash between the indigenous and European traditions and the tensions between the sacred and secular.

- **Character analysts** concentrated on how individuals within the drama changed throughout the film, and how the changes mirrored changes in the relationships between Spain, Portugal, the Guarani, and the Roman Catholic Church.

- **Historical researchers** investigated the accuracy of the film's representation of the conflicts and also provided additional historical context.

- **Connectors** looked for similarities between the film's South American circumstances and the situation in North America, and also connected the historical events to contemporary cultural and political events.

Each team was given a private discussion board to talk about the film in general and the specific findings of each task member. By a specific date, each team was required to send to Professor Vexploration their team's comprehensive analysis of the film. The professor read the reports, collated the important points, added points that students had missed, and posted his synthesis along with the team reports for general class viewing.

ONLINE IMPLEMENTATION   Form student groups, create a separate forum for each group with the posted prompt, assign individual roles, and have students respond to the prompt according to their assigned role. Consider having groups write a team analysis that presents their findings that can be posted in a whole class threaded discussion, or create a Web page for group viewing.

VARIATIONS AND EXTENSIONS
- Assign the different roles to teams instead of individuals.
- Give each group a different assignment to critique that is related to the same issue. The follow-up whole-class discussion will be particularly engaging if students read critiques that represent different sides of the issue.
- Extend this activity for more than one class session. For example, teams can read an entire book with individuals rotating roles every chapter.

OBSERVATIONS AND ADVICE   "Analytic Teams" accomplishes several purposes. By dividing the process into parts and assigning these parts to individuals, students are able to focus on learning and performing one aspect at a time. "Analytic Teams" is also useful for promoting active learning. Listening to a lecture, watching a video, or reading an assignment can be passive activities for students. Forming structured teams in which each member is assigned a distinct task may increase opportunities for participation as well as confidence in the value of the contribution. Each student can say, "My job is to be a critic" (or to think of questions, or to look for examples, and so on). Additionally, "Analytic Teams" is useful for preparing students for more complex problem-solving assignments in which they must assume multiple roles individually.

The most challenging aspect in preparing for this technique is selecting an assignment that is complex enough to yield a useful analysis when divided into component tasks. If the task is not sufficiently complex, one or more of the individual team members will be bored or unable to participate fully.

To reduce the amount of time required for this activity in class, have the actual listening, viewing, or reading take place out of class.

One of the significant challenges of this SET is determining how to follow up on the group work in a way that will help students meaningfully synthesize the various information and opinions they have heard. Consider SET 20, "Poster Sessions," or one of the following reporting-out strategies (Barkley, Cross, & Major, 2005, p. 80):

- Panel: Students make a series of brief presentations to the class, followed by discussion in which panel participants receive and answer questions from the audience.

- Team Rotation: Team A moves to Team B to present their ideas while members of Team B listen and ask questions. Teams then reverse roles.

- Three Stay, One Stray: A person from Team A is designated to move to Team B to report while the other team members remain behind to hear from a traveling team member from Team C.

Students typically prefer some roles to others. They may even resist being assigned certain roles and request that they be assigned roles with which they have already developed both comfort and skill. Yet it is important that students develop their abilities in multiple roles.

To encourage students to develop their abilities and to move out of their comfort zone, consider creating profiles of analytic process roles. Each profile can consist of brief descriptions of the kinds of skills each role requires. Create two or three questions that will assess students' affinity for the various roles and ask each student to answer these questions for themselves. Awareness and class discussion of this may also motivate students to stretch their analytical skills by working to develop their abilities in less comfortable or more challenging roles.

KEY RESOURCES   Barkley, E. F., Cross, K. P., & Major, C. H. (2005). *Collaborative learning techniques: A handbook for college faculty*. San Francisco: Jossey-Bass.

Johnson, D. W., Johnson, R., & Smith, K. (1998). *Active learning: Cooperation in the college classroom*. Edina, MN: Interaction Book Company.

S T U D E N T
E N G A G E M E N T
T E C H N I Q U E

14

Book Club

Essential Characteristics

PRIMARY MODE	Collaborative
ACTIVITY FOCUS	Reading, Discussing, Presenting
DURATION OF ACTIVITY	Multiple Sessions
ONLINE TRANSFERABILITY	High

DESCRIPTION AND PURPOSE This SET offers a mechanism to help students become actively engaged in discussion of instructor-designated books. The teacher selects 3–5 books on core course topics and develops reading guides with discussion questions specific to each book. Students are allowed to choose the book they wish to read and then join a "Book Club" of 5–7 students that meet to discuss the book.

Although discussion must address the instructor-developed guide, students are also encouraged to generate their own discussion topics as they participate in an open, natural conversation about the book. Discussions can be held during face-to-face class time, outside of class, or online. When finished, each book club gives a formal presentation to the whole class, using their responses to the reading guide as the basis for a synthesis of what they learned.

STEP-BY-STEP DIRECTIONS
1. Select 3–5 books that offer different insights or perspectives on course-related topics. Create a reading guide of discussion questions keyed to book sections (such as questions for Chapters 1–3).
2. Determine a calendar that divides up and distributes the reading to fit the course schedule.
3. Decide the basic parameters for where, when, and how students will read and discuss the books. Prepare a handout with directions and deadlines.

4. Write a brief description of each book, explaining how the book fits with the course's learning goals and why students may find the book interesting, and create a separate sign-up sheet to generate groups of 5–7 students. Depending upon class size, there may be more than one group reading the same book.

5. Select and implement procedures for book selection and book club membership.

6. Student groups meet together to discuss the book and, when finished, to prepare their final report in an oral presentation to the whole class.

EXAMPLE

Introduction to American Government and Politics

Professor Manuel Recount wanted students to develop a deeper understanding of and appreciation for the personal dimension of the American presidency. He chose five respected, engaging biographies of presidents from different historical periods and created reading guides that prompted students to look for connections between the president's life (such as family, education, relationships) and the policies and legislation enacted during his presidency, to reflect upon the personal sacrifice and toll the presidency had on the president, and so forth. Students signed up on a first come, first served basis to participate in a book club that focused on one of the biographies. Professor Recount set aside time in class for the book clubs to meet for the first time to set up their own parameters and schedule for discussion outside of class, and then allowed ten minutes of class time once a week for students to solve any logistical problems. Each book club made a fifteen-minute formal presentation to the whole class during the last week of the term, sharing a synthesis of their insights and responses to the reading guide prompts.

ONLINE IMPLEMENTATION

Write up activity directions, including a time frame with clear deadlines. Determine a method for book club sign-ups (for example, create separate forum threads identified by each book's title and ask students to post a response on the appropriate thread to indicate their choice by a specified date). Form groups based on student choice and assign each group its own closed-access threaded discussion area so that members can communicate privately. Have final text reports posted in a public forum for all members of the class to view. For closure, create an assignment that requires all students to view the various reports and, for example, to answer specific questions or compare and evaluate the final reports.

VARIATIONS
AND EXTENSIONS

- Instead of having different groups of students reading different books, choose 3–4 books, describe the merits of each book, and then have the class select a book by ballot that everyone will read.

- Use this technique in foreign language courses, having students read books or texts in the language they are studying that are appropriate to their skill level (such as children's books, young adult literature, or excerpts on history and culture from travel guides).

- Create a blog or threaded discussion forum for each book club to provide an online mechanism for students to plan and discuss.

OBSERVATIONS
AND ADVICE

Use a unifying theme when selecting books. Themes may be genre-specific (such as biographies, historical fiction) or offer different perspectives on a single topic (such as developing multicultural competency).

Some colleges have institution-wide "common book experience" programs or sponsor author series. Selecting books from these lists offers opportunities for students to connect with the larger campus community and to meet authors for book signings. (Examples include the Foothill College Author Series at http://preznet.fhda.edu/fas.html and the Eastern Michigan University Common Reading Experience at http://www.emich.edu/campuslife/?p=orientation-reading.)

There are several categories from which to choose books, including nonfiction (for example, biography, autobiography, persuasive narratives) and fiction (for example, historical fiction, short stories, science fiction). Even disciplines or courses not generally associated with reading beyond textbooks may find works that are engaging, have literary merit, and can deepen student knowledge and understanding of core ideas in the course or discipline.

Rather than determining a single reading/discussion schedule for all groups, give students the final deadline and allow each book club to determine its own schedule.

If you have determined that book clubs will meet primarily outside of regular class time, set aside some class time for students to meet, plan, and solve logistical problems.

Students may assume a rotating assortment of task roles such as facilitator, recorder, planning coordinator, and so forth.

KEY RESOURCE   Literature Circles Resource Center, College of Education, Seattle University. *Literature Circles.com.* Retrieved from http://www.literaturecircles.com/.

S T U D E N T
E N G A G E M E N T
T E C H N I Q U E

15

Small Group Tutorials

Essential Characteristics

PRIMARY MODE	Individual and Collaborative
ACTIVITY FOCUS	Writing
DURATION OF ACTIVITY	Single or Multiple Session
ONLINE TRANSFERABILITY	Low

DESCRIPTION AND PURPOSE

Students write essays in preparation to meet with the teacher in groups of 4–6. As each student reads his or her essay, the teacher interrupts at will to make points or ask questions.

This traditional British-style format provides a more focused framework for teachers to nurture students' individual intellectual growth and higher-order academic skills. In addition to learning from the teacher's comments on their own work, students benefit from hearing the interchange between the teacher and the other members of the group. This SET also provides students with more personalized and meaningful contact with their teachers.

STEP-BY-STEP DIRECTIONS

1. Prior to the beginning of the academic term, decide how often and for how long you will meet with groups, and plan group size and the course calendar accordingly.

2. Within the first week of the term, assign students to a group and designate the day, time, and location for each group's tutorial session.

3. Decide on the writing task and prepare a handout with directions.

4. On the day of the tutorial, organize chairs or desks into a circle, and decide which student will read first. As each student reads his or her essay, interrupt and comment as appropriate and conclude with any summary comments or recommendations. Consider inviting students to offer their insights or reactions.

EXAMPLE

Introduction to Philosophy

Professor Watts Itmene decided to use "Small Group Tutorials" to provide formative feedback to students while they were working on their final paper. He formed groups and set aside one hour a few weeks before the essay was due for each group to meet with him during regular class hours. The students had been asked to consider the question, What is the difference between appearance and reality? and then select one of the philosophers they were studying during the semester and write an essay on how that philosopher had addressed the topic. As each student read through the draft of his or her essay during the tutorial, Professor Itmene offered critical comments and recommendations. While some feedback pertained only to a specific student's essay, most of his comments addressed aspects of critical thinking that could be applied to the other students' work as well. Students were encouraged to revise their essays based on the feedback and told to attach this early draft to their final draft at the submission deadline.

ONLINE IMPLEMENTATION

This technique is most effective when teachers are able to interact with students in the moment. If this activity seems as though it would be useful in the online course, synchronous tools such as teleconferencing and chat sessions that also have chalkboard tools offer one possibility for adaptation.

VARIATIONS AND EXTENSIONS

- Instead of essays, use tutorials to direct course capstone projects, monitor independent study, expand research skills, or discuss a program of guided reading.
- Invite students to offer feedback to their peers in the group. Explicit instruction at the beginning of the tutorial on how to criticize constructively can eliminate discomfort or hurt feelings and ensure that the tutorial gets off to a good start.
- Consider training more advanced students or using TAs to perform the tutor role.

OBSERVATIONS AND ADVICE

The major challenge is setting limits and providing a supportive structure within which students are encouraged to exercise independence and responsibility. Most teachers are naturally predisposed to be helpful, but the primary purpose of this type of tutorial is to help students become independent learners. This requires teachers to exercise restraint and be patient as they let students struggle to think through problems and find solutions on their own.

Teaching students on a more individualized basis requires greater sensitivity to interpersonal interactions than is generally needed when conducting large classes. For example, take care to offer candid feedback but not to engender defensiveness, to allow students to ask questions but to discourage them from being dependent, to maintain an appropriate degree of authority and control but still relate to the students as adults, and to encourage students to be independent but offer guidance and help when needed.

Students are more likely to speak up in a small group. They may also tend to stray off task or to start talking too personally. To manage the tutorial time effectively, have clear objectives and keep the discussion focused.

The greater personal contact that is the benefit of the tutorial setting may be uncomfortable for some teachers or students who prefer (or are simply accustomed to) the more distant, objective relationships that characterize traditional, large-group classroom instruction.

KEY RESOURCE   Lowman, J. (1995). *Mastering the techniques of teaching*. San Francisco: Jossey-Bass, pp. 216–219.

Chapter 14

Synthesis and Creative Thinking

CREATIVITY IS A complex phenomenon that has been studied from several different perspectives and has consequently been defined in many ways. A definition adopted by Angelo and Cross (1993) captures an important way creativity manifests itself in the college classroom: creative thinking is "the ability to interweave the familiar with the new in unexpected and stimulating ways" (p. 181). Similarly, synthesis is the process by which pre-existing ideas, influences, or objects are combined in such a manner as to make a new, unified whole. The student engagement techniques (SETs) in this chapter engage students by challenging their creativity and ability to synthesize and by asking them, in one way or another, to use what they know or have done as the basis for generating something new and original.

S T U D E N T
E N G A G E M E N T
T E C H N I Q U E

16

Team Concept Maps

Essential Characteristics

PRIMARY MODE	Collaborative
ACTIVITY FOCUS	Diagramming
DURATION OF ACTIVITY	Single Session
ONLINE TRANSFERABILITY	Low

DESCRIPTION AND PURPOSE

This SET is an example of a graphic organizer. Because a picture can be worth a thousand words, graphic organizers are powerful tools for converting complex information into meaningful displays. They can be used for many different purposes, including helping students pull background knowledge forward, assessing how well knowledge is remembered and understood, and fostering creativity as participants generate new ideas.

In "Team Concept Maps," student teams draw a diagram that conveys members' combined ideas or understanding of a complex concept, procedure, or process. This SET engages students by challenging them to synthesize and be creative as they organize their hierarchy of associations into a meaningful graphic. Diagramming words, ideas, tasks, or principles is identified by many different names, including "Word Webs," "Mind Maps," and "Cognitive Maps." The name "Concept Maps" is used here because this term is used in the literature to describe a broad, inclusive approach and this SET will be most effective if teachers are creative in deciding what should be diagrammed and students are encouraged to be creative in choosing what is the most appropriate graphic.

STEP-BY-STEP DIRECTIONS

1. Choose a concept, procedure, or process for students to map that is important to your course and that is rich in associations and connections.

2. Brainstorm for a few minutes, writing down terms and short phrases that represent the most important components of the concept.

3. Choose a graphic image that you believe best captures the relationships of the concept (for example, a spoked wheel, a flowchart, a network tree, or a fishbone) and map the concept yourself so that you can uncover potential problems. Your own diagram can also serve as a model against which to assess group work.

4. Map a parallel concept to demonstrate the process to students.

5. Decide what to use as a shared writing space (for example, flip charts, large pieces of paper, the whiteboard) and bring it and colored markers or crayons to class.

6. Describe and demonstrate the process to students.

7. Form teams, distribute paper and markers, and present the central concept that you want students to graph.

8. Have students sketch out a diagram starting with the central idea or first step in a process and adding words, phrases, or images connected by lines or arrows.

ONLINE IMPLEMENTATION   This technique is most effective when students are able to interact in the moment. Consider using a whiteboard tool during a synchronous session. The outcome can be captured as a screenshot to be uploaded onto a forum and shared with other students. If this SET will be an ongoing activity in your course, consider purchasing a software package that assists in the development of concept maps, such as Inspiration (http://www.inspiration.com/) or use presentation or word-processing software that includes drawing tools. Each person adds to the diagram in different color fonts.

EXAMPLES

Statics

Professor Alec Tricity used "Team Concept Maps" to help students synthesize and demonstrate their understanding of the elements and processes of an electric charge. He explained what he wanted students to do, using an overhead projector to demonstrate the concept of an electric field as an example. He formed groups of three and provided each group with newsprint and markers. After about ten minutes, he asked each group to select a reporter who then explained its map to the whole class.

• • •

History of the United States from 1877

In a freshman history course, Professor Rose E. Riveter wanted students to synthesize their understanding of the complex effects of World War II on the United

States. She organized the class into groups of four, and gave each group a large piece of newsprint paper and four different colored markers. Using "WW II's effects on the continental U.S." as the central theme, she asked students to generate ideas and to show the relationship of their ideas in a graphic. For example, students in one group identified women, education, and the economy as core ideas, with each student who had the idea writing it on the paper with his or her marker. The next step was to identify and graph details and supporting elements. Under *Economy*, students mentioned that World War II provided many jobs in defense, boosted American markets, and brought the United States out of the depression. Again using their markers in different colors, students were able to demonstrate relationships (for example, that jobs in defense offered opportunities for women). The groups turned in their "Team Concept Maps" to Professor Riveter for evaluation, and because students used different colored markers, Professor Riveter could assign individual participation grades (adapted from Kagen, 1992; Barkley, Cross, & Major, p. 227).

• • •

Basic Two-Dimensional Design

This course introduces students to basic design concepts and their application. Professor Pat Tern Uses "Team Concept Maps" throughout the class to help students analyze and synthesize ideas and represent them visually. As the term progresses and students become more adept at diagramming, she encourages them to enhance the graphic by choosing various shapes, lines, images, and values and arranging them to create a unified visual statement. Figure 14.1 is a copy of a "Team Concept Map" a group of students created the first day of class in response to her prompt "What is design?" (Barkley, Cross, & Major, 2005, pp. 227–228).

VARIATIONS AND EXTENSIONS

- Use different kinds of graphics to represent different relationships. For example, graphs may resemble a spoked wheel with the central idea at the hub, or a solar system with the stimulus in the sun's position, or a geographical map (Angelo & Cross, 1993, p. 200). There are many models for organizing information.

  - The "Series of Events Chain" in Figure 14.2 is useful for describing the stages of an event.

  - The "Spider Map" in Figure 14.3 demonstrates a more layered approach to charting ideas related to a central concept.

  - Additional ideas include "Network Tree" (Figure 14.4) to organize a hierarchical set of information and "Fishbone Map" (Figure 14.5) for nonredundant cause-effect relationships.

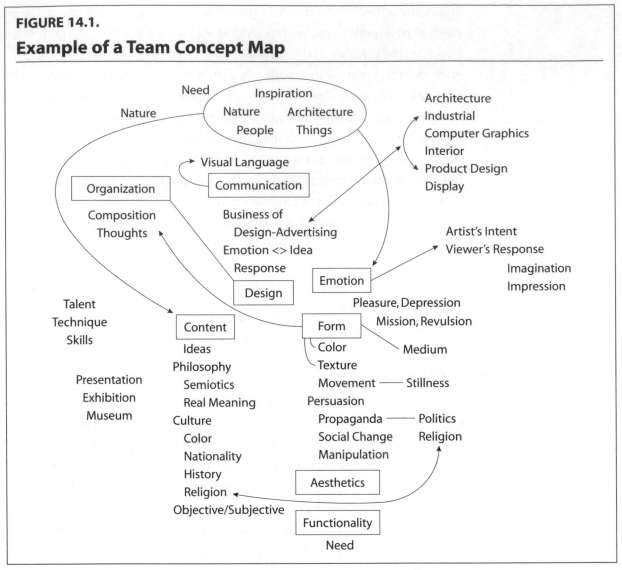

FIGURE 14.1.

Example of a Team Concept Map

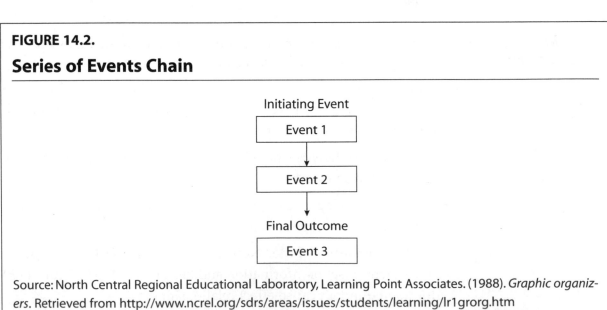

FIGURE 14.2.

Series of Events Chain

Initiating Event

Event 1

Event 2

Final Outcome

Event 3

Source: North Central Regional Educational Laboratory, Learning Point Associates. (1988). *Graphic organizers*. Retrieved from http://www.ncrel.org/sdrs/areas/issues/students/learning/lr1grorg.htm

FIGURE 14.3.

Spider Map

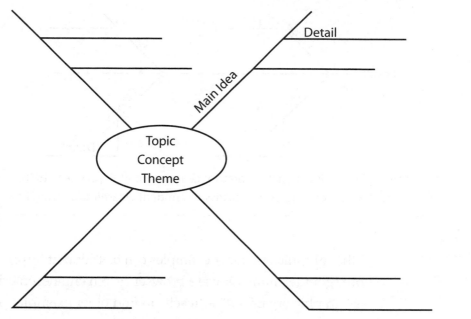

Source: North Central Regional Educational Laboratory, Learning Point Associates. (1988). *Graphic organizers*. Retrieved from http://www.ncrel.org/sdrs/areas/issues/students/learning/lr1grorg.htm

FIGURE 14.4.

Network Tree

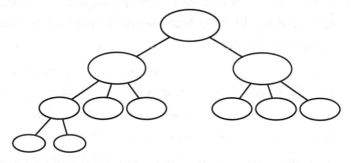

Source: North Central Regional Educational Laboratory, Learning Point Associates. (1988). *Graphic organizers*. Retrieved from http://www.ncrel.org/sdrs/areas/issues/students/learning/lr1grorg.htm

FIGURE 14.5.

Fishbone Map

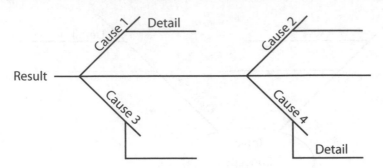

Source: North Central Regional Educational Laboratory, Learning Point Associates. (1988). *Graphic organizers*. Retrieved from http://www.ncrel.org/sdrs/areas/issues/students/learning/lr1grorg.htm

Other graphic organizer examples can be found at http://www.graphic.org/goindex.html. Or use a browser search engine, entering terms such as "graphic organizer" + "teach" to find other examples on the Internet.

- Instead of having students generate the list of ideas constituting the components of a concept, provide them with a list and ask them to graph out the relationships between the items, adding any new ideas.

OBSERVATIONS AND ADVICE Angelo and Cross (1993, pp. 197–202) offer the following considerations regarding use of concept maps.

- Asking students to create concept maps helps educators and students pay attention to the schemata—or conceptual networks—that we use to organize what we learn.

- Because concept maps organize information graphically, this activity appeals to students with strong visual learning skills. Conversely, students with well-developed verbal skills and weaker visual skills may find this activity frustrating and believe that it is a waste of time.

- Although some students may find it difficult to generate ideas or distinguish between levels of ideas, it may be even more difficult for them to identify relationships. Therefore, take sufficient time to introduce this activity so that you can demonstrate the process and clarify your expectations.

- Comparing groups' concept maps can be difficult unless you limit items to a closed list of terms or phrases. Although comparisons will be easier, this limitation diminishes student creativity, breadth, and depth.

See Nilson (2007) for an insightful discussion on the benefits of graphics for learning. She also explicates the features that distinguish concept maps from mind maps.

How you close this activity depends upon your purpose for having students construct the concept map. Teachers often use this activity to prepare students for a second, more extensive activity. For example, you may want teams to create concept maps to generate and organize their ideas for the teaching stage in a jigsaw activity (SET 33, "Jigsaw") or to create a topic overview for a "role play" (SET 19, "Role Play"). Or you may want to use the concept maps as the basis for a whole-class discussion, asking team spokespeople to show and explain the ideas and associations in their group's concept map. Another option is to have teams submit their concept maps to you for evaluation. If each student on a team uses a different colored marker, it is possible to assess individual participation.

KEY RESOURCES   Angelo, T. A., & Cross, K. P. (1993). *Classroom assessment techniques*. San Francisco: Jossey-Bass, pp. 197–202.

Barkley, E. F., Cross, K. P., & Major, C. H. (2005). *Collaborative learning techniques, A handbook for college faculty*. San Francisco: Jossey-Bass, pp. 226–231.

Graphic.org. (n.d.). Graphic Organizers. Retrieved from http://www.graphic.org/goindex.html.

Nilson, L. B. (2007). *The graphic syllabus and the outcomes map: Communicating your course*. San Francisco: Jossey-Bass.

S T U D E N T
E N G A G E M E N T
T E C H N I Q U E

17

Variations

Essential Characteristics

PRIMARY MODE	Individual
ACTIVITY FOCUS	Variable
DURATION OF ACTIVITY	Single Session
ONLINE TRANSFERABILITY	High

DESCRIPTION AND PURPOSE

"Variations" challenges students' creativity as they imagine and evaluate alternatives to a given stimulus in order to build something new.

Students create an altered version of the original, such as rewriting the ending of a story, imagining the consequences of a changed event in history, composing a different conclusion to a famous musical composition, or using an iconic art image as the basis for a new work of art.

STEP-BY-STEP DIRECTIONS

1. Select the item you wish to use as the stimulus or starting point for this activity.

2. Reflect upon the stimulus yourself and brainstorm ideas for how you might create the variation, noting your thought processes as well as any problems you encounter.

3. Use your experiment in #2 as the basis for writing assignment directions.

4. Explain the activity to students, perhaps using your experiment as an illustration, and answering any questions.

5. Students create and submit their projects.

EXAMPLES

Music Theory and Composition

As one of the final projects in the theory and composition course sequence, Professor Harmon I. Zashun chose "Variations" to challenge his students to synthesize their understanding of historical style principles. He selected a well-known folk song melody and asked students to arrange it as a short keyboard piece in the style of any one of the following composers: Bach, Mozart, Beethoven, Chopin, Debussy, Bartok, or Ives.

• • •

Christian Thought and Church History

Professor Zeke N. Yeshallfind wanted students to understand more deeply the significance of theological differences in the Christian church. He selected several defining moments in the two-thousand-year history of the Christian church (for example, the Council of Nicaea, the coronation of Charlemagne, the schism between East and West, and the Reformation) and used these as a topical framework of entry points into the context for theological differences. After they had studied the issues and events surrounding each defining moment, he organized students into groups of five and had each group imagine what would have happened had these events occurred differently. For example, for the Reformation, he asked students, "What do you think would have happened had Martin Luther not been excommunicated as a heretic?" He believed that by challenging students to look at the events from this imagined perspective, they developed greater appreciation and understanding of the importance of these critical incidents (concept adapted from Mark Noll's *Turning Points: Decisive Moments in the History of Christianity*, 2001).

ONLINE IMPLEMENTATION   This SET is easily implemented online as an assignment. If the assigned variation involves something other than text (such as a three-dimensional model), students can hand deliver or mail their projects or upload filmed or photographed images of their work.

VARIATIONS AND EXTENSIONS

- Students can do this project in pairs or in small groups.

- Instead of a single variation, use the concept of "theme and variations," in which students create multiple versions altering different components. For example in music, in which theme and variations is a well-established compositional form, one variation might be to change the harmony from major to minor mode, another variation might change the rhythmic organization, and a third variation might change the texture from homophonic to polyphonic.

- Have students share their variations with each other as a presentation during class, uploaded to a Web site, or a class book (SET 21) or in a poster or exhibit (SET 20).

- Instead of creating a variation, students can look at a stimulus from varied perspectives. For example in a process called "Cubing" (Writing Center, 2009), students respond to a topic from six different directions (analogous to the six sides of a cube):

    1. Describe it.

    2. Compare it.

    3. Associate it.

    4. Analyze it.

    5. Apply it.

    6. Argue for and against it.

OBSERVATIONS AND ADVICE   Students who feel that they are not creative may resist this assignment. Explain that creativity requires taking a risk, and that ideas will flow more freely if they quiet their internal judgmental voice.

Use brainstorming techniques to help students generate ideas for variation.

Consider providing students with additional support by encouraging them to work with a partner or by scaffolding this technique and breaking the process down into manageable parts.

KEY RESOURCE   Writing Center, University of North Carolina at Chapel Hill. Brainstorming. *Handouts and links.* Retrieved from http://www.unc.edu/depts/wcweb/handouts/brainstorming.html

STUDENT
ENGAGEMENT
TECHNIQUE

18

Letters

Essential Characteristics

PRIMARY MODE	Individual
ACTIVITY FOCUS	Reading, Writing
DURATION OF ACTIVITY	Single Session
ONLINE TRANSFERABILITY	High

DESCRIPTION AND PURPOSE

Students assume the identity of an important or famous person in the discipline and write a letter explaining their thoughts on an issue, theory, or controversy to another important or famous person who holds a different perspective. The letter can be to a contemporary or it can be an imaginative juxtaposition between people of different eras.

This SET requires students to draw from their knowledge of the ideas and historical/social context of both people and to capture the essence of the personality and opinions of the person whose identity they are assuming. It is a challenging activity that can help develop students' ability to draw inferences from or conclusions about material they are studying and then synthesize and present their insights in an interesting and creative manner.

STEP-BY-STEP DIRECTIONS

1. Select an issue, theory, decision, or set of beliefs in your discipline that represents a "big idea" and is important to your course.

2. Identify two famous people associated with different perspectives and jot down the defining characteristics that distinguish each person's views.

3. Choose one of the personalities and write a letter expressing his or her viewpoint, starting the letter with a brief summary of the addressee's perspective or ideas. Although this is not a required step, writing your

own letter can help you uncover unexpected problems or challenges with the assignment and provide a model for assessing your students' letters.

4. Create a handout that includes directions and assessment and evaluation criteria.

5. Distribute the handout and explain the assignment, allowing time for questions.

EXAMPLES

Honors Institute Seminar in Science

In this course designed for students who had demonstrated strong academic motivation and ability in the sciences, Professor Al Kali wanted to incorporate an assignment that would be fun, interesting, and challenge students' higher-order thinking skills. He asked students to choose two scientists from any of the science disciplines who had different theories or viewpoints and write a letter assuming the perspective of one of the scientists. As an example, he assumed the identity of Jean-Baptiste Lamarck and wrote a letter to Charles Darwin arguing his theories of transmutation within a generation to oppose Darwin's theory of gradualism. When students had completed the assignment, he formed them into small groups and asked each individual to bring sufficient copies of their letter to distribute to each group member. Students took turns reading their letter to the group, explaining the thinking and research underlying their letter, and answering group members' questions regarding the represented scientists' views.

• • •

History of Constitutional Law

To help students internalize and personalize the controversies underlying the development of constitutional law, this professor formed students into pairs and asked them to research and choose a famous or historically significant court decision about constitutional law that had not already been covered in class. Student As were to write a letter to the editor of a national news magazine such as *Time* or *Newsweek* that represented the plaintiff's perspective, and Student Bs were assigned to write a letter representing the defendant's perspective. When both letters were written, the professor formed groups of 8–10 students and had pairs take turns reading their letters to the group, followed by a brief Q & A period in which group members were encouraged to make comments or ask questions. Each group was asked to vote for the set of letters they found most interesting and persuasive, and then the authoring dyads were asked to read these to the whole class. She found that the activity challenged students to investigate and think about the historical cases in an engaging, novel way and that reading the letters in groups and to the whole class exposed students to the ideas underlying important constitutional law cases in a memorable manner.

ONLINE IMPLEMENTATION This SET is easily adapted to online classes. Consider using the collaborative variation and form student pairs, with one student assigned to writing the original letter and the other writing the response. Set a deadline for Student As to send the original letter to their partner as an e-mail attachment, and set a subsequent deadline for Student Bs to send the response. The letters can be submitted to the instructor for assessment and evaluation.

VARIATIONS AND EXTENSIONS
- Divide the class in half and form students into pairs. Have one student assume one identity and write the original letter and the second student assume the second identity and write a response.

- Instead of a letter, have students invent a dialogue between two people. Students create the dialogues by selecting and weaving together actual quotes from primary sources, or by inventing reasonable quotes given the student's knowledge and understanding of the speakers and context. Angelo and Cross (1993) offer several examples of dialogues. To illustrate contemporary but opposing perspectives, they suggest a dialogue between an abolitionist and a slaveholder in the United States in 1855. To illustrate a dialogue between people of different eras, they suggest a conversation between Alexander, Caesar, and Napoleon on the leadership skills required to conquer an empire and those needed to maintain one. (This technique is described fully in CAT 17, "Invented Dialogues," in Angelo and Cross, 1993, pp. 203–207).

OBSERVATIONS AND ADVICE This activity helps teachers assess students' understanding of the fundamental differences between different theories, historical epochs, genres, and so forth. It can be motivating because it gives students the opportunity to be creative. On the other hand, because it requires high-order thinking skills, it may be overwhelming and frustrating to students who do not feel creative or do not yet understand the material deeply enough to write a convincing and interesting letter.

KEY RESOURCE Angelo, T. A., & Cross, K. P. (1993). *Classroom assessment techniques: A handbook for college teachers* (2nd ed.). San Francisco: Jossey-Bass, pp. 203–207.

**STUDENT
ENGAGEMENT
TECHNIQUE**

19

Role Play

Essential Characteristics

PRIMARY MODE	Collaborative
ACTIVITY FOCUS	Performing
DURATION OF ACTIVITY	Single Session
ONLINE TRANSFERABILITY	Moderate

*DESCRIPTION
AND PURPOSE*

Students apply course concepts as they assume fictional identities or envision themselves in unfamiliar situations.

"Role Play" is a creative, participatory activity that provides the structure for students to experience the emotional and intellectual responses of an assumed identity or imagined circumstance. The word *role* indicates that students actively apply knowledge, skills, and understanding to successfully speak and act from an assigned perspective. The term *play* indicates that students use their imaginations and have fun, acting out their parts in a nonthreatening environment.

*STEP-BY-STEP
DIRECTIONS*

1. It is critical to spend thoughtful time designing the scenario for your role play. Appropriate scenarios require interaction from stakeholders with multiple perspectives. Therefore, identify the perspectives and define the type and number of characters and the framework for their actions.

2. In addition to the roles for the scenario, you may also want to assign group-process roles such as Moderator (who can, for example, intervene if a person falls out of character) and Observer (who interprets and comments on the action).

3. As you craft the basic story line, it is best to initiate the action through a critical event that the players must respond to, such as a comment by one of the actors or an incident that has just occurred.

4. Identify resources (if any) for each of the play's roles, and decide how the activity will end. For example, will you set a time limit, or will you let the scenario end naturally?

5. Ask students to form groups with enough members in each group to assume each stakeholder role.

6. Present the scenario and allow time for discussion of the problem situation. It is important to allow sufficient time for students to ask questions on any aspects of the scenario that are unclear.

7. Assign or ask students to assume a stakeholder role. If you have decided to assign group-process roles such as Moderator and Observers, make sure students are clear on their tasks.

8. Inform students of the time limit or other parameters that will signify the end of the activity. The role play should run only until the proposed behavior is clear, the targeted characteristic has been developed, or the skill has been practiced.

9. Follow the role play with a discussion within the small groups or with the whole class, or both. Discussion should focus on the students' interpretations of the roles and the motivations for and consequences of their actions.

ONLINE IMPLEMENTATION Chat sessions or Virtual Reality Environments (VREs) offer frameworks for implementing role-playing online. Chat sessions occur in real time, whereas VREs offer the option of either synchronous or asynchronous interaction. Because teachers can provide students with the option of assuming roles anonymously, the self-consciousness that sometimes accompanies face-to-face role play is eliminated. If this SET fits well with your teaching goals, investigate the considerable number of software products that have been developed for designing and delivering online role plays. To find them, conduct a search online starting with simple keywords such as "role play" + "teaching." Or consult the technology advisors for teaching on your campus.

EXAMPLES

Psychology of Prejudice

The purpose of this course is to help students understand the complex psychological patterns that develop among different majority and nonmajority groups as a result of the effects of overt and covert discrimination. In order to increase his students' awareness of the nature of prejudiced interactions as well as to help them identify appropriate ways to respond, this professor uses "Role-Play" frequently in his class. He typically organizes his students into groups of three and assigns group members one of three roles: Prejudiced Speaker, Responder, or Social Observer. Throughout the academic term, he crafts a variety of simulated situations and creates characters representing different perspectives (for example, ethnic, racial, gender, socioeconomic background, physical disability). One situation is a business-meeting scenario in which the Prejudiced Speaker is a manager who makes an offending racist remark, the Responder is a subordinate representing the targeted race and must determine an appropriate response, and the Social Observer describes his or her feelings when watching the scene. At the end of the activity, the students share their reactions first with their group and then with the whole class, critiquing the response and the reaction. The class then participates in a post-exercise discussion that focuses on a range of topics that emerged from the exchange (Plous, 2000).

• • •

Oral Communication Skills I

Professor Ann Glishlerner knew that many of the students in her beginning ESL class were extremely self-conscious about speaking up. As nonnative speakers, they came from many countries around the world and feared that they would make mistakes and that other students would not understand them. Yet it was essential that they practice extensively in order to develop vocabulary, grammatical accuracy, and clear pronunciation. Professor Glishlerner discovered that if she asked students to pretend they were someone else, it reduced some of their anxiety. Furthermore, if the scenario was based on an everyday situation, it motivated them because they immediately saw the usefulness of the exercise. She created scenarios such as ordering dinner at a restaurant or asking for directions to the main campus library that emphasized everyday English. She then formed small groups so that students had more opportunities to practice speaking and so that the context would be less threatening than speaking before the whole class.

• • •

History of the Vietnam War

In this hybrid class on the Vietnam War, the professor believed it was important to use classroom time for lecture, but he also wanted his students to understand the war's complexity and to be able to empathize with the viewpoints of the war's various stakeholders. This goal was particularly important to him since he knew that his class attracted many students who had had personal experience with the war. His students included Vietnam vets, immigrant students from Vietnam, returning adult students who had actively protested the war, and parents whose children had died or been injured in the war. Thus many of his students came into the course with strong feelings and beliefs about the war's issues. He worked with his institution's technology department to establish a Virtual Reality Environment for his class and then created scenarios that correlated with his lecture topics. Rather than establishing individual roles, he developed generic role categories, such as American Soldier and South Vietnamese Villager. Each student selected a role and then adopted an appropriate name. He retained for himself the role of Moderator so that he could intervene if exchanges become too emotional or inappropriate. He provided students with the option of entering the VRE anonymously, but if they wished to earn participation credit, they messaged him privately with the moniker they had assumed in the role play. At regular, scheduled intervals throughout the term, he devoted class time to discussion of the themes that emerged (Swensen, personal communication, 2003).

● ● ●

Management Practices

A professor teaching an online course decided to use a role play to teach concepts and content. He formed six groups with four students each, with each group representing a company and with each student assuming one of the following roles: CEO, Financial Officer, Operations Chief, or Marketing Executive. The companies competed against each other for three phases of the companies' life cycles (start-up, growth, and independence). The game simulated nine years during nine weeks of the course. For each year the students in each company established crucial input data, such as prices, advertising, purchase, production, and size of sales force. The instructor collected data and compiled them for the game, creating output data for each company that consisted of units sold, back orders, market share, operating income, income tax, net income, and so forth. The professor evaluated the companies based on results after nine years. Each company met in regular conference, during which the employees discussed data. In another conference called "Managers' Corner," the students participated in management-related discussions (adapted from Hsu, 1989.)

VARIATIONS AND EXTENSIONS

- Allow students to help determine the scenario, identify the major stakeholders, and create the roles.

- Give students time to practice and then have student groups perform the role play in front of the class. Or instead of having multiple groups participating in multiple role plays, have one group role-play in front of the rest of the class. Assign Observers specific tasks for interpreting the action and dialogue of the role play.

- After the initial performance is finished, re-enact the role play, changing characters or redefining the scenario.

- Combine this activity with a "Fish Bowl," by having one group perform the role play while another group watches, and then have the groups trade places.

- Especially in VREs, consider creating roles for students to manipulate the environment. For example, a Manipulative Devil sets up obstacles and creates challenges for the characters, or an Improvising Storyteller creates extensions to the scenario adapting to unforeseen twists in the action. The Australian University Teaching Committee's "Learning Designs" Web site describes these and other roles as well as aspects of effective online role play design (www.learningdesigns.uow.edu.au/guides/info/G1/more/ModeratorsGuide.html#roles).

OBSERVATIONS AND ADVICE   Spend sufficient time before the activity to ensure that students understand the purpose of the role play. If they don't understand your learning goals, students may get off track or the role play may fall flat and seem artificial.

Students must also understand the nature and character of the roles they are assuming. If they know who they are, then they will be more effective in the role. If the role is a complicated one, then they may need time to reflect or conduct research prior to enacting their role.

Although many students will be drawn to this SET with enthusiasm, others will feel self-conscious and uncomfortable about assuming a role. They may resist this activity, protesting that it seems silly. To reduce their discomfort, take care to create a nonthreatening environment and consider preparing students earlier in the term with icebreaker activities (see T/S 30, "Use icebreakers to warm up the class," in Chapter 9). Also, reassure students that although acting is important in this SET, you are not trying to develop acting ability but rather to achieve specific learning goals. Finally, consider allowing these students to assume Observer roles.

The closure stage of this activity is very important. Take time to debrief on the lessons learned through the experience. Don't expect students to develop deep understanding of human situations after a limited exposure in a single role play. Help students relate the role play to their own lives.

The real value of "Role Play" occurs when students form general opinions about course concepts that they developed and internalized as a consequence of assuming a new identity or acting in a new situation.

This SET can be effective, but as with any teaching strategy, be careful not to use it excessively. If it is overused, it can become tedious and feel artificial or silly.

To assess or grade "Role Play," consider videotaping the role plays or having students create their own videotape. Groups can view the videotape and discuss the specific problems or general principles revealed in the tapes, perhaps summarizing and synthesizing their observations into an essay.

KEY RESOURCES Barkley, E. F., Cross, K. P., & Major, C. H. (2005). *Collaborative learning techniques: A handbook for college faculty*. San Francisco: Jossey-Bass, pp. 150–155.

Naidu, S., Ip, A., & Linser, R. (2000). Dynamic goal-based role-play simulation the web: A case study. *Educational Technology and Society 3*(3), pp. 190–202.

Plous, S. (2000). Responding to overt displays of prejudice: A role-playing exercise. *Teaching of Psychology 27*(3), pp. 198–200.

S T U D E N T
E N G A G E M E N T
T E C H N I Q U E
20

Poster Sessions

Essential Characteristics

PRIMARY MODE	Individual
ACTIVITY FOCUS	Multiple
DURATION OF ACTIVITY	Multiple Sessions
ONLINE TRANSFERABILITY	High

DESCRIPTION AND PURPOSE

Students create posters or exhibits that illustrate their understanding of key course topics, issues, or ideas. On presentation day, the class divides and half the students walk around and view displays while others stay with their display to explain and answer questions.

This SET engages students on multiple levels. Students must (1) do an initial activity (such as constructing a model, researching a topic, or analyzing an issue) well enough to produce something to exhibit; (2) be creative as they generate possible ways to represent and display their idea or product; (3) evaluate possibilities and choose their best display design; (4) devise a workable implementation plan; (5) carry out their plan and construct the poster or exhibit; and (6) reflect upon what they learned so that they are able to summarize, synthesize, and share their learning with others on presentation day. In addition, "Poster Sessions" provides teachers and students with an alternative to conventional written reports, thus meeting the needs of a wider range of learners. Finally, this activity can help students deepen their knowledge and understanding as they view and discuss the exhibits of their peers.

STEP-BY-STEP DIRECTIONS

1. Determine topic, content and design parameters, and how exhibits will be displayed.

2. Choose the exhibit day (or days). If projects are complex, consider working backward to schedule check points and creating a rubric to guide students in their thinking and to use to submit a plan to you.

3. Create a handout that includes directions as well as evaluation criteria.

4. Have students brainstorm potential topics that fit within your parameters and generate a prioritized list of two or three ideas that they submit to you. (Having students present multiple ideas allows you to review all topics, ensure that topics support class learning goals, and prevent duplication.)

5. Review the lists and work with students to select the topics.

6. Discuss design parameters and exhibit day logistics with students.

7. Give students time to organize their efforts and (if appropriate) prepare a prospectus in which they will formulate their core idea, identify goals and the resources they will need, and create a schedule for completion of the tasks.

8. Prepare for exhibit day by organizing a display schedule that allows at least half of the students to view the exhibits while the other half remains with the display to explain and answer questions. Allow for sufficient time for students to then switch roles.

EXAMPLES

Advanced Ceramics

This class enrolled students with a wide range of skills. Professor Sarah McGlaise wanted students to practice articulating their artistic visions verbally and to learn creative ideas and technical solutions from each other regarding glazing and hand-built, wheel-thrown, and combination forms. At regular intervals throughout the term, she used the "Poster Session" strategy and had students select two or three works that they felt represented both their successful and unsuccessful attempts to grapple with artistic or technical challenges and share these with their peers.

●　●　●

Introduction to Physics

To help students gain a deeper understanding of the principles of gravitation, Professor Moe Shunenforse formed students into teams of five to design and build a "hot-air balloon" out of flat pieces of tissue paper. To share results, students were asked to create an exhibit that included the following components:

Design: All equations and data used for calculating balloon size, including the formulas used for volume and surface area, the data students collected about different types of materials, estimates about size and mass, "slop" factors, additional load parameters, and so forth

Construction: The steps used to construct the sphere, including an initial prototype model

Test and analysis: Atmospheric data measured on launch day, predictions of flight from the buoyancy equation and gas laws, final temperatures (inside and outside the balloon), and a report of what happened at the launch, including why it worked if it worked, and what might have happened if it did not work

Students were encouraged to include photographs, graphs, preliminary models, video clips, and any other information they believed would best communicate what they had learned to their fellow students. On exhibit day, each team was given space for their exhibit and asked to determine a schedule that would allow them to take turns walking among exhibits or remaining with the exhibit to serve as spokesperson. Spokespeople were instructed to be prepared to reflect on whether the team felt the design was a good one and why or why not, what things would they do differently to improve the design, and so forth (D. Parker, personal communication, 2008).

• • •

Music of Multicultural America

In this online class, the professor wanted her students to be able to recognize the influence of historical genres such as blues, jazz, Cajun, and gospel on the popular music to which they listened. She also wanted students to understand how their favorite musician's individual style had been shaped by the social, historical, racial, and ethnic context in which the musician had grown up. Students were asked to choose a musician and then design and construct a Web page "portrait" that would be part of the course's online "Portrait Gallery." The Web page was to contain the following components:

Visual representation: A visual identity such as a copyright-free photo or a student drawing

Personal significance: A serious, fresh, substantive but concise explanation of why the student chose this musician and why this musician is (or will be) important for others to know about

Biography: A narrative section that addresses the social/historical context in which the musician grew up, musician-specific information including ethnic/racial roots, the styles and artists that had influenced the musician, and the musician's influence on subsequent artists

Discography: An annotated list of recordings

Music examples: Three representative listening excerpts converted for delivery on the Internet

Critical commentary: An analysis of listening examples for structural components (rhythm, melody, harmony, and so forth), genre and/or genre influences (blues, jazz, gospel, folk, and so forth), and ethnic influences (Latin clave rhythms, African melodic ornamentation, and so forth). If the selection is a song with lyrics, inclusion of the lyrics and the student's interpretation of the lyrics.

For more information: 3–5 Web sites that provide additional information either on the artist, genre, or historical and social context

Bibliography: A list of books, articles, and Web sites consulted

She found that the project motivated students, provided a framework for bringing together several aspects of the course, and made a significant contribution to the learning repository for the class because the "Portrait Gallery" was cumulative, with new artists added each term.

ONLINE IMPLEMENTATION Have students create a Web page as their presentation medium. The Web page can contain text, images, or video and links to other sites. How you display the multiple Web pages will depend upon your course-delivery software and may range from students' posting the URL for their page along with an explanation on a threaded discussion to sophisticated programs that allow for multimedia streaming with mechanisms for viewers to submit comments.

VARIATIONS AND EXTENSIONS • Make this a collaborative activity by forming teams to create exhibits. Give teams time to organize their efforts such as preparing a prospectus in which they formulate their research questions, identify goals and the resources they will need to carry out their investigation, choose their methods of investigation, and divide up and assign the tasks. On exhibit day, at least one student can stand by the exhibit and answer questions as other students walk around and view the exhibits of their peers (CoLT 18, "Group Investigation" in Barkley, Cross, and Major, 2005, pp. 199–204).

OBSERVATIONS AND ADVICE "Poster Session" is a presentation strategy, with two characteristics distinguishing it from the typical manner in which students present to the class. First, students display their work simultaneously (which is more efficient than a series of presentations), and second, during the viewing and exhibiting, students interact informally in small groups to discuss the exhibits. This can be less intimidating and may result in more candid, individually relevant discussion than would be generated in a formal presentation with Q & A involving the whole class along with the teacher.

Although elaborate science fair exhibits with the attendant organizational issues may come to mind, "Poster Sessions" can be implemented very simply, with 3-D material displayed on a designated subset of desks and 2-D material tacked or taped to the walls at locations around the room. Displayed items vary based on course content and instructional goals, but they might include written documents (such as letters, content summaries, quotes), visual documents (charts, photographs, art reproductions), objects (models, cultural artifacts, biological specimens), and media (audio and film recordings).

KEY RESOURCE   Colorado State University. *Writing Guides: Poster Sessions.* Retrieved from http://writing.colostate.edu/guides/speaking/poster/pop2a.cfm

**STUDENT
ENGAGEMENT
TECHNIQUE**

21

Class Book

Essential Characteristics

PRIMARY MODE	Individual
ACTIVITY FOCUS	Writing
DURATION OF ACTIVITY	Variable
ONLINE TRANSFERABILITY	High

DESCRIPTION AND PURPOSE   Toward the end of a course, individual students submit an essay assignment that they believe represents their highest quality work. Submissions are collected and bound together as a "Class Book" that will be available to future students in the same course. This SET offers an opportunity for students to create a record of their cumulative course experience, motivates students to strive for personal excellence, and provides students in subsequent classes with models of quality work done by their peers.

STEP-BY-STEP DIRECTIONS

1. Choose what kinds of assignments will be used in the class book and develop guidelines or rules for submission that specify content, format, and quality expectations.

2. Decide on the scope and quality of the final product (for example, simple stapled copies or a more elaborate, bound document using desktop publishing software) and whether you will produce it yourself or assign production to students.

3. Determine a production schedule that is late enough in the term so that students have a reasonable number of assignments from which to choose their best work, yet also allows sufficient time to produce the class book.

Composition, Critical Reading, and Thinking

This course provides students with techniques and practice in expository and argumentative writing based on critical reading and thinking about nonfiction texts. Professor S. A. Rider incorporates collaborative activities extensively in order to help students at this commuter college feel part of a community and because he believes it is the best pedagogical approach for his learning goals. To motivate and challenge students to do their personal best, Professor Rider informs students on the first day of the term that two weeks before the semester ends, they will select what they consider to be their best essay for publication in a class compilation called *Showcase*. He explains that *Showcase* will provide them with a keepsake to remind them of their course experience, and it will give future students models of exemplary work. He asks for volunteers to serve on the production committee who, for extra credit, will be responsible for organizing, editing, and printing the compilation.

Although the first time he implemented the assignment the students produced a simple, spiral-bound document, subsequent classes were motivated to outshine the previous classes and used desktop publishing software to produce high-quality, hard-covered editions that included a preface and photographs with short bios of the students. The cumulative *Showcase* editions are displayed in the English department office.

ONLINE IMPLEMENTATION

There are many ways to implement this SET in an online course. One of the simplest ways is to have students submit their assignments as portable document files (PDFs) and create a list of links on a Web page or forum. A more sophisticated approach would be to create an online magazine, sometimes referred to as a zine, ezine, webzine, or cyberzine. There are several software packages that streamline the production process for online magazines, and they can be located by using a simple search with words such as "ezine publishing."

VARIATIONS AND EXTENSIONS

- Ask students to volunteer or vote on a group of in-class peers to serve as an editorial board responsible for vetting what goes into the class book.
- Have students develop a class memoir that is included as the preface or introduction to the book. This memoir can encourage students to reflect on their learning experiences, build class community, and offer advice to subsequent students on how to learn the most and be successful in the course.

- Instead of a hard-copy class book, create a Web-based magazine, with each class creating the next edition of the online publication.

- This SET is well-suited to courses in the visual and performing arts, with students submitting film clips, images, or music compositions that are compiled on a class CD or DVD.

- In addition to selecting and submitting the assignment, ask students to write a few paragraphs that comment or explain the submission (for example, why they feel it was their best work, the challenges they faced and overcame as they created the work, or analysis and interpretation of the work).

- Have students create individual portfolios out of which they select their best work for the course portfolio.

OBSERVATIONS AND ADVICE

Emphasize that intellectual quality is the criterion for inclusion in the book and that the goal is to produce a book of high-quality work, not just a pretty book.

Students may get too focused on the production of the class book, losing sight of the basic goal of doing excellent work on all their assignments and using evaluation skills to choose their best individual assignment.

KEY RESOURCE

Watkins, R. (2005). *75 e-Learning activities: Making online learning interactive.* San Francisco: Pfeiffer, pp. 198–200.

S T U D E N T
E N G A G E M E N T
T E C H N I Q U E

22

WebQuests

Essential Characteristics

PRIMARY MODE	Collaborative
ACTIVITY FOCUS	Reading, Writing, Presenting
DURATION OF ACTIVITY	Multiple Sessions
ONLINE TRANSFERABILITY	Moderate

DESCRIPTION AND PURPOSE

Student teams participate in an inquiry-oriented activity in which most or all of the information is drawn from the Internet. Using primarily instructor-specified Web sites, team members investigate an open-ended question and participate in a highly structured group process that aims to help them synthesize and apply their understanding to a task that replicates real-world challenges.

"WebQuests" helps students learn to use the Web for research in ways that encourage analysis and judgment rather than simply copying or summarizing information. Because the task is authentic—a scaled-down version of things adults do as citizens or workers—"WebQuests" creates a bridge between what is learned in the classroom and the world outside of the classroom, demonstrating how and why classroom-based knowledge is important.

STEP-BY-STEP DIRECTIONS

1. Decide on a topic that connects course material to current events or select an area that is inadequately covered in available texts.

2. Design a task that utilizes Web information to achieve a specified goal. Dodge and March's WebQuest Design Patterns page (http://webquest .sdsu.edu/designpatterns/all.htm) describes dozens of categories of tasks.

   For example, in the category "Analyzing for Bias," students analyze sources of information for bias and use their analysis to articulate a point of view and demonstrate its impact. An example of a topic is "Botox: Effects, Risks, and Truths."

In the category "Time Capsule," students investigate, evaluate, and select a number of artifacts that capture the essence of a particular period of history. An example of a topic is "The Rise of the Civil Rights Movement in the 1950s: The Contradiction Between American Idealism and Racism."

3. Identify the roles students will assume and the steps they'll follow to complete the activity.

4. Identify the online resources available on the topic by brainstorming a list of related words and using the list to search for relevant sites. As you search, create a list of current, accurate, engaging, and task-appropriate sites that can be used to guide students in their inquiry. San Diego State University's WebQuest page Four Nets for Better Searching provides strategies for searching for such sites (http://webquest.sdsu.edu/searching/fournets.htm).

5. Develop a comprehensive grading rubric that specifies how each component of the WebQuest will be evaluated. San Diego State University's WebQuest portal provides rubrics that can be used to assess the pedagogical soundness of the assignment as well as student performance (http://webquest.sdsu.edu/webquestrubric.html).

6. Create a Web page or hard-copy document that provides assignment details.

EXAMPLES

Organic Chemistry

One of the aims of the chemistry program at this university is to provide opportunities for scientific study and creativity within global contexts that will stimulate and challenge students. To help achieve this goal in an organic chemistry course, Fiona Clark, a chemistry professor at International Baccalaureate World School, created a WebQuest titled "Organic Chemistry in the News."

She gives students a memo (supposedly) written by the editor-in-chief of the local newspaper, in which he tells students that he is being bombarded with questions regarding four topics that have recently been in the news: a proposed pipeline for carrying natural gas, trihalomethanes (THMs) in the local water supply, chemical warfare, and the use of various man-made organic chemicals. He informs students that the paper's science editor is out of town on another project and the newspaper needs credible local experts to investigate the topics. He asks students to research the topics and write an editorial that he can publish by a specified date. He also explains that in order to satisfy the local scientific community, he needs students to prepare a laboratory experiment that could be used to test their findings.

The professor assigns students to groups that will focus on one of the four topics. First, they are asked as individuals to divide a piece of paper into two columns and write everything they already know about the topic in Column A, and what they think they still need to learn in Column B. They then discuss what they wrote with their group and select a role such as Reporter/ Editor, Lab Technician, and Graphic Designer. Each group is given a list of 6–8 Web sites to begin their investigation. The results of their investigation are summarized in an essay written as a newspaper editorial (Clark, 2008).

● ● ●

Advanced Spanish

This is an adaptation of a WebQuest titled "Cuba en Crisis" developed by Christen Savage and Daniel Woolsey (n.d.) for advanced Spanish students. Students are organized into teams of five and presented with the following fictional scenario based on the death of Fidel Castro and the assassination of Raúl Castro:

> With the recent deaths of both Fidel and Raúl Castro, Cuba is in crisis. A prominent news magazine wants to run a special edition on Cuba and take an in-depth look at the current situation. This will involve researching not only the present, but also the history of Cuba and why the nation is in this predicament. Your team of reporters is assigned to the story and requested to make a prediction about Cuba's future based on your findings.

Students are given one week to gather information and one week to organize their findings. They then give a final group presentation that includes data as well as a prediction as to what will happen next in Cuba.

Following is a step-by-step process:

1. **Class discussion:** As a whole class, students read and discuss articles in Spanish that provide contrasting views on the two Castro regimes.
2. **Individual expert:** Students are organized into teams of five. Each team member is responsible for one of the following five areas: history, politics, economy, human rights, and public opinion.
3. **Research:** Team members choose from a list of Web sites provided by the instructor for each expertise area as well as general Web sites and additional video/audio resources (such as tapes of Castro's speeches). Students are required to read a minimum of three articles, with only one in English.

4. **Individual paper:** Each student writes a summary of his or her research and provides this to other group members and to the instructor.

5. **Group discussion:** Groups reconvene and use their summary papers as the basis for discussing and coming to a conclusion regarding the future of Cuba.

6. **Group presentation:** Each group presents their findings to the whole class. Presentations are oral and in Spanish, but may take the form of computer presentation slides, a creative skit, a news report, a Web magazine, a documentary, and so forth. Each student takes on a specific role for the presentation. Roles include Group Summarizer, Issues Reporter (Pros), Issues Reporter (Cons), Artistic Director, and Materials Expert. Groups must prepare and provide a handout for the rest of the students.

7. **Reflection paper:** Students individually write a paper reflecting on the way in which their opinion has or has not changed since the beginning of the activity. The paper also includes a self-assessment on their personal contribution to the information-gathering process, group discussion, and class presentation.

Students are provided with a comprehensive grading rubric that specifies how each component of the WebQuest will be evaluated.

ONLINE IMPLEMENTATION

To be successful with online students, WebQuests must be highly structured. Form groups and assign each group its own threaded discussion area so that members can communicate aspects of the investigation privately. Break the process into its various parts and outline tasks so that students are clear on their responsibilities. Establish a time frame with clear deadlines. Have final text reports or Web pages posted in a public forum for all members of the class to view. For closure, consider creating an assignment that requires all students to view the various reports and, for example, to answer specific content questions or compare and evaluate the investigation results.

VARIATIONS AND EXTENSIONS

- WebQuests are complex, highly scaffolded activities. Teachers can simplify any of the components to make them less elaborate. For example, rather than making the WebQuest a group project in which group members adopt different roles, Deanya Lattimore, a professor at Syracuse University, has individual students look at information through different "frames." The WebQuest she designed is called "Literacy and the Person," and students look at what it means to be "a person" from the perspectives of metaphysics, anthropology, psychology, sociology, and philosophy as preparation for an essay.

OBSERVATIONS AND ADVICE   WebQuests are based on the research of Bernie Dodge and Tom March at San Diego State University. Just as they are complex and challenging for students to do, they are complex and challenging for teachers to create. Dodge and March's comprehensive site (http://webquest.org), hosted by the Educational Technology Department at San Diego State University, provides a wealth of information and advice, including a discussion blog, design templates, and WebQuest examples with a search tool that sorts WebQuests by discipline and educational level.

Because WebQuests were originally designed for K–12 students, there is limited information on how to apply this technique within a college environment.

KEY RESOURCES   Clark, F. *Organic Chemistry in the News.* Retrieved from http://www3.ns .sympatico.ca/chemfifi/Organic%20WebQuest/index.htm.

Dodge, B., & March, T. *WebQuests.* Retrieved from http://webquest.sdsu.edu/.

Savage, C., & Woolsey, D. *Cuba en Crisis.* Retrieved from http://mypage.iu.edu/ ~dwoolsey/cuba_en_crisis/.

Chapter 15

Problem Solving

DEVELOPING STUDENTS' ability to solve problems efficiently and effectively is a goal almost all teachers share. *Problems* can be generally described as puzzles that exercise the mind, but what constitutes a problem varies widely across the disciplines. For example, when we think about a math problem, we are thinking about a statement or proposition that is amenable to being analyzed and solved with the methods of mathematics. When we think about a social problem, we are thinking about a particularly difficult situation in society such as poverty, violence, injustice, or discrimination. Problems can be well defined and have correct answers, or they can be loosely defined "confusing messes incapable of technical solution" (Schön, 1983, p. 42). Whether the problems we want students to grapple with are straightforward tasks designed to produce a specified result or complex quandaries that seem incapable of resolution, problem solving is fundamental to most disciplines. The student engagement techniques (SETs) in this chapter are designed to engage students in learning and practicing problem-solving strategies.

STUDENT
ENGAGEMENT
TECHNIQUE
23

What's the Problem?

Essential Characteristics

PRIMARY MODE	Individual
ACTIVITY FOCUS	Reading, Writing
DURATION OF ACTIVITY	Single Session
ONLINE TRANSFERABILITY	High

DESCRIPTION AND PURPOSE One of the first steps in good problem solving is being able to correctly identify what kind of problem one is dealing with in order to determine the appropriate principles and techniques needed to solve the problem. To do this, students must be able to look beyond surface differences among problems and perceive underlying similarities. In this activity, students work in pairs, looking at examples of common problem types in order to identify the particular type of problem each example represents. In this way, students support each other as they try to increase their efficiency and effectiveness in problem solving by learning to generalize problem types instead of seeing problems as isolated exemplars.

STEP-BY-STEP DIRECTIONS
1. Identify two or more types of problems that students find difficult to distinguish.
2. Choose or craft several examples of each type.
3. Depending upon your teaching goals and the skill level of your students, decide on the complexity of the task. Will you provide them with information about the types of problems and ask them simply to match type with example? Will you provide them only with the examples and ask them to name the problem type?
4. Consider trying out your examples on a colleague or an advanced student to see whether he or she agrees that your examples are clear rep-

resentatives of a particular problem type. This can help you assess how difficult the task is and how long it will take students to complete. (As a general rule, allow students two to three times as long as it took your colleague to do the task.)

5. Make a handout, or a presentation slide, or an overhead-projector transparency containing the problem examples.

6. Form students into pairs and explain the directions, allowing time for questions.

7. Students work through the examples, identifying the type of problem each example represents.

EXAMPLES

Critical Reading and Thinking

To help her students learn to read more critically, Professor Ima Nerer wanted them to develop skills in identifying fallacies in arguments. She decided that by the end of the course, she wanted them to be able to recognize quickly a minimum of twenty fallacy types. She started with five common types (confusing cause and effect, red herring, straw man, ad hominem, and post hoc) and created an overhead transparency with a series of short paragraphs such as the following:

> Presidential candidate X claims that the federal government should not fund the acquisition and construction of the Seawolf class of Attack Submarines. Presidential candidate Y says he deeply opposes this position, claiming it will leave the country defenseless.

After explaining the fallacies to students in a presentation, she posted the transparency and asked students to turn to a neighbor to discuss and identify the type of fallacy each paragraph represented. As a follow-up, she offered bonus points to students who found examples of any of the five fallacies in the media. A few weeks later, she added five more common fallacies, and so on, building up students' knowledge of the types of fallacies as well as improving their ability to recognize them in day-to-day contexts. She found that students enjoyed working together to practice identifying fallacy types and discovering how this skill helped them look more critically at information they encountered in everyday life.

• • •

Music Theory and Composition

The fundamental goal of this course was for students to learn, understand, and apply the voice-leading rules known as Eighteenth-Century Common Practice Technique (for example, avoid parallel fifths and octaves, leading tones must resolve to the tonic, and never make a melodic movement of an augmented interval). Professor Paul Ifanick was frustrated that although students appeared to know the rules, they often did not recognize when they violated them in their harmonization assignments. To help students become better at recognizing errors, he created worksheets of four-measure harmonic progressions, with each progression containing two or three errors. On a separate sheet, he created a numbered list of the basic rules. He then asked student pairs to go through the examples, find and circle the errors and write in the number of the rule the harmonization had violated.

ONLINE IMPLEMENTATION   Synchronous tools such as teleconferencing or chat sessions that also have chalkboard tools offer one possibility for using this SET in an online environment. Alternatively, invite students to contact a classmate and talk through the problem set on the telephone or through instant messaging. Or consider giving student pairs the assignment with problem-type examples and have each student first identify the problems independently and then compare with their teammate and reach consensus, and then submit that as a joint assignment.

VARIATIONS AND EXTENSIONS

- Ask students to create or locate their own examples of the problem types.

- Ask students to provide a detailed explanation of the critical attributes of each problem type, and identify the clues an expert would seek to distinguish the types.

- Once students know how to recognize a problem type, pair this SET with SET 25, "Think-Aloud-Pair-Problem Solving," to help them practice how to solve the problems.

OBSERVATIONS AND ADVICE   This SET naturally lends itself to disciplines that contain well-defined problems with correct answers. But there are also disciplines (or types of problems within disciplines) that are messier and more complex, that include a huge array of relevant variables both known and unknown, and that may not have a single correct solution. If you are using these kinds of problems, inform students that there may be multiple solutions and ask them to choose one, justifying their response with reference to the evidence provided in the example.

Real-world problems are often complex and multifaceted and do not fit into a single category. To keep students focused on identification skills, simplify the examples to highlight the distinctions between problem types, but explain the need for and the limitations of these streamlined example problems to students.

KEY RESOURCE   Angelo, T. A., & Cross, K. P. (1993). *Classroom assessment techniques.* San Francisco: Jossey-Bass, pp. 214–217.

Think Again!

Essential Characteristics

PRIMARY MODE	Individual, Collaborative
ACTIVITY FOCUS	Problem Solving
DURATION OF ACTIVITY	Single Session
ONLINE TRANSFERABILITY	High

DESCRIPTION AND PURPOSE   In this SET, the teacher presents a common misconception in the discipline and then takes a quick, informal poll asking students to agree or disagree with the statement. The teacher then tells students that the statement is untrue and assigns students a task that requires them to prove why it is untrue.

This activity challenges students by creating cognitive dissonance, requiring them to subject their belief to critical analysis and use the knowledge and understanding they are acquiring in the course to gather the appropriate evidence to demonstrate why a commonly held belief is untrue.

STEP-BY-STEP DIRECTIONS

1. Identify and write a common misconception in your discipline on a presentation slide or overhead transparency.

2. Decide on the task that students will do to prove the statement is untrue.

3. Tell students you are going to share with them a statement and that you would like them to agree or disagree, assuring them that their choice will not affect their grade.

4. Display and read the statement and ask students who agree with it to raise their hands.

5. Assuming the majority agree, tell students that the statement is untrue and then ask them to turn to a partner and complete a task that requires

them to prove why it is untrue. (If a considerable number of students disagree, pair them with those who agree so that together they can complete the task proving why the statement is untrue.)

Algebra

Professor Polly Nomeal presented students with the following statement: "The maximum speed of a sailboat occurs when the boat is sailing in the same direction as the wind." She took a quick poll, and 80 percent of the students agreed. She then explained that their intuitive answer was wrong. She formed groups of three and told students, "Sailboats can actually go much faster when they sail across the wind. How so? Using what you have been learning in vector algebra, explain why sailboats can sail faster when the wind blows sideways to their direction of travel rather than from directly behind them. Make your explanation clear enough for the general public to understand. You can use diagrams if that helps" (adapted from Bean, 1996, p. 27).

• • •

Introduction to Physics

To keep students actively engaged throughout the lecture portion of a large introductory physics class, this professor sometimes presents a scenario with two or three possible outcomes. For example, to introduce the topic of conservation of energy, he projects an image of three identical skateboarders prepared to race down three differently shaped ramps at precisely the same time. He asks students to decide which skateboarder would win the race—the skateboarder on the (a) straight ramp, (b) the cycloid ramp, or (c) the parabola ramp? Since the lecture hall is equipped with an automatic response system (clickers), he has students first vote individually on a, b, or c. Without revealing the result, he asks students to turn to someone sitting next to them and explain their reasoning. Then he asks them to come to consensus on a choice and vote again. He displays the results of the individual and paired responses and uses them as the basis for an explanation on the principles involved in the example. He often performs a live experiment in front of the class to demonstrate which response was correct.

ONLINE IMPLEMENTATION Save time by skipping the step of asking students to indicate whether they agree or disagree with the statement. Simply present the task as an assignment, asking students to prove why this commonly held belief is untrue. It will be easiest if you have students complete the assignment individually, but if you wish to garner the benefits of collaborative learning, form student pairs who can communicate through private messaging and e-mail, or form groups and set up a closed-access threaded discussion forum for each group to work out their solution.

VARIATIONS AND EXTENSIONS

- This basic technique can also be used to engage students in solving problems related to course content rather than common misconceptions in the field, as indicated in the physics example above.

- As a follow-up activity to proving why the misconception is untrue, ask students to figure out how to explain it in clear, simple language to the general public.

OBSERVATIONS AND ADVICE

Consider posing the question as "Raise your hand if you think most people on the street would agree with this statement."

If students are savvier than you had thought and the majority of them disagree with the statement, tell them they are right and ask them to explain why.

KEY RESOURCE

Bean, J. C. (1996). Engaging ideas: *The professor's guide to integrating writing, critical thinking, and active learning in the classroom.* San Francisco, Jossey-Bass, p. 27.

STUDENT
ENGAGEMENT
TECHNIQUE

25

Think-Aloud-Pair-Problem Solving (TAPPS)

Essential Characteristics

PRIMARY MODE	Collaborative
ACTIVITY FOCUS	Problem Solving
DURATION OF ACTIVITY	Single Session
ONLINE TRANSFERABILITY	High

DESCRIPTION AND PURPOSE   In "Think-Aloud-Pair-Problem Solving" student pairs receive a series of problems as well as specific roles—problem solver and listener—that switch with each problem. The problem solver thinks aloud, talking through the steps of solving a problem, while the partner listens, following the steps, attempting to understand the reasoning behind the steps, and offering suggestions if there are missteps.

TAPPS places the emphasis on the problem-solving process rather than the product. Articulating one's own process and listening carefully to another's process helps students practice problem-solving skills and learn to diagnose errors in logic. Depending upon the problems used, it can also help increase student awareness of the range of successful (and unsuccessful) approaches to problem solving. TAPPS improves analytical skills by helping students to formalize ideas, rehearse concepts, understand the sequence of steps underlying their thinking, and identify errors in someone else's reasoning. Since it requires students to relate information to existing conceptual frameworks and to apply existing information to new situations, it can also promote deeper understanding. Finally, it can help foster metacognitive awareness, as it provides a structure for students to observe both their own and another's process of learning.

1. Spend sufficient time developing an appropriate set of field-related problems that students can solve within a limited time frame. The problems should engage students in basic problem-solving skills such as identifying the nature of the problem, analyzing the knowledge and skills required to reach a solution, identifying potential solutions, choosing the best solution, and evaluating potential outcomes. To be most effective, the problems should challenge students, requiring them to concentrate and focus their attention, whether they are solvers or listeners.

2. Create a worksheet with a series of problems.

3. Ask students to form pairs and explain to students the roles of problem solver and listener. The role of the problem solver is to read the problem aloud and talk through the reasoning process in attempting to solve the problem. The role of the listener is to encourage the problem solver to think aloud, describing the steps to solve the problem. The listener may also ask clarification questions and offer suggestions, but should refrain from actually solving the problem.

4. Ask students to solve a set of problems, alternating roles with each new problem.

5. Call completion when students have solved all problems.

ONLINE
IMPLEMENTATION

The need for synchronous communication between pairs makes this SET cumbersome online. However, if you believe that modeling and receiving feedback on problem solving is important to your course, consider asking students to teleconference. An alternative would be to organize students into pairs, have them individually work through a problem (or problem set), explain their thinking at each step, and then send their assignment for feedback either as an e-mail attachment or a post on a discussion board.

EXAMPLES

English as a Second Language

An English professor was teaching a course in grammar to ESL students. He decided to use sentence diagramming to help students understand the relationship of the various parts of speech. First he explained diagramming to the students, demonstrating the process by parsing and graphing several sample sentences on the board. When students indicated that they understood the steps, he formed pairs and gave each pair a set of several sentences. He asked students to take turns diagramming the sentences, talking out loud to explain why they were making their choices while their partner listened and offered suggestions when necessary. The professor closed the activity by asking each pair to select the most challenging sentence from the set and go to the board, sharing both their diagramming and the reasoning behind the diagramming with the whole class.

• • •

Elementary Statistics

Professor Marge N. O'Vera decided to use TAPPS in an introductory statistics class to have students practice regression analysis. She prepared a handout that included a scenario with an attached printout of data. She then asked students to use this data to solve ten problems. Professor O'Vera asked students to pair with the student sitting next to them. She explained the roles of problem-solver and listener. The students worked on the problems, alternating between problem-solver and listener until all of the problems were completed. She then held a full class discussion to review the answers and to clarify questions regarding the problem-solving process.

• • •

Programming in BIOPERL

The purpose of this course was to teach students to create utility software programs using a specific scientific programming language. To achieve this goal, students needed to become competent in a complex problem-solving process of retrieving, manipulating, and analyzing sequences from a variety of databases. The instructor noticed that some of his students caught on and were able to go through the steps relatively easily. Others tended to make process mistakes that resulted in programming errors that were time-consuming and frustrating to find later. Historically, these struggling students simply dropped the course at this point, so the instructor was searching for ways to reduce attrition and alleviate student anxiety. He decided to use TAPPS to structure practicing the problem-solving process with a peer, and to use recent quiz scores to partner a student who was having difficulties problem solving with a student who was doing well. The result was that students not only gained competence sooner than in the previous semester when they had worked independently, but it also significantly reduced student attrition.

VARIATIONS AND EXTENSIONS

- This SET is typically used for a series of close-ended problems, but it can also be used for more open-ended problem solving. The activity may take more time, so plan for fewer problems.
- If all pairs have worked on the same problem set, select pairs at random to report out their solution, or take a vote on the most challenging

problems and share and examine solutions along with tips for improvement as a class.

Many students, especially new students, will not have highly developed problem-solving skills. Consider preparing students by having students practice problem solving as a class prior to this activity.

Student problem-solvers may not be comfortable having their logic exposed to other students. Student listeners may not be trained in logic so they may not be able to note difficulties. Because of the level of risk students may feel, it is important to have established a high level of trust in your class prior to using this activity. Thus, it may also be a good idea to use this technique with pairs who work together throughout the term or at least over several sessions.

Students will solve problems at different speeds. In this SET, it is particularly important to have an additional problem (an "extension") on hand for students who complete the problems quickly so that they do not sit around bored waiting for the other students to finish. Consider crafting a particularly challenging bonus question for extra credit.

Monitor students to ensure they are reinforcing correct information and problem-solving processes.

Either to get a rough measure of students' problem-solving ability prior to implementing TAPPS, or as a follow-up activity to assess how much they have learned, provide students with a few examples of common problem types and ask them to recognize and identify the particular type of problem each example represents. This activity can help you assess how well your students can recognize various problem types, which is the first step in matching problem type to solution method (Angelo and Cross, pp. 214–217).

If you are most interested in assessing how students solve problems and how well they understand and can describe problem-solving methods, have them individually track the steps that they took in solving the problem in TAPPS and submit this to you for review. Angelo and Cross also suggest ideas for adapting and extending the assessment (pp. 224–225):

- Give students two problems: one of low and the other of medium difficulty. The results of their efforts to solve the problems can help you to gauge the best level at which to begin whole-class or small-group instruction.

- Ask students with elegant, well-documented responses to explain their solutions to a partner, a small group of students, or even to the whole class.

- Since most students have little or no experience reflecting on their own problem-solving processes, you may have to help them learn how to do this. Also, to ensure that peers give each other thoughtful and thorough responses, you may need to give students credit for this activity.

To grade this SET, students can submit a record of the solutions with the solver for each problem identified (for example, by initials). You may also wish to have the listener identified and to have the listener include his or her suggestions for problem-solving improvement.

KEY RESOURCES   Barkley, E. F., Cross, K. P., & Major, C. H. (2005). *Collaborative learning techniques: A handbook for college faculty*. San Francisco: Jossey-Bass, pp. 172–176.

Lochhead, J., & Whimby, A. (1987). Teaching analytical reasoning through thinking-aloud pair problem solving. In J. E. Stice (Ed.), *Developing critical thinking and problem solving abilities: New directions for teaching and learning, 30*. San Francisco: Jossey-Bass, pp. 72–93.

MacGregor, J. (1990). Collaborative learning: Shared inquiry as a process of reform. In M. D. Svinicki (Ed.), *The changing face of college teaching: New directions for teaching and learning, 42*. San Francisco: Jossey-Bass, pp. 19–30.

Millis, B. J., & Cottell, P. G., Jr. (1998). *Cooperative learning for higher education faculty*. Phoenix, AZ: Oryx Press, p. 114.

STUDENT
ENGAGEMENT
TECHNIQUE

26

Proclamations

Essential Characteristics

PRIMARY MODE	Collaborative
ACTIVITY FOCUS	Reading, Writing
DURATION OF ACTIVITY	Single Session
ONLINE TRANSFERABILITY	High

DESCRIPTION AND PURPOSE

Student teams identify and analyze a problematic situation in the local community. They then write a speech for a government official that persuades others of the urgency of the problem and offers strategies for solving the problem.

Researching and proposing solutions to problems helps students develop critical and creative thinking skills. Working on a real problem in the community can deepen understanding of theoretical concepts, demonstrate the relevance and importance of academic work, and help foster a greater sense of social and civic responsibility. Since students present their analysis and solution strategies in a persuasive speech, this SET can also help students develop communication skills.

STEP-BY-STEP DIRECTIONS

1. Spend time thinking through the parameters of this assignment. What kinds of community problems do you want students to identify? For example, can the problems be general (graffiti, reckless driving, noise, ethnic conflict, and so forth) or should they be discipline specific (art-related community problems might include insufficient amateur artist exhibit opportunities, lack of information on how and where to dispose of art-related hazardous waste materials, and artists' sense of social isolation). Will you determine, or will you allow students to determine, the type of government official and audience for which the

speech will be written (such as the mayor, Chamber of Commerce, school district Board of Trustees, city planning department)?

2. Determine how students will report out (will you ask the team to submit the speech as a written document or require a team representative to actually give the speech to the class?).

3. If the skill level of your students is such that they require more scaffolding, consider identifying sample problems and writing a model speech yourself to help clarify your expectations.

4. Ask students to use newspapers, media, the Internet, personal experience, and other sources to identify two or three local community problems that they would like to investigate.

5. Select the problems yourself by choosing from the lists submitted by students, or have students participate in the process. One method is to type out or write on the board all of the potential choices and then ask individuals to vote for their top three choices. The class's most popular topics can then be designated as the available choices.

6. Form teams based on topic interest.

7. Give teams time to organize their efforts such as preparing a prospectus in which they state the problem, give specific examples of the problem, and identify possible reasons for the problem.

8. Allow time for students to analyze the problem, identify solutions, and decide on the central idea they are trying to convey. Consider providing them with guidance on writing speeches, such as suggesting that they create an outline, number points so audience members can follow, and after each point return to the main theme.

EXAMPLE

Race and Ethnic Relations

This course focuses on the evolving meaning of race and ethnicity as it relates to intergroup relations in the United States. The professor decided to use "Proclamations" to help students better bridge theory and practice and to help them recognize their potential power as change agents for improving relations in their community. He asked students to write on a piece of paper a list of five problems that they observed in their community that seem to have some basis in the area's changed racial and ethnic demographics. He collected the papers, made a synthesized, composite list, and distributed the list to the class, asking students to number their top five choices. Based on the students' votes, he formed groups and assigned each group to focus on one of the five problems. Their assignment included discussing the problem, coming to agreement on strategies to solve the problem, and then writing their choice of a speech or a letter to an appropriate government or civic leader.

OBSERVATIONS AND ADVICE

Since there is no official definition of *community problem*, consider establishing parameters such as "the problem should have two or more of the following criteria: it occurs frequently, has lasted for a while, affects many people, is disturbing and possibly intense, deprives people of legal or moral rights, or is perceived as a problem by a significant number of people" (Berkowitz, 2007).

Encouraging students to work on problems that are authentic and relevant to them is refreshingly different from just reading about problems and issues in a textbook, thus engaging students in working for solutions that they find important and interesting.

Real community problems are often complex, resisting clear analysis and solution and persisting despite concerted efforts. Encourage students to take the time and make the effort to think hard about the problem and untangle its varied components; the many dimensions may involve multiple reasons for the problem, the costs of solutions, multiple solutions with different types of actions, the stakeholders, opposition to proposed solutions, and so forth. It is also possible that problems are too complex and involve factors that are beyond a community's control (general economic decline, for example, that prevents the community from having the necessary resources; Watts, 2007). Recognizing what is within one's control and what is not is an important life lesson.

KEY RESOURCES

Berkowitz, B. (2007). *The community tool box: Bringing solutions to light.* Work Group for Community Health and Development, University of Kansas. Retrieved from http://ctb1.ku.edu/en/tablecontents/.

Watts, M. M. (2007). *Service learning.* Upper Saddle River, NJ: Pearson/Prentice Hall.

S T U D E N T
E N G A G E M E N T
T E C H N I Q U E

27

Send-a-Problem

Essential Characteristics

PRIMARY MODE	Collaborative
ACTIVITY FOCUS	Discussing
DURATION OF ACTIVITY	Single Session
ONLINE TRANSFERABILITY	Moderate

DESCRIPTION AND PURPOSE

In "Send-a-Problem," groups of students each receive a problem, try to solve it, and then pass the problem and solution to a nearby group. Without looking at the previous group's solution, the next group works to solve the problem. After as many passes as seem useful, groups analyze, evaluate, and synthesize the responses to the problem they received in the final pass and report the best solution to the class.

"Send-a-Problem" thus involves two activity stages: solving problems and evaluating solutions. The purpose of the first stage is to provide students with an opportunity to practice together and learn from each other the thinking skills required for effective problem solving. The purpose of the second stage is to help students learn to compare and discriminate among multiple solutions.

STEP-BY-STEP DIRECTIONS

1. Determine the number of problems you will need in order to have all groups working simultaneously.

2. Decide how you will present the problem. Consider attaching each problem to the outside of a file folder or an envelope into which groups can then insert their solutions.

3. Think carefully about the instructions you will give to students regarding time limits and the order in which they should pass the problem (such as clockwise). Being clear with students can help to reduce any confusion.

4. Form groups of 4–6 students, describe the activity, give instructions, and answer questions.

5. Distribute a different problem to each group, asking each group to discuss the problem, generate possible solutions, choose the best solution, and record and place their response in the folder or envelope.

6. Call "Time," and instruct teams to pass to the next group; each group receives a new folder or envelope. Upon receiving new problems, students again brainstorm responses and record results until time is called and they again pass the problem to a new group.

7. Repeat the process for as many times as seems useful and appropriate for the problem.

8. Students in the final group review and evaluate the responses to the problem, adding any additional information they wish.

9. The activity concludes as teams report on the responses contained in the envelope or folder they evaluated. As groups report out, add any points that groups missed and reinforce correct processes and solutions.

EXAMPLES

Urban Planning

This professor decided to use "Send-a-Problem" so that students could evaluate different groups' solutions to a residential rezoning problem. She gave each group a manila envelope that included the data required to solve the problem and two 5 × 7 index cards. She asked students to discuss and agree upon a solution, write the solution on one of the cards and place it in the envelope, and pass the envelope to the next group. The next group also discussed a solution, recorded their responses on the second index card and placed it in the envelope. This group sent their solution to a third group, who reviewed the responses from the first two groups and selected what they believed was the best solution. The instructor asked these third, final groups to report on which solution they felt was best and to describe why.

• • •

Advanced Pathophysiology and Patient Management

To review assessment and treatment of patients with respiratory disease, Professor Xavier Breath divided the class of twenty students into three groups. He then gave each group an envelop with a patient's specific symptoms written on the outside. Professor Breath asked groups to review the symptoms, diagnose the disease, and recommend and write down appropriate treatment and therapy. After each group had discussed the first problem for fifteen minutes, the instructor asked students to put their responses in the envelope and pass it to a group sitting nearby who repeated the process. After another fifteen-minute discussion, students sent the envelopes to a final group. When the final group received the envelope, they synthesized the responses from the two previous groups and added additional responses. They then selected the most likely disease causing the patient's symptoms and selected the best treatment. The professor called on each group and wrote the best responses on the chalkboard, incorporating a review of diagnosis protocol, symptoms, diseases, and treatment.

● ● ●

English Literature

In this online class, Professor Fitz William wanted students to think deeply about cultural and social conditions surrounding the development of the novel *Pride and Prejudice*. He decided to have students participate in an online adaptation of "Send-a-Problem." He organized students into three groups and created a forum for each group. He then developed three questions relating the text to the historical context of the nineteenth century and posted one of the questions on each of the group forums. He gave students in each group one week to respond to their first question and a second week to respond to their second question. During the third week, he gave students access to all forums, and asked groups to evaluate the responses to their final question.

ONLINE IMPLEMENTATION An adaptation of this SET can be effective in the online environment. Determine problems and organize students into as many groups as you have problems. Create a protected-access forum for each group. Post problem prompts and ask students to solve the appropriate problem as listed in Table 15.1 for Stage 1. During Stage 2, permit forum access to all students to respond to the solutions that were posted in the preceding two weeks.

TABLE 15.1.

Stages of Problem Solving

		Stage 1: Problem Solving	Stage 2: Solution Evaluation
	Time frame 1	*Time frame 2*	*Time frame 3*
Group A	Solve problem 1	Solve problem 2	Evaluate solutions for problem 3
Group B	Solve problem 2	Solve problem 3	Evaluate solutions for problem 1
Group C	Solve problem 3	Solve problem 1	Evaluate solutions for problem 2

VARIATIONS AND EXTENSIONS

- Allow students to generate their own list of problems that they would like to see the class solve. For example, individuals may wish to have additional coverage of a certain type of problem that they find consistently confusing. Or perhaps there are issues in a reading assignment that they found particularly intriguing and would like to hear what other students think. While you may have specific topics that you must cover, giving students some control over the problems/topics can generate more engagement and investment in this SET.

- Consider using this SET as a review before an examination. Bring in copies of old tests for students to take and compare their answers.

- For closure, have groups write the numbers of the problems on the board, and ask the evaluating teams to report which group's solution they determined was best, recording the team's name under the problem's number. Then ask the evaluating team to summarize the winning team's solution and state why they felt that solution was best. Offer the winning team the opportunity to add any additional comments.

OBSERVATIONS AND ADVICE

Interpret *problem* to include a variety of complex questions and issues (such as text, diagnosis, and identification of a physical element).

"Send-a-Problem" is most effective for developing several thoughtful solutions for more complex problems that do not have a single right answer. In some situations, it may be effective for close-ended problems that students just learned in a lecture or reading assignment. In this way, it can replace traditional drill-and-practice exercises by adding in higher-order thinking skills during the second solution-evaluation stage.

Prepare the problems and work through the solutions yourself so that you can determine the amount of time it will take groups to solve the problems. Depending on the complexity of the problem, you will need to estimate how long each stage of this activity will take to allow enough time for thinking and reflection. Try to select problems that are roughly equal in complexity and that take approximately the same amount of time to solve.

If you are teaching a large class, you may want to have several groups work on the same problem, but you will find that this works better if groups with the same problems are not seated next to each other.

Be fairly specific about time limitations and be thorough in the instructions introducing the activity. This will give students an idea of how much thought they can give to their responses and it will help ensure that the activity proceeds smoothly. Be prepared to extend the time limit if the majority of the groups seem to still be on task or to call time sooner than you anticipated if the majority of the groups seem to be wrapping up.

Despite your best efforts at developing comparable problems and setting time limits, groups may well work at different rates, and they need sufficient flexibility to do that. In order to prevent any group from having to sit idle or from having to pass the problem before they are ready, have several extensions (additional problems) ready to fill in. Final groups can report on more than one problem, or you can pick up the additional problems and respond.

Having participated in "Send-a-Problem," students should be relatively skilled at solving specific problem types and evaluating problem-solving processes. If students have been working on different types of problems, provide them with a few problems and ask them to state the principle that best applies to each problem. This will help you to evaluate their ability to associate specific problems with the general principles used to solve them and to determine their skill at transferring what they have learned to new problem situations.

KEY RESOURCES   Barkley, E. F., Cross, K. P., & Major, C. H. (2005). *Collaborative learning techniques: A handbook for college faculty*. San Francisco: Jossey-Bass, pp. 177–181.

Kagen, S. (1992). *Cooperative learning* (2nd ed.). San Juan Capistrano, CA: Resources for Teachers, pp. 10–11.

Millis, B. J., & Cottell, P.G., Jr. (1998). *Cooperative learning for higher education faculty*. Phoenix, AZ: Oryx Press, pp. 103–105.

**STUDENT
ENGAGEMENT
TECHNIQUE**

28

Case Studies

Essential Characteristics

PRIMARY MODE	Collaborative
ACTIVITY FOCUS	Reading, Writing
DURATION OF ACTIVITY	Single Session
ONLINE TRANSFERABILITY	High

DESCRIPTION AND PURPOSE   Case studies involve an in-depth analysis of a single situation or set of circumstances over time. Among the most popular and enduring methods for getting students involved in problem solving and teamwork, their use has spread beyond the professional fields such as medicine, law, and business in which they originated to include the humanities.

A well-designed case requires analysis, problem solving, decision-making, and justification. The case study approach engages students because of its emphasis on active learning, its real-world application, the drama and excitement that may characterize a particular case, and its opportunities for students to identify personally with the decision makers and the problems they confront.

STEP-BY-STEP DIRECTIONS   1. Using the Internet, newspapers, journal or magazine articles, your own experiences, or the experiences of professionals and practitioners in your field, find a situation or set of circumstances that poses a challenging problem.

2. Write up the case along with a series of questions to guide students in their analysis. McKeachie, Hofer, Svinicki, Chism, Van Note, and Chu (2002) suggest the following prompts to guide students in their approach to the case:

   What is the problem?

   What might have caused the problem?

What evidence can be gathered to support or discount any of the hypotheses?

What conclusions can be drawn? What recommendations?

3. Decide how you will have groups report out (written or oral statement?).

4. Form groups of 4–6 students and distribute the handout to each team, allowing time for students to ask questions and clarify the task.

5. Students study the case, sorting out factual data, identifying the problems and the issues, and reflecting on their relevant experience as they move toward recommending actions that resolve the dilemma in the case. (The amount of time depends upon the complexity of the case, but may extend over several class sessions.)

6. Facilitate a whole-class discussion of the case, posing questions and guiding the discussion toward points of major importance, but avoiding telling students the "right" answers (Davis, 1993, p. 164).

EXAMPLE

Physical Geology

This course was designed for students who were not science majors and were enrolled in the class to fulfill general education requirements. The professor wanted to engage students by helping them to relate mineral properties to real-life uses and hazards. Minerals are the first topic covered in the semester, and the professor used a real case that had been tried in their county's legal system as the last component of the class discussion of minerals. The title of the activity was "A Question of Responsibility: Whose Asbestos Caused Her Lung Disease?" The professor knew that most students were aware that asbestos is a health hazard, but don't know that *asbestos* refers to a variety of minerals with both useful and harmful properties. Students were presented with a case study describing the an asbestos-related personal injury lawsuit and asked to apply what they had learned to the lawsuit presented in the case. They then participated in a follow-up activity in which they weighed the risks of leaving asbestos in public buildings against the risks of removing it (Branlund, 2008).

VARIATIONS AND EXTENSIONS

• Instead of a written case study, use a film excerpt or a role play to present the problem situation (McKeachie, 1999, p. 178).

• Partner with community members or professionals in your field to craft real cases and then invite these people to share their decisions and the consequences of their choices after students have analyzed the case.

- Create a "Cross Case Comparison" in which you select two different cases and ask students to examine the cases to discover similarities and differences between them.

- After students have studied a case, change one or more variables and ask them to speculate on how this would have affected the outcome.

***OBSERVATIONS
AND ADVICE***   Be concise. Although providing many details can make the case seem more real, and one of the goals of the case study method is to teach students to select the most important factors from a complex mesh of facts and data, too much information overwhelms and frustrates students.

Good case studies have the following features (Davis, 1993, p. 162; Davis, 2009, p. 223):

Tells a "real" story

Applicable to all students in your class

Rich in characterizations, to allow for competing interpretations of motives

Promotes empathy with the central characters

Complex enough to raise interesting questions and alternatives

Simple enough to prevent students from becoming lost in extraneous details

Lacks an obvious or clear-cut right answer

Encourages students to think and take a position

Demands a decision

KEY RESOURCES   Barkley, E. F., Cross, K. P., & Major, C. H. (2005). *Collaborative learning techniques: A handbook for college faculty*. San Francisco: Jossey-Bass, pp. 182–187.

Barnes, L., Christensen, C. R., & Hansen, A. (1994). *Teaching and the case method: Text, cases, and readings*. Boston: Harvard Business School.

Chapter 16
Application and Performance

IN MANY WAYS, the knowledge and skills students learn in our classes gain relevance and value when students can apply them. The student engagement techniques (SETs) in this chapter provide activities for students to connect what they are learning to their personal lives or the real world, to carry out an action or accomplish a task that they otherwise know only theoretically, or to demonstrate what they know and how well they can transfer and apply what they know in a new or different context.

STUDENT ENGAGEMENT TECHNIQUE

29

Contemporary Issues Journal

Essential Characteristics

PRIMARY MODE	Individual
ACTIVITY FOCUS	Writing
DURATION OF ACTIVITY	Multiple Sessions
ONLINE TRANSFERABILITY	High

DESCRIPTION AND PURPOSE

Students are more motivated to learn things that they believe are worth learning. In this SET, students look for connections between course material and recent events or developments that they find via online news sites, printed news sources, or broadcast media. They then write in a journal or post on a blog how course material applies to these current affairs.

This technique deepens student understanding of course-related ideas and concepts and helps them to appreciate the value of what they are learning in the classroom by making it easier for them to see its relevance to the real world.

STEP-BY-STEP DIRECTIONS

1. Decide the journal parameters ahead of time. For example,
   - What will be the journal medium (a lined tablet, a word-processing file, a bound booklet, an online blog)?
   - How frequently should students make entries, and will the journal be for a course segment or the whole term?
   - What should a typical entry look like? Consider a three-part entry: (1) date of journal entry and news source, (2) summary (who, what, where, when, why, how), and (3) the principles, ideas, and concepts from the course that the event reflects.

2. Determine how you will assess the journal.

3. Consider creating a handout that includes directions, clarifies your expectations, and provides examples.

4. Students look for and record or post journal entries that connect course material to news events.

EXAMPLES

Applied Ethics

Professor Howie Aktud wanted students to examine ethics by observing actual choices made by people in real situations. He asked students to monitor the news for stories of conflict related to controversial issues such as abortion, rationing of health care, animal rights, environmental concerns, gun control, homosexuality, and capital punishment; record at least one item per week in a journal; and write a single-paragraph analysis using the terms and principles they were learning in class. He collected the journals twice during the term, assigning grades based on the number of entries and the quality of the analyses. For the final exam, students selected an event in their journal and used the conceptual tools of metaethics and normative ethics they had learned during the term to write an extensive essay analyzing the main issue from multiple perspectives, and closing with the steps they believed could be taken to resolve the conflict in the specific news incident.

•   •   •

Music Business

In this course, students study the legal and business aspects of the music industry with an emphasis on publishing, licensing, and promotion. To keep the course up-do-date, this instructor requires students to monitor the online site *Music Industry News Network* throughout the term, looking for current news stories that relate to course topics such as the rapidly changing copyright law in the multimedia industry and the Internet. Students write the date, source, and a synopsis of the news story, and identify the relevant laws or principles in a journal in preparation for the first class session of the week. During the first five minutes of class, students share their findings with partners as the instructor walks around the room, making a plus, check, or minus next to student names in the grade book based on a quick assessment of that week's entry. He then invites students to share their findings and interpretations with the whole class, using these reports as a basis for discussion and drawing connections to what will be studied during the upcoming week.

ONLINE IMPLEMENTATION

This SET can be easily adapted to an online course through use of a blog for students to write their entries. In this way, students can incorporate text, images, and links to Web pages, media, and other blogs that enrich their journal. Set up preferences so that each student's blog is kept private from other students but allows you access as the instructor. Tell students you will be spot-checking blogs randomly throughout the term, or set up a formal evaluation schedule. Consider creating a single-threaded discussion forum for students to share insights from their blogs, or set up multiple forums dedicated to separate topics.

VARIATIONS AND EXTENSIONS

- Ask students to expand their entries by including questions they have about the event, especially aspects that appear to be course-related but which have not yet been covered in class.

- Use the journal for reflective purposes, asking students to think about the event and relate it to their personal lives, answering questions such as "Have you experienced anything similar in your own life?" and "Given what you have learned about X in this course, what might you advise the participants to do now that would help them to move forward most productively?"

- Consider having students follow up this activity with a formal essay in which they analyze, synthesize, or evaluate the information in their journal entries.

- If appropriate to course goals, ask students to monitor online news sites from other English-speaking countries and, for example, compare and contrast coverage of a single event from different international perspectives. Or ask students in foreign language courses to look for events or articles in the media of that country and translate and interpret their findings. *News and Newspapers Online* from the libraries of the University of North Carolina at Greensboro (http://library.uncg.edu/news/) provides links to news sites from all over the world.

- Make this a collaborative learning activity by using "Dialogue Journals" in which students exchange journals with a peer who reads and responds to the entry with comments and questions. To create a Dialogue Journal, students draw a vertical line about one-third of the page from the right margin (or use word-processing software to create a two-column table). The writer writes in the left, the responder writes in the right. Journal writing can be particularly effective when writers know that someone who is interested in the topic will read and respond to their entries. Since reading and responding to students can be a time-consuming task, peer exchange helps ensure students receive immediate and critical feedback without adding to instructor workload (Barkley, Cross, & Major, 2005, pp. 236–240).

- Consider creating a communal journal. Keep the journal on a desk or table in the classroom or your office or maintain an online forum or blog that is available for entries and responses by any class member.

OBSERVATIONS AND ADVICE   Students will come to class with preconceptions about journal writing; therefore, be clear on your parameters for their entries.

It is important for the instructor (or a peer, as described in Variations and Extensions) to review the journal and respond to the entries or students may feel that the assignment is busy work.

Check journals regularly or tell students you will be evaluating them on a random basis to discourage them from waiting until the last minute to do all the entries.

KEY RESOURCE   Bean, J. C. (1996). *Engaging ideas: The professor's guide to integrating writing, critical thinking, and active learning in the classroom.* San Francisco: Jossey-Bass, p. 109.

S T U D E N T
E N G A G E M E N T
T E C H N I Q U E

30

Hearing the Subject

Essential Characteristics

PRIMARY MODE	Individual, then Collaborative
ACTIVITY FOCUS	Discussing
DURATION OF ACTIVITY	Single Session
ONLINE TRANSFERABILITY	Low

DESCRIPTION AND PURPOSE

Students "listen" to a text passage, film clip, or image, paying close attention to its forms of expression but refraining from evaluating or interpreting the work. Then in small groups, they paraphrase as much of what they witnessed as possible to their team members as a warm-up to a large-group or whole-class discussion in which they make meaning of what they perceived.

In a culture characterized by high speed and multitasking, some faculty have expressed concerns that students have difficulty being still and taking the time needed to really focus and concentrate. This SET provides a procedure for students to practice this kind of mental activity, a skill that is particularly important as they approach tasks that are difficult and require sustained effort to accomplish.

STEP-BY-STEP PROCEDURES

1. Select a work that is rich with meaning that is best understood through careful, sustained reflection.

2. Take the time to really "listen" to it yourself, jotting down words, shapes, colors, textures, or whatever kinds of characteristics best capture your experience. Note how much time this takes you. You can use your work to model the process to students who must then apply the process to a new subject or to help you facilitate student discussion on the same subject.

3. Explain the purpose and model the process to students. Tell them the amount of time they will be asked to sit quietly studying the subject, then answer any questions.

4. Instruct students to quietly and independently study the subject for a designated amount of time, jotting down the types of descriptive characteristics that are appropriate for the subject.

5. Ask students to form groups of 2–3 and share their observations, but refrain from commenting on how they feel about the subject or interpreting its meaning.

6. Combine small groups to form groups of 4–6 or move to a whole-class discussion, first addressing the experience of intensely "listening" to the subject and sharing how the process helped or hindered students' enjoyment of the subject before moving to discussion about the subject's meaning.

EXAMPLES

Art Appreciation

In this introductory survey course, Professor Ike O'Nogrephy found that many students looked at images quickly and superficially, paying attention only to surface details such as the image's topic. Students felt satisfied with their approach when they were dealing with art that was representational and realistic, but he knew that this method would leave them bewildered and resistant as the course moved toward more abstract art. He decided to use "Hearing the Subject" to challenge them to take the time to look at images more closely. First, he reviewed a number of general concepts such as form, space, area, plane, axis, proportion, scale, value, and so forth. Then he asked students to have these concepts in mind as they spent five minutes quietly and independently studying Hans Hofmann's expressionist painting *Effervescence*. He encouraged students to jot down words, shapes, colors, textures, and so forth as they "listened" to what Hofmann was "saying." When the five minutes were up, he turned the projector off and asked students to form groups of three and share their observations, recalling as much detail as possible from the painting but refraining from evaluating or interpreting it. He then facilitated a whole-class discussion in which students talked about the patience and stillness required to look closely at an image and how the process in which they had just participated could help them approach particularly difficult works of art.

•   •   •

Introduction to American Literature

This professor knew that students had a difficult time with e. e. cummings's poetry because of the way cummings breaks from the conventions of syntax, punctuation, and typography. To challenge students to make the effort required to move beyond their initial resistance, he distributed a handout with two of cummings's poems—"look at this)" and "he does not have to feel because he thinks." He asked students to look intently at the poems for five minutes, concentrating on the way the words looked on the page (the use of capitals, punctuation marks, the physical layout of the words, and so forth). He then asked students to share observations with the whole class, such as "He mixes everything up in "'a) s w (e loo) k'" or "The title of 'look at this)' ends with a closed parenthesis while the last phrase of the poem begins with an open parenthesis." After students shared all their observations about the poems' visual display of the words, he formed them into small groups and asked them to now read the poems, choose one, and then brainstorm creatively looking for connections between the meaning of the words and cummings's use of punctuation and text layout.

ONLINE IMPLEMENTATION

The effectiveness of this SET is largely dependent upon a group of students first sitting quietly for a designated amount of time as they focus on the subject, followed by small-group and then large-group discussion. Although using synchronous tools such as teleconferencing or chat sessions offer one possibility for implementing this in the online environment, the "silence" time would be awkward. A possible adaptation would be to ask students to study the subject individually and on their own, then post in a threaded forum the subject's characteristics by a deadline. Follow this with another threaded discussion in which students offer interpretations of the subject.

VARIATIONS AND EXTENSIONS

- This technique can also be used on a literal level to help students listen better. For example, students could be asked to listen to a person speak, but concentrate on body language, speech inflections, speed of delivery, and so forth, rather than the words themselves. Or as students listen to an example of music, they could concentrate on embedded attributes (such as individual lines within the texture, the micro organization of the rhythm, repetition and variation of motifs, and so forth) rather than attending only to the dominant elements such as melody, words, and beat. This achieves the SET's purpose of moving students beyond superficial observations to deeper examination and understanding, using an auditory task as the medium.

- In a variation of this approach called "Controversial Statements," teachers generate a discussion by stating a strongly worded statement taken from the public domain or created by the teacher. The provocative (or even inflammatory) statement should challenge assumptions that students take for granted or cling to fiercely. After the statement has been made, students in small groups try to understand the reasoning and circumstances that frame the statement. Why would someone hold those views? What in their experience could have led to such ideas? What possible grounds could we advance to support the making of such an argument?

- This activity asks students to come up with evidence and rationales outside their usual frames of reference. By examining the grounds for a view that is contrary to their own, they may learn to be more understanding and tolerant of opinions with which they disagree. It can engage students at an emotional level and deepen student thinking by challenging them to look at what they are learning from new perspectives (Brookfield and Preskill, 2005, pp. 70–71).

OBSERVATIONS AND ADVICE This technique challenges students to concentrate on something just as they would if they were listening carefully to someone speak, but the process is not necessarily auditory and the focus is on the subject rather than another person. It teaches students to attend sympathetically to even the most confusing or off-putting works and derive a certain level of understanding instead of dismissing the works out of hand. It can help students appreciate the amount of effort and attention that is sometimes required to make sense of experiences and ideas that are difficult, complex, and multifaceted.

Peter J. Frederick (2002) has created a similar technique that he calls "Evocative Visuals and Textual Passages" and describes how he uses it in large-lecture settings to help students learn and practice "close reading" (pp. 60–62). In addition to text passages, paintings, photographs, or video clips, he suggests using quantitative charts or graphs. For example in his large history class, he uses transparencies of census data, ship manifests of the sex, age, occupation and homes of passengers, military muster rolls, and so forth. He then asks students two questions: What do you see? (or What's going on here?) and What does it mean to you? (or What do you think it means?). He explains that invariably, numerous differing interpretations emerge, which challenges students to consider the complexity of knowledge and make decisions about which interpretations they think make the most sense for them. He also notes that this activity helps students learn the skills of doing history, rather than just covering content.

KEY RESOURCES Brookfield, S., & Preskill, S. (2005). *Discussion as a way of teaching: Tools and techniques for democratic classrooms.* San Francisco: Jossey-Bass, pp. 92–94.

Frederick, P. J. (2002). Engaging students actively in large lecture settings. In C. A. Stanley (Ed.), *Engaging large classes: Strategies and techniques for college faculty.* Bolton, MA: Anker, pp. 60–62.

S T U D E N T
E N G A G E M E N T
T E C H N I Q U E

31

Directed Paraphrase

Essential Characteristics

PRIMARY MODE	Individual
ACTIVITY FOCUS	Writing
DURATION OF ACTIVITY	Single Session
ONLINE TRANSFERABILITY	High

DESCRIPTION AND PURPOSE

This SET provides a structured activity that helps students take an idea or concept and "make it their own" by integrating it into their own words and understandings. Students paraphrase concepts that are complex or are typically conveyed using highly specialized vocabulary into simpler language that will be understood by a designated audience. The process of translating complicated language or concepts into simpler, straightforward, more personally relevant language helps students remember what they have learned longer. It also gives students practice restating their learning into a form that a specific audience can understand (for example, patients, clients, or customers), a skill that is essential for success in many professions.

STEP-BY-STEP DIRECTIONS

1. Identify an important principle, theory, concept, or argument that students have studied, preferably one that has implications outside of the classroom.

2. Determine an appropriate, realistic, and challenging audience for which students could craft their translations.

3. Try paraphrasing the information yourself to see how realistic the assignment is. Also consider paraphrasing a concept that is similar in complexity so that you can model the process and goal for students.

4. Explain and model the process to students and tell them the topic as well as the audience.

Statics

To help students in their comprehension and recall of highly technical information, Professor Alec Tricity provides students with a list of key topics for each major unit of study. He asks students to read the detailed discussion of these topics in the textbook until they feel confident that they understand them, then set aside the book and write their own rendition of the essential information and ideas on a note card. After checking their version with the original to make sure that it accurately expresses key concepts but in their own words and making any adjustments or changes as needed, students submit their note cards for his review.

• • •

Radiation Oncology

This course focused on preparing health professionals who would be caring for people who were receiving radiation therapy. The teacher knew that an important skill would be to be able to explain medical terms and therapies to patients who were anxious, scared, and unfamiliar with the medical terminology. To help students practice this skill, she asked them to pair up and take turns, responding to prompts such as, "Explain to a patient the differences between sterotactic radiation therapy, remote brachytherapy, and unsealed internal radiation therapy."

ONLINE ADAPTATION

Preparation and procedures are essentially the same as for a face-to-face class, but with students receiving directions and submitting their paraphrases using your course's assignments tool.

VARIATIONS AND EXTENSIONS

• Some teachers have expressed concern that students are cobbling together information from various sources in their essays and research papers without properly citing the original source. Use this SET to help students practice how to legitimately use information and ideas they find elsewhere by providing them with examples of original passages, and then asking them to paraphrase and cite appropriately.

OBSERVATIONS AND ADVICE

You may want to point out the difference between paraphrasing and summarizing. A paraphrase must be entirely in one's own words with the purpose of expressing another person's ideas in one's own language, while a summary means to distill the most essential points of someone else's work in a manner that is much shorter than the original.

KEY RESOURCE

Angelo, T. A., & Cross, K. P.. (1993). *Classroom assessment techniques*. San Francisco: Jossey-Bass, pp. 281–284.

S T U D E N T
E N G A G E M E N T
T E C H N I Q U E

32

Insights-Resources-Application (IRAs)

Essential Characteristics

PRIMARY MODE	Individual
ACTIVITY FOCUS	Writing
DURATION OF ACTIVITY	Single Session
ONLINE TRANSFERABILITY	Designed for Online

DESCRIPTION AND PURPOSE

In conjunction with an assigned reading, students complete a written assignment that includes three components: new perceptions or understandings (Insights), a resource they have found that amplifies the reading's themes or information (Resources), and an example from the student's personal experience that relates to the reading (Application).

This SET engages students by challenging them to reflect upon and identify what they have learned, connect what they have learned to their personal experience, and search out additional sources that deepen their knowledge or understanding of the reading's themes or information.

STEP-BY-STEP DIRECTIONS

1. Identify a reading that lends itself to the kinds of reflection and personal connections required by this SET. Create directions that ask students to write a brief assignment that includes the following three components:

   a. **Insights (I):** Three one-sentence bullet points that represent new understandings about the meaning or nature of the reading's topic.

   b **Resource (R):** One additional resource such as a book, article, Web site, film, or news item that has similar thoughts, ideas, or themes that amplify the reading.

   c. **Application (A):** A paragraph that relates the reading to an example from the student's current or past experience.

2. Create a threaded discussion forum for the IRAs and ask students to post their IRAs and then read and comment on at least two other students' IRAs by a deadline. Encourage students to make substantive comments by suggesting they identify similarities and differences between various students' postings, connecting ideas to previous readings, providing additional supportive insights or resources, and so forth.

EXAMPLE

Survey of International Business

Professor Sal Ling wanted her students to connect theory and practice in their study of the global commercial community. She used IRAs in conjunction with a set of reading assignments on international marketing functions, creating a discussion forum for students to post both their own essays and to comment upon the essays of their peers. She believed the exercise helped students by deepening their understanding of key topics, encouraging them to find personal relevance by connecting what they were learning to their own experiences, and providing them with a peer-developed bibliography of resources for later reference.

ONLINE IMPLEMENTATION   This SET is designed for online delivery.

VARIATIONS AND EXTENSIONS

- Instead of using this SET in conjunction with a reading, use it to conclude a more general unit of study or for other kinds of learning activities such as discussion follow-up or video viewing.

- Use this SET within a face-to-face setting by having students bring their written assignments to class and then exchange them with a partner. Give students a few minutes to read their partner's assignment, and then ask them to compare and contrast their ideas.

KEY RESOURCE   Conrad, R., & Donaldson, J. A. (2004). *Engaging the online learner*. San Francisco: Jossey-Bass, p. 80.

STUDENT
ENGAGEMENT
TECHNIQUE

33

Jigsaw

Essential Characteristics

PRIMARY MODE	Collaborative
ACTIVITY FOCUS	Discussing
DURATION OF ACTIVITY	Multiple Sessions
ONLINE TRANSFERABILITY	High

DESCRIPTION AND PURPOSE

Students work in small groups to develop knowledge about a given topic and to formulate effective ways of teaching it to others. These "expert" groups then break up, and students move to new "jigsaw" groups, each one consisting of students who have developed expertise in different subtopics.

"Jigsaw" is helpful in motivating students to accept responsibility for learning something well enough to teach it to their peers. It also gives each student a chance to be in the spotlight. When students assume the role of Teacher, they lead the discussion, so even students who are reticent to speak up in class must take on leadership roles.

STEP-BY-STEP DIRECTIONS

1. Spend sufficient time designing the learning task. The topic should be simple enough for students with a good grasp of the subject to teach it to their peers, but complex enough to require discussion and the design of interesting strategies for instruction. The topic should divide usefully into a number that will allow you to form expert groups of equal numbers of students. Be aware that the number of subtopics dictates the number of students in the second jigsaw group.

2. Develop a list of topics for developing expertise, making the division of the material into component parts clear.

3. Either through teacher assignment or by interest areas, students form groups charged with developing expertise on a particular topic then work in these expert groups to master the topic. They also determine

ways to help others learn the material, exploring possible explanations, examples, illustrations, and applications.

4. After expert groups have developed their expertise and pedagogical strategies, students move from their expert group to a new jigsaw group in which each student serves as the only expert on a specific topic. In the jigsaw groups, experts teach the material and lead the discussion on their particular topic.

5. Students return to their expert groups, debrief, and the whole class reflects on the group discoveries in a closure activity.

EXAMPLES

Masterpieces of American Literature

Professor Paige Turner taught a Southern writers course. Toward the end of the semester, she decided to have her class examine the topic of how Southern writers used people and events from their own lives as elements in their fiction. She selected five authors for the assignment: William Faulkner, Flannery O'Connor, Eudora Welty, Walker Percy, and Thomas Wolfe. Each student selected one author to research in homework. At the next class, students worked in small expert groups organized by author to develop a list of biographical facts that appeared in the short stories of their author. Each group created a comprehensive list of information about their author and also determined how to present the material to other students so that it could be learned within a ten-minute small-group discussion. In the subsequent class session, Professor Turner formed new jigsaw groups, each with one expert for each author who took turns leading the discussion. For closure, Professor Turner conducted a whole-class discussion in which students compared the amount and type of biographical facts that they found in each of the author's short stories.

• • •

Introduction to Cultural Anthropology

Wanting her students to gain an understanding of several primitive cultures, Professor Sara McShards decided to have her students participate in a "Jigsaw." She believed that this collaborative technique would give her students an opportunity to learn by engaging in research, by interacting with each other, and by teaching other students. Professor McShards divided the class into six groups of six students each, informing students that they would be responsible for studying one culture, and then teaching their peers about that culture. "Teachers" would also conduct follow-up evaluations of their peers' understanding of the material that they taught them by creating, administering, and evaluating a practice quiz. At the conclusion of that segment of the course, all students would take a comprehensive examination, testing and grading them on all six of the cultures.

She advised students to consider the major religious beliefs, economic practices, governance structure, and class systems that produced each culture. To prepare them to assume the teaching role effectively, she led a class discussion about various teaching methods (including the use of outlines, definition pages, worksheets, and sample quizzes). After the groups became knowledgeable about their assigned culture, Professor McShard reassigned students to new jigsaw groups, with one member from each of the first teacher groups. Each Teacher took a turn providing information and leading a discussion in which they asked and answered questions about their culture. To close the group activity, each Teacher gave the practice quiz to the students in the jigsaw group. After the Teachers had evaluated the quizzes, they submitted them to Professor McShard, who reviewed them and used them to guide the development of her study guide for the comprehensive exam.

• • •

Web Site Publishing Tools

This online course is an introduction to Web site design and management, and one of the course objectives is for each student to create a professional functioning Web site using a variety of tools and techniques. Halfway through the term, the instructor assigns each student to an Expert Team and a Jigsaw Team. There are six Expert Teams based on six features of the design software program that she has not covered in class. Although it is possible for students to create fully functioning Web sites without these features, implementing them into their final sites will enhance their projects and add to the professionalism of the e-portfolios they are creating to demonstrate their skills to prospective employers or clients.

Students can select which Expert Team they would like to join on a first come, first served basis, but she assigns students to the Jigsaw Team so that she can ensure one expert is on each team. Each Expert Team is given their own private forum on the course's discussion board and one week to do a "Knowledge Quest" in which they research their specific feature. Team members can use Web resources, books, or external discussion boards or Listservs to research their topic, using their Expert Team's in-class forum to pool their information. At the end of one week, they take their shared knowledge and develop a strategy to teach their topic. Expert Teams have one more week to create a learning unit to present to the Jigsaw Teams. These presentations must include screenshots, incorporate the researched feature, list references, and recommend the two best resources for further information.

At the end of the third week, everyone on the Jigsaw Team has learned basic information about each of the six tools, and the professor opens up all forums and presentations to the entire class. Students are then required to include one of the new features that they learned in the Expert Team and another feature that they learned in the Jigsaw Team into their final projects.

ONLINE IMPLEMENTATION

Identify 4–5 specific topics you want students to teach each other. Identify each topic as Topic A, Topic B, and so forth, and create an Expert Group Forum for each of these topics. Thus Expert Group Forum A will be for students who will become experts in Topic A. Determine possible ways the topics could be taught online, such as through text documents, Web pages, or forums on a discussion board. Part of the SET is having students determine the best way to teach it, which deepens their knowledge of it. Assess the skill level of your students and the ease with which these teaching strategies could be incorporated into your online class. For example, know how many of your students possess the skills and resources to create Web pages—and know whether your course management system allows you or your students to upload Web pages relatively easily—before you offer this as an option for the teaching stage of this activity.

The simplest and most generally accessible format is to have students create instructional modules from text documents. These decisions, combined with the size of your class, will help determine the parameters you will want to establish for the assignment. Provide sufficient time for expert groups to work on their assignments individually, to pool their ideas, to ask questions of each other, to become experts on that topic, and to determine and develop their teaching materials. Form jigsaw groups that include one expert for each of the topics. Thus individual members of Expert Groups A, B, C, D, and E will form into multiple jigsaw groups, each with ABCDE membership. Create separate forums for each jigsaw group and have each expert teach his or her topic to other group members.

VARIATIONS AND EXTENSIONS

- Use this technique for complex problem-solving tasks and have expert groups learn a skill necessary to solve the problem.

- Increase student interest in this exercise by asking students to help generate the lists of topics.

- Instead of calling students "experts," call them "teachers."

- Instead of asking students to work in two different groups (the Expert one for mastery, and the Jigsaw one for teaching), have students work with only one group, with pairs forming and breaking off to develop expertise on a specific topic, and then rejoining the full group for teaching. This variation is called "Within Team Jigsaw" (Millis & Cottell, 1998, pp. 133–134).

- Give students a list of the key points that represent your initial thinking on how you would teach the topic, and invite students to critique your approach and then either go beyond it or think differently and come up with an alternative way to teach the topic.

- Ask groups to choose a spokesperson for an all-class review. The spokespersons make a presentation to the whole class, and remaining group members can elaborate or contribute additional views.

- Give students an individual quiz on the topics. Consider grouping individual scores into team scores. This variation is called "Jigsaw 2" (Slavin, 1995).

- One way of ensuring preparation for jigsaw group work is to test individually for content knowledge prior to the discussion in the expert group, and re-test after expert group discussion.

OBSERVATIONS AND ADVICE Experienced teachers know that teaching something to others requires an understanding of the subject matter beyond surface learning. As students develop strategies for teaching to their peers, they may discover examples, anecdotes, or analogies that enhance their comprehension. They may design charts or graphs that illustrate relationships visually. They may create quiz questions or discussion questions that probe for new levels of meaning. These are learning activities that deepen the Teacher's understanding and also benefit the Learners.

Students who are not familiar with collaborative learning and are not comfortable in being so self-directed may complain that they are "doing the teacher's work." Explain the purpose of this collaborative technique to students before the exercise, and have a closure activity for reflection on what students have learned.

Acquiring expert knowledge also encourages interdependence. In the initial Expert Group assignment, students must take advantage of the knowledge, skills, understanding, and creativity of their fellow students since this will benefit them in their role as Teacher. In their role as Teachers in the jigsaw group, peers reward their classmates for good teaching, or rebuke students who don't know their subject well enough to teach it.

If students are to realize the advantages of the peer-teaching role, they must take the challenges of teaching seriously. Consider engaging students in a preliminary, whole class discussion about what good teaching entails: clear explanations, practical examples, visual aids, provocative questions, and the like. Take time to present the challenges of teaching explicitly so that students can come up with creative ideas for communicating effectively with their peers about academic subject matter.

Any peer-teaching technique depends on how well prepared students are for their assignment. The focus of "Jigsaw" is to learn something well enough to teach it. But the learning group may also need advance preparation. For many topics, one cannot expect a peer teacher to work with a group that has not done any background reading or preparation. Thus, it may be important to assign homework that prepares students for both roles: teachers and learners.

Providing closure for this activity is essential. If you don't have a good closing activity, students may feel like you are shirking your duty as the instructor by making the students teach themselves and providing them with no feedback. Hold a whole class discussion on how they fulfilled the assignment, where they fell short, and where they exceeded the learning requirements. An additional or alternative activity is to ask groups to reflect on, and then share, something that members did that helped the group to learn. Or give students a quiz or test on the material to stress its importance.

"Jigsaw" has been used effectively across a wide spectrum of levels, from K–12 to university. Because of its highly contrived structure, however, this technique should not be overused. Once or twice a semester preserves the novelty and freshness.

Since "Jigsaw" tends to be a time-consuming technique and includes a variety of purposes, it is important to evaluate the process. The most direct assessment might be to solicit student answers to a brief survey. Survey questions should be those that really concern you, derived from your experience in preparing the exercise or from your observations of the group process. Questions might be both specific and general: On a scale of 1 to 10, how helpful was this exercise in deepening your understanding of _____? Did you find this an effective use of class time? How well was the teaching role performed in your group? What were the major advantages of "Jigsaw" to you? Major disadvantages? What did you learn from assuming the role of Teacher? How could the exercise be improved? You will receive the most candid answers if survey responses are anonymous.

Since "Jigsaw" is distinctive for its emphasis on students assuming the role of teacher for their area of expertise, an assessment technique such as SET 31, "Directed Paraphrase," can focus on how well students perform the teaching function. Consider stopping after the first small-group session to ask a few students who will serve as experts in their next group to paraphrase briefly for the entire class their introductory statement. The paraphrase should be brief, hit the high points of the past discussion, and be understandable to their peers new to the concepts. This provides an opportunity for the instructor to make any necessary corrections as well as to gain insight into the discussions taking place in the groups.

KEY RESOURCES   Angelo, T. A., & Cross, K. P. (1993). *Classroom assessment techniques: a handbook for college teachers* (2nd ed.). San Francisco: Jossey-Bass, pp. 232–235.

Aronson, E., Blaney, N., Stephin, C., Sikes, J., & Snapp, M. (1978). *The jigsaw classroom.* Beverly Hills, CA: Sage.

Aronson, E. (2000). *The jigsaw classroom.* Retrieved from http://www.jigsaw.org/

Barkley, E. F., Cross, K. P., & Major, C. H. (2005). *Collaborative learning techniques: A handbook for college faculty.* San Francisco: Jossey-Bass, pp. 156–163.

Johnson, D. W., Johnson, R., & Smith, K. (1998). *Active learning: Cooperation in the college classroom.* Edina, MN: Interaction Book Company. pp. 2:24–2:25.

S T U D E N T
E N G A G E M E N T
T E C H N I Q U E

34

Field Trips

Essential Characteristics

PRIMARY MODE	Collaborative
ACTIVITY FOCUS	Visiting a Site
DURATION OF ACTIVITY	Single Session
ONLINE TRANSFERABILITY	High

DESCRIPTION AND PURPOSE   Groups of students visit an off-campus location for first-hand observation or research.

Field trips provide students with a course-related experience that cannot be replicated in the classroom. Going to physical locations such as research laboratories, medical facilities, museums, art exhibits, environmental centers, or sites with unique geological or botanical characteristics help students understand the value and meaning of what they are learning in the classroom as well as see how this knowledge can be applied in different and novel situations. Finally, going off-campus can also be a refreshing change of pace and provide an opportunity for students to bond together as a learning community.

STEP-BY-STEP DIRECTIONS   1. Because field trips take students off campus, there are increased expenses and risks. To mitigate liability, most institutions have formalized field trip procedures that require preapproval of forms. Places that are not generally open to the public and that may put students at some level of risk (such as prisons and hospitals) may require students to sign waivers. Therefore, as a first step, check your institution's policies and procedures so that you know requirements regarding field trips.

2. Attend to basic planning details.

    a. Contact the appropriate host site personnel to determine that the location is open to group visits and to see if staff can provide support, such as arranging for guided tours, special presentations, or access to areas not normally available to the public.

    b. If possible, visit the site yourself so that you can uncover any potential problems in advance.

    c. Work with host site staff to select the date and time.

    d. Prepare students by alerting them to any additional costs, appropriate dress codes (for example, in medical or research facilities), standards of behavior, and so forth.

    e. Determine how students will travel (on their own? car pool? institution-provided buses or minivans?). Consider forming students into groups with a leader who will be responsible for communicating with you via cell phone.

3. Craft a follow-up activity such as whole class discussion or a written essay that guides students to reflect upon what they have learned and connect the field trip experience to what they have learned or are learning in class.

EXAMPLES

Introduction to Sociology

In this large, general education course at the University of Michigan, students are divided into groups and visit nearby Detroit to observe how various sociological phenomena such as race, ethnicity, gender, socio-economic class, social stratification, urban renewal, mobility, sense of community, and so forth play out in different neighborhoods (Wright, 2000).

• • •

Humanities and the Modern Experience

To enrich student experience in this online course, Professor Art X. Ibit incorporates virtual field trips to prominent museums with noted and specialized collections. He creates worksheets of prompts designed for each site that require students to locate specific information but also includes a thought-provoking prompt to which students respond on a threaded discussion forum.

• • •

DNA Sequencing and Bioinformatics

This course is designed to help students understand, use, and perform DNA sequencing and cloning techniques in a research and production setting. Professor Jean Poole knew of a local research laboratory that had established a DNA Learning Center that provided students with the opportunity to work with the same computer tools and data that the lab's genome scientists used. The center had developed computer-based modules that provided students with hands-on computer exercises in which they analyzed human, plant, bacterial, and viral genomes; studied how variations in DNA sequence contribute to disease; and learned about new strategies for developing therapeutic drugs. The center also scheduled a Q&A session with one of their scientists for students to ask questions about the research and bioinformatics as a career (adapted from Cold Spring Harbor Laboratory's DNA Learning Center "Bioformatics Field Trips" http://www.dnalc.org/ddnalc/field_trips/hsbioinform.html).

ONLINE IMPLEMENTATION

If your course enrolls only students who live locally, you can prepare for and implement this SET in much the same way you would for a face-to-face class. To minimize logistical challenges, consider creating worksheets and then telling students to visit the site on their own. Or consider creating a forum and encouraging students to coordinate with peers to visit the site in small groups. Alternatively, create a virtual field trip (see Variations and Extensions).

VARIATIONS AND EXTENSIONS

- Organize a virtual field trip to one of the many Web sites created for this purpose. *Virtual Field Trips* (http://www.internet4classrooms.com/vft.htm) is a comprehensive clearinghouse for site information on 100+ locations from all around the world.
- Assign individual students or student teams with topics to research on the field trip for which they must gather information, take digital photos, and then summarize and display their findings on a series of presentation slides. Either combine the slides into a single presentation to serve as the stimulus for a whole-class discussion, or ask students to conduct their own presentations.

OBSERVATIONS AND ADVICE

Field trips generally take place outside of regular class meeting times, and since most students have intense schedules involving other classes, work obligations, internships, and domestic responsibilities, one of the challenging aspects of organizing a field trip is finding a time that everyone can meet. Do your best to find a date and time that works for most students, but then simply provide alternative assignments for students who cannot participate due to scheduling conflicts. This also addresses unforeseen circumstances where students cannot participate due to illness or emergencies.

The larger the class, the more difficult it is to organize field trips. Consider dividing a large class into multiple smaller groups and staggering the scheduling of the trip.

If the logistical aspects of organizing the trip seem overwhelming, create worksheets or field trip guides and give students responsibility for visiting the sites on their own either individually or in small groups but within a specified time framework.

KEY RESOURCE   Wright, M. C. (2000). Getting more out of less: The benefits of short-term experiential learning in undergraduate sociology classes. *Teaching Sociology* 28(2): 116–126.

Chapter 17

Attitudes and Values

HELPING STUDENTS to understand and recall information and then use this knowledge in a variety of contexts to solve problems and think critically and creatively is an important goal for most college teachers. But many educators are striving for more than cognitive-based learning. They want students to *care*—about life, about themselves, about what they are trying to teach them. The student engagement techniques (SETs) in this chapter provide learning activities that help students gain greater understanding of their own feelings, opinions, and principles as well as those of others.

S T U D E N T
E N G A G E M E N T
T E C H N I Q U E

35

Autobiographical Reflections

Essential Characteristics

PRIMARY MODE	Individual
ACTIVITY FOCUS	Writing
DURATION OF ACTIVITY	Single Session
ONLINE TRANSFERABILITY	High

DESCRIPTION AND PURPOSE Self-awareness is an important component of engaged learning. In this SET, students write an essay in response to a prompt that asks them to reflect upon their personal history in relation to the course or discipline. As students think about and tell their story, they connect their own life and experience to what they are studying, exploring their beliefs, attitudes, values, preferences, background knowledge, learning problems, biases, and so forth.

This SET can be very helpful to students because it requires them to become more conscious of the experiences, values, and attitudes they bring to the course. Such knowledge can help students more easily find meaning and relevance in what they are learning. The increased understanding that comes from this self-assessment can also empower students to build on their strengths as well as identify areas in which they would like to improve.

STEP-BY-STEP DIRECTIONS
1. Decide the scope of the project and which aspects of their life you wish students to describe (past experiences that have shaped their attitude toward the discipline, learning experiences in similar courses, involvement in related activities, and so forth).
2. Further limit the autobiography by establishing parameters regarding the chronological periods and personal areas (academic, family, work, and so forth) you wish students to address.

3. To ensure that the autobiography is focused and pertinent to learning goals, construct explicit directions that include length, rubrics, or specific questions for students to answer.

Elementary Algebra

In conjunction with an objective, diagnostic assessment quiz on math skills, Professor Anna Logue gives students the following in-class assignment on the first day:

> Within the next fifteen minutes, and in less than a page, please describe one of your most memorable learning experiences in prior math classes.
>
> If an experience was positive, explain why. If an experience was negative, explain why and try to identify what might have been done differently (either by you, the teacher, or your peers) that would have helped improve the situation.

Before students submit their papers, she asks them to turn to a partner and share and compare experiences. She then asks students to report out, writing on the board the specific behaviors both she (in one column) and the students (in another column) can do to help make their learning experiences in her class positive and successful.

• • •

Music of Multicultural America

To help students connect their personal experience to course content and to deepen their appreciation of how historical, cultural, and social context influences music preferences, this instructor gives the students the following assignment at the beginning of the term:

> Write a 1,000-word autobiographical essay that correlates your family background with the evolution of your personal tastes in music. Divide your essay into clear periods of your life corresponding to the time frame provided below:
>
> • Prior to your birth: What was happening in your family in the approximately 25 years before you were born? Where were they living, what was going on in their world, and what kinds of music were your parents and/or grandparents listening to?

- Ages 0–5: What musical experiences did you have as a child? Describe any lullabies, children's or folk songs you remember. To what extent, if any, did ethnicity and race shape these experiences? Were there any other significant experiences in your life at this time that have a connection with music?

- Ages 6–12: What music did you hear during this period? Describe any musical experiences that were important to you (such as activities in school, studying an instrument, hearing music at family gatherings or from older siblings, and so forth).

- Ages 13–21: This is typically a critical period in which your musical tastes are shaped for the rest of your life. What music were you listening to during this period and what do you think shaped your preferences? Did your preferences change over this period and if so, how and why?

- If you are older than 21, what musical experiences have you had since you turned 21 and have your musical tastes changed? How and why?

- Now reflect upon your cumulative experience: How old are you now? To what extent and in what ways do you believe the environment in which you grew up shaped your current musical likes and dislikes? How do you think this compares and contrasts with other students who are similar to you in terms of age, ethnicity, gender, and so forth?

ONLINE ADAPTATION This SET adapts easily to the online environment. As an alternative to a written assignment and if students are appropriately skilled, consider having them construct a Web page autobiography that includes images, sound clips, or video.

VARIATIONS AND EXTENSIONS
- To increase the degree of self-awareness, ask students to explain how and why the events they described were meaningful.

- Have students use multimedia (photographs, documents, music examples, and so forth) to enhance their narrative.

- If your directions have asked students to focus on starting points, skills, capabilities, and self-confidence, consider retaining the essays and returning them at the end of the term for students to write a postscript in which they describe their learning and personal growth in the course.

OBSERVATIONS AND ADVICE Focusing on attitudes toward learning course content is particularly useful in introductory courses, especially those in which students are likely to feel high levels of anxiety, such as mathematics, statistics, and public speaking. It can also serve as a tool for more effectively gauging student starting points.

Fink (2003, p. 47) has observed that when students learn more about themselves, they inevitably learn about others. Thus this SET may be useful in helping students achieve social learning goals such as developing empathy and interpersonal skills. This reciprocal relationship (developing a self that is capable of interacting with others in a more effective way) underlies many major educational goals. For example, learning how to interact effectively with people of different race and ethnicity is an important component in developing multicultural competence.

If, after reading through the essays, you discover that many students feel substantial anxiety about the course, consider sharing recurring themes with the whole class to reassure students that many of their peers are also anxious and are starting at similar places in their learning.

Some students may feel uncomfortable revealing personal information, so don't require students to disclose information that may be considered too private. Also, be sure to explain how the assignment relates to course learning goals and consider offering an alternative assignment for students who don't wish to participate.

Because autobiographies can be time-consuming to write and to read, make sure they are limited in scope and length.

Students are likely to invest a good deal of effort and emotion into their personal stories, so be sure to allocate sufficient time to read and respond to them.

Autobiographies can yield a great deal of information that can be used for setting instructional goals appropriate to the particular mix of students. Additionally, they can uncover expertise that could be used to invite students to give special presentations or to solicit student leaders or tutors.

KEY RESOURCES   Angelo, T. A., & Cross, K. P. (1993). Focused autobiographical sketches. *Classroom assessment techniques*. San Francisco: Jossey-Bass, pp. 281–284.

Fink, L. D. (2003). *Creating significant learning experiences: An integrated approach to designing college courses*. San Francisco: Jossey-Bass.

S T U D E N T
E N G A G E M E N T
T E C H N I Q U E

36

Dyadic Interviews

Essential Characteristics

PRIMARY MODE	Collaborative
ACTIVITY FOCUS	Discussing
DURATION OF ACTIVITY	Single Session
ONLINE TRANSFERABILITY	High

DESCRIPTION AND PURPOSE

Student pairs take turns interviewing each other, asking questions that address individual values, attitudes, beliefs, and prior experience as these relate to course content or learning goals.

Using questions that draw out students' experience and knowledge from outside of class can help engage students by validating their existing expertise and by bridging the gap between the academic and the real worlds. Interviews require the interviewee to express their individual thoughts and feelings, and because students are more likely to say what they truly think, feel, or believe to a single peer than they are to a group, this activity encourages them to make a high degree of personal commitment to the learning task.

STEP-BY-STEP DIRECTIONS

1. Develop a list of interview questions prior to the class session.

2. Divide students into pairs.

3. Explain the procedure:

   • Emphasize that Student A will interview Student B for a designated time (such as ten minutes) until you say "Time to switch."

   • Clarify that the role of the interviewer is to ask questions, listen, and probe for further information but not to evaluate or respond with his or her own ideas.

- Tell students that they will be writing an essay summarizing their partner's responses.

4. Students interview their partners, reversing roles when you say, "Time to switch." Then they write and submit their summary essays.

Introduction to Modern Literature

This instructor used "Dyadic Interviews" to encourage students to read thoughtfully and make connections between what they read and their personal lives. He crafted questions for selected literature assignments that he distributed in advance, telling students that they would be required to provide in-depth responses to the prompts in an interview with one of their peers. For example, as they read Tim O'Brien's short story "The Things They Carried," students knew they would later be asked, "What item did the soldiers carry that you found to be most surprising, and why?" and "What effect did the switch from third person to first person have on you as you realized the narrator was actually one of the soldiers?" After the interviews, he moved to a whole-class discussion. He found that because the interview required students to formulate personal opinions and provided a low-risk opportunity to collect their thoughts and rehearse their responses before going public with the whole class, the ensuing discussion was noticeably rich.

• • •

Dental Hygiene

In an advanced course in dental hygiene, Professor Perry Dontal wanted to prepare his students for their clinical practicum. He used "Dyadic Interviews" to help students anticipate how they might respond to challenging situations they were likely to encounter in the clinics. He used his professional experience to create a worksheet with a series of "What would you do if …?" questions. He formed student pairs and asked students to use the questions to interview each other. After the interviews, he organized three pairs into groups of six and asked students to give a brief summary of their partner's responses to the group. Groups were then asked to choose the question that had concerned them most. The instructor used their responses as the basis for a whole-class discussion on how best to handle the most anxiety-provoking scenarios. Professor Dontal hoped the activity would reduce students' anxiety and prepare them to respond effectively to problems they would face during their clinical practicum.

ONLINE
IMPLEMENTATION

Creating a sense of community in online classes is a challenge for many instructors. Implementing "Dyadic Interviews" can help students get to know other students in the class. Divide the class into pairs and give partners a designated amount of time to interview each other through private messaging or e-mail. Give students additional time to synthesize responses and ask them to submit their summaries either as a written assignment or as a posting on a threaded discussion.

VARIATIONS
AND EXTENSIONS

- Instead of creating the interview questions yourself, decide upon a general topic and then ask students to develop interview questions either individually or as a class.

- Use the interviews as a warm-up for whole class discussion. Providing students with an opportunity to collect their thoughts and rehearse their responses in a low-risk situation before going public with the whole class tends to promote richer discussion.

- Have students take notes or even record and transcribe the interview, then use the information to write an assignment such as a biographical essay about the person they interviewed. Consider having interviewers write up their findings in a format appropriate for the course (such as executive summary, descriptive essay, or newspaper article).

- Expand the time and the intent of the activity to foster more in-depth interviews. Form pairs and then ask them to spend the entire hour (or class period) going for a walk or having coffee so that they can gather information at a deeper level. When the group reconvenes, give pairs a task to do together that enables them to start working on a more complex and challenging course activity. Consider making the pairs long-term learning partnerships or encouraging students to follow up the activity by forming such a partnership (Silberman, 1995, pp. 56–57).

- Expand this to a larger-group activity by using "Three-Step Interview" (Barkley, Cross, and Major, 2005, pp. 121–125). In this activity, student pairs take turns interviewing each other and then report what they learn to another pair. The three steps are (1) Student A interviews Student B, (2) Student B interviews Student A, (3) Students A and B summarize their partner's responses for Students C and D and vice versa.

- Have three teammates interview a fourth in depth; this variation is called a "Team Interview" (Kagen, 1992).

- Instead of requiring that the interviewee be a classmate, have students interview someone from their work, their neighborhood, or their family. For example, you might suggest they identify someone who they perceive as being very different from themselves. Characteristics that might define differences include generation, ethnicity, sexual orientation, religion, and country of origin. Based on the interview, have students write a profile of the person. This activity requires students to encounter an "other" whose experience, values, and attitudes may differ extensively from theirs and to try to understand this person at a deeper level. In the process, they may find surprising commonalities that could challenge stereotypes (adapted from Bean, 1996, p. 94).

OBSERVATIONS AND ADVICE   Interviews help students get to know a classmate better and to find the commonalities that lead to a sense of community.

Dividing the class into pairs allows for more individuals to talk simultaneously, thus providing students with an opportunity to explore ideas in more depth and with greater personal relevance than generally possible in whole class discussions.

It is often best to try to form pairs from students who do not know each other. Following are some strategies for randomly selecting students to form pairs or groups (Barkley, Cross, and Major, 2005, pp. 46–50):

- Odd-Even: Walk through classroom aisles saying "Odd," "Even," "Odd," "Even," for each row, and then ask students in the "odd" row to turn around and pair up with the student immediately behind them in the "even" row.

- Playing Cards: Give a playing card to each student, distributing four cards for each kind (for example, four aces, four kings, four queens). Students find the other students with the same card rank to form groups of four and can subdivide into pairs by matching color.

- Created Cards: Cut up heavy stock paper or use index cards and write on each card A-1 (for Group A, Member 1), A-2, B-1, B-2, and so forth. You can also purchase index cards in different colors and patterns that students can hold up, allowing them to easily locate pair or group members.

- Line Up and Divide: Ask students to line up by some criteria such as birthdays, or in alphabetical order of their first or last names, or by height; then break the line to form pairs or groups with the number of students needed.

Try to create interview questions that are likely to generate a wide array of interesting responses, as interviews will lack energy if the questions elicit predictable and similar answers.

Consider pairing students intentionally to maximize diversity and to prevent students from interviewing someone they already know. This way the interview is fresh and generates new information and insights.

KEY RESOURCES Barkley, E.F., Cross, K.P., & Major, C. H. (2005). *Collaborative learning techniques: A handbook for college faculty.* San Francisco: Jossey-Bass, pp. 246–250.

Millis, B. J., & Cottell, P. G. (1998). *Cooperative learning for higher education faculty.* Phoenix, AZ: Oryx Press.

S T U D E N T
E N G A G E M E N T
T E C H N I Q U E

37

Circular Response

Essential Characteristics

PRIMARY MODE	Collaborative
ACTIVITY FOCUS	Discussing
DURATION OF ACTIVITY	Single Session
ONLINE TRANSFERABILITY	High

DESCRIPTION AND PURPOSE   Students sit in a circle and take turns expressing their thoughts in response to an instructor-designated prompt, but by making a brief summary of the preceding speaker's comments and using that as a springboard for their own remarks.

This technique helps students learn to listen to others attentively and respectfully, integrate what they hear into their current understandings, and then use this new insight as the basis for their own ideas. The circular process provides a platform for each individual to speak, thus democratizing participation and reducing opportunities for individuals to remain passive and uncommitted.

STEP-BY-STEP DIRECTIONS

1. Craft an engaging question that has many potential responses. Try responding to the question yourself, and make adjustments as necessary.

2. Decide how you are going to present the question (handout, presentation slide, whiteboard) and if you are going to have a follow-up activity.

3. Ask students to move chairs or desks to form a circle. If the class is large, form multiple smaller circles of 6–9 students, designating one student in each group to serve as process monitor.

4. Explain the purpose of the activity and the directions. Here is an example:

> *Moving clockwise around the circle once, you will each take a turn responding to the prompt, starting with a summary of the preceding*

student's comments and connecting what you have to say with what you just heard. Take the time you need to speak thoughtfully, and try to express your ideas succinctly. Please don't interrupt or speak out of turn. If I believe you are taking too much time, I will give you the following hand signal indicating that you must wrap it up.

5. Ask one student to begin the activity by responding to the prompt. Consider starting with the student to your right so that you can model summarizing and connecting their comments to your own.

EXAMPLES

Survey of American Literature

In this course, students studied representative works from the pre–Civil War period to the beginning of World War I. To help students recognize the enduring nature of the literary themes and to help them connect to the material personally even though the stories were from historical periods remote to the students' experience, the professor used "Circular Response", asking prompts such as "Do the characters seem real and believable to you?" "In what ways can you relate to their predicaments?" "To what extent do they remind you of yourself or someone you know?" Because all students were required both to listen carefully and to contribute their own thoughts, he believed the activity helped keep students engaged as it exposed them to a wide range of ideas regarding literature.

• • •

Intermediate French

Professor May Whee used "Circular Response" to give students practice speaking and understanding French. Instead of responding to a single prompt, she asked students to "create a story" that wove together the preceding student's contribution with what the speaking student could imagine might happen next. For example, she started one activity by saying, in French, "This morning I woke up and it was a beautiful day. The sky was blue and the sun was bright, so I decided to walk down to the café and have breakfast." The next student would need to understand and integrate what she had said and then add to it by saying something like "As I walked to the café, I started to plan what I would order to eat for breakfast. I knew I wanted a café au lait, but I wasn't sure if I wanted something as filling as an omelet or something simpler, such as a croissant." Students found the activity fun and engaging, recognizing its value in requiring them to listen attentively and practice new vocabulary and grammatical structures in a practical, relevant communication task.

VARIATIONS
AND EXTENSIONS
- Use this technique to help students develop creativity by requiring them to generate an imaginative response to a prompt and build upon each other's ideas to weave a story (as in the French example above).

- "Circle of Voices" is a variation that is used in some Native American, First Nation, and Aboriginal cultures to give each person an equal chance to contribute to the discussion. It is typically used in the middle of discussion to allow those who haven't yet spoken some time designated for their voices alone. To implement this in the classroom, the instructor invites four or five students to form a circle and then asks the whole class to be silent for a few minutes to allow the students in the circle to gather and organize their thoughts. When it is time to start the activity, each student is given a designated amount of uninterrupted time to express his or her thoughts. After the circle is completed, the discussion opens into a more free-flowing format, but discussants are allowed only to talk about the students' ideas that were expressed in the "Circle of Voices" (Brookfield and Preskill, 205, pp. 78–79).

KEY RESOURCE   Brookfield, S. D., & Preskill, S. (1999). *Discussion as a way of teaching: Tools and techniques for democratic collaborative learning classrooms.* San Francisco: Jossey-Bass, pp. 79–81.

STUDENT
ENGAGEMENT
TECHNIQUE

38

Ethical Dilemmas

Essential Characteristics

PRIMARY MODE	Collaborative
ACTIVITY FOCUS	Discussing
DURATION OF ACTIVITY	Single Session
ONLINE TRANSFERABILITY	High

DESCRIPTION AND PURPOSE This SET, an adaptation of "Everyday Ethical Dilemmas" (Angelo and Cross, 1993, pp. 271–274), helps students think through their values within the context of real-world and course-related situations. Students are presented with an ethics-based, discipline-related scenario in which somebody must choose a course of action between two or more difficult alternatives. Students are given time to think about the dilemma quietly and independently. They then choose from a few options how they believe they would respond and submit their choice anonymously to the teacher, who uses the students' distribution of choices as the basis for discussion of the issues. This activity provides them with a forum to probe the motivations underlying and the consequences resulting from ethics-based choices in a safe environment, and may prepare them to make better choices when they encounter similar situations in the future.

STEP-BY-STEP DIRECTIONS

1. Choose one specific ethical issue or question to focus on.

2. Locate or create a short case that poses the essential dilemma realistically.

3. Write two or three questions that require students to take a position on the dilemma and to explain or justify that position.

4. Ask students to write short, honest, anonymous responses.

5. Allow enough class time for students to write responses, or make this a take-home assessment exercise.

Freshman Seminar: Study Skills/Personal Development

This interdisciplinary course serves several aims—among them, introducing first-year college students to the values and standards of the academic community. To get a sense of her students' views on academic integrity, this psychology instructor prepared a half-page case that she wrote and distributed to the class. The case concerned a college student, Anne, and her roommate, Barbara. Barbara told Anne that she was planning to take her boyfriend's final exam for him in a required science class, a class that Anne was also taking. The assessment asked the Freshmen Seminar students to respond anonymously, in less than half a page, to the following two questions: (1) What, if anything, should Anne do about the plans Barbara and her boyfriend have for cheating on the final exam? (2) Depending on your answer to Question 1, why should or shouldn't Anne do something?

The instructor allowed students ten minutes of class time to respond to the dilemma; she then collected the cases. When she read them after class, she was somewhat surprised to find that nearly 60 percent of the students thought that Anne should not do anything about the planned cheating. The reasons they gave were varied, but more centered on Anne's relationship to her roommate. Another quarter of the students thought that Anne should confront Barbara and try to talk her out of it, and a few favored notifyng some campus authority. The instructor shared these results with the class and asked them to uncover the values behind various answers. A lively discussion of academic integrity ensued (Angelo & Cross, 1993, p. 272).

● ● ●

Microcontroller Programming

To challenge his students to think about social and ethical issues in this otherwise technical course, this professor created the following scenario:

> You are a software engineer at a small start-up company developing code for an embedded microcontroller in a product that controls patient life support systems in hospital intensive care units. The product that contains your group's software is key to the company's survival, and if the product is not released, the company will fail and you and the other employees will be out of a job at a time when the job market is dismal. The ship date has been set, and there's a big press conference scheduled to demonstrate the product. Unfortunately, after your group's software was integrated into the product, you discover a bug that, although highly unlikely, could possibly disable the device. The first software update for the product is scheduled three months

after the product has started shipping, and you know the boss will not approve an interim fix. What do you do?

He projected two choices on an overhead: (a) ship the product or (b) report the bug. He first asked students to think about how they would respond and to use their personal-response-system clickers to indicate their choice. Before revealing the results, he asked students to choose how they thought most people would respond. He then asked students to turn to a partner to share and compare thoughts about the scenario and the values underlying each choice, before moving to a whole-class discussion of the issues (adapted from Jacobson, 2002).

• • •

Statistics

Professor Anne Alesis decided to use "Ethical Dilemmas" as a warm-up to a presentation she had prepared on the role of ethics in statistics. She described to her students a situation that she had encountered when she was still a graduate student: one of her peers was finishing his doctorate and working as a research assistant for the chair of his dissertation committee. The chair had a contract with a large pharmaceutical firm and was in charge of providing statistical analysis on one of the firm's products. The chair essentially told the student, "Here's the data. Make it work."

After the instructor presented the dilemma, she asked students to think quietly about what they would do in a similar situation, then write this down on a slip of paper. She collected the slips and then formed students into groups of five and had them discuss their responses. She asked them to focus in their discussion not on which decision was ethical (that was obvious), but rather discuss the challenges individuals face when trying to act ethically. While students were involved in their small-group discussions, she tallied the responses. In her follow-up presentation, she shared the aggregated data, then talked about a range of documented ethical violations of the national statistical system and closed with a homework assignment based on the American Statistical Association's "Ethical Guidelines for Statistical Practice" (http://www.amstat.org/profession/index.cfm?fuseaction=ethicalstatistics).

ONLINE IMPLEMENTATION To ensure students respond candidly, it is important for them to be able to respond anonymously. If your course delivery software has a surveying tool that allows for anonymous responses, have students respond to the dilemma, do a simple statistical analysis of the results, and use the distribution of responses as the prompt for the discussion. If your course does not have this tool, consider presenting the dilemma on a forum, with students discussing hypothetical responses to the dilemma on a threaded discussion.

VARIATIONS AND EXTENSIONS

- Ask students to create a dilemma or assign them the task of discovering a dilemma in the discipline, profession, or from the everyday real world that relates to the course.
- Consider adding a performance element to the task by having students role-play the situation or work in teams to argue one side of the dilemma.

KEY RESOURCE   Angelo, T. A., & Cross, K. P. (1993). *Classroom assessment techniques*. San Francisco: Jossey-Bass, pp. 271–274.

STUDENT
ENGAGEMENT
TECHNIQUE

39

Connected Communities

Essential Characteristics

PRIMARY MODE	Collaborative
ACTIVITY FOCUS	Discussing
DURATION OF ACTIVITY	Multiple Sessions
ONLINE TRANSFERABILITY	High

DESCRIPTION AND PURPOSE

Students enrolled in different but related courses join together to discuss instructor-developed prompts. Although paired classes can be at the same institution, technology such as online discussion forums and desktop video-conferencing makes it possible to connect students from different institutions.

This SET exposes students to a wider range of perspectives and ideas, motivates students to discuss topics with peers at a deeper level, and provides a structured context to explore linkages that extend beyond the usual confines of a single course.

STEP-BY-STEP DIRECTIONS

1. Determine a learning goal or theme for students to explore that would be enhanced by interaction with individuals other than class members.

2. Decide on the scope and structure of the interaction (a single conversation or several? discussion only, or multiple projects? face-to-face or virtual?).

3. Identify the community with which students will be interacting and work with the leadership of the designated community to develop and implement a plan for interaction.

EXAMPLES

History of the Middle East and Comparative World Religions

Two faculty members at the same institution but in different departments were committed to interdisciplinary learning and to promoting a greater sense of community among their students. They discovered that they were both interested in making their course content more relevant to current events by helping students explore the struggle over forms and meanings in Muslim culture and politics. As a simple way to achieve their goals, they created a single online discussion forum for both courses. Students shared insights drawing from the historical and philosophical perspectives of the two courses as they responded to prompts addressing this struggle and its implications for religious authority, gender roles, and notions of citizenship, civil society, and democracy.

• • •

Intermediate French

Students in an intermediate-level French class at an American university were connected through videoconferencing with graduate students studying teaching French as a foreign language in Lyon, France. Students communicated through both face-to-face audiovisual exchanges as well as synchronous written chat as they responded to a series of pedagogical modules intended to develop their linguistic ability and cultural knowledge (Williams, 2007).

• • •

Triad Learning Community: Psychology as a Natural Science, Intro to Anthropology, and Composition—Social Issues

This institution organized a Freshman Interest Group Learning Community whose core theme was the spectrum of human behavior. The students co-registered for all three courses. Faculty worked together to coordinate integrated learning goals and assignments, but taught the courses separately. The students met together as a cohort in three auxiliary meetings during the academic term for orientation, progress monitoring, and program assessment (adapted from MacGregor, Smith, Matthews, & Gabelnick, [n.d.]).

VARIATIONS AND EXTENSIONS

• Ask students to connect course material with a real-world setting or with a professional organization or group.

• If the course is a sequence in a major, ask students to connect the course to prior coursework in the major.

OBSERVATIONS AND ADVICE

In the initial planning stages of "Connected Communities," assume administrative logistics have been successfully worked out and engage in boundary-crossing curricular brainstorming focused on what students could learn. This allows you to be creative as you explore ideas for themes that might intrigue you and your students.

To locate a faculty member to partner with in the design and implementation of "Connected Communities," consider a colleague you already know (at your own institution, a neighboring institution, or someone you've met at disciplinary or educational conferences) who has similar pedagogical values and with whom you already feel a level of interpersonal and professional comfort. It may be helpful to build on existing related educational initiatives on campus, such as student affairs/academic affairs partnerships, diversity, writing across the curriculum, critical thinking, and so forth that also have support service people who can be helpful in implementing plans.

If you are considering implementing "Connected Communities" on a fairly extensive basis, discuss ideas with colleagues or staff already involved in formal Learning Communities initiatives. The Learning Communities National Resource Center (http://www.evergreen.edu/washcenter/project.asp?pid=73) offers extensive information, including a national directory of campus programs, links to publications on implementation and assessment, and residential summer institutes and workshops to guide campus teams and regional networks on activities.

Working with colleagues on this SET can help overcome the sense of isolation many faculty members and their students feel.

Technology offers exciting opportunities for linking classes from very different institutions or distant locations. Although this can be achieved relatively simply through online discussion forums, videoconferencing has the advantages of synchronous interactive telecommunication technologies that allow people in two or more locations to interact via two-way video and audio transmissions. Use of the technology for educational purposes has become easier due to wider availability of high-speed Internet connectivity and decreased cost of video capture and display. Video teleconference systems based on a Webcam or personal computer system with software compression have made videoconferencing even more accessible and affordable. Although technology is widely available for videoconferencing, there are currently two challenges that undermine its effectiveness:

- **Technical challenges:** Perceived (or real) unreliability, different standards, features and qualities of teleconferencing systems that require special configurations to successfully connect, as well as the fact that many faculty do not feel capable of using or comfortable with the technology, means that faculty will need institutional support both for setup and fast assistance.

- **Eye contact:** Effective group communication requires eye contact for conversational turn-taking, perceived attention, and intent. Current videoconferencing technology gives the impression that participants are avoiding eye contact.

KEY RESOURCES   MacGregor, J., Smith, B., Matthews, R., & Gabelnick, F. (n.d.) *Learning community models* (PowerPoint PDF). Retrieved from http://www.evergreen.edu/wash center/project.asp?pid=73

The Washington Center. *Designing a learning community in an hour.* Retrieved from http://www.evergreen.edu/washcenter/resources/lchour/lchour.htm.

S T U D E N T
E N G A G E M E N T
T E C H N I Q U E

40

Stand Where You Stand

Essential Characteristics

PRIMARY MODE	Collaborative
ACTIVITY FOCUS	Discussing
DURATION OF ACTIVITY	Single Session
ONLINE TRANSFERABILITY	High

DESCRIPTION AND PURPOSE In preparation for class, students read two essays related to a controversial issue, with one essay in support of and the other in opposition to a particular idea or viewpoint. In class, the teacher presents a statement that reflects one of the two sides. Students individually decide whether they agree or disagree, writing down their rationale. They then go stand in front of one of four signs the teacher has posted around the room (Strongly Agree, Agree, Disagree, and Strongly Disagree) and take turns presenting their rationales for the position they have assumed. They are then invited to move to another sign if the arguments they hear persuade them to change their minds.

This activity encourages students to think critically, gives them opportunities to practice developing and presenting arguments, and to listen carefully to others' points of view. Additionally, by requiring each student to choose the corner that represents their position and articulate their rationale for that position, it ensures all students make some level of personal commitment to the issue.

STEP-BY-STEP DIRECTIONS

1. Identify a controversial topic important to your course and locate one or more essays that clearly support each side of the controversy.

2. Reproduce sufficient copies to create one set for each student and distribute essays and assign reading.

3. Create—and on the day of the class post—signs in the four corners of the room stating Strongly Agree, Agree, Disagree, or Strongly Disagree.

4. Present students with a statement that reflects one of the two sides and ask students to individually decide whether they agree or disagree with the statement and to write down their rationale, using arguments, evidence, and quotes from the essays to support their position.

5. When students have finished writing down their views, ask them to go stand in front of the sign that most closely reflects their position on the statement.

6. Ask students at each station to take turns orally presenting their rationales for the position they have assumed.

7. Invite students to move to another sign if they were persuaded to change their minds after hearing their peers' arguments.

8. Conclude the activity with a whole class discussion in which students share how their perspectives were or were not altered as a result of the activity.

EXAMPLE

Introduction to Sociology

To help students explore their ideas, values, and belief systems regarding the concept of the nuclear family, this professor decided to use "Stand Where You Stand" to address the topic of adoption of children by same sex couples. She collected two essays, one in favor and the other opposed. She had students read the essays prior to class. When students gathered in the classroom, she asked them to choose their position in response to the statement "Gay couples should be given the same legal rights as heterosexuals in adopting children," and go stand under the appropriate sign. As students individually reported the rationales for their position, she made a list of the pros and the cons. When students had finished, she summarized the arguments for each side and invited students to move to a different sign if their opinion had changed. Students then were asked to return to their seats, and she closed with a whole-class discussion of student reactions to the activity in general before moving into a presentation on the specific sociological concepts underlying their arguments.

VARIATIONS AND EXTENSIONS

• Have students individually or in small groups make a persuasive speech presentation or write a letter to the editor of the local newspaper about their stand. Students could pair up to offer feedback to peers on their letters to the editor.

KEY RESOURCE   Brookfield, S. D., & Preskill, S. (1999). *Discussion as a way of teaching: Tools and techniques for democratic classrooms.* San Francisco: Jossey-Bass, pp. 117–118.

Chapter 18

Self-Awareness as Learners

STUDENTS WHO reflect on their learning are better learners than those who do not. With greater understanding of what and how they are learning, they are able to develop strategies to increase the effectiveness of their learning and to exert more control over their learning. The student engagement techniques (SETs) in this chapter offer ideas for activities to help students become more mindful of their own learning preferences, abilities, and styles.

STUDENT ENGAGEMENT TECHNIQUE

41

Learning Logs

Essential Characteristics

PRIMARY MODE	Individual
ACTIVITY FOCUS	Writing
DURATION OF ACTIVITY	Multiple Sessions
ONLINE TRANSFERABILITY	High

DESCRIPTION AND PURPOSE

Instructors create a series of prompts that challenge students to reflect on their learning in different ways throughout the academic term. Students write out their responses in a journal that is submitted as a course assignment.

"Learning Logs" provide a formal medium for students to explore their individual learning strategies and styles. Reflecting on and writing about their learning can help students see patterns and preferences, diagnose learning strengths and weaknesses, and generate solutions to learning-related problems. This SET helps students take responsibility for their learning and practice the skills necessary to become independent, self-directed learners. It can also provide them with the insights necessary to ensure that they are working in their optimal challenge zone.

STEP-BY-STEP DIRECTIONS

1. Decide the journal parameters ahead of time. Identify the kinds of learning-related topics, issues or skills you wish students to reflect upon and craft corresponding prompts. To do this, you might write out content-based learning objectives or goals and then craft prompts such as, "How well do you feel you have achieved this goal?" or "What strategies or resources did you use to achieve this goal?" Another approach is to craft prompts related to specific activities, such as "What enabled you to learn the most from this experience?" "What would you do differently if you had more time?" "How did today's

discussion build upon yesterday's?" "What one idea did you find most interesting and why?" Other parameters include the medium (a computer file? a lined tablet?), the frequency with which students will make entries and submit the journal to you, and the criteria by which you will evaluate it.

2. Create a handout that explains the purpose of the journal, includes directions, clarifies your expectations, and provides examples.

EXAMPLES

Freshman Seminar

The team of professors who taught this freshman seminar used this SET as part of a multistrategy approach to help freshman succeed. Students were given a template that provided columns/rows in which to make weekly entries recording the amount of time they spent studying for different classes, the specific activities they used to study, the grades they were receiving in their assignments, and so forth. At regular intervals, students met with a mentor to review their "Learning Logs" and identify strategies and resources to help them be more successful.

● ● ●

Speech Communications

In her syllabus for a speech and communications course, Weimer (2002, pp. 207–208) provides twenty-two prompts for a "Learning Log" that students are invited to select from and respond to throughout the academic term. The first three prompts are provided here to show the kinds of entries students are asked to make in their journal:

> **Entry 1:** Develop a game plan for the course indicating which assignments you plan to complete. Why have you selected these options? What do you think your choices indicate about your learning preferences? Why do you think a teacher would give students a choice about assignments? How do you think this strategy will affect your performance in class?

> **Entry 2:** Why does the university require a course in speech communication? If this course wasn't required, would you take it? Why? Why not? Overall, how would you assess your communication skills? Reread pp. 22–23 in the text, and set at least one goal for yourself in this class.

> **Entry 3:** Write about your experiences working in groups. What made those group experiences effective or ineffective? What responsibilities do individuals have when they participate in groups? Can individual members do anything to encourage other members to fulfill these responsibilities?

ONLINE IMPLEMENTATION   This SET is easily adapted to online classes as a regular assignment. If the kinds of prompts you have developed do not require students to divulge material they may wish to keep private, consider setting up a blog for students to share their insights.

VARIATIONS AND EXTENSIONS

- Consider making this a collaborative activity by assigning it as a "Dialogue Journal." In a "Dialogue Journal," students make entries on one side of a page that is divided by a vertical line. Students exchange journals with a peer who reads and responds to the entry with comments and questions (Barkley, Cross, & Major, 2004).

- Instead of assigning specific prompts, provide students with a list of sentence starters and allow them to choose the starter they feel best fits their individual situation. Following is a sample of a variety of starters (adapted from http://www.bcps.org/offices/lis/models/diseases/sentstarters.html):

  1. Today my efforts to learn were very successful (or unsuccessful) because . . . .

  2. Today I had a problem trying to . . . . Tomorrow I will try to solve that problem by . . . .

  3. Today I made an important breakthrough in my understanding. The thing that helped me was . . . .

  4. Today I was finally able to make progress because I . . . .

  5. The easiest (or hardest) part of (the research for this project, this assignment, sitting in class) was . . . .

  6. I need help with . . . so tomorrow (or tonight, or after class), I will . . . .

  7. I am proud of myself today because I . . . .

  8. Today, I changed the way I . . . because . . . .

  9. One thing I learned today about how I learn is . . . .

  10. I used time well today because I . . . .

  11. I need to do a better job of . . . during the next class session because . . . .

OBSERVATIONS AND ADVICE   Journaling can be fairly time consuming for students, so make sure you have spent sufficient time crafting good prompts that make clear connections to course content and that you have explained the journal's purpose so that students do not think of the assignment as busy work.

It is important to have students turn journals in regularly so that they do not wait until the last minute to write all the entries.

KEY RESOURCE   Weimer, M. (2002). *Learner-centered teaching: Five key changes to practice.* San Francisco: Jossey-Bass, pp. 207–208.

S T U D E N T
E N G A G E M E N T
T E C H N I Q U E

42

Critical Incident Questionnaire (CIQ)

Essential Characteristics

PRIMARY MODE	Individual
ACTIVITY FOCUS	Writing
DURATION OF ACTIVITY	Single or Multiple Session
ONLINE TRANSFERABILITY	High

DESCRIPTION AND PURPOSE

At regular intervals throughout the semester, students write responses to the same five questions that ask them to focus on critical moments or actions related to their learning. The questionnaire is constructed on a single sheet of NCR (no carbon required) paper so that it creates a copy. Students turn in the original but keep the copy for themselves, reviewing their responses over time to identify patterns in how their own behavior and the actions of their peers help or hinder their learning.

The "Critical Incident Questionnaire" (CIQ) helps students become more aware of themselves as learners and encourages them to take an active role influencing class climate so that it is most conducive to their learning. It also helps teachers gather the information they need to more accurately assess classroom environment and to better understand and address problems when they arise.

STEP-BY-STEP DIRECTIONS

1. Create a form that asks on a single 8½ × 11–inch paper one or more questions such as

    a. At what moment in class or in doing your homework this week were you most engaged as a learner?

    b. At what moment in class this week were you most distanced as a learner?

    c. What action did anyone in the class take this week that you found most affirming or helpful?

    d. What action did anyone in the class take this week that you found most puzzling or confusing?

    e. What surprised you most about the class this week?

Allow space for students to write a response.

2. Decide how frequently you will be distributing the CIQ, determine the number of forms needed, and arrange to have these printed as NCR forms through your institution's print shop or enter "NCR Form" as keywords in an Internet search engine to find online or local printing services.

3. Decide on other logistical aspects, such as how and where students will submit forms, whether their responses will be anonymous or named, and so forth.

4. Early in the academic term, explain to students the purpose of the CIQ, emphasizing how it will both help them become better learners and help you ensure that the class is most conducive to their learning. Go over submission logistics (how often, when, and in what manner students will fill out and turn in the CIQ) and answer any questions about the process.

5. On the designated day, distribute the CIQ, allow time for students to fill out the form, and ask learners to leave the top copy of the CIQ facedown on a table by the door as they exit the room.

6. Share each week's results with the students at the beginning of the subsequent week, using the answers to point out trends in students' awareness and understanding of their own learning skills, performance, and habits and addressing problems such as students who talk too much, imbalance between teacher and student voice, discrimination, and so forth.

EXAMPLES

General Psychology

This general education introductory course was one of the university's mega-classes taught in a large lecture hall. In the past, Professor Watts D. Matta had experienced problems with student incivility that ranged from simple lack of consideration and respect (talking to a neighbor while he was lecturing) to overt hostility and aggression (arguing too vehemently during discussion). He believed these behaviors were undermining the sense of community and seriously disrupting the learning environment. He decided to add a question to his first-day student survey: "In your opinion, what makes a classroom environment particularly conducive to learning?" Students responded with comments like: engaging lectures, good discussion, prepared students, respect for different opinions, wide participation, trust between students and between students and teacher, and so forth. The next day, he reported to students what they wanted in the class. He explained that he shared their ideals, and was inviting them to work with him to create such an environment. He then described how he was instituting the CIQ activity to help them all monitor how well they were succeeding in achieving the excellent learning environment they all wanted (adapted from a posting by Kathleen Donegan on the teach-net@berkeley.edu listserv on January 28, 2008, describing her work).

•   •   •

Microbiology

Professor Penny Cillen wanted to help her students assess how productive their behavior was while listening to lectures. She decided to use CIQs to achieve this and created a form with the following questions:

1. How fully and consistently were you concentrating during these twenty minutes of lecture? Did you get distracted at any point? If so, how did you bring your attention back into focus?
2. What were you doing to record the information you were receiving? How successful were you?
3. How were you connecting the new information you were hearing to what you already know?
4. What do you expect to come next in the lecture, and why?
5. What strategies might you use to improve your ability to learn from my lectures? What suggestions do you have for how I might improve my lectures so that you can learn better?

Early in the course, she stopped her lecture on the use of Beta-lactam antibiotics in the treatment of bacterial infections and asked students to reflect upon their behaviors—both mental and physical—during her presentation. She gave them two minutes to recall their behavior and then distributed the CIQ form and asked students to respond to the prompts.

She then asked students to turn to a partner and share their insights as well as ideas on how they might modify their listening, focusing, and note-taking behavior to improve their learning. She repeated the CIQ in the middle and close to the end of the semester. In one of the questions on the end-of-term class evaluation, she asked students to comment on whether their lecture-listening behaviors had changed during the term and if so, how.

ONLINE IMPLEMENTATION If your course software program has an anonymous survey tool, use this to gather students' responses. Include the statistical distribution of responses with any insights or comments you have about student responses in regular announcements, or include this information on a threaded discussion forum and invite students to post their own comments about the distribution.

OBSERVATIONS AND ADVICE Although implementing this activity at the end of the last class of the week gives students the broadest perspective from which to review the past week, they may hurry and answer superficially. Brookfield and Preskill (1999) recommend implementing it slightly earlier in the last hour, allotting a specified amount of time (they suggest ten minutes), and then moving into a final wrap-up prior to class dismissal.

Student anonymity ensures that students will not feel hesitant to provide candid, truthful feedback regarding the class, their classmates, or the instructor. If the development of self-awareness skills is an explicit learning goal for the course and you are considering assessing and evaluating skill development, you may want to know who filled out the form and track progress. Finding the balance between these two is a personal decision based on many factors. One solution might be to alternate between anonymous and signed responses.

KEY RESOURCE Brookfield, S. D., & Preskill, S. (1999). *Discussion as a way of teaching: Tools and techniques for democratic classrooms.* San Francisco: Jossey-Bass, pp. 48–50.

STUDENT
ENGAGEMENT
TECHNIQUE

43

Go for the Goal

Essential Characteristics

PRIMARY MODE	Individual
ACTIVITY FOCUS	Writing
DURATION OF ACTIVITY	Single or Multiple Session
ONLINE TRANSFERABILITY	High

DESCRIPTION AND PURPOSE

Goal setting can be a powerful focusing activity for helping students to become conscious of what they hope to accomplish and encouraging them to accept responsibility for their learning. In this SET, students generate and prioritize a list of their learning goals at the beginning of the academic term, a unit of study, or a specific learning activity.

Identifying what they want to learn can also help students organize their time and resources so that they can better recognize and resist distractions. It also provides students with a framework against which to measure progress, giving them guidance on how to get back on track if they have strayed.

STEP-BY-STEP DIRECTIONS

1. Take time to identify and write out your teaching goals so that you have a reference point for comparing what you want students to learn with what students say they want to learn. If your teaching goals differ from students' learning goals, decide to what extent you would be willing to substitute or alter your goals to accommodate their interests on either a class or individual basis.

2. Decide whether to use this SET at the course, unit, or activity level; whether it will be a one-time activity (such as at the beginning of the course or before a major project) or used multiple times throughout the term; and how you or your students will monitor progress.

3. Consider creating a handout that provides students with guidance on identifying appropriate learning goals (see Observations and Advice later in this SET).

EXAMPLE

Elementary Statistics

Professor Sam Pell knew that many students were fearful about his course. Because of their anxiety, they tended to focus on surface learning strategies that would help them perform well on the tests, consequently missing the bigger picture that he knew would be more meaningful to them in the long run. To help students develop a more positive and constructive orientation toward the course, he worked with them during the first day of the term to develop deep learning goals. He then formed small groups and asked them to brainstorm strategies they could use to help themselves and each other to be successful in their efforts to achieve the goals. In the whole-class discussion that followed, he listened to their ideas and, where appropriate and possible, pointed to ways he could make adjustments in the course activities or course calendar to support their efforts.

ONLINE IMPLEMENTATION

This SET is easily implemented online, but how you do so will depend on what you are trying to accomplish. If, for example, you are using the activity to guide students in clarifying their class goals at the beginning of the term, have students generate and prioritize their lists individually and then ask students to post one or two of their highest priority goals on a threaded discussion, but adding only ones that have not already been posted by other students. Consider responding to the students' list with a list of your own goals as well as comments regarding how teacher/learner goals compare or contrast and any accommodations, if any, you intend to make. On the other hand, if you are using the activity to help students monitor their personal progress, you may want students to generate their lists and then include a follow-up assignment such as periodic journal reflections throughout the term reflecting on how well they are or are not meeting their goals.

VARIATIONS AND EXTENSIONS

- Use this SET throughout the academic term to help students see goals not as terminal destinations but rather as guideposts to measure progress, to reassure them that they are headed in the right direction, and to provide them with feedback to make adjustments if necessary to get back on track.

- Ask students to prioritize their goals by relative importance, then to prioritize the goals based on other criteria such as "difficulty to achieve" or "amount of time needed to accomplish the goal."

- Have students elaborate by writing next to each goal answers to questions such as Why do I want to accomplish this goal? or What kinds of support structures (people, place, things) do I need to accomplish this goal?

- Consider having students break down large goals into incremental, small, concrete steps that they can take to achieve the goal.

- Use this SET in conjunction with a strategy such as "Choice Boards" in order to promote student autonomy. To implement a "Choice Board," the teacher creates a menu of options for learning or assessment usually displayed on a grid. The choices can be designed around any aspect of the course from developing skills and processing information to synthesizing and reflecting upon key understandings. For example, a nine-cell "Choice Board" might allow students to choose (1) a subject to research from three topical areas, (2) to do this research individually, with a partner, or in a group of 3–5, and (3) to communicate their understanding by either writing a traditional research paper, constructing a Web page with hyperlinks, or giving a formal presentation to the class. "Choice Boards" can also be tiered in terms of complexity or effort required and weighted accordingly (Dodge, 2005, pp. 64–71). Combining this with goal-setting encourages students to accept responsibility for their choices.

- Implement an activity at the end of the academic term that helps students recognize and celebrate their achievements.

OBSERVATIONS AND ADVICE Most students will need guidance on how to identify learning goals. To help them get started, you may wish to provide them with a list and then have students use this as the basis from which to craft personal learning goals. For these purposes, consider the Teaching Goals Inventory (TGI) developed by Angelo and Cross. This inventory is available in *Classroom Assessment Techniques* (Angelo & Cross, 1993, pp. 393–397) and online (enter "Teaching Goal Inventory" as a search phrase in your browser). The TGI consists of a series of fifty-two goal statements such as "Develop analytic skills," "Develop ability to think creatively," "Improve writing skills," "Develop an informed concern about contemporary social issues," and "Improve ability to organize and use time effectively." The inventory organizes these fifty-two goals into six clusters: Higher-Order Thinking Skills, Basic Academic Success Skills, Discipline-Specific Knowledge and Skills, Liberal Arts and Academic Value, Work and Career Preparation, and Personal Development. While the TGI can help you or your students identify broad goals, you will still need to personalize and contextualize the goals for a specific course.

Goal theory research suggests we help students develop "learning" rather than "performance" goal orientations. Students who approach academic activities with performance goals treat the activities as tests of their ability to perform; their primary concern is preserving their self-perceptions and public reputations as capable individuals. Thus, they tend to avoid challenging tasks, conceal their difficulties, give up easily, and rely on surface-level learning strategies such as rote memorization. In contrast, students who approach academic activities with learning goal orientations focus on acquiring the knowledge, skills, and understanding that the activities are designed to develop. When they encounter difficulties, they are buoyed by the belief that their efforts will pay off and are more likely to seek help or persist with their own self-regulated learning efforts. Additionally, they tend to adopt deep-learning strategies such as paraphrasing the material into their own words and connecting it to prior knowledge. (Brophy, 2004, pp. 90–91).

Additional guidance on identifying learning goals can be acquired from the assessment and learning outcomes literature. Several of the characteristics developed for learning outcomes could be adapted for use in guiding students on the crafting of effective goals. For example, effective goal statements

- focus on the learning resulting from an activity rather than on the activity itself,
- focus on important, non-trivial aspects of learning,
- focus on skills and abilities central to the discipline,
- are general enough to capture important learning but clear and specific enough to be measurable, and
- focus on aspects of learning that will develop and endure (adapted from Huba & Freed, 2000, p. 98).

KEY RESOURCE   Angelo, T. A., & Cross, K. P. (1993). *Classroom assessment techniques*. San Francisco: Jossey-Bass, pp. 290–294.

STUDENT
ENGAGEMENT
TECHNIQUE

44

Post-test Analysis

Essential Characteristics

PRIMARY MODE	Individual
ACTIVITY FOCUS	Analyzing, Writing
DURATION OF ACTIVITY	Single Session
ONLINE TRANSFERABILITY	High

DESCRIPTION AND PURPOSE   This technique is designed to help students develop greater awareness of their test-preparing and test-taking skills. It is a two-stage process that is divided into several steps. The first stage occurs after students have completed an exam but before they submit the exam to the instructor. At this stage, students predict their score, list their study strategies, rate their effort, and identify what was easiest and what was most difficult for them about the exam. This process helps students learn to gauge the correlation between their effort and perception of performance and how well specific study strategies prepared them for the exam.

In the second stage—after students have received their graded exams—students are asked to write about their emotional response to their score, compare their score with their prediction, and then go through the exam analyzing each exam question for the thinking skills it required (such as recall, application, analysis) and the source of the question (book, lecture, homework assignments). The second stage clarifies understanding of what is meant by different levels of thinking skills, helps students recognize their strengths and weaknesses, and guides them to specific changes they can make to help them to be more successful on future exams. They then reflect on and decide if they will make any changes in preparation for the next exam.

STEP-BY-STEP
DIRECTIONS

1. Choose a learning taxonomy with clearly identified levels of skills that best reflects your pedagogical values. Bloom's original taxonomy of educational objectives for the cognitive domain (Bloom, Engelhart, Furst, Hill, & Krathwohl, 1956) is the most widely known but there are others, including Anderson, Krathwohl, and Bloom's (2001) revision of that taxonomy, Fink's (2003, pp. 27-60) "taxonomy of significant learning," and Shulman's (2002) table of learning.

2. As you construct your exam, include questions that target each of the taxonomy's levels. Label the question appropriately (e.g., apply, analyze, evaluate) and identify the source (book, lecture, homework assignment). This is for your own use to compare against students' determination of the thinking required and the source for each question.

3. Add directions for Stage 1 of this technique at the end of the exam that include the following procedural steps.

> *After you have completed the exam but before you submit the exam to me, please*
>
> a. *predict your exam score;*
>
> b. *rate your effort in studying for the exam on a scale of 1 (lowest) to 10 (highest);*
>
> c. *list the specific learning strategies you used to study for the exam (for example, memorized definitions through flashcards, rewrote and reviewed lecture notes, created outlines of reading assignments, and so forth); and*
>
> d. *identify what you found easiest and most difficult about the exam and why.*

Stage 2 of this technique occurs after students have received their graded exams. Students can complete the steps for this stage in class immediately after the return of their exams, or they can complete the steps outside of class time during the following week. Create a separate worksheet that includes the taxonomy and the following procedural steps, and ask students to complete the worksheet, attach it to their exam, and submit to you.

> *Now that you have received your graded exam, please*
>
> a. *describe your emotional response to your exam score (surprised? disappointed? relieved? and so forth);*
>
> b. *compare your actual score with your predicted score;*

c.   *go back through each exam question and identify the level of the learning taxonomy used in each exam question;*

d.   *calculate the proportion of items you answered correctly or incorrectly at each classification level;*

e.   *determine the source of each question (book, lecture, homework assignment);*

f.   *reflect upon and describe any changes in strategies or amount of time studying you plan to do to prepare for the next exam; and*

g.   *offer me any feedback on how your peers or I could help you better prepare for the exam.*

EXAMPLE

General Biology

Professor Mike Robe was concerned about the high rate of student attrition and final exam failure in this introductory course. He decided to incorporate "Post-test Analysis" as part of a more comprehensive strategy for redesigning the course to promote greater student success. He used this SET for the two midterms and found that it helped many students develop the awareness and study and test-taking skills that enabled them to be more successful on the final exam.

ONLINE IMPLEMENTATION

The preparation and procedure steps for this SET are essentially the same for an online class as they are for a face-to-face class.

VARIATIONS AND EXTENSIONS

• Some institutions are looking for strategies to address high rates of course withdrawal or failing grades, often in a select group of students, such as freshmen classes. This SET could provide an effective tool for helping teachers and students identify more precisely the problems and the solutions for reducing attrition and increasing the percentage of students who pass the course.

• Adapt this SET for use with written assignments and other projects.

• Consider using students' evaluations as an element in the determination of their final course grade.

• Ask students to use their evaluation to set a goal for their preparation for the next test and then to reflect on how well they accomplished their goal.

OBSERVATIONS This SET requires teachers to spend a significant amount of time both to
AND ADVICE design effective tests and to set up the structure for students to do the post-
test analysis.

Since the purpose of this SET is to help students improve their skills in
preparing for and taking exams, it should be done early enough in the academic term to allow students to apply what they have learned to subsequent exams.

KEY RESOURCE Achacoso, M. V. (2004). Post-test analysis: A tool for developing students' meta-
cognitive awareness and self-regulation. In M. V. Achacoso & M. D. Svinicki
(Eds.) *Alternative strategies for evaluating student learning*. San Francisco: Jossey-
Bass, pp. 115–119.

Chapter 19

Learning and Study Skills

STUDENTS WHO EXCEL in school have developed a variety of skills to help make their learning more efficient and effective. For example they know how to plan, how to take good notes, how to find information, how to prepare for an exam, and how to contribute well to whole-class discussions or participate in a small-group project. The student engagement techniques (SETs) in this chapter offer ideas for learning activities in which students focus on learning or improving some of these basic learning and study skills.

S T U D E N T
E N G A G E M E N T
T E C H N I Q U E

45

In-class Portfolio

Essential Characteristics

PRIMARY MODE	Individual
ACTIVITY FOCUS	Note-Taking
DURATION OF ACTIVITY	Multiple Sessions
ONLINE TRANSFERABILITY	Low

DESCRIPTION AND PURPOSE

Students collect and organize lecture notes, essay responses to prompts presented during class, summaries of small- and whole-group discussion, personal reflections, and so forth into a portfolio and submit these for evaluation two or three times per academic term.

This SET provides teachers with a mechanism to help students stay focused and attentive during face-to-face class sessions. Students know that they must take complete and accurate notes, listen carefully to discussions, participate thoughtfully during group work, and think deeply about instructor-developed prompts so that they can summarize or synthesize what they learned in their portfolios.

STEP-BY-STEP DIRECTIONS

1. Organize class sessions using a variety of activities so that in addition to listening to lectures or observing demonstrations, students are actively integrating and applying what they are learning by writing, discussing, and problem solving.

2. Determine portfolio parameters (schedule of submission, size and format, and so forth).

3. Decide how portfolios will be evaluated and write up grading rubrics.

4. Create a cover sheet, make copies to distribute, and explain the process and your expectations to students.

General Psychology

Professor Hugh Menature organizes face-to-face class sessions to involve multiple learning activities including lecture, demonstration, small-group work, whole class discussions, and so forth. To ensure students are actively engaged in all activities, he requires students to take comprehensive lecture notes and to write reflections, responses, and discussion summaries to document all other in-class work. Students compile their in-class work as a portfolio and submit these at the midterm and end of the semester. Because the class is large and he does not have the time to read all portfolios herself, and because he believes it deepens students' learning if they have the opportunity to read through another student's work, he uses a peer review process (see Exhibit 19.1). He finds that the strategy helps ensure students are attentive and actively participating during class, provides documentation of what students learn, and helps students develop valuable organization and note-taking skills. Using peer review helps ensure the portfolios are read and evaluated thoughtfully but in a way that does not add significantly to his workload. (See the cover sheet form in Exhibit 19.1.)

VARIATIONS AND EXTENSIONS

- Offer an extra credit option for students to search out additional resources and expand upon any topics covered in class that they found unclear or particularly intriguing.
- Add in a self-assessment section for students to reflect upon their learning or a feedback section for students to make comments to you.

OBSERVATIONS AND ADVICE

Because students will be evaluated on how well they take notes, present material in ways that help students take good notes. For example, speak slowly, provide handouts of complicated graphs and figures so that students can keep up, use the overhead projector or presentation slides to show overall structure. Consider providing students with guidance about how to take good notes in a mini-lecture, a handout, or by providing examples of effective notes (Davis, 1993, p. 182).

For advice on how to create a grading rubric for this activity, see T/S 25, "Use rubrics to give students frequent and useful feedback" in Chapter 8 of this book or Stevens and Levi (2005), *Introduction to Rubrics: An Assessment Tool to Save Grading Time, Convey Effective Feedback, and Promote Student Learning.*

It is important that students' portfolios are read carefully. This is time-consuming, so if your class is large or your workload does not permit sufficient time for reading the portfolios, consider incorporating a peer review process.

EXHIBIT 19.1.

Cover Sheet for Peer Review

In-Class Portfolio

Cover and Grading Sheet

Last Name _____ First Name _____

Peer Evaluators _____ and _____

Date										Total
Organization (0–10)										
Quality (0–50)										

Total without Peer Review Bonus

Students' Portfolios You Evaluated	50
_____and_____	

Total with Peer Review Bonus

☐ APPEALS PROCESS: I believe my portfolio was evaluated inappropriately for the specific reasons I state on the reverse side. If we agree, you will receive the higher points and the person who evaluated your portfolio may have their Bonus adjusted accordingly. If we do not agree, you will receive a "frivolous complaint" 25-pt. penalty. Appeals must be done when portfolio is submitted so that it can be resolved prior to point posting.

Organization (0–8 Points): Day, date, class time, and topic at the top of that day's notes, with that day's notes clearly distinguished as a new day and in correct order (2 pts per item).

QUALITY (0–50 POINTS):

Level 1 Excellent (41–50 points): The notes are excellent, written in an exceptionally organized and legible manner and appearing to include 90–100% of the info from the presentation slides as well as additional comments from the lecturer. For any group work or responses to in-class questions, there is a paragraph of at least 100 words (about the length of the directions in this Level 1 paragraph) written in a manner that clearly demonstrates that the student responded to the question or participated in the group assignment in a serious and substantive manner.

Level 2 Very Good (31–40 points): The notes are very good, written neatly and legibly, and appear to include most of the info from the presentation slides. The group work or responses to in-class questions are also very good, but are either not long enough or do not demonstrate serious effort and critical thinking.

Level 3 Adequate (21–30 points): The notes and any written work are adequate, but they appear incomplete, are difficult to read, or the group work summaries or responses are short and/or superficial.

Level 4 (10–20 points) or Half Credit: The notes are too difficult to read or are clearly incomplete. (This level requires more of a judgment call and if you feel unprepared to make this call, consult with the instructor.) If a student had to leave early, he or she should have written across the top of that day's notes "Half Credit." In this case, determine the level and give half of the top points (e.g., half of Very Good/40 would be 20 points).

Peer review reduces instructor workload and also provides students with an opportunity to read other students' ideas, to review the material that was covered in class, and to see the range of quality work submitted by their peers. If you use peer review, students should be informed of this at the beginning of the term.

To implement peer review, set aside one hour of class time on the submission date to guide students through the process. Provide students with the option of having their portfolios instructor-graded, but encourage them to participate in peer review by explaining how this will help their own learning or by giving them a small grade point bonus. Instituting an appeals process for students to challenge their peer-assigned grades may alleviate student anxiety. It is also useful to have a "frivolous complaint" penalty to discourage trivial, unwarranted appeals. Although peer review can be done individually, it is helpful for the review to be done by pairs who can help support each other in the process and ensure a more balanced reading.

1. On peer review day, students organize notes sequentially, fill out and attach a cover sheet, and submit their portfolios to the instructor.

2. The instructor forms students into groups of two and redistributes the portfolios so that each dyad receives two other students' portfolios. (A simple way to do this that prevents students from receiving their own portfolio to grade is to ask students to submit portfolios into stacks based on gender, and then distribute the women's portfolios to the men and men's to the women.)

3. The instructor guides students through a brief review of each day's content to remind them of the lecture topic and any active learning prompts, allowing time for student pairs to read through the notes, write comments, and evaluate the portfolio according to instructor-specified rubrics.

4. The instructor collects the evaluated portfolios and returns them to their authors, who read through the comments, and—if they choose to challenge their peers' evaluation—fill out an appeals form that includes their specific reasons for challenging their grade.

5. The instructor collects the portfolios again, reviews any contested grades, spot-checks the evaluations, records grades, and returns portfolios to their authors.

KEY RESOURCE   Stevens, D. D., & Levi, A. (2005). *Introduction to rubrics: An assessment tool to save grading time, convey effective feedback, and promote student learning.* Sterling, VA: Stylus.

S T U D E N T
E N G A G E M E N T
T E C H N I Q U E

46

Resource Scavenger Hunt

Essential Characteristics

PRIMARY MODE	Individual
ACTIVITY FOCUS	Reading, Writing
DURATION OF ACTIVITY	Single Session
ONLINE TRANSFERABILITY	High

DESCRIPTION AND PURPOSE
Students engage in fact-finding and information-processing exercises using instructor-specified library and Internet sources.

This SET challenges learners to locate and think about course-related information as they explore essential resources that will be useful or required for their future study. The answers they find to the questions expand their content knowledge and understanding in an engaging activity that also helps them to become more effective users of research resources.

STEP-BY-STEP DIRECTIONS

1. Identify encyclopedias, dictionaries, journals, and Web sites (disciplinary and professional associations, Internet libraries, topic-specific Web pages, and so forth) that students should be familiar with to effectively complete course assignments.

2. Find at least one specific fact within each resource that is beneficial for learners and construct a corresponding question.

3. Create additional follow-up questions that challenge students to process the information.

4. Craft final questions that require students to use their knowledge of the resources to evaluate which resource would be best for a specific task.

5. Create an assignment that includes directions and questions and distribute to students.

Music History

Professor Grace Note uses this SET as one of the first activities in her online course to help students find Internet-based resources that they can use to augment the information she provides them within her course structure. She creates two questions for each resource. The first asks for the answer to a basic information retrieval question that could only be answered using that source; for example, "The Internet Public Library's Music History Laboratory (http://www.ipl.org/div/mushist/) includes summaries, images, and sound files of representative music of the major historical periods in Western music. In the section on the Renaissance, what piece is provided as an example of English madrigals?" The second question requires students to process the information in that source; for example, "In what ways does the composer of the madrigal example use tempo and texture to reinforce the message of the poem?" After students have answered questions on the specific sources, she asks them to use their cumulative knowledge to identify which sites would be best for specific purposes; for example, "If I needed to *see* what the score of an English madrigal looked like, as opposed to *hearing* what an English madrigal sounded like, which of the ten sources in this 'Resource Scavenger Hunt' would be most likely to provide that information?" Finally, she asks students to use their own research skills to locate and describe three additional Web-based resources and to post this on the follow-up threaded discussion.

ONLINE IMPLEMENTATION   The preparation and procedures for this SET are the same for both face-to-face and online classes.

VARIATIONS AND EXTENSIONS
- Have students individually or in teams create scavenger hunts for other students. Select a course-related topic and determine an appropriate number of scavenger hunt items each learner is to create for the topic. Create sample scavenger hunt items to serve as models. Consider having students post their scavenger hunt questions on an online discussion board and then requiring the other students to complete one or more of the scavenger hunts posted by their peers. End the activity by having each student post the answers to his or her scavenger hunt.

KEY RESOURCE   Watkins, R. (2005). *75 e-Learning activities: Making online learning interactive.* San Francisco: Pfeiffer, pp. 147–149.

S T U D E N T
E N G A G E M E N T
T E C H N I Q U E

47

Formative Quiz

Essential Characteristics

PRIMARY MODE	Individual or Collaborative
ACTIVITY FOCUS	Discussing
DURATION OF ACTIVITY	Single Session
ONLINE TRANSFERABILITY	Low

DESCRIPTION AND PURPOSE

The teacher posts a question on a presentation slide or overhead projector that is similar to those that will be used on major exams, gives students an appropriate amount of time to decide on an answer quietly and independently, then asks students to share their answers with a partner, a small group, or with the whole class. After students have shared their responses, the teacher gives the correct answer, clarifies misunderstood material, or builds upon student responses to craft a more complete answer.

This SET challenges students to make a personal commitment as they use their knowledge and understanding of course content to express to a partner or a group their answer to the instructor's questions. Since students receive immediate feedback, any misunderstandings are quickly corrected just as their correct understandings are validated and reinforced. This technique also helps the teacher assess student learning. Finally, it can reduce student anxiety about the kinds of questions that will be on major exams and point to areas that warrant further study.

STEP-BY-STEP DIRECTIONS

1. Write out a series of questions that are similar to those that will be asked on exams.
2. Create overhead transparencies or presentation slides that allow you to display the questions one at a time, with an additional transparency or slide showing the answer.

3. Decide whether students will answer individually or as small groups and determine how they will report their answer.

4. Explain the process to students, answer any questions, and then present a question on an overhead transparency or presentation slide and give students time to think through an answer individually.

5. Ask students to share their answer with a partner, small group, or the whole class.

6. Show the transparency or slide with the correct answer and explain why the answer is correct. Take time to find out why students answered incorrectly so that you can clarify misunderstandings before moving on to the next slide.

EXAMPLES

Radiologic Technology State Board Preparation

This course is designed to help students at the end of their Radiologic Technology academic program prepare for the State Board examinations. Professor Flo Roskopi uses "Formative Quizzes" as one of many strategies to help students review information and hone the test-taking skills that will help them have successful exam experiences. She provides students with sample quizzes containing 10–15 objective-style questions similar to those they will find on the exam. Students complete the quiz individually within a specified time limit. They then join their team (three pre-organized groups of five students) and work together to reach consensus on the team's quiz answers. Teams then exchange their completed team quiz, Professor Roskopi posts an overhead transparency showing the correct answers, and the team scores another team's answer sheet. The teams that earn a perfect score win a point, which Professor Roskopi posts on the "Scoreboard," a section of the whiteboard on which she records cumulative scores for the week.

• • •

Beginning Algebra

This professor distributes three index cards of different colors to each student, organizes students into pairs, and then presents overhead transparencies with the kinds of math problems that will be on the exam. For example, one problem is

Simplify the expression $2(a − 3) + 4b = 2(a − b − 3) + 5$.

She gives students a few moments to solve the problem individually and then projects a transparency with three possible choices and asks individuals to commit to an answer by raising their cards to vote for answer A (green), B (yellow), or C (blue). She quickly tallies their responses. She then asks students to turn to a partner, discuss the problem, and agree on a single answer to which they commit as a dyad, tallying the answers again. Next she shows a slide that solves each problem step by step. She finds that this process is an engaging way to review material, uncover and clarify misunderstandings, motivate students, and help her gauge how prepared students are for the exams.

ONLINE IMPLEMENTATION As structured, this SET does not transfer well to the online class environment. If you want to provide students with opportunities to practice taking tests, consider creating parallel versions of automatically graded tests that students can take, but set up preferences such that the grades are not sent to the official grade book.

OBSERVATIONS AND ADVICE The easiest kinds of questions to use in this SET are short-answer or objective questions—true/false, multiple choice, and fill-in-the-blank. McKeachie, Hofer, Svinicki, Chism, Van Note, Zhu, et al. (2002, pp. 78–81) and Davis (2009, pp. 393–398) offer extensive advice on how to construct good multiple-choice and true/false questions, from which the following is excerpted:

- Problem stems should be brief but complete so that students understand the problem before reading the answers, and they should be stated in the positive rather than the negative.

- Ask students to select the best answer rather than the correct answer, and avoid using words like *always, never, all*, or *none.* This minimizes arguments from contentious students.

- Possible answers should be as brief as possible, contain only familiar words, and avoid irrelevant clues to the correct answer (for example, longer or more elaborate answers).

- Make sure you use good distractors (incorrect answers) that are plausible and that represent errors commonly made by students, thus requiring students to make meaningful discriminations.

To really determine whether students understand a concept, offer a series of questions—typically three—each with different wording and structure but all designed to test the same concept (Gorder, 2008).

Some institutions are investing in technology known as Automatic Response Systems (or "clickers"). To use these systems, teachers display or speak prepared or ad hoc questions, students key in answers with their remote, and responses are tallied and displayed on a projection screen. Since tallying and displaying results occur immediately, both the teacher and students get the information they need quickly to assess understanding. The more sophisticated systems can display results using a variety of graphs (bar charts, pie charts, scatter graphs, and so forth) and can also allow for embedded video and sound files for multimedia presentations. Teachers can choose whether or not student responses are recorded for grading purposes.

For a low-tech method of tallying student responses, provide students in advance with two or three different-colored index cards to indicate true/false; a, b, or c; agree/disagree/no opinion; or yes/no/not sure. Ask for a simultaneous showing of cards (Davis, 1993, p. 134).

KEY RESOURCE   Bonwell, C. C. (1966). Enhancing the lecture: Revitalizing a traditional format. In T. E. Sutherland & C. C. Bonwell (Eds.), *Using active learning in college classes: A range of options for faculty.* San Francisco, Jossey-Bass, pp. 35–36

**STUDENT
ENGAGEMENT
TECHNIQUE**

48

Crib Cards

Essential Characteristics

PRIMARY MODE	Individual
ACTIVITY FOCUS	Writing
DURATION OF ACTIVITY	Single or Multiple Session
ONLINE TRANSFERABILITY	Low

DESCRIPTION AND PURPOSE Asking students challenging, open-ended exam essay questions that require them to think deeply is an effective teaching strategy, but some students struggle with writing or cannot think clearly during exams due to distractions or test-taking anxiety. "Crib Cards" offsets these problems by allowing students the time they need to think the problem through in advance and by requiring them to select and organize information they believe will be most useful as a support structure.

Early in the term, the instructor gives students a handout with a list of essay questions from which a subset will be chosen for the midterm and final exam. Students create a 3 × 5 index card for each question, writing whatever information they believe will be useful to them during the exam except the essay itself (a thesis statement and outline, key topics and concepts, lists of supporting data, and so forth). Crib cards are used during the exam and are turned in with the exam, including cards for questions not asked.

STEP-BY-STEP DIRECTIONS

1. Craft essay questions that test for high-level thinking (application, synthesis, and evaluation) rather than recall of facts.
2. Write out a model answer yourself, tracking the time it takes you so that you can estimate how long it will take students to write theirs (generally, two or three times as long).

3. Revise the question as needed and follow the same process for additional questions.

4. Develop guidelines for grading and create a handout that includes directions, the essay questions, and grading rubrics.

5. Consider creating a few sample crib cards showing a range of styles (outline, list of key topics or principles, graphic organizers with facts and data for support arguments, and so forth) that students can use as models.

6. Distribute the handout that includes directions, essay questions, and grading rubrics to students early in the term.

7. Explain the process, giving students guidance on how to create the crib cards and distributing the model crib cards for students to review.

8. On the day of the exam, collect both the essays and all of the crib cards (including those for questions not asked).

EXAMPLE

Introduction to Sociology

In order to help her students learn at a deep level, Professor Jen Der aims to have her students grapple with the enduring, big ideas at the heart of sociology as a discipline rather than having them simply memorize facts and data. She assesses student understanding through a series of essay questions. The essay questions require students to deal with abstract, counterintuitive, and often misunderstood ideas. Professor Der recognizes that it takes students time to think through their answers, and so she uses "Crib Cards" to help students prepare for and succeed on the comprehensive final exam.

ONLINE IMPLEMENTATION If you require proctored, on-campus exams in your online course, this SET can be implemented as is, but it is not transferable to online courses in which the exams are open resource.

VARIATIONS AND EXTENSIONS
- "Exam Preparation Journals" are an alternative strategy but with a similar goal of helping support students during the exam process. Early in the course, teachers give students a list of essay questions from which the midterm and final exam questions will be drawn. Students are instructed to divide a journal into sections, with each section corresponding to one of the essay questions. As the course material builds and develops, students write in each journal section the appropriate facts and ideas they acquire from the readings, lectures, and discussions that will enable them to answer the questions. Teachers can choose to

allow students to use their preparation journals during the exam, walking around the room and perhaps assigning bonus points to students who have done a conscientious job of responding to each question (Bean, 1996).

- Provide students with a list of the key concepts that will underlie exam questions rather than the essay questions themselves.

- Instead of using this SET for essay questions, use "Crib Cards" for problem solving in courses such as mathematics, economics, and science and ask students to include on their cards formulas, theorems, or other kinds of appropriate numerical data.

OBSERVATIONS AND ADVICE   "Crib Cards" helps students develop metacognitive skills by requiring them to think out and plan for answers, encouraging them to extend and refine their line of thinking, gather supporting evidence, develop arguments, and practice articulating a complex position precisely.

KEY RESOURCE   Bean, J. C. (1996) *Engaging ideas: The professor's guide to integrating writing, critical thinking, and active learning in the classroom.* San Francisco: Jossey-Bass, p. 190.

**STUDENT
ENGAGEMENT
TECHNIQUE**

49

Student-Generated Rubrics

Essential Characteristics

PRIMARY MODE	Collaborative
ACTIVITY FOCUS	Discussing
DURATION OF ACTIVITY	Single Session
ONLINE TRANSFERABILITY	Low

DESCRIPTION AND PURPOSE   Teachers provide student groups with three examples of outstanding course work such as an essay, research paper, musical composition, mathematical proof, or scientific lab report. Students analyze the works to determine the common characteristics and then develop assessment rubrics for the assignment that include a list of the most important traits and a corresponding scoring scale. The teacher facilitates a whole-class discussion to reach consensus on a set of rubrics that will be used to assess future assignment submissions.

This SET helps teach students how to identify the features of excellent work and internalize the meaning of high standards. It also results in a set of grading rubrics that contain explicit criteria and standards. This, in turn, guides students as they do their assignments and makes grading more effective and efficient. Finally, involving students in the process of developing the rubrics gives them greater control over the outcome, which can be motivating.

STEP-BY-STEP DIRECTIONS
1. Take time to think about your overall course objectives so that you can identify an assignment (or assignment type) that is important to the class and requires students to work at sophisticated levels of thinking.

2. Locate three exemplary models done by professionals, prior students, more advanced students, or students of colleagues. Note for yourself why each work exemplifies excellence.

3. Go through the steps using the models to create a simple evaluation rubric yourself, noting the characteristics that come to mind. This will help you to ensure the assignment is feasible and point out any adjustments or changes that need to be made.

4. Using your own experience as a guide, create a handout that directs students through the steps to develop a simple rubric. Here is an example:

   Look at these three model examples and

   a. *Identify and list the criteria, dimensions, or traits that stand out to you in each model (for example, "The essay has a clear thesis statement" or "The portfolio is visually attractive and well-organized").*

   b. *From your three lists, select five traits that seem to be essential and that all three of the models share.*

   c. *Describe the qualities that make that dimension or trait excellent (the thesis is clear to the reader, seems to be appropriately limited in scope, shows synthesis and original thought, and so forth).*

5. Duplicate the models so that you have a set of three for each group of 4–6 students.

6. Explain to students that you are providing them with examples of work that meet your highest expectations for the assignment they will be doing. Tell them that you want them to analyze the works to identify the specific characteristics that make the examples so good.

7. Distribute the handout and talk through the steps, answering any questions.

8. Form groups of 4–6 students, consider asking them to identify roles such as recorder, reporter, and facilitator, and provide each group with a set of the exemplary models.

9. Students create a simple grading rubric.

10. Ask groups to report out, writing out their ideas on the board and using this as a basis for a whole-class discussion on what constitutes excellence.

11. Either use the discussion to create a rubric that you will use, or collect the rubrics students have created and say you will review their models and use these as the basis for a single, consolidated rubric that will be used to evaluate their own versions of the assignment.

EXAMPLE

Principles of Marketing

As the final project in this class, Professor Sal N. Stuff formed groups of students and assigned them to identify a product and then develop a marketing strategy for the product. To increase the sense of "real world" applicability of the assignment, she had students make a presentation on their strategy to the class as though they were talking to a group of business managers. She decided to use "Student-Generated Rubrics" to help students see what was required for a high-quality presentation. She formed students into groups of five, and directed them to take careful notes as they observed three videotapes of past student presentations, noting what the students were doing that made the presentations so effective. She then asked students to pool their ideas and compile a list of shared qualities. Groups reported out ideas such as "good eye contact," "clear introduction that set out the plan for the presentation," "spoke loudly, slowly, and with modulated voice quality." She wrote the groups' ideas on the board, helped the group come to consensus on which attributes were most important, and told them she would be using their ideas to create a rubric with which they would assess their peers' presentations.

ONLINE IMPLEMENTATION

This SET is most effective when students can look at the models and interact "in the moment" to discuss the attributes that make it excellent. If having students generate grading rubrics seems as though it would be particularly valuable in your course, consider presenting students with 1–3 models, set up a threaded discussion forum in which students post their observations, and then use these to create an evaluation rubric.

VARIATIONS AND EXTENSIONS

- Instead of three examples of excellent work, give students examples that represent a range of quality (such as excellent, average, poor) and ask them to identify how the examples differ.

KEY RESOURCE

Stevens, D. D., & Levi, A. (2005). *Introduction to rubrics: An assessment tool to save grading time, convey effective feedback, and promote student learning.* Sterling, VA: Stylus.

S T U D E N T
E N G A G E M E N T
T E C H N I Q U E

50

Triad Listening

Essential Characteristics

PRIMARY MODE	Collaborative
ACTIVITY FOCUS	Discussing
DURATION OF ACTIVITY	Single Session
ONLINE TRANSFERABILITY	Low

DESCRIPTION AND PURPOSE

This SET provides students with a structured activity to practice the speaking and listening skills that create classroom conditions in which students are comfortable taking risks and expressing their true thoughts. Groups of three students practice speaking and listening skills as they perform specific roles (Speaker, Reflective Listener, and Referee).

STEP-BY-STEP DIRECTIONS

1. Take the time to explain to students why good communication skills are important for your class. For example, consider something along this line:

   In my class, I want you to be an active, engaged participant in our discussions, which means that you need to speak up and say what you truly think, feel, and believe. This requires that you take some level of risk. Although the degree to which one is willing to take risks varies, we know that we are more likely to take risks in situations in which we feel safe and supported than in those in which we fear we will be criticized or challenged aggressively for what we say. This activity is designed to help you practice the kinds of communication skills needed for us to have effective discussions in this class.

2. Create a handout that clarifies the roles and identifies the steps in this process.

Roles

Speakers aim to state their ideas simply and clearly, supporting the main idea with concrete examples, and avoiding counterproductive communication behaviors such as aggression, cynicism, and sarcasm.

Reflective Listeners try to forget themselves momentarily and concentrate on the other person, attempting to understand the main idea of what the person is saying, while avoiding counterproductive behaviors such as judging, advising, sympathizing, or kidding. They then use their own words to summarize back to the speaker what he or she said as accurately and completely as possible.

Referees oversee the exchange, making sure participants stick to the rules and interrupting only to clear up misunderstandings. If the Referee (or the Speaker) feels that the Reflective Listener's summary is inaccurate, the Referee interrupts and helps clear up the misunderstanding.

Steps

Step 1: The Speaker talks first. The speaker should a) state her idea as concisely as possible (do not digress, joke around, introduce irrelevancies, or meander) and b) amplify and clarify the idea.

Step 2: The Reflective Listener says back to the Speaker what the Speaker has said, but using his or her own words. Reflective Listeners should try to be (a) as thorough and accurate as possible and (b) avoid simply repeating the same words, but rather try to use their imagination and creative use of language to capture the essence of what the Speaker has said.

3. Distribute the handout, explain the process (roles and steps), and answer any questions.

4. Form groups of three, and tell students that they will be taking turns playing the role of Speaker, Reflective Listener, and Referee and allow them to decide who will take which role for the first round.

5. Present the prompt.

6. The Speaker responds to the prompt.

7. The Reflective Listener paraphrases what the Speaker said.

8. The Referee monitors the process.

9. Students rotate roles and follow the process for the same or a new prompt.

ONLINE
IMPLEMENTATION
This SET does not adapt to online classes.

EXAMPLE

Intercultural Communication/Speech

This class focuses on the dynamics of intercultural communication. The professor regularly uses "Triad Listening" to help students better understand cultural concepts, language style, ethnic perspectives, and stereotypes as they facilitate or hinder effective verbal and nonverbal interaction across cultural barriers.

OBSERVATIONS
AND ADVICE
Consider preparing students for this activity by giving a presentation or facilitating a discussion on the elements of effective communication. For example, Luotto and Stoll (1996), the teachers who wrote the book from which this technique was drawn, provide students with descriptions of the emotional components underlying effective active listening. They also describe ineffective listening responses ("blocks") that communicate to the speaker that it's not acceptable to have his/her feeling. Following are some of the examples they use to illustrate (Luotto and Stoll, 1996, pp. 41–42).

1. **Ordering, demanding:** "You must try"; "You have to stop" (Don't have that feeling, have some other feeling.)

2. **Persuading, arguing, lecturing:** "Do you realize?" "The facts are" (Here are some facts so you won't have that feeling.)

3. **Criticizing, blaming, disagreeing:** "You aren't thinking about this properly." (You're wrong if you have that feeling.)

4. **Reassuring, sympathizing:** "Don't worry"; "You'll feel better" (You don't need to have that feeling.)

5. **Interpreting, diagnosing:** "What you need is" "Your problem is" (Here's the reason you're having this feeling.)

6. **Kidding, using sarcasm:** "When did you last check the news?" "My old aunt had the same . . ." (You're silly if you persist in having that feeling.)

Some students may resist this SET, making fun of the activity or saying they don't need help in communication skills. At the beginning of their course on developing effective communication skills, Luotto and Stoll (1996) discuss "flight behaviors" and provide students with descriptions of the many ways people run away from things they don't want to face. By addressing most of the reasons underlying potential student resistance up front, they find that students recognize the value of the activity and are more cooperative. Drawing from Gerald Egan's book, *You and Me: The Skills of Communicating and Relating to Others* (1977), they describe twelve common flight behaviors. Following is an abbreviated, modified excerpt from descriptions they provide students of four of these behaviors (Luotto and Stoll, 1996, pp. 28–31):

- **Boredom**: Boredom is an insult to yourself. A person who is bored sees himself or herself as a victim of what's happening—and tends to put the blame "out there," saying that the interaction isn't interesting. A bored person is one who has given up taking the initiative and is just letting things happen. A bored person is a burden. Since he or she is really not engaged, he or she becomes a distraction. People will notice someone who is bored and eventually others feel that they have to deal with this bored person. You are responsible for your own boredom; it is a choice.

- **People who don't need skills training**: These people will run away from this kind of training saying that they already possess the skills. All of us can use a check-up from time to time. Most people will find that it is invigorating to polish skills we already possess or to discover ways to improve skills we haven't used in some time.

- **Humor**: Humor is a two-edged sword. It can be used to lighten the effect of a confrontation, but it can also be used to run away from a situation that may not be comfortable. A genuinely humorous person can often get a confrontation across in a lighthearted way but still make the confrontation serious and meaningful. On the other hand, some people, when things get too tense, dissipate the tension with humor, failing to realize that a reasonable amount of tension can help keep people working toward their goals. Whenever individuals adopt humor as a consistent part of their style, it is no longer serving a useful function, and needs to be faced and addressed.

- **Hostility**: Hostility is one of those strong emotions that many of us fear. There was a time in the development of human-relationship training when the expression of raw hostility toward others was seen as liberating. Those days have passed; raw hostility is now seen by most as a form of aggression rather than of assertiveness. Any use of hostility should be examined—not because hostility is evil in itself, and not because a certain amount of hostility isn't normal in human relationships, but because hostility may really be a cover-up for something else, and it undermines the sense of a learning community that contributes to student engagement.

KEY RESOURCE   Luotto, J. A., & Stoll, E. L. (1996). *Communication skills for collaborative learning.* Dubuque, IA: Kendall/Hunt, pp. 35–39.

Key to Courses and Professors in SET Examples

SET	Course	Professor Name and Translation
1 Background Knowledge Probe	Political Science	
	Human Anatomy and Physiology	Tish Oosells (tissue cells)
	Music of Multicultural America	
2 Artifacts	Remedial Math	
	Art History	Al E. Gorical (allegorical)
	American History	Emma Grashun (immigration)
3 Focused Reading Notes	English Literature	Rita Booke (read a book)
	Music History	
4 Quotes	Introduction to Shakespeare	Rose N. Crantz (Rosencrantz, a character in *Hamlet*)
	Principles of Advertising	

SET	Course	Professor Name and Translation
5 Stations	African American Literature	
	Math	Al Gorithem (algorithm)
	U.S. History	
6 Team Jeopardy	History of the United States	James Town (Jamestown)
7 Seminar	Intro to American Literature	Sal Inas (Salinas, the California town where Steinbeck was born)
	Cultural Anthropology	
8 Classify	Art Appreciation	Dee Sign (design)
	Comparative Animal Physiology	
9 Frames	Introduction to American Government and Politics	Frank N. Privilige (franking privilege)
	Workshop on the Scholarship of Teaching and Learning	
10 Believing and Doubting	General Biology	Jenn Ettics (genetics)
11 Academic Controversy	Art History	Anne Cestral (ancestral)
12 Split-Room Debate	Education Leadership	Vi S. Principal (vice principal)
13 Analytic Teams	History of the Americas	A. Joe Vexploration (Age of Exploration)
	Management Seminar	

SET	Course	Professor Name and Translation
14 Book Club	Introduction to American Government and Politics	Manuel Recount (manual recount)
15 Small Group Tutorial	Intro to Philosophy	Watts Itmene (What's it mean?)
16 Team Concept Maps	Statics	Alec Tricity (electricity)
	Basic Two-Dimensional Design	Pat Tern (pattern)
	History of the U.S. from 1877	Rose E. Riveter (Rosie the Riveter)
17 Variations	Music Composition and Theory	Harmon I. Zashun (harmonization)
	Christian Thought and Church History	Zeke N. Yeshallfind (Seek and ye shall find)
18 Letters	Honors Institute Seminar in Science	Al Kali (alkali)
	History of Constitutional Law	
19 Role Play	Oral Communication Skills I	Ann Glishlerner (English learner)
	History of the Vietnam War	
19 Role Play	Psychology of Prejudice	Sara Bellum (cerebellum)
	Management Practices	
20 Poster Sessions	Introduction to Physics	Mo Shunenfors (motion and force)
	Advanced Ceramics	Sarah McGlaise (ceramic glaze)
	Music of Multicultural America	

SET	Course	Professor Name and Translation
	U.S. History	Vi O'Lashuns (violations)
21 Class Book	Composition, Critical Reading, and Thinking	S. A. Rider (essay writer)
22 WebQuests	Organic Chemistry	
	Advanced Spanish	
23 What's the Problem?	Music Theory and Composition	Paul Ifanick (polyphonic)
	Critical Reading and Thinking	Ima Nerrer (I'm an error)
24 Think Again!	Algebra	Polly Nomeal (polynomial)
	Introduction to Physics	
25 TAPPS	Elementary Statistics	Marge N. O'Vera (margin of error)
	English as a Second Language	
	Programming in BIOPERL	
26 Proclamations	Race and Ethnic Relations	
27 Send-A-Problem	English Literature	Fitz William (Fitzwilliam, first name of Darcy, a main character in *Pride and Prejudice*)
	Urban Planning	
	Advanced Pathopyshiology and Patient Management	Xavier Breath (save your breath)
28 Case Studies	Physical Geology	

SET	Course	Professor Name and Translation
29 Contemporary Issues	Applied Ethics	Howie Aktud (how he acted)
	Music Business	
30 Hearing the Subject	Art Appreciation	Ike O'Nogrephy (iconography)
	Introduction to American Literature	
31 Directed Paraphrase	Statics	Alec Tricity (electricity)
	Radiation Oncology	
32 IRAs	Survey of International Business	Sal Ling (selling)
33 Jigsaw	Masterpieces of American Literature	Paige Turner (page turner)
	Introduction to Cultural Anthropology	Sara McShards (ceramic shards)
	Web Site Publishing Tools	
34 Field Trip	Humanities and the Modern Experience	Art X. Ibit (art exhibit)
	Introduction to Sociology	
	DNA Sequencing and Bioinformatics	Jean Poole (gene pool)
35 Autobiographical Reflections	Elementary Algebra	Anna Logue (analog)
	Music of Multicultural America	

SET	Course	Professor Name and Translation
36 Dyadic Interviews	Dental Hygiene	Perry Dontal (periodontal)
	Introduction to Modern Literature	
37 Circular Response	Intermediate French	May Whee (mais oui)
	Survey of American Literature	
38 Ethical Dilemmas	Statistics	Anne Alesis (analysis)
	Microcontroller Programming	
	Freshman Seminar: Study Skills/Personal Development	
39 Connected Communities	History of the Middle East and Comparative World Religions	
	Intermediate French	
	Triad Learning Community Involving Three Courses: Psychology as a Natural Science, Intro to Anthropology, and Composition – Social Issues	
40 Stand Where You Stand	Introduction to Sociology	
41 Learning Logs	Freshman Seminar	
	Speech Communications	
42 Critical Incident Questionnaire	General Psychology	Watts D. Matta (What's the matter?)

SET	Course	Professor Name and Translation
	Microbiology	Penny Cillen (penicillin)
43 Go for the Goal	Elementary Statistics	Sam Pell (sample)
44 Post Test Analysis	General Biology	Mike Robe (microbe)
45 In-Class Portfolio	General Psychology	Hugh Menature (human nature)
46 Resource Scavenger Hunt	Music History	Grace Note (grace note)
47 Formative Quiz	Radiologic Technology State Board Preparation	Flo Roskopi (fluoroscopy)
	Beginning Algebra	
48 Crib Cards	Introduction to Sociology	Jen Der (gender)
49 Student-Generated Rubrics	Principles of Marketing	Sal N Stuff (selling stuff)
50 Triad Listening	Intercultural Communication/Speech	

Appendix B

NSSE/SET Crosswalk Tables

THE NATIONAL SURVEY of Student Engagement (NSSE) gathers information about collegiate quality on a national basis. Established in 1998 and headquartered at Indiana University in the Center for Postsecondary Research and Planning, it uses a specially developed survey instrument consisting of questions that address empirically confirmed "good practices" in undergraduate education that promote student engagement. There are several survey projects that work in partnership with NSSE, including the Community College Survey of Student Engagement (CCSSE), The Faculty Survey of Student Engagement (FSSE), and The Beginning College Survey of Student Engagement (BCSSE).

The following crosswalk tables provide a mechanism for correlating survey questions with the Student Engagement Techniques (SETs) and the Student Engagement Tips and Strategies (T/S). The NSSE survey item format is the one that is used, since that is the parent survey. The complete survey can be accessed at www.nsse.iub.edu/html/survey_instruments_2009.cfm. The SETs and T/S are recommended for addressing a specific survey item. For example, Survey Item 1a addresses how often students ask questions in class or contribute to class discussions. The recommended SETs are those that structure class discussions in ways that promote participation by all students and the recommended T/S are those that offer teachers ways to create a sense of classroom community so that all students feel comfortable speaking up in discussions and asking questions.

Crosswalk Table A: NSSE Survey Items to Student Engagement Techniques (SETs) and *Tips and Strategies (T/S)* (in italics)

NSSE Survey Items	Student Engagement Techniques, *Tips and Strategies*
1. ACADEMIC AND INTELLECTUAL EXPERIENCES	
a. Asked questions in class or contributed to class discussions.	SET 2, 4, 7, 8, 12, 14, 15, 27 *and T/S 29, 30, 32, 34*
b. Made a class presentation	SET 8, 13, 14, 15, 19, 20, 26, 33
c. Prepared two or more drafts of a paper or assignment before turning it in	SET 15, 21 *and T/S 42*
d. Worked on a paper or project that required integrating ideas or information from various sources	SET 5, 9, 11, 13, 15, 17, 18, 20, 21, 22, 26, 28, 31 *and T/S 42*
e. Included diverse perspectives (different races, religions, genders, political beliefs, etc.) in class discussions or writing assignments	SET 4, 7, 9, 11, 12, 13, 18, 22, 26, 40 *and T/S 27, 32*
f. Come to class without completing readings or assignments	SET 3, 4, 6, 7, 14, 15, 20 *and T/S 24*
g. Worked with other students on projects during class	SET 2, 6, 8, 9, 11, 13, 16, 19, 20, 21, 25, 26, 28, 33, 36 *and T/S 35*
h. Worked with classmates outside of class to prepare class assignments	SET 6, 9, 13, 18, 19, 20, 21, 22, 26, 34 *and T/S 24, 31*
i. Put together ideas or concepts from different courses when completing assignments or during class discussions	SET 1, 7, 8, 16 *and T/S 38*
j. Tutored or taught other students (paid or voluntary)	SET 31, 33
k. Participated in a community-based project (e.g., service learning) as part of a regular course	SET 34, 36
l. Used an electronic medium (listserv, chat group, Internet, instant messaging, etc.) to discuss or complete an assignment	SET 22, 32, 39 *and T/S 31*
m. Used e-mail to communicate with an instructor	*T/S 31*
n. Discussed grades or assignments with an instructor	SET 43 *and T/S 25*

NSSE Survey Items	Student Engagement Techniques, *Tips and Strategies*
o. Talked about career plans with a faculty member or advisor	
p. Discussed ideas from your readings or classes with faculty members outside of class	
q. Received prompt feedback from faculty on your academic performance (written or oral)	*T/S 25*
r. Worked harder than you thought you could to meet an instructor's standards or expectations	SET 21 *and T/S 41, 42*
s. Worked with faculty members on activities other than coursework (committees, orientation, student life activities, etc.)	
t. Discussed ideas from your readings or classes with others outside of class (students, family members, co-workers, etc.)	
u. Had serious conversations with students of a different race or ethnicity than your own	SET 14, 15, 28, 36, 39, 50
v. Had serious conversations with students who are very different from you in terms of their religious beliefs, political opinions, or personal values	SET 7, 11, 13, 14, 15, 36, 39, 50

2. MENTAL ACTIVITIES

NSSE Survey Items	Student Engagement Techniques, *Tips and Strategies*
a. Memorizing facts, ideas, or methods from your courses and readings so you can repeat them in pretty much the same form	SET 6 *and T/S 20, 21, 22*
b. Analyzing the basic elements of an idea, experience, or theory, such as examining a particular case or situation in depth and considering its components	SET 7, 8, 9, 10, 11, 12, 13, 16, 22, 24, 26, 28, 30, 33, 40

NSSE Survey Items	Student Engagement Techniques, *Tips and Strategies*
c. Synthesizing and organizing ideas, information, or experiences into new, more complex interpretations and relationships	SET 8, 15, 16, 17, 18, 20, 26, 33
d. Making judgments about the value of information, arguments, or methods, such as examining how others gathered and interpreted data and assessing the soundness of their conclusions	SET 9, 11, 12, 18, 20, 21, 22, 24, 25, 26, 27, 28, 29
e. Applying theories or concepts to practical problems or in new situations	SET 5, 10, 13, 18, 19, 20, 24, 25, 26, 27, 28, 31, 32

3. READING AND WRITING

NSSE Survey Items	Student Engagement Techniques, *Tips and Strategies*
a. Number of assigned textbooks, books, or book-length packs of course readings	SET 3, 4, 7, 14
b. Number of books read on your own (not assigned) for personal enjoyment or academic enrichment	SET 3, 4, 7, 14
c. Number of written papers or reports of 20 pages or more	
d. Number of written papers or reports between 5 and 19 pages	SET 15, 21
e. Number of written papers or reports of fewer than 5 pages	SET 9, 15, 17, 18, 21, 26, 29, 31, 32, 35

4. PROBLEM SOLVING

NSSE Survey Items	Student Engagement Techniques, *Tips and Strategies*
a. Number of problem sets that take you more than an hour to complete	SET 23, 25
b. Number of problem sets that take you less than an hour to complete	SET 23, 25, 27

5. EXAMS

NSSE Survey Items	Student Engagement Techniques, *Tips and Strategies*
To what degree examinations have challenged you to do your best work	SET 47, 48

6. ADDITIONAL COLLEGIATE EXPERIENCES

NSSE Survey Items	Student Engagement Techniques, *Tips and Strategies*
a. Attended an art exhibit, gallery, play, dance, or other theatre performance	SET 34

NSSE Survey Items	**Student Engagement Techniques,** *Tips and Strategies*
b. Exercised or participated in physical fitness activities	
c. Participated in activities to enhance your spirituality (worship, meditation, prayer, etc.)	
d. Examined the strengths and weaknesses of your own views on a topic or issue	SET 7, 14, 18, 19, 24, 29, 35, 36, 40
e. Tried to better understand someone else's views by imagining how an issue looks from his or her perspective	SET 2, 4, 11, 17, 18, 19, 24, 26, 27, 28, 29, 30, 31, 40, 50
f. Learned something that changed the way you understand an issue or concept	SET 2, 4, 7, 10, 11, 12, 13, 14, 15, 17, 18, 19, 24, 26, 27, 28, 29, 30, 34, 35, 37, 38, 40, 41

7. ENRICHING EDUCATIONAL EXPERIENCES

a. Practicum, internship, field experience, co-op experience, or clinical assignment	SET 34
b. Community service or volunteer work	SET 26, 29
c. Participate in a learning community or some other formal program where groups of students take two or more classes together	SET 39
d. Work on a research project with a faculty member outside of course or program requirements	
e. Foreign language coursework	
f. Study abroad	
g. Independent study or self-designed major	SET 20, 41 *and T/S 41*
h. Culminating senior experience (capstone course, senior project or thesis, comprehensive exam, etc.)	SET 15, 20, 21, 26, 39

8. QUALITY OF RELATIONSHIPS

a. Relationships with other students	SET 42, 50 *and T/S 27, 28, 29, 30, 31, 33, 36, 37*
b. Relationships with faculty members	SET 15 *and T/S 26, 29, 32, 33, 37*
c. Relationships with administrative personnel and offices	

NSSE Survey Items	Student Engagement Techniques, Tips and Strategies
9. TIME USAGE	
a. Preparing for class (studying, reading, writing, doing homework, analyzing data, rehearsing, and other academic activities)	SET 3, 4, 6, 7, 13, 14, 15, 18, 19, 20, 22, 43, 48 *and T/S 40, 41, 42*
b. Working for pay on campus	
c. Working for pay off-campus	
d. Participating in co-curricular activities (organizations, campus publications, student government, fraternity or sorority, intercollegiate or intramural sports, etc.)	
e. Relaxing & socializing (watching TV, partying, etc.)	
f. Providing care for dependents living with you (parents, children, spouse, etc.)	
g. Commuting to class (driving, walking, etc.)	
10. EDUCATIONAL AND PERSONAL GROWTH	
a. Acquiring a broad general education	
b. Acquiring job or work-related knowledge and skills	SET 31, 32, 34
c. Writing clearly and effectively	SET 9, 15, 18, 21, 26, 31, 35 *and T/S 25, 42*
d. Speaking clearly and effectively	SET 4, 7, 11, 12, 14, 15, 19, 20, 33, 36, 37 *and T/S 25, 42*
e. Thinking critically and analytically	SET 4, 7, 8, 9, 10, 11, 12, 13, 14, 15, 16, 17, 18, 22, 23, 24, 25, 26, 27, 28, 30, *and T/S 25, 42*
f. Analyzing quantitative problems	SET 23, 25, 27
g. Using computer and information technology	SET 22, 32, 39, 46 *and T/S 31*
h. Working effectively with others	SET 7, 11, 15, 16, 19, 25, 33, 36, 37, 38, 39, 42, 49, 50
i. Voting in local, state, or national elections	
j. Learning effectively on your own	SET 3, 5, 22, 29, 32, 35, 41, 45, 46, 48, 49 *and T/S 17, 40*
k. Understanding yourself	SET 1, 2, 7, 10, 12, 14, 18, 19, 35, 36, 38, 41, 43, 44, 45, 50
l. Understanding people of other racial and ethnic backgrounds	SET 2, 12, 14, 15, 18, 19, 28, 36

NSSE Survey Items	Student Engagement Techniques, *Tips and Strategies*
m. Solving complex real-world problems	SET 10, 12, 13, 19, 20, 23, 24, 25, 26, 27, 28, 38 *and T/S 7*
n. Developing a personal code of values and ethics	SET 19, 35, 36, 38, 49
o. Contributing to the welfare of your community	SET 26, 34
p. Using computer and information technology	SET 22, 32, 39, 46 *and T/S 31*
q. Developing a deepened sense of spirituality	

Crosswalk Table B: Student Engagement Techniques (SETs) to NSSE Survey Items

Student Engagement Technique (SET)	NSSE Survey Items
1. Background Knowledge Probe	11k
2. Artifacts	1a, 1g, 6e, 1i, 6f, 11e, 11l, 11l
3. Focused Reading Notes	1f, 3a, 3b, 9a, 11j
4. Quotes	1e, 1f, 3a, 6e, 6f, 9a, 11d, 11e
5. Stations	1f, 6e, 6f, 11d, 11e
6. Team Jeopardy	1f, 1g, 1h, 2a, 9a
7. Seminar	1a, 1i, 1e, 1f, 1v, 2b, 3a, 3b, 6d, 6f, 9a, 11d, 11h, 11k
8. Classify	1a, 1b, 1i, 1g, 2b, 2c, 10e
9. Frames	1d, 1e, 1g, 1h, 2b, 2d, 3e, 11c, 11e
10. Believing and Doubting	1e, 2b, 2e, 6f, 11e, 11m
11. Academic Controversy	1d, 1e, 1g, 1v, 2b, 2d, 6e, 6f, 11d, 11e, 11h, 11k
12. Split-Room Debate	1a, 1b, 1e, 2b, 2d, 6f, 11d, 11e, 11h, 11k, 11l, 11m
13. Analytic Teams	1b, 1d, 1e, 1g, 1h, 1v, 2b, 2e, 6f, 9a, 11e, 11m
14. Book Club	1a, 1b, 1d, 1f, 1u, 1v, 2d, 3a, 3b, 6d, 6f, 9a, 11d, 11e, 11k, 11l
15. Small Group Tutorials	1a, 1b, 1c, 1d, 13, 1f, 1u, 1v, 2c, 3d, 3e, 6f, 7h, 8b, 9a, 11c, 11d, 11e, 11h, 11l
16. Team Concept Maps	1b, 1i, 1g, 2b, 2c, 11e, 11h, 11k
17. Variations	1d, 2b, 2c, 3e, 6e, 6f, 9a, 11e

Student Engagement Technique (SET)	NSSE Survey Items
18. Letters	1d, 1e, 1g, 1h, 2c, 2d, 2e, 3e, 6d, 6e, 6f, 9a, 11k, 11l, 11m
19. Role Play	1b, 1g, 1h, 2e, 6d, 6e, 6f 9a, 11d, 11h, 11k, 11l, 11m, 11n
20. Poster Sessions	1b, 1d, 1f, 1g, 1h, 2c, 2d, 2e, 7g, 7h, 9a, 11d, 11m
21. Class Book	1c, 1d, 1g, 1h, 2c, 2d, 2e, 3d, 3e, 7g, 7h, 9a, 11c
22. WebQuests	1d, 1e, 1h, 1l, 2b, 2d, 9a, 11e, 11g, 11j
23. What's the Problem?	1g, 4a, 4b, 11e, 11f, 11j, 11g, 11m
24. Think Again	2b, 2d, 2e, 6d, 6e, 6f, 11e, 11m
25. Think-Aloud-Pair-Problem Solving (TAPPS)	1g, 2b, 2d, 2e, 4b, 11e, 11f, 11h, 11m
26. Proclamations	1b, 1d, 1e, 1g, 1h, 2b, 2c, 2d, 2e, 3e, 6e, 6f, 7b, 7h, 11c, 11m 10o
27. Send-a-Problem	1a, 2b, 1d, 1e, 1g, 2b, 2c, 2d, 2e, 6e, 6f, 10h, 10l, 10m, 11o
28. Case Studies	1a, 2b, 2d, 2e, 4b, 6e, 6f, 11e, 11f, 11m, 11l
29. Contemporary Issues Journals	3e, 6d, 6e, 6f, 7b
30. Hearing the Subject	1a, 2b, 2d, 6f, 11e, 11j
31. Directed Paraphrase	1d, 1j, 2e, 3e, 6e, 11b, 11c
32. Insights-Resources-Application (IRAs)	1m, 2e, 3e, 11g, 11b, 11c, 11j
33. Jigsaw	1b, 1g, 1j, 2b, 2c, 2d, 11c, 11d, 11h
34. Field Trips	1h, 1k, 1t, 6a, 6f, 7a, 11b, 11o
35. Autobiographical Reflections	3c, 3e, 6d, 6f, 11c, 11j, 11k, 11n
36. Dyadic Interviews	1g, 6d,11h, 11l, 11k, 11n
37. Circular Response	6e, 11c, 11d, 11h
38. Ethical Dilemmas	6f, 11h, 11m, 11k, 11n
39. Connected Communities	1v, 7c, 7h, 11g, 11h,
40. Stand Where You Stand	2b, 6d, 6e, 6f
41. Learning Logs	6f, 7g, 11j, 11k
42. Critical Incident Questionnaire (CIQ)	8a, 11h
43. Go for the Goal	1n, 9a, 11k
44. Post-test Analysis	11k
45. In-class Portfolio	11j, 11k
46. Resource Scavenger Hunt	11g, 11j
47. Formative Quiz	11j
48. Crib Cards	2c, 9a, 11c
49. Student-Generated Rubrics	11h, 11j, 11n
50. Triad Listening	6e, 8a, 11h, 11k

References

About.com: Continuing Education. (n.d.). *Ice Breakers*. Retrieved from http://adulted.about.com/od/icebreakers.

Achacoso, M. V. (2004). Post-test analysis: A tool for developing students' metacognitive awareness and self-regulation. In M. V. Achacoso and M. D. Svinicki (Eds.), *Alternative strategies for evaluating student learning*. San Francisco: Jossey-Bass.

Alexander, B. (2008). *Games for education: 2008. EDUCAUSE Review* 43(4). Retrieved from http://connect.educause.edu/Library/EDUCAUSE+Review/Gamesfor HigherEducation20/46975?time=1231765247

Anderson, L. W., Krathwohl, D. R., and Bloom, B. S. (2001). *A taxonomy for learning, teaching, and assessing: A revision of Bloom's taxonomy of educational objectives*. New York: Longman.

Angelo, T. A. (2001). Opening Plenary Session of the Central California Conference on Assessing Student Learning, California State University, Fresno, April 27. In M. Allen, Course Assessment Workshop Handouts, Student Learning Outcomes Convocation, October 31, 2008, Foothill College.

Angelo, T. A., and Cross, K. P. (1993). *Classroom assessment techniques: A handbook for college teachers* (2nd ed). San Francisco: Jossey-Bass.

Annenberg Media Learner.org. (n.d.). Math in daily life: Savings and credit. *Interactives*. Retrieved from http://www.learner.org/interactives/dailymath/savings.html.

Aronson, E. (2000). *The jigsaw classroom*. Retrieved from http://www.jigsaw.org/

Aronson, E., Blaney, N., Stephan, C., Sikes, J., and Snapp, M. (1978). *The jigsaw classroom*. Beverly Hills, CA: Sage.

Association of American Colleges and Universities. (2007). *College learning for the new global century: A report from the National Leadership Council for Liberal Education and America's Promise*. Retrieved from http://www.aacu.org/advocacy/leap/documents/GlobalCentury_final.pdf

Astin, A. (1968). *The college environment*. Washington, DC: American Council on Education.

Astin, A. (1993). *What matters in college?* San Francisco: Jossey-Bass.

Ausubel, D. P. (1968). *Educational psychology: A cognitive view*. New York: Holt, Rinehart & Winston.

Ausubel, D. P. (1977). The facilitation of meaningful verbal learning in the classroom. *Educational Psychologist, 12*, 162–178.

Bain, K. (2004). *What the best college teachers do.* Cambridge, MA: Harvard University Press.

Bandura, A. (1977). Self-efficacy: Toward a unifying theory of behavioral change. *Psychological Review, 84*(1), 191–215.

Bandura, A. (1982). Self-efficacy mechanism in human agency. *American Psychologist, 37*(2), 122–147.

Barkley, E. F. (2006a). Capturing change: A tale of two portfolios. Retrieved from http://gallery.carnegiefoundation.org/gallery_of_tl/castl_he.html

Barkley, E. F. (2006b). *Crossroads: Finding the intersections between learning goals and outcomes.* Retrieved from http://web.mac.com/elizabethbarkley/CoursePortfolio/Portfolio_Entrance.html

Barkley, E. F. (2006c). Honoring student voices, offering students choices: Empowering students as architects of their own learning. *National Teaching and Learning Forum, 13*(3).

Barkley, E. F. (2008). *Defining student engagement (faculty and student perspectives): Feedback from the International Society for the Scholarship of Teaching and Learning (ISSOTL) Special Interest Group on Student Engagement.* Compiled by E. Barkley from e-mail and conversations with faculty and posted on http://groups.google.com/group/issotl—student-engagement-special-interest-group/web

Barkley, E. F. (2009). Teachers talk: Perspectives on student engagement. Web page on *Student Engagement Techniques.* Retrieved from http://web.me.com/elizabethbarkley/Student_Engagement_Techniques/Teachers_Talk.html

Barkley, E. F., Cross K. P., and Major, C. H. (2005). *Collaborative learning techniques: A handbook for college faculty.* San Francisco: Jossey-Bass.

Barnes, L., Christensen, C. R., and Hansen, A. (1994). *Teaching and the case method: Text, cases, and readings.* Boston: Harvard Business School.

Bautista, V. (2000). *Improve your grades: How to become an honor student.* Warren, MI: Bookhaus Publishers.

Bean, J. C. (1996). *Engaging ideas: The professor's guide to integrating writing, critical thinking, and active learning in the classroom.* San Francisco: Jossey-Bass.

Berkowitz, B. (2007). *The community tool box.* Work Group for Community Health and Development, University of Kansas. Retrieved from http://ctb1.ku.edu/en/tablecontents/

Blankstein, A. M., Cole, R. W., et al. (2007). *Engaging every learner.* Thousand Oaks, CA: Corwin Press.

Bloom, B. S. E., Engelhart, M. D., Furst, E. J., Hill, A. H., & Krathwohl, D. R. (1956). *Taxonomy of educational objectives: Handbook I: Cognitive comain.* New York: David McKay.

Blumberg, P. B. (2009) *Developing learner-centered teaching: A practical guide for faculty.* San Francisco: Jossey Bass.

Boettcher, J. V. (2004). *Faculty guide for moving teaching and learning to the web.* Phoenix, AZ: League for Innovation in the Community College.

Bonwell, C. C. (1996). Enhancing the lecture: Revitalizing a traditional format. In T. E. Sutherland and C. C. Bonwell Sutherland (Eds.), *Using active learning in college classes: A range of options for faculty.* San Francisco: Jossey-Bass.

Bonwell, C. C., and Eison, J. A. (1991). *Active learning: Creating excitement in the classroom.* Washington, DC: School of Education and Human Development, George Washington University.

Bowen, S. (2005, Winter,). Engaged learning: Are we all on the same page? *Peer Review.* Retrievedfrom http://findarticles.com/p/articles/ml_qa4115/is_2000501/ai_n13634584

Brandt, R. (1995, September). Punished by rewards: A conversation with Alfie Kohn. *Educational Leadership, 53*(1).

Branlund, J. M. (2008, July 29). Case teaching notes for "A question of responsibility: Whose asbestos caused her lung disease?" National Center for Case Study Teaching in Science, State University of New York at Buffalo. Retrieved from http://library.buffalo.edu/libraries/projects/cases/case.html

Breaux, A. L. (2003). *101 "answers" for new teachers and their mentors: Effective teaching tips for daily classroom use*. Larchmont, NY: Eye on Education.

Breaux, A. L., and Breaux, E. (2004). *Real teachers, real challenges, real solutions: 25 ways to handle the challenges of the classroom effectively*. Larchmont, NY: Eye on Education.

Brewster, C., and Fager, J. *Increasing student engagement and motivation: Time on task to homework*. Retrieved from http://www.nwrel.org/request/oct00/textonly.html

Brookfield, S., and Preskill, S. (2005). *Discussion as a way of teaching: Tools and techniques for democratic classrooms*. San Francisco: Jossey-Bass.

Brophy, J. E. (1987). Synthesis of research on strategies for motivating students to earn. *Educational Leadership, 5*(2) 40–48.

Brophy, J. E. (2004). *Motivating students to learn*. Mahwah, NJ: Erlbaum.

Brown, A. L., Bransford, J. D., Ferrara, R. A., and Campione, J. C. (1983). Learning, remembering, and understanding. In P. H. Mussen (Ed.), *Handbook of child psychology*. New York: Wiley.

Brown, J., and Weiner, B. (1984). Affective consequences of ability versus effort ascriptions: Controversies, resolutions, and quandaries. *Journal of Educational Psychology, 76*, 146–158.

Browne, M. N., Freeman, K. E., and Williamson, C. L. (2000, September). The importance of critical thinking for student use of the Internet. *College Student Journal*. Retrieved from http://findarticles.com/p/articles/mi_m0FCR/is_3_34/ai_66760560/pg_1.

Bruffee, K. A. (1993). *Collaborative learning: Higher education, interdependence, and the authority of knowledge*. Baltimore, MD: Johns Hopkins University Press.

Bruffee, K.A. (1995). Sharing our toys: Cooperative learning versus collaborative learning. *Change, 27*(1), 12–18.

Burgstahler, S. (2008). *Universal design of instruction: Definition, principles, and examples*. University of Washington. Retrieved from http://www.washington.edu/doit/Brochures/Academics/instruction.html

Chapman, A. (1975). *Bloom's taxonomy—Learning domains: Cognitive, affective, psychomotor domains—Design and evaluation toolkit for training and learning*. In R. J. Armstrong (ed.), *Developing and writing behavioral objectives*. Tucson: Educational Innovators Press.

Chickering, A. W., and Gamson, Z. F. (1987). Seven principles for good practice in undergraduate education. *Wingspread Journal 9*(2).

Christakis, D., et al. (2004). Early television exposure and subsequent problems in children. *Pediatrics 113*(4), 708–713.

Clark, F. (2008). *Organic chemistry in the news*. Webquest. Retrieved from http://www3.ns.sympatico.ca/chemfifi/Organic%20WebQuest/index.htm

Connolly, S. (2007). *Learning communities*. Upper Saddle River, NJ: Pearson/Prentice Hall.

Conrad, R. M., and Donaldson, J. A. (2004). *Engaging the online learner: Activities and resources for creative instruction*. San Francisco: Jossey-Bass.

Coomes, M. D., and DeBart, R. (Eds.). (2004). *Serving the millennial generation*. San Francisco: Jossey-Bass.

Cooper, J. L. (2000, Spring). Getting started: Informal small-group strategies in large classes. In J. MacGregor, J. L. Cooper, K. A. Smith, and P. Robinson (Eds.), *Strategies for energizing large classes, 81*. San Francisco: Jossey-Bass.

Corno, L., and Mandinach, E. B. (1983). The role of cognitive engagement in classroom learning and motivation. *Educational Psychologist, 18*(2), 88–108.

Covington, M. V. (1993). A motivational analysis of academic life in college. In J. C. Smart (Ed.), *Higher education: Handbook of theory and research*, Vol. 9. New York: Agathon Press.

Covington, M. (2000). Intrinsic versus extrinsic motivation in schools: A reconciliation. *Current Directions of Psychological Science 9*, 22–25.

Covington, M. V., and Roberts, B. (1994). Self-worth and college achievement: Motivation and personality correlates. In P.R. Pintrich, D. R. Brown, and C. E. Weinstein (Eds.), *Student motivation, cognition, and learning* (pp. 157–187). Hillsdale, NJ: Erlbaum.

Cranton, P. (2006). *Understanding and promoting transformative learning: A guide for educators of adults* (2nd ed.). San Francisco: Jossey-Bass.

Crawford, M., & Chaffin, R. (1986) The reader's construction of meaning: Cognitive research on gender and comprehension. In E. A. Flynn & P. P. Schweickart (Eds.), *Gender and reading: Essays on readers, texts, and contexts*. Baltimore: Johns Hopkins.

Cross, K. P. (1988). In search of zippers. *AAHE Bulletin*, June 1988.

Cross, K. P. (1993a). *Closing the gaps between teaching and learning.* Speech presented at the College Reading and Learning Association, Kansas City, April 2.

Cross, K. P. (1993b). *The coming of age of experiential education.* Speech presented at the 22nd Annual National Conference of The National Society for Experiential Education, San Francisco, CA, October 27.

Cross, K.P. (1993c). *Environments for learning.* Speech presented at the annual conference of the Association for California College Tutorial and Learning Assistance, Sacramento, CA, November 19.

Cross, K. P. (1997). *Developing professional fitness through classroom assessment and classroom research.* Cross Paper 1. Mission Viejo, CA: League for Innovation in the Community College.

Cross, K. P. (1998a). *Opening windows on learning.* Cross Paper 2. Mission Viejo, CA: League for Innovation in the Community College.

Cross, K. P. (1998b). *Putting together the puzzle of the college experience.* Speech presented at the Third Pacific Rim Conference on The First Year in Higher Education: Strategies for Success in Transition Years. Auckland, New Zealand, July 7.

Cross, K. P. (1998c). *Learning communities.* Speech presented at Bridgewater State College, April 17.

Cross, K. P. (1999). *Learning is about making connections.* Cross Paper 3. Mission Viejo, CA: League for Innovation in the Community College.

Cross, K. P. (2001, February). *Motivation: Er . . . will that be on the test?* Mission Viejo, CA: League for Innovation in the Community College.

Cross, K. P. (2003). *Techniques for promoting active learning.* Mission Viejo, CA: League for Innovation in the Community College.

Cross, K. P., and Steadman, M. (1996). *Classroom research: Implementing the scholarship of teaching.* San Francisco: Jossey-Bass.

Csikszentmihalyi, M. (1978). The hidden costs of reward: New perspectives on the psychology of human motivation. In *Intrinsic rewards and emergent motivation*. Hillsdale, NJ: Erlbaum.

Csikszentmihalyi, M. (1993). *The evolving self: A psychology for the third millennium.* New York: Harper Collins.

Csikszentmihalyi, M. (1997). Intrinsic motivation and effective teaching: A flow analysis. In J. Bess (Ed.), *Teaching well and liking it: Motivating faculty to effectively* (pp. 72–89). Baltimore: Johns Hopkins Press.

Cummins, P. F. (2004). *Proceed with passion: Engaging students in meaningful education.* Los Angeles: Red Hen Press.

Czerner, T. B. (2001). *What makes you tick?: The brain in plain English*. New York: Wiley.

Davis, B. G. (1993). *Tools for teaching*. San Francisco: Jossey-Bass.

Davis, B. G. (2009). *Tools for teaching*. San Francisco: Jossey-Bass.

Deci, E. (1992) On the nature and functions of motivation theories. *Psychological Science, 3*, 167–171.

Deci, E., Koestner, R., and Ryan, R. (1999). A meta-analytic review of experiments examining the effects of extrinsic rewards on intrinsic motivation. *Psychological Bulletin, 125*, 627–668.

Deci, E., and Ryan, R. (1985). *Intrinsic motivation and self-determination in human behavior*. New York: Plenum.

Deci, E., and Ryan, R. (Eds.). (2002). *Handbook of self-determination research*. Rochester, NY: University of Rochester Press.

de Groot, A. (1966). Perception and memory versus thought: Some old ideas and recent findings. In B. Kleinmuntz (Ed.), *Problem solving*. New York: Wiley.

Designing a learning community in an hour. Retrieved from http://www.evergreen.edu/washcenter/resources/lchour/lchour.htm.

Diamond, M., and Hopson, J. (1998). *Magic trees of the mind*. New York: Dutton.

Diamond, R. M. (1998). *Designing and assessing courses and curricula: A practical guide*. San Francisco: Jossey-Bass.

Dodge, B., and March, T. (n.d.). Webquests. http://webquest.sdsu.edu/.

Dodge, J. (2005). *Differentiation in action*. New York: Scholastic.

Edgerton, R. (1997). *Higher education white paper*. Pew Charitable Trusts.

Egan, G. (1977). *You and me*. Monterey, CA: Brooks/Cole.

Eifler, K. (2008, June-July). Academic "speed-dating." *Teaching Professor*.

El-Shamy, S. (2004). *How to design and deliver training for the new and emerging generations*. San Francisco: Pfeiffer.

Erickson, B. L., Peters, C. B., and Strommer, D. W. *Teaching first-year students*. San Francisco: Jossey-Bass, 2006.

Fenton, C., and Watkins, B.W. (2008). *Learner-centered assessment: Real strategies for today's students*. Phoenix, AZ: League for Innovation in the Community College.

Fink, L. D. (2003). *Creating significant learning experiences: An integrated approach to designing college courses*. San Francisco: Jossey-Bass.

Finkelstein, J. (2006). *Learning in real time: Synchronous teaching and learning online*. San Francisco: Jossey-Bass.

Frederick, P. J. (2002). Engaging students actively in large lecture settings. In C. A. Stanley (Ed.), *Engaging large classes: Strategies and techniques for college faculty*. Bolton, MA: Anker.

Friedrich, K. A., Sellers, S. L., and Burstyn, J. (2007). *Thawing the chilly climate: Inclusive teaching resources for science, technology, engineering, and math*. In D. R. Robertson and L. B. Nilson (Eds.), *To improve the academy: Resources for faculty, instructional, and organizational development* (Chap. 9). San Francisco: Jossey-Bass.

Garrison, D. R., and Vaughan, N. D. (2008). *Blended learning in higher education: Framework, principles, and guidelines*. San Francisco: Jossey-Bass.

Gorder, P. F. (2008). Students who use "clickers" score better on physics test. *Research News*. Retrieved from http://researchnews.osu.edu/archive/clickers.htm.

Graff, G., and Birkenstein, C. (2006). *"They say/I say": The moves that matter in academic writing*. New York: Norton.

Graphic organizer. (n.d.). Retrieved from http://www.graphic.org/goindex.html.

Hall, R.M., and Sandler, B.R. (1982). *The classroom climate: A chilly one for women?* Project on the Status and Education of Women. Washington, DC: Association of American Colleges.

Harnish, J. (2008). *What is a seminar? Seminar process to encourage participation and listening. Identifying good seminar behaviors.* Handouts distributed at Collaborative Learning Conference II: Working Together, Learning Together, Everett Community College, Everett, WA, February 22–23.

Harward, D. W. (2007). Engaged learning and the core purposes of liberal education: Bringing theory to practice. *Liberal Education 93*(1, Winter), 6–15.

Heppner, F. H. (2007). *Teaching the large college class: A guidebook for instructors with multitudes.* San Francisco: Jossey-Bass.

Hochstetler, D. (2006). Using narratives to enhance moral education in sports. *Journal of Physical Education, Recreation and Dance, 77*(4), 37–44.

Holladay, J. (2007). Managing incivility in the college classroom. *Division of Instructional Innovation and Assessment: Graduate Student Instructor Program.* Retrieved from http://www.utexas.edu/academic/diia/gsi/tatalk/incivility.php.

Hopkins, G. (2000). Icebreakers 2000: Getting-to-know-you activities for the first days of school. *Education World.* Retrieved from http://www.education-world.com/a_lesson/lesson/lesson196.shtml

Howe, N., and Strauss, W. (2000). *Millennials rising: The next great generation.* New York: Vintage.

Howe, N., and Strauss, W. (2007). *Millennials go to college: Strategies for a new generation on campus.* Washington, DC: American Association of Collegiate Registrars and Admissions Officers.

Howell, C. (2006). "Call me Doctor!"—Notes on classroom civility. *EDUCAUSE Connect: Transforming education through information technologies.* Retrieved from http://connect.educause.edu/blog/catherine/callmedoctornotesonclassr/2323.

Hsu, E. (1989.) Role event gaming simulation in management education: A conceptual framework. *Simulation and Games, 20,* pp. 409–438.

Huba, M. E., and Freed, J. E. (2000). *Learner-centered assessment on college campuses: Shifting the focus from teaching to learning.* Boston: Allyn and Bacon.

Involvement in learning: Realizing the potential of American higher education. (1984) Washington, DC: National Institute of Education.

Jacobson, D. (2002). Getting students in a technical class involved in the classroom. In C. A. Stanley (Ed.), *Engaging large classes: Strategies and techniques for college faculty.* Bolton, MA: Anker, pp. 214–216.

Johnson, D. S., Johnson, R. T., and Smith, K. A. (1998). *Active learning: Cooperation in the college classroom.* Edina, MN: Interaction Book Company.

Joint Educational Project, University of Southern California. (n.d.). *Service learning: Potential problems.* Retrieved from http://www.usc.edu/dept/LAS/jep/sl/problems.htm.

Jones, S. (2003). *Let the games begin: Gaming technology and entertainment among college students.* Pew Internet and American life project. Retrieved from http://www.pewinternet.org/PPF/r/93/report_display.asp

Kagen, S. (1992). *Cooperative learning.* San Juan Capistrano, CA: Resources for Teachers.

Knowles, M. S. (1986). *Using learning contracts.* San Francisco: Jossey-Bass.

Kohn, A. (1993). *Punished by rewards.* Boston: Houghton Mifflin.

Krathwohl, D. R., Bloom, B. S., and Masia, B. B. (1964). *Taxonomy of educational objectives, the classification of educational goals. Handbook II: The affective domain.* New York, David McKay.

Kuh, G. D. (2005). *Assessing conditions to enhance educational effectiveness: The inventory for student engagement and success.* San Francisco: Jossey-Bass.

Kuh, G. D., Kinzie, J., Schuh, J. H., and Witt, E. J. (2005). *Student success in college: Creating conditions that matter.* San Francisco: Jossey-Bass.

Lacayo, R. (2008). Who owns history? *Time.* March 3, 61–65.

Lattimore, D. (n.d.). *The WebQuest goes to college.* The Writing Program, Syracuse University. Retrieved from http://web.syr.edu/~mdlattim/essays/webquest _goes2college.html.

Learning Communities National Resource Center. Retrieved from http://www .evergreen.edu/washcenter/lcfaq.htm.

Literature Circles Resource Center, College of Education, Seattle University. Literature Circles.com. Retrieved from http://www.literaturecircles.com/.

Lochhead, J., and Whimby, A. (1987). Teaching analytical reasoning through thinking-aloud pair problem solving. In J. E. Stice (Ed.), *Developing critical thinking and problem solving abilities: New directions for teaching and learning, 30* (pp. 72–93). San Francisco: Jossey-Bass.

Love, J. (2007). Meeting the challenges of integrative learning: The Nexia concept. In D. R. Robertson and L. B. Nilson (Eds), *To improve the academy: Resources for faculty, instructional, and organizational development* (Chap. 17). San Francisco: Jossey-Bass.

Lowman, J. (1995). *Mastering the techniques of teaching.* San Francisco: Jossey-Bass.

Luotto, J. A., and Stoll, E. L. (1996). *Communication skills for collaborative learning.* Dubuque, IA: Kendall/Hunt.

MacGregor, J. (1990). Collaborative learning: Shared inquiry as a process of reform. In M.D. Svinicki (Ed.), *The changing face of college teaching* (pp. 19–30). San Francisco: Jossey-Bass.

MacGregor, J., Cooper, J. L., Smith, K. A., and Robinson, P. (2000). *Strategies for energizing large classes: From small groups to learning communities.* San Francisco: Jossey-Bass.

MacGregor, J., Smith, B. L., Matthews, R., and Gabelnick, F. (n.d.). *Learning community models.* Retrieved from http://www.evergreen.edu/washcenter/project .asp?pid=73.

Martinez, M. E. (1998). What is problem solving? *Phi Delta Kappan 79*(April), 605–609.

McKeachie, W. J. (1994). *Teaching tips: Strategies, research and theory for college and university teachers.* Lexington, MA: D. C. Heath.

McKeachie, W. J, and Gibbs, G. (1999). *Teaching tips: Strategies, research, and theory for college and university teachers.* Boston: Houghton Mifflin.

McKeachie, W. J., Hofer, B. K., Svinicki, M. D., Chism, N., Van Note, N., Zhu, E., et al. (2002). *McKeachie's teaching tips: Strategies, research, and theory for college and university teachers.* Boston: Houghton Mifflin.

McTighe, J., and Wiggins, G. (1999). *The understanding by design handbook.* Alexandria, VA: Association for Supervision and Curriculum Development.

Meyers, C., and Jones, T. B. (1993). *Promoting active learning: Strategies for the college classroom.* San Francisco: Jossey-Bass.

Michaelsen, L. K., Knight, A. B., and Fink, D. L. (2002). *Team-based learning: A transformative use of small groups.* Westport, CT: Praeger.

Miller, J. E., Trimbur, J., and Wilkes, J. M. (1996). Providing structure: The critical element. In T. E. Sutherland and C. C. Bonwell (Eds.), *Using active learning in college collaborative learning classes: A range of options for faculty* (pp. 17–30). San Francisco: Jossey-Bass.

Millis, B. J., and Cottell, P. G. (1998). *Cooperative learning for higher education faculty.* Phoenix, AZ: Oryx Press.

Naidu, S., Ip, A., and Linser, R. (2000). Dynamic goal-based role-play simulation the web: A case study. *Educational Technology and Society 3*(3), 190–202.

National Survey on Student Engagement (NSSE). (2009). [Web site]. Indiana University Center for Postsecondary Research. Retrieved from http://www.nsse .iub.edu/index.cfm

Newquist, H. P. (2004). *The great brain book: An inside look at the inside of your head.* New York: Scholastic Reference.

Nilson, L. B. (2003). *Teaching at its best: A research-based resource for college instructors.* Bolton, MA: Anker.

Nilson, L. B. (2007). *The graphic syllabus and the outcomes map: Communicating your course.* San Francisco: Jossey-Bass.

Noam, G. G. (Ed.). (2006). *The case for twenty-first century learning.* San Francisco: Wiley Periodicals.

Noll, M. (2001). *Turning points: Decisive moments in the history of Christianity* (2nd ed.). Grand Rapids, MI: Baker Academic.

Nuhfer, E. B. (2005). De Bono's red hat on Krathwohl's head: Irrational means to rational ends—More fractal thoughts on the forbidden affective (*Educating in Fractal Patterns* XIII). *The National Teaching and Learning Forum, 14*(5), 7–11.

Nuhfer, E., and Knipp, D. (2003). The knowledge survey: A tool for all reasons. *To improve the academy, 21,* 59–78. Retrieved from http://www.isu.edu/ctl/facultydev/KnowS_files/KnowS.htm

Nunley, K. F. (2006). *Differentiating the high school classroom: Solution strategies for 18 common obstacles.* Thousand Oaks, CA: Corwin Press.

Oates, K. K., and Leavitt, L. H. (2003). *Service-learning and learning communities: Tools for integration and assessment.* Washington, DC: Association of American Colleges and Universities.

Ouimet, J. A., and Smallwood, R. A. (2005, November–December). CLASSE—The class-level survey of student engagement. *Assessment Update, 17*(6).

Palmer, P. J. (2007). *The courage to teach: Exploring the inner landscape of a teacher's life.* San Francisco: Jossey-Bass.

Pascarella, E. T., and Terenzini, P. T. (1991). *How college affects students: Findings and insights from twenty years of research.* San Francisco: Jossey-Bass.

Pascarella, E. T., and Terenzini, P. T. (2005). *How college affects students: A third decade of research.* San Francisco: Jossey-Bass.

Perry, W. G. (1998). *Forms of ethical and intellectual development in the college years: A Scheme.* San Francisco: Jossey-Bass.

Perry model of intellectual and cognitive development. (n.d.). Reprinted from G. A. Thoma (1993, Spring), The Perry framework and tactics for teaching critical thinking in economics, *Journal of Economic Education,*128–136. Retrieved from http://www.lib.uconn.edu/~mboyer/burcha2.html

Pintrich, P. R. (2003). A motivational perspective on the role of student motivation in learning and teaching contexts. *Journal of Educational Psychology, 95* (4), 667–686.

Piskurich, G. M., and Piskurich, J. F. (2006). *Rapid instructional design: Learning ID fast and right.* San Francisco: Pfeiffer.

Plous, S. (2000). Responding to overt displays of prejudice: A role-playing exercise. *Teaching of Psychology 27*(3), 198–200.

Provitera-McGlynn, A. (2001). *Successful beginnings for college teaching: Engaging your students from the first day.* Madison, WI: Atwood.

Raffini, J. P. (1996). *150 ways to increase intrinsic motivation in the classroom.* Boston: Allyn and Bacon.

Ratey, J. J. (2002). *A user's guide to the brain: Perception, attention, and the four theaters of the brain.* New York: Pantheon Books.

Rhem, J. (2007). CLASSE: The missing link? *The National Teaching and Learning Forum 16*(4), 1–4.

Rhem, J. (2008). "They say/I say"—Teaching thinking. *The National Teaching and Learning Forum 17*(3), 1–3.

Rogers, S. (1997). *Motivation and learning: A teacher's guide to building excitement for learning and igniting the drive for quality.* Golden, CO: Peak Learning Systems.

Rogers, S. (2005). *Teaching tips: 105 ways to increase motivation and learning.* Evergreen, CO: Peak Learning Systems.

Rozycki, W. (1999, April). Just-in-time teaching. *Research and Creative Activity, 22*(1). Indiana University Office of Research and the University Graduate School. Retrieved from http://www.indiana.edu/~rcapub/v22n1/p08.html

Sandler, B.R., and Hoffman, E. (1992). *Teaching faculty members to be better teachers: A guide to equitable and effective classroom techniques.* Washington, DC: Association of American College.

Sandler, B. R., Silverberg, L. A., and Hall, R. M. (1996). *The chilly classroom climate: A guide to improve the education of women.* Washington, DC: National Association for Women in Education.

Sansone, C., and Harackiewicz, J. (2000). *Intrinsic and extrinsic motivation: The search for optimal motivation and performance.* San Diego: Academic Press.

Savage, C., and Woolsey, D. (n.d.). *Cuba en Crisis.* http://mypage.iu.edu/~dwoolsey/cuba_en_crisis/

Schön, D. A. (1983). *The reflective practitioner.* New York: Basic Books.

Schoop, M. (2007). From classrooms to learning spaces: Teaching by design. *Cross Paper 10.* Mission Viejo, CA: League for Innovations.

Shulman, L. S. (2002). Making differences: A table of learning. *Change 34*(6): 36–44. Retrieved from The Carnegie Foundation for the Advancement of Teaching (Publications) at http://www.carnegiefoundation.org/publications/sub.asp?key=452&subkey=612

Silberman, M. (1995). *101 ways to make training active.* San Francisco: Jossey-Bass/Pfeiffer.

Silberman, M. (1996). *Active learning: 101 strategies to teach any subject.* Needham Heights, MA: Allyn & Bacon.

Silberman, M. (2004). *The best of active training.* San Francisco: Pfeiffery.

Silberman, M., and Clark, K. (1999). *Active learning: 101 ways to make meetings active: Surefire ideas to engage your group.* San Francisco: Jossey-Bass/Pfeiffer.

Singham, M. (2005) Moving away from the authoritarian classroom. *Change 37*(3), 50–57

Slavin, R.E. (1995) Cooperative learning: theory, research and practice. (2nd Ed.) Boston: Allyn and Bacon.

Smallwood, R. (2009). *CLASSE: Classroom survey of student engagement.* Retrieved from http://www.assessment.ua.edu/CLASSE/Overview.htm.

Smith, K.A. (1996). Cooperative learning: Making "group work" work. In T. E. Sutherland and C. C. Bonwell (Eds.), *Using active learning in college classes: A range of options for faculty* (pp. 71–82). San Francisco: Jossey-Bass.

Snooks, M. K. (2004). Using practice tests on a regular basis to improve student learning. In M. V. Achacoso and M. D. Svinicki (Eds.), *Alternative strategies for evaluating student learning.* San Francisco: Jossey-Bass.

Sorcinelli, M. D. (2002). Promoting civility in large classes. In C. A. Stanley and M.E. Porter (Eds), *Engaging large classes: Strategies and techniques for college faculty.* Bolton, MA: Anker.

Sousa, D. A. (2006). *How the brain learns.* Thousand Oaks, CA: Corwin Press.

Stanley, C.A. (2002). Involved in the classroom. In C. A. Stanley and M.E. Porter (Eds.), *Engaging large classes: Strategies and techniques for college faculty.* Bolton, MA: Anker.

Stanley, C. A., and Porter, M. E. (2002). *Engaging large classes: Strategies and techniques for college faculty.* Bolton, MA: Anker.

Stevens, D. D., and Levi, A. (2005). *Introduction to rubrics: An assessment tool to save grading time, convey effective feedback, and promote student learning.* Sterling, VA: Stylus.

Sugar, S. (1998). *Games that teach: Experiential activities for reinforcing learning*. San Francisco: Jossey-Bass/Pfeiffer.

Sutherland, T. E., and Bonwell, C. C. (Eds). (1996). *Using active learning in college classes: A range of options for faculty*. San Francisco: Jossey-Bass.

Svinicki, M. D. (1999). *Teaching and learning on the edge of the millennium: Building on what we have learned*. San Francisco: Jossey-Bass.

Svinicki, M. D. (2004a). Authentic assessment: Testing in reality. In M. V. Achacoso and M. D. Svinicki (Eds.), *Alternative strategies for evaluating student learning*. San Francisco: Jossey-Bass.

Svinicki, M. D. (2004b). *Learning and motivation in the postsecondary classroom*. Bolton, MA: Anker.

Swaner, L. E. (2007). Linking engaged learning, student mental health and well-being, and civic development: A review of the literature. *Liberal Education 93*(1, Winter), 16–25.

Tannenbaum, J., and Bush, V.C. (2005). *Jump write in!* San Francisco: Jossey-Bass.

Teaching tips: Classroom civility. *University of California Santa Cruz's Teaching Toolbox*. Retrieved from http://ic.ucsc.edu/CTE/teaching/tips-civility.html

Tervaniemi, M., and Hugdahl, K. (2003). Lateralization of auditory-cortex function. *Brain Research Reviews 43*(3), 231–246.

Thalheimer, W. (2008). Providing learners with feedback—Part 1. *Research-based recommendations for training, education, and e-learning*. Retrieved from http://learningtechnologiesconference.wordpress.com/2008/06/20/the-importance-of-good-feedback-in-learning/

Thiagarajan, S. (2006). *100 favorite games*. San Francisco: Pfeiffer.

Tileston, D. W. (2004). *What every teacher should know about student motivation*. Thousand Oaks, CA: Corwin Press.

Tinto, V. (1994) *Leaving college: Rethinking the causes and cures of student attrition*. Chicago: University of Chicago Press.

Tomlinson, C. A. (1999). *The differentiated classroom: Responding to the needs of all learners*. Alexandria, VA: Association for Supervision and Curriculum Development.

Tomlinson, C. A. (2001). *How to differentiate instruction in mixed-ability classrooms*. Alexandria, VA: Association for Supervision and Curriculum Development.

Tomlinson, C. A., and Eidson, C. C. (2003). *Differentiation in practice: A resource guide for differentiating curriculum, grades K-5*. Alexandria, VA: Association for Supervision and Curriculum Development.

Tomlinson, C. A., and Strickland, C. A. (2005). *Differentiation in practice: A resource guide for differentiating curriculum*. Alexandria, VA: Association for Supervision and Curriculum Development.

Vygotsky, L. S. (1978). *Mind in society: The development of higher psychological processes*. Cambridge, MA: Harvard University Press.

Walvoord, B. E. F., and Anderson, V. J. (1998). *Effective grading: A tool for learning and assessment*. San Francisco: Jossey-Bass.

Watkins, R. (2005). *75 e-Learning activities: Making online learning interactive*. San Francisco: Pfeiffer.

Watson, G. (2003). *190 ready-to-use activities that make science fun*. San Francisco: Jossey-Bass.

Watts, M. M. (2007). *Service learning*. Upper Saddle River, NJ: Pearson/Prentice Hall.

Weimer, M. (2002). *Learner-centered teaching: Five key changes to practice*. San Francisco: Jossey-Bass.

Weimer, M. (2009). Student engagement techniques: A handbook for college teachers, *Manuscript Review*, February 15.

Weiner, B. (1979). A theory of motivation for some classroom experiences. *Journal of Educational Psychology, 71*, 3–25.

Weiner, B. (1985). An attributional theory of achievement motivation and emotion. *Psychological Review, 92*(4), 548–573.

Weiner, B. (1986). *An attributional theory of motivation and motion.* New York: Springer-Verlag.

Wesch, M. (2007). *A vision of students today* [video]. Digital ethnography project, Cultural Anthropology. Kansas State University. Retrieved from http://www .youtube.com/watch?v=dGCJ46vyR9o

White, C. P. (2004). Student portfolios: An alternative way of encouraging and evaluating student learning. In M. V. Achacoso and M. D. Svinicki (Eds.), *Alternative strategies for evaluating student learning.* San Francisco: Jossey-Bass.

Wiggins, G. P. (1998). *Educative assessment: Designing assessments to inform and improve student performance.* San Francisco: Jossey-Bass.

Wiggins, G. P., and McTighe, J. (1998). *Understanding by design.* Alexandria, VA: Association for Supervision and Curriculum Development.

Williams, V. K. (2007, October 31). Posting on UC Berkeley Graduate School of Education Community listserv.

Wilson, K., and Korn, J. H. (2007). Attention during lectures: Beyond ten minutes. *Teaching of psychology. 34*(2), 85–89.

Wlodkowski, R. J. (2008). *Enhancing adult motivation to learn: A comprehensive guide for teaching all adults.* San Francisco: Jossey-Bass.

Wright, M. C. (2000). Getting more out of less: The benefits of short-term experiential learning in undergraduate sociology classes. *Teaching Sociology* 28 (2), 116–26.

Writing Center, University of North Carolina at Chapel Hill. (2009). Brainstorming. *Handouts and links.* Retrieved from http://www.unc.edu/depts/wcweb/ handouts/brainstorming.html.

Yaman, D., and Covington, M. (2006). *I'll take learning for 500: Using game shows to engage, motivate, and train.* San Francisco: Pfeiffer.

Index